When a vast image out of *Spiritus Mundi*

Troubles my sight: somewhere in sands of the desert

'The Second Coming' —W. B. YEATS

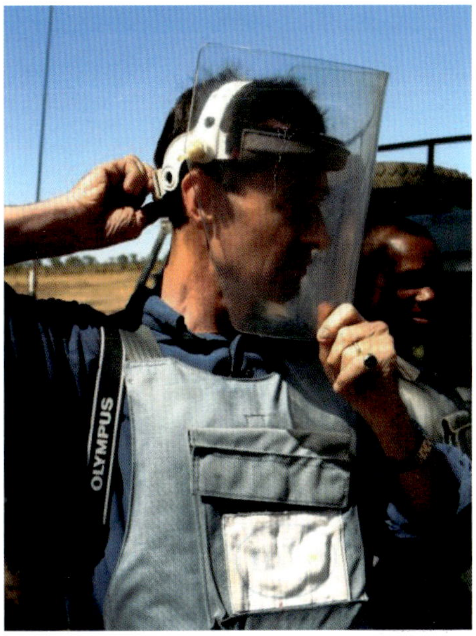

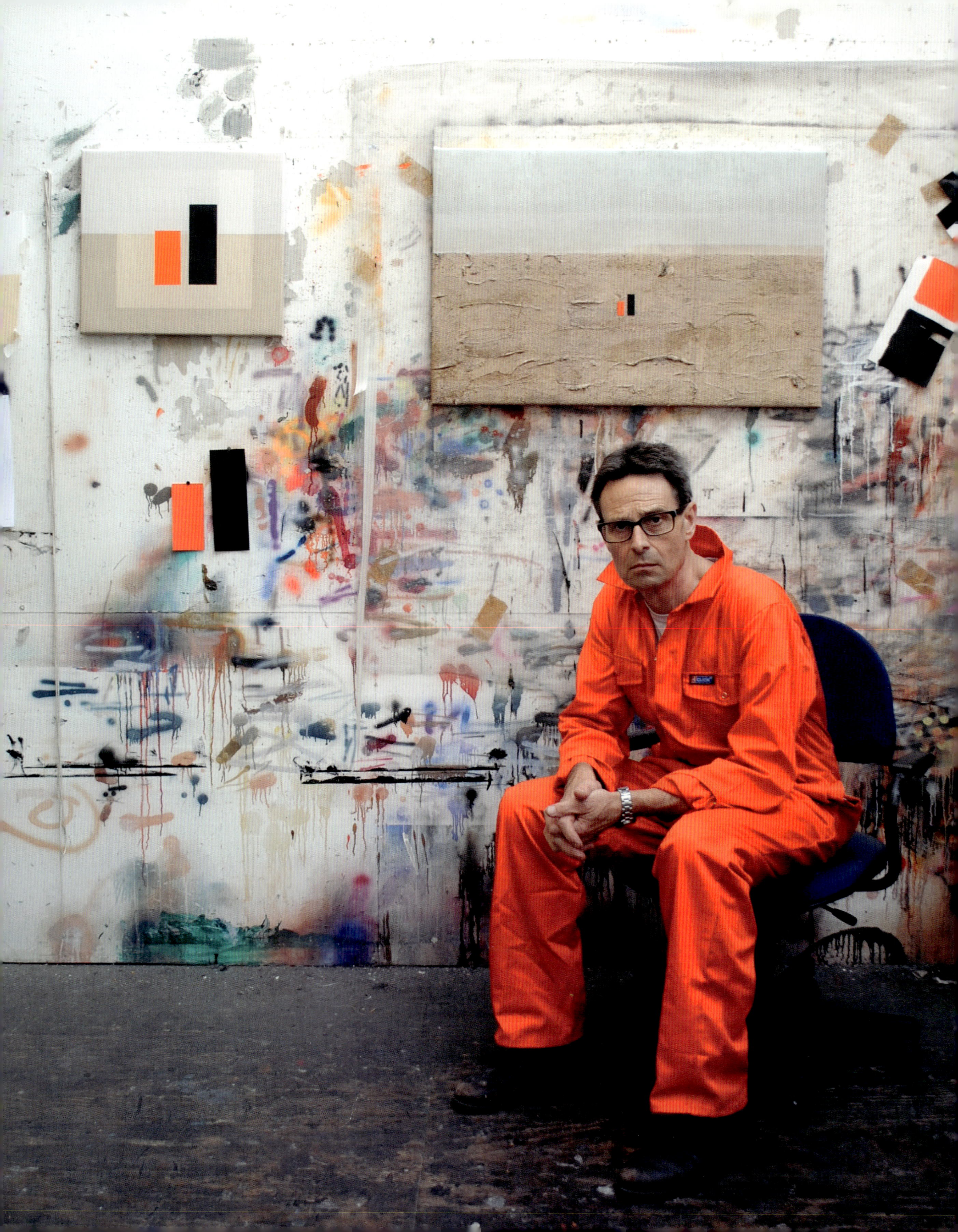

TROUBLES MY SIGHT
THE ART OF
JOHN KEANE

MARK LAWSON

INTRODUCTION BY

ALEX DANCHEV

FOREWORD BY

BRIAN ENO

FLOWERS GALLERY

First published in Great Britain in 2015 by Flowers

FLOWERS
82 Kingsland Road
London E2 8DP
TEL: +44 (0) 20 7920 7777
info@flowersgallery.com

21 Cork Street
London W1S 3LZ
TEL: +44 (0) 20 7439 7766
info@flowersgallery.com

529 West 20th Street
New York NY 10011
TEL: +1 (212) 439 1700
newyork@flowersgallery.com

www.flowersgallery.com

ISBN 981-1-906412-68-5

Co-ordinators: Matthew Flowers, Juliette O'Leary and Alexandra Peake
Photography: Antonio Parente
Design: Katy Homans
Printing: Empress, London

Cover image: *Sixty Selfie*, 2014, oil on canvas, 140 x 120 cm / 55⅛ x 47¼ in
Inside cover images: *Armageddon Now* (virtual image) 1 and 2, 2004
page 1: John Keane in Angola, photograph by Karen Lobo-Morell, 2006
Frontispiece: John Keane in his studio, in front of *Distillation of Terror*, 2014; self-portrait photograph

A catalogue record for this book is available from the British Library.

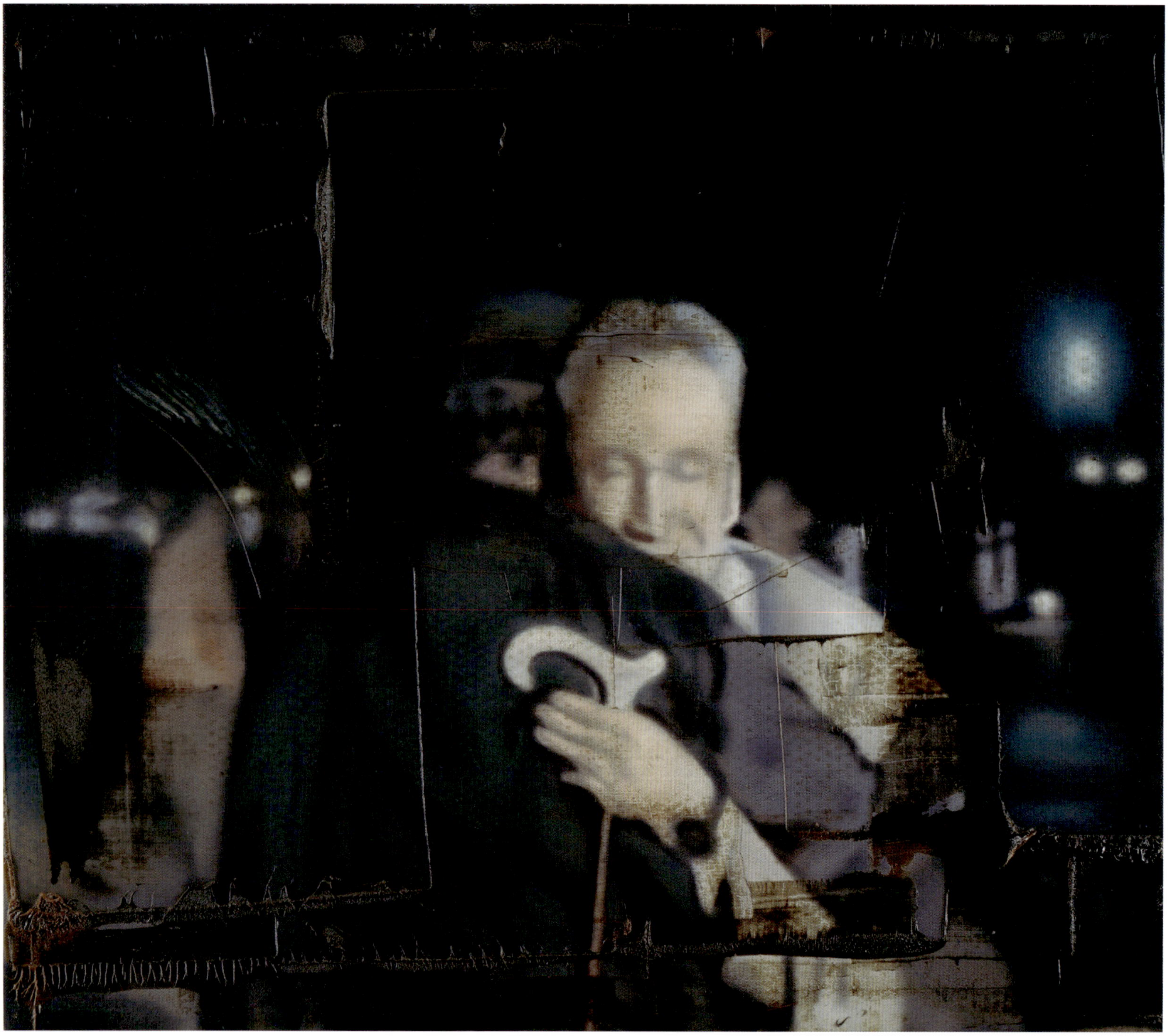

The Contentious Return of Abdelbaset Al-Megrahi, 2009
Oil on linen
76 x 86 cm / 30 x 34 in
Private Collection, UK

JOHN KEANE

BRIAN ENO

In December 1988, a 747 took off from London Heathrow, heading for New York. The plane blew up over Lockerbie in Scotland with a loss of 270 lives.

By a very unsettling coincidence, I had connections with three people on that flight. One was an ex-girlfriend, and another an ex-assistant. And there was a courier—carrying a video tape of some of my work for showing in America.

That tape was among the debris found after the crash. Six months later, after it had been cleared as evidence, it was returned to my office in London. It was slightly battered. It sat on a desk and nobody wanted to touch it. It was charged with its own history, with a sense of having been part of something terrible.

Something of that ominous charge is present in many of John Keane's paintings. Although their subjects are often horrific, what is more unsettling about them is the sense of *having been present*. They don't feel like pictures *about* the scenes they show; instead they seem to come right out of those scenes, as if they were there as they were happening.

They do this not by being more explicit and graphic than the sea of photographs and video to which we're exposed daily, but by being blurrier, vaguer, dreamier, messier . . . *less* definite. The pictures transform the specific into the archetypal. In a time of increasingly explicit detail, Keane realises that it's the *distillation* of detail that catches our imagination, that makes us engaged. The power of the experience is predicated not on what is shown, or what is missing—but on what we, the audience, can't resist imagining.

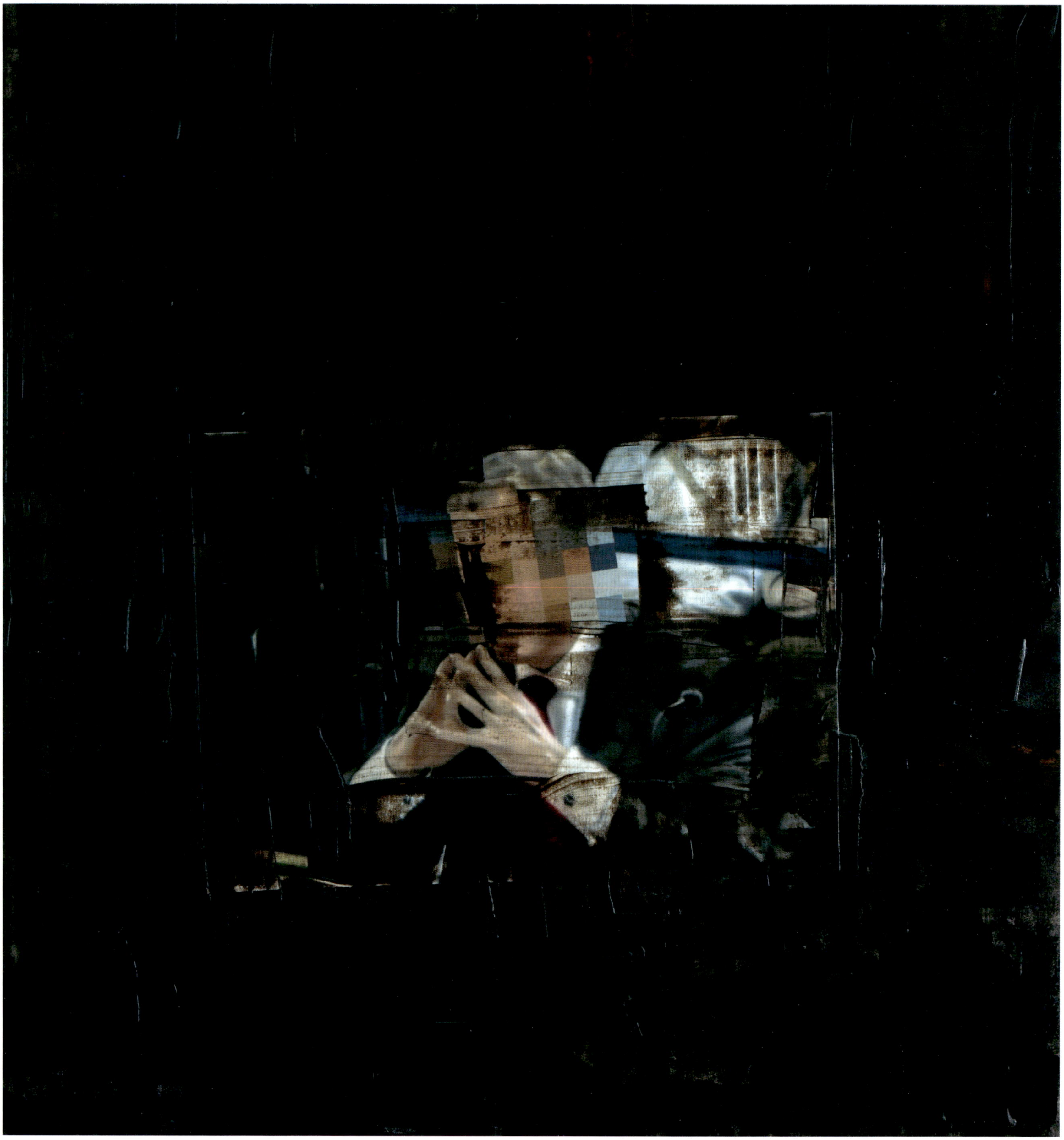

INTRODUCTION

THE ARTIST AND THE MERCURIALIST

ALEX DANCHEV

mercurial, mercurialist

A person born under the influence of the planet Mercury; a person having the qualities attributed to such a birth, esp. eloquence, ingenuity, or aptitude for trade. Also occas. with unfavourable connotation: a sharper, a thief.

1556 T. Hill tr. B. Cocles *Brief Epitomye Phisiognomie* sig.D3v The face leane declareth that man to be warye or wittie, circumspect in hys doings, fatigable, of a good understandying as the mercuriales haue . . . and dysdaynfull.

1615 T. Tomkis *Albumazar* i.i.sig.B Come brue Mercurials sublim'd in cheating, . . . fellow-souldiers I'th'watchfull exercise of Theevery.

1622 Bacon *Hist. Raigne Henry VII* 113 This Youth ... was such a Mercuriall, as the like has seldome beene knowne.

1650 R. Gentilis tr. V. Malvezzi *Considerations Lives Alcibiades & Coriolanus* 156 The Mercurials with their swiftnesse run over all things.

1702 W. Penn *More Fruits of Solitude* §76.30 The Mercurial too often happen to leave Judgment behind them, and sometimes make Work for Repentance.

Oxford English Dictionary

ON FRIDAY 29 JANUARY 2010, JOHN KEANE spent the whole day glued to his computer screen. He was watching a political spectacle: the Iraq Inquiry, live from the Queen Elizabeth II Conference Centre in London. He was watching the trial of Tony Blair as the Chairman of the Inquiry, Sir John Chilcot, insisted it was not the first session of oral evidence from the Prime Minister and prime mover of that disastrous enterprise, a public hearing before an audience whose members had lost loved ones in Iraq (as Chilcot put it) and others drawn by ballot, recorded for posterity, and now freely available on the Inquiry's website, together with the transcript of the proceedings.

As he watched online, he took screengrabs of Blair in full flow. Over the next few months, the screengrabs metamorphosed into a series of oil paintings, of teasing anonymity and tremendous power, *Figure at an Inquiry* (2010) — a faster rate of production than the benighted Inquiry, which has yet to report, five years on, notwithstanding the blithe words of the Chairman that day: 'We aim to deliver our report by the end of this year.'

Figure at an Inquiry No.5, 2010
Oil on linen
215 x 200 cm / 84½ x 78½ in
Collection: Nick Taylor

John Keane is a political painter, as Mark Lawson's acute and affectionate study serves to remind us. Lawson notes 'the persistent oppositional instinct in Keane's art'; and that shrewd observation accords well to the paintings of *Figure at an Inquiry*. Characteristically, the artist himself pinpoints a fundamental truth (and neatly skewers his subject) when he remarks that these works 'dwell on the mercurial appearance of Tony Blair at the Chilcot Inquiry', as he puts it as a way of introducing the exhibition in which they first appeared, 'Scratching the Surface, Joining the Dots' (2012). 'Mercurial' is *le mot juste*. Blair prides himself on his judgment, and on his sincerity—he is soused in sincerity—but the mercurial too often happen to leave Judgment behind them, and sometimes make Work for Repentance, as William Penn truly said. If ever a man made work for repentance, it is the God-Bothering Tony Blair.

He returned to that famous day in his memoirs, *A Journey* (2010). 'As I thought on how to answer the question that was put to me at the end of my evidence to the Chilcot Inquiry,' he writes, 'I felt sick, a mixture of anger and anguish.' The question was whether he had any regrets. It was put twice, by Chilcot himself, and on Blair's own account his answer was deliberately incomplete. He spoke of a sense of responsibility; he expressed no regrets. He seems to feel that he was set up. 'The anger was at being put in a position in an inquiry that was supposed to be about lessons learned, but had inevitably turned into a trial of judgment, and even good faith; and in front of some of the families of the fallen, to whom I wanted to reach out, but knew if I did so, the embrace would be immediately misused and misconstrued.' The anger was mutual. Some members of the public could no longer contain themselves (though their interventions are suppressed in the transcript). One man stood up and shouted politely, 'Come on, Mr Blair, there must be one regret.' Two bereaved mothers broke down in tears. Another man yelled, 'Surely you regret the death toll?' Blair ignored them. 'But [my] anger was selfish,' he concludes, 'trivial—comparatively at any rate—and transient.' As he left the room, someone cried out, 'Murdering bastard Blair!'

There remains the anguish. 'The principal part of that is not selfish,' he continues. 'Some of it is, to be sure. Do they really suppose I don't care, don't feel, don't regret with every part of my being the loss of those who died?' Now, he says, he is beyond tears, beyond sympathy, beyond sorry. He is in a different place, a place of perpetual burden. 'Regret can seem bound to the past. Responsibility has its present and future tense.' Piteous yet unrepentant, Tony Blair feels your pain.

However uncomfortable he may have felt at the beginning or the end—and he was not entirely nerveless as his hand shook as he opened a bottle of water at the start of the session—Blair's appearance at the Chilcot Inquiry was of a piece with his appearance at all the other inquiries at which he is inclined to boast. Inquiries are theatre. Blair is nothing if not a consummate performer on the political stage. He is defined by his wars and his starring roles. The two are connected, not least in his own mind. Arraigned before Chilcot, he was in his element. He was well-practised—his appearance at the Hutton Inquiry in 2003 was a tour de force of frank-seeming phrases—and he was well-rehearsed.

John Keane scrutinized him on screen, at once fascinated and appalled. The upshot of that scrutiny is a fine demonstration of what an artist can do: the contribution he can make to ethical and political life. *Figure at an Inquiry* succeeds triumphantly (that is to say, quietly) in capturing the mercurialist in the moment, as if anatomizing the performance, and at the same time trapping or caging him for our edification or gratification, as it may be. As Cézanne knew, painting is truth-telling. John Keane's truth is worth attending to. In 'Figure at an Inquiry No. 5', the hands have it.

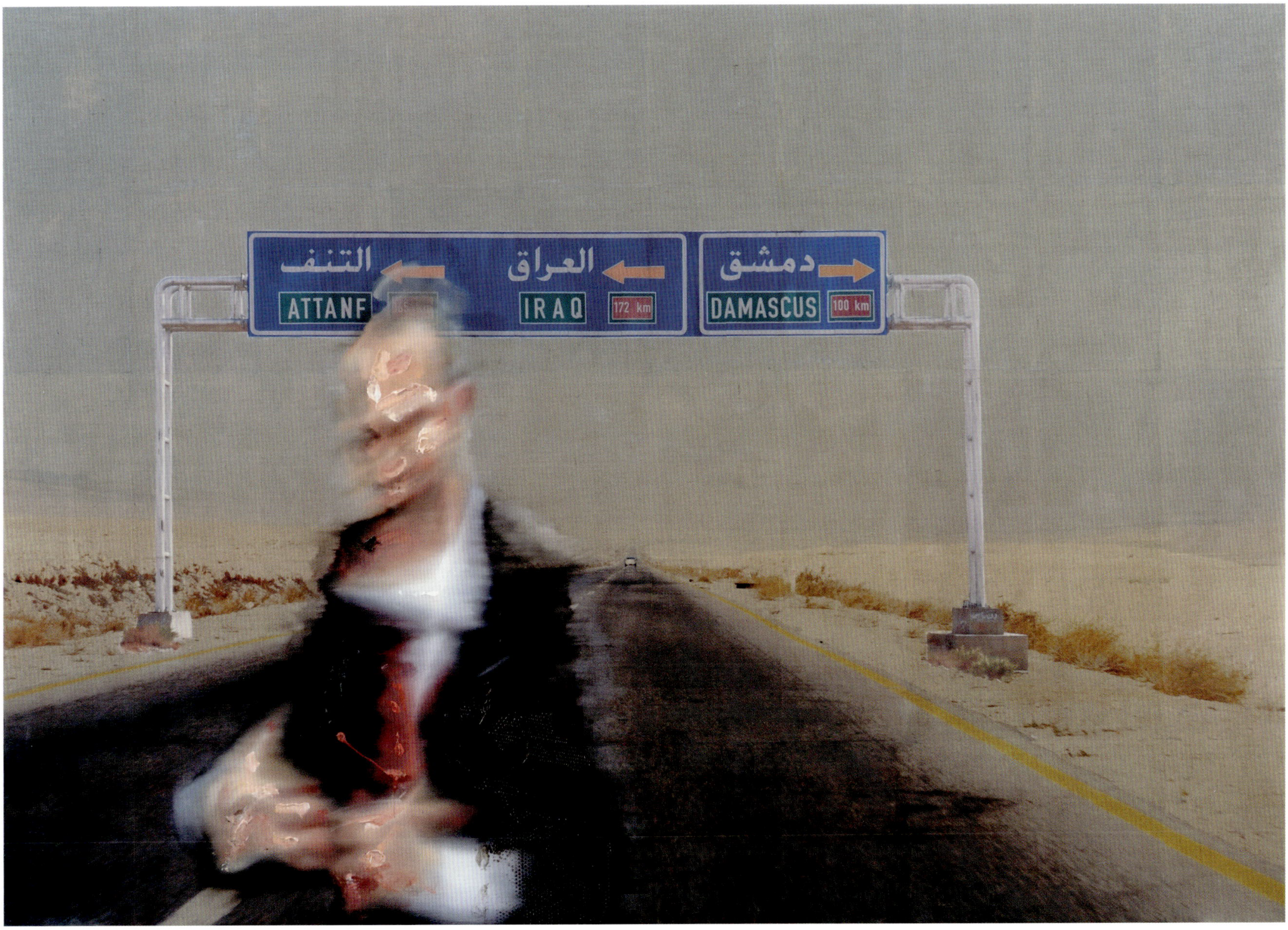

Sign from God, 2009
Oil and inkjet transfer on jute
207 x 280 cm / 81½ x 110¼ in
Private Collection, UK

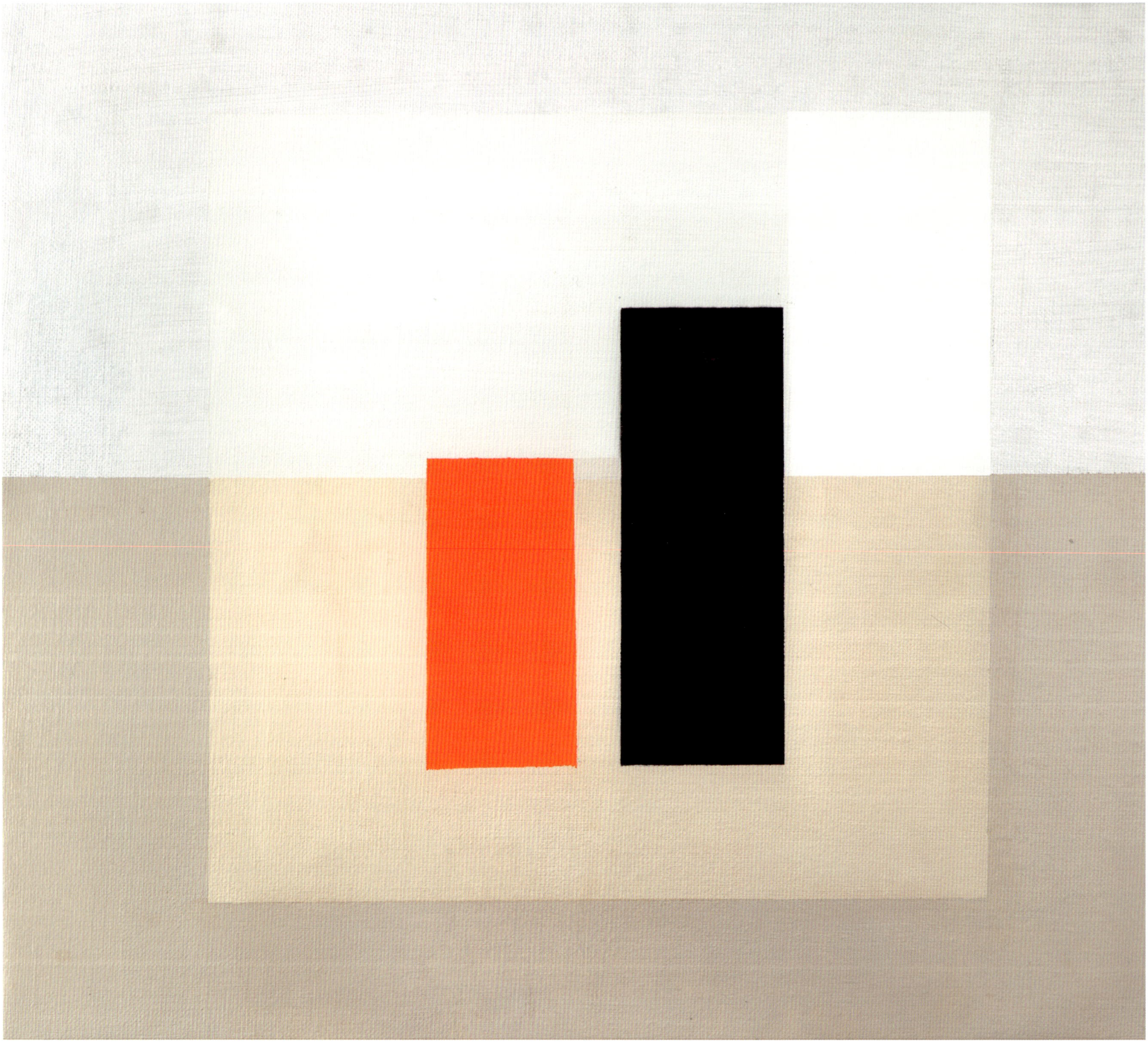

Distillation of Terror, 2014
Oil on linen
40 x 45 cm / 15¾ x 17¾ in

TROUBLES MY SIGHT

THE ART OF JOHN KEANE

MARK LAWSON

This book is based on my observation of John Keane's work in galleries and catalogues over a period of more than 30 years, and on four long conversations with the artist, recorded at his studio between November 2014 and January 2015. A small amount of quotation and analysis concerning the earlier work overlaps with passages in John Keane: *Conflicts of Interest* (Mainstream, 1995) but the structure and language are in most cases changed.

—MARK LAWSON

CHAPTER ONE

WORK IN PROGRESS

THE FIRST INTERVIEW WITH JOHN KEANE FOR THIS BOOK was due to begin at the 11th hour of the 11th day of the 11th month, 2014—96 years to the minute since the ending of the First World War. In the event, the conversation was slightly delayed because the train on which the interviewer was traveling to the artist's studio stopped before 11am in order to allow staff and passengers to observe the two-minute silence that has become an annual British ritual, its significance raised even further on this occasion by the almost year-long commemorations of the start of the 1914–18 conflict.

Our date had been made some weeks earlier, through a casual reconciling of diaries, with neither of us noticing that we would start talking after this historically weighted pause. But, once spotted, it seemed entirely fitting because the conflicts that followed the war to end all wars have been a recurrent subject in Keane's work. And, as I would discover that morning, he had just begun a new strain of work provoked by the latest—militarily unorthodox, visually shocking—manifestation of the West's tension with its ideological enemies.

Walking from Old Street tube station to Keane's studio, you pass—fittingly for a visit to an artist—a visual institution: Moorfields Eye Hospital. In one of the many nearby streets of converted warehouses, Keane's workspace is a long, high-ceilinged room divided, by equipment and furniture, into four distinct parts: an office area for dry work, bordered by desks, filing cabinets and flat-screen computers; a large L-shaped brushwork zone that is marked out by two walls showing substantial splatter-spill from spray painting; a small square of kitchen and a meeting zone configured by right-angled sofas.

With tea and biscuits from the kitchen, we faced each other across the sofas, with my line of sight including the walls of the painting space, from where glared distorted portraits of Vladimir Putin, media tycoon Rupert Murdoch and former Murdoch executive and *News of the World* editor Rebekah Brooks, as if in a Chamber of Horrors for liberals.

We talked about the rituals of British military remembrance, amplified on this November 11th by the landmark anniversaries of the First World War. Keane had made a few WWI-themed pictures for a group exhibition on the subject curated by Flowers Gallery, his representatives for three decades. He had also been asked by the Royal Mint to put in proposals for coins commemorating 1914. Submitting artists were given a list of suggested subjects and themes, divided into sub-sections. From a biographical category, Keane chose the nurse Edith Cavell and the writer T.E. Lawrence and, under Technology, was inspired by gas warfare, but all of his designs were rejected by the presiding committee. When Keane's civil service intermediary suggested doing something on battles, and he had the idea of making the reverse of the coin look as if it had been found on a battlefield: the metal cratered and pitted. But that was turned down as well. All creative careers are a struggle to turn ideas into money but, in his failed flirtation from the Royal Mint, Keane had suffered the poignant frustration of failing to turn coins into cash.

When the conversation moved on to Keane's long concern as an artist with war (chapters three and four), the conversation took an intriguing turn towards current work:

> JK: I think we're living in particularly interesting times now, when it's perhaps less easy to look at the subject of war with the detachment that we once had. I'm fascinated by now—the whole jihadi movement and the ideology that holds human life with such contempt.
>
> ML: And also that young men and women from Britain are going off to the Middle East prepared to die.
>
> JK: Yes, well that is fascinating and disturbing. You see jihadist beheadings on video, you hear about massacres in the desert and you think: I want to be part of that. What is it you find appealing? It's like: let's go and join the Nazis.

During the latter part of 2014, an Islamist jihadist group most commonly known as ISIL (Islamic State of Iraq and the Levant)—which has also operated as ISIS (Islamic State of Iraq and Syria) and Islamic State—posted online footage of a number of foreign hostages being murdered by beheading. The victims included the American journalist James Foley and two Englishmen: aid worker David Haines and Alan Henning, a Lancastrian taxi-driver who was using his holiday to work as a supply driver for a humanitarian charity. They were killed by the so-called "Jihadi John", a black-clad figure who seemed from the videos to speak with an English accent.

Appalled by the actions at a moral level, Keane was also professionally intrigued by the apparently artful visual decisions in the video. For their deaths, the hostages were dressed in the bright orange work garments which, borrowed from the US prison system, were given to the inmates at Guantanamo Bay, the American military prison off Cuba that was set up by the adminstration of President George Bush to hold, usually without process or trial, those suspected of involvement in or support for anti-American terrorism. The giving of these clothes to the hostages decapitated by ISIL jihadists showed America that a circuit of hurt was being reversed on the perpetrator.

> ML: If you were a playwright or novelist, you might think: this is a subject that I'd like to write about. But artistic inspiration is more mysterious to me: would you ever think, as formally as that, I want to do a painting *about* this?
>
> JK: I think there has to be some emotional response. But then the difficulty is how to render that visually. It's finding a route in.
>
> ML: But you seem obsessed with the jihadi issue. So it is going to become something?

JK: Er, yes, it is. But it's getting a way in. Because the desert beheadings are already so theatrical, so carefully staged.

ML: But I'm interested in the idea of cultural taboos. Would you hesitate to use the beheading images for ethical or moral reasons? The feelings of the families?

JK: Well, this is what I'm struggling with. Look. . . .

He led me to the support wall that serves as his main easel for work in progress: in this case, a picture called 'Aggregation of Terror'. On an inkjet-printed background of sand, familiar as the desert setting of the ISIL video hostage-killings, were placed a black rectangle and, beside it, a smaller version of the same shape in an orange shade immediately recognisable — as the executioners had assumed Western viewers would — as the colour of the Guantanamo Bay jumpsuits that ISIL's victims had been forced symbolically to wear. In another version of this conceit, the video image reduced even more to stripes of fawn, orange and black. Once you had got the key, the darkest strip of paint clearly represented the robes of the jihadist murderer, Jihadi John.

Such mysterious depiction is a new departure in Keane's art. Apart from a few Mondrian homages as a student, almost all of his work — except for the possible complication of some of the images in the *Guantanamerica* series (chapter three) — has been representational or figurative rather than abstract. This is inevitable because his political and journalistic intentions would be almost impossible to communicate through grids and patterns, although this didn't protect the Russian abstractionist Kazimir Malevich from being censored by the Communists because his preference for the oblique over socialist realism was considered decadent. (Conversely, abstract painting is currently very popular in China, perhaps because its political meanings are almost impossible to identify and suppress.)

'Aggregation of Terror', however, is a fascinating combination of the abstract — the two strips of colour — and the political because a viewer who has seen the ISIL videos can easily see sand, victim and killer.

JK: The visceral, graphic element in the beheading videos is so repulsive that I didn't want to use it. So I took a screen-grab and digitalised and pixilated it beyond all recognition. So, I'm playing around with it. But it is experimental. As I was doing it I was greatly enjoying that sense of tonal and colour relationships on a flat surface that is one of the pleasures of abstract painting.

ML: Although it's abstract, it leads back to the videos. To reduce it to *The Sun* newsdesk phone-call. If they rang up and said: the relatives of a murdered hostage are really angry about this?

JK: Yes, it would worry me. It's like 9/11: there are a couple of paintings relating to the figures who jumped off the Twin Towers but you have to be sure about why you are using this kind of stuff and what you do with it.

In early December, my next visit to the studio, we talked about portraits and self-portraits (see chapter four) before I asked about the progress of what might be called a redacted portrait: 'The Aggregation of Terror'. Keane said that he had refined the image of the two stripes of colour — black and orange — against the sand but had abandoned the project:

JK: I haven't really done much more on that. I think I'm finished with that particular subject now. It's such a difficult area to deal with, especially as I want to avoid very graphic images but somehow to address the phenomenon, the issue, and what it raises. I'm still thinking about it and I'm not sure where it can go: how you can make something of it.

ML: Your use of paint in these pictures — it's a sort of video-screen finish, very smooth; there's no piling up of paint.

JK: No. I'd done that in the past and I moved away from it. But, yes, I think it is influenced by working from video images.

ML: Visually we're very much in a flat-screen visual culture at the moment?

JK: Yes. I'm not sure that I'm consciously commenting on that; it's more that there's a visual aesthetic in video and HD that I enjoy and want to try to bring to painting. With ink-jet printing, there is a rather beautiful finish that I suppose I am trying to reproduce by hand.

And, at that point, Keane gave the impression that he had also achieved another kind of finish — that his artistic response to the ISIL killings was also over. But, in late December, the next visit, my peripheral vision picked up, just through the door, a flash of bright orange. My first thought was that it was the familiar mid-winter sight, especially in the workspaces of freelance artists and writers: the warming bars of an electric fire.

Walking in, I saw at the far end of the room new canvases showing orange jumpsuits, empty but hanging with arms and legs stretched out in the air: a Guantanamo Calvary.

Christmas plans swapped, courteous tea and biscuits and then:

ML: It's always fascinating for me to walk in here and see what's happened while I was away. And today it's: bang, those crucified jumpsuits. So take me through them.

JK: Well, we'd been talking last time about how I wanted to address that imagery of the Islamic State beheadings but without including gruesome viscera and so on. So it was hard to find a way in. And I recently struck on this idea of the jumpsuit: the theatre and costume element, the way that IS had taken the outfit of the Guantanamo Bay detainees and turned it on its head and used it against the Americans and British as a provocative theatrical gesture. So I sent off for my very own jumpsuit.

ML: You just put 'jumpsuit' into a search engine?

JK: Yes, I Googled 'orange jumpsuit' and loads of them came up on eBay. Actually, you can buy them as costumes, as fancy dress because some people apparently like to go to parties dressed as a Guantanamo detainee. But I wanted a more authentic work-suit. And, when I got it, I didn't know what to do, so I pinned it up.

ML: Did you put it on?

JK: Yes, I photographed myself wearing it. But pinning it up in the attitude of a crucifixion, that gave it a new resonance and the shape the image would take began to fall into place. And it also coincided with rediscovering Yeats' poem 'The Second Coming', which is filled with religious imagery, and, I think, written some years after the First World War.

In scriptural prophecy and Christian dogma, the 'Second Coming' refers to the assertion that Jesus Christ will return to Earth, beginning the end of the world. But Yeats inverts — *perverts*, the bishops and priests of his Ireland would have said — this imagery, so that the cult to come is anti-Christian.

Almost 100 years on, the poem seems astonishingly topical. With a prescience that would be the envy of many diplomats and journalists over the last century, Yeats even places this messianic backlash in the same hot, sandy Middle Eastern terrain where the earlier faith was made, where *reel shadows of the indignant desert birds*. And, in words at which successions of school English students including John Keane have essayed meaning, the future super-being is a *rough beast* who *slouches towards Bethlehem to be born*.

So the anti-Christ will have the same birth-place as the Christ, although the first religious leader's work will be reversed. In a phrase risking blasphemy by the strictures of the time, Yeats violently tips over the baptismal font, its holy water diluted by something stronger: *the ceremony of innocence is drowned*.

Yeats even places this spiritual crisis close to our own time. The moment is post-Millennial (a date long considered apocalyptic) as *twenty centuries* have passed, rather than the nineteen and a fifth that had elapsed at the time of writing. But it was two lines in particular that triggered Keane's artistic imagination. The vision of the poet-prophet includes: *somewhere in sands of the desert / A shape with lion body and head of a man*.

The artist does not, as a Nostradamus scholar might, try to explain away the leonine line but simply acknowledges its irrelevance. However, the man's head somewhere in the desert made him see the beheading videos, from which his mind then jumped to jumpsuits.

Although Keane, as readers of this book will learn, is an avowed atheist, these paintings—in which he puts the IS into Christ while both the pose of the clothes and poetry of Yeats are full of Christian imagery—are not the only place in which he plays with religious iconography. In the case of some of his foreign correspondent projects (in Latin and South America), this was because the Catholic Church was a powerful historical and political player in those regions. In the jumpsuit pictures, a non-believing artist seems to be conducting a complex religious dialogue. The post- or anti-Christian imagery of 'The Second Coming' is complicated by the presentation of the IS killings as crucifixions.

ML: In using that image, are you trying to suggest a religious war between Islamic State and Christian nations?

JK: Well, all those possibilities are there. I'm sure there are people in Islamic State who would like to see it in those terms.

ML: And indeed there are—from the other side—in the American neo-conservative movement?

JK: Absolutely. But, with the pose, it seemed to me that kneeling would be too obvious somehow. And the crucifixion, although it obviously has strong Christian associations, people were also crucified who weren't Christian. And so I was interested in the ideas of martyrdom and sacrifice, which ISIS is also using, although to a different religious purpose. It had a resonance without being too literal.

ML: You're always reluctant to explain these flashes of inspiration. But, when you talk about 'rediscovering' the poem and being 'struck by' the jumpsuit?

JK: Well, as you know, I'd already been playing with the colour orange and I suddenly thought of getting a jumpsuit. Quite often things come to me on my walk to work, which is 35–40 minutes from home, when cogs start turning. With the poem, I remember suddenly thinking of those lines: 'The best lack all conviction, while the worst are filled with passionate intensity.' And it seemed to fit.

ML: It could refer to President Obama and Islamic State, for example?

JK: Exactly. It seems very resonant now and so I looked up the poem again and there were all these lines about the desert sand and the 'head of a man'. And there seemed to be a sort of congruence and it seemed fertile territory to explore. Although it's very hard to talk about work in progress.

January 2015: the start of a year that would see general elections in Britain and Israel and the declaration of presidential candidates in the US — three of Keane's most fertile territories. Unseasonably warm post-Christmas temperatures of 54F perhaps vindicated another of his artistic interests: global warming and environmental damage. The day before we talked — confirming the urgency of his latest concern with East-West culture clashes — 12 people, including several of France's leading cartoonists, had been murdered by gunmen, apparently Islamist terrorists, at the offices of the French satirical weekly magazine *Charlie Hebdo*.

As we exchanged new year greetings and Keane made tea, I checked on the jumpsuit picture: the lurid crucified uniform now floating against a black background. To its left the actual outfit was posed and pinned on a step-ladder in a more submissive position.

MK: This is my fourth visit and the jumpsuit image looks complete to me?

JK: Yes. It is. You saw it in its early stages but it's pretty much finished now. I think I told you before I was toying with the title 'Second Coming'? And then I thought 'Shroud'. But — because it is already in that crucifixion attitude — it already has a quasi-religious aspect and I didn't want to underline it too much and so I'm just going to call it 'Jump'.

This reference to both the garment's name and the disembodied figure in mid-air is, as subsequent chapters will show, typical of the artist's delight in word-playing titles. The new title may also encourage viewers to connect the floating clothes with the bodies of American workers who hurled themselves from the roofs of the blazing skyscrapers of the World Trade Centre in 2001: a vision of horror that inspired some Keane paintings (chapter four). If that connection is intended, it is fitting because 9/11, Guantanamo Bay and the ISIL beheadings fed and encouraged each other in a loop of cruelty between the US and UK.

But the clothing also proved to be a suitable jumping-off point for another picture. The suit against the wall was, it turned out, artfully positioned.

JK: I'm going to do a second one with the jumpsuit, but with the attitude kneeling. Which is a bit more difficult to get. But I rather like the clumsiness of the posture.

ML: And what will that be called?

JK: Good question. 'Jump II'? I haven't got that far yet.

ML: And those two pictures will be the end of this idea?

JK: I think so at the moment. We'll see where it goes.

Three days after that conversation, when he e-mailed me jpegs of the ISIL pictures, Keane added the note: 'By the way, I think I've decided that 'Aggregation of Terror' will become 'Distillation of Terror'.'

But, while the artist went back to work on selecting the paintings intended for a May 2015 exhibition 'The Wisdom of Hindsight', this book applies hindsight to an aggregation — or distillation — of the work and life of John Keane.

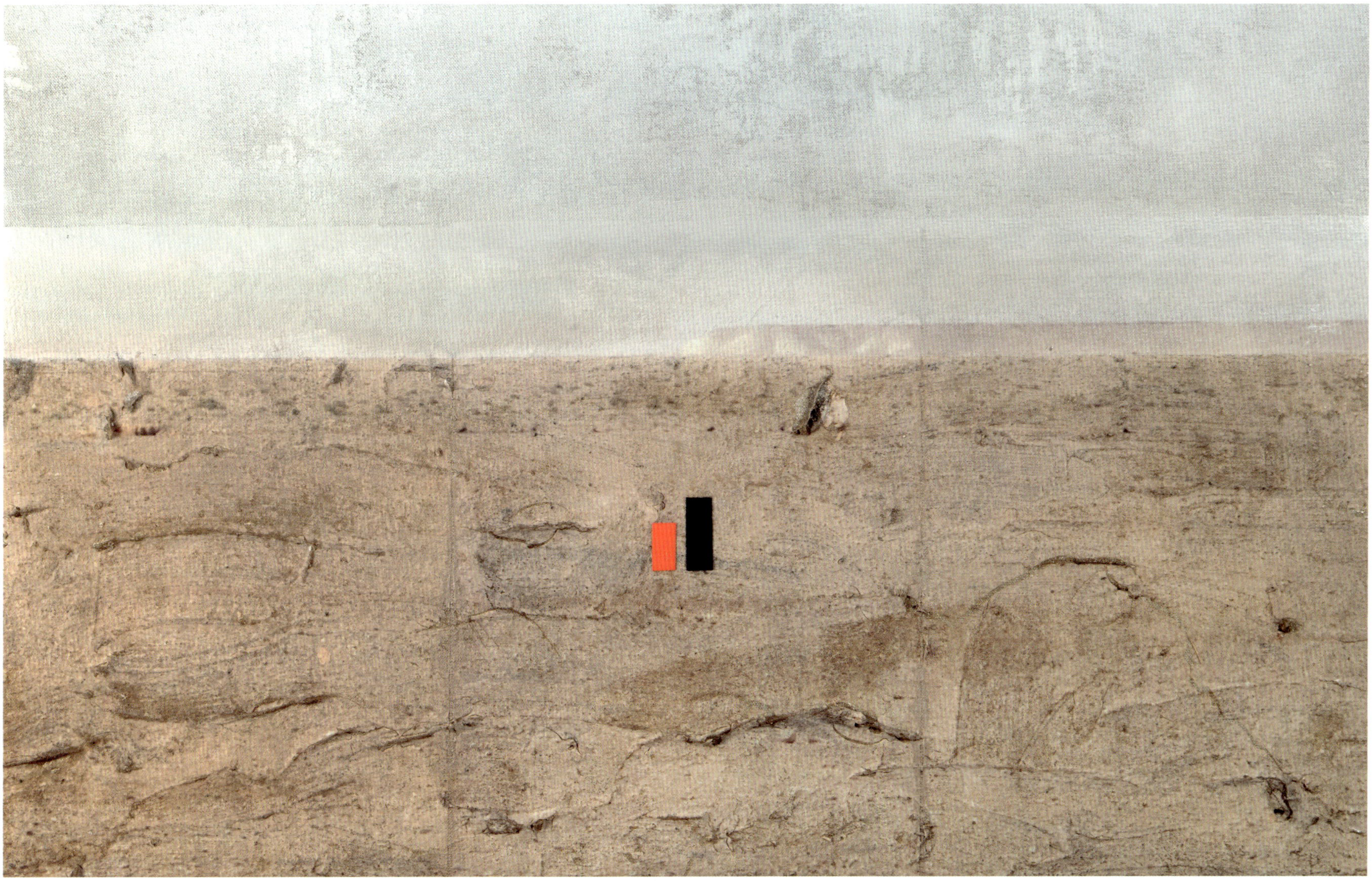

Second Coming, 2014
Oil on canvas
56 x 87 cm / 22⅛ x 34¼ in

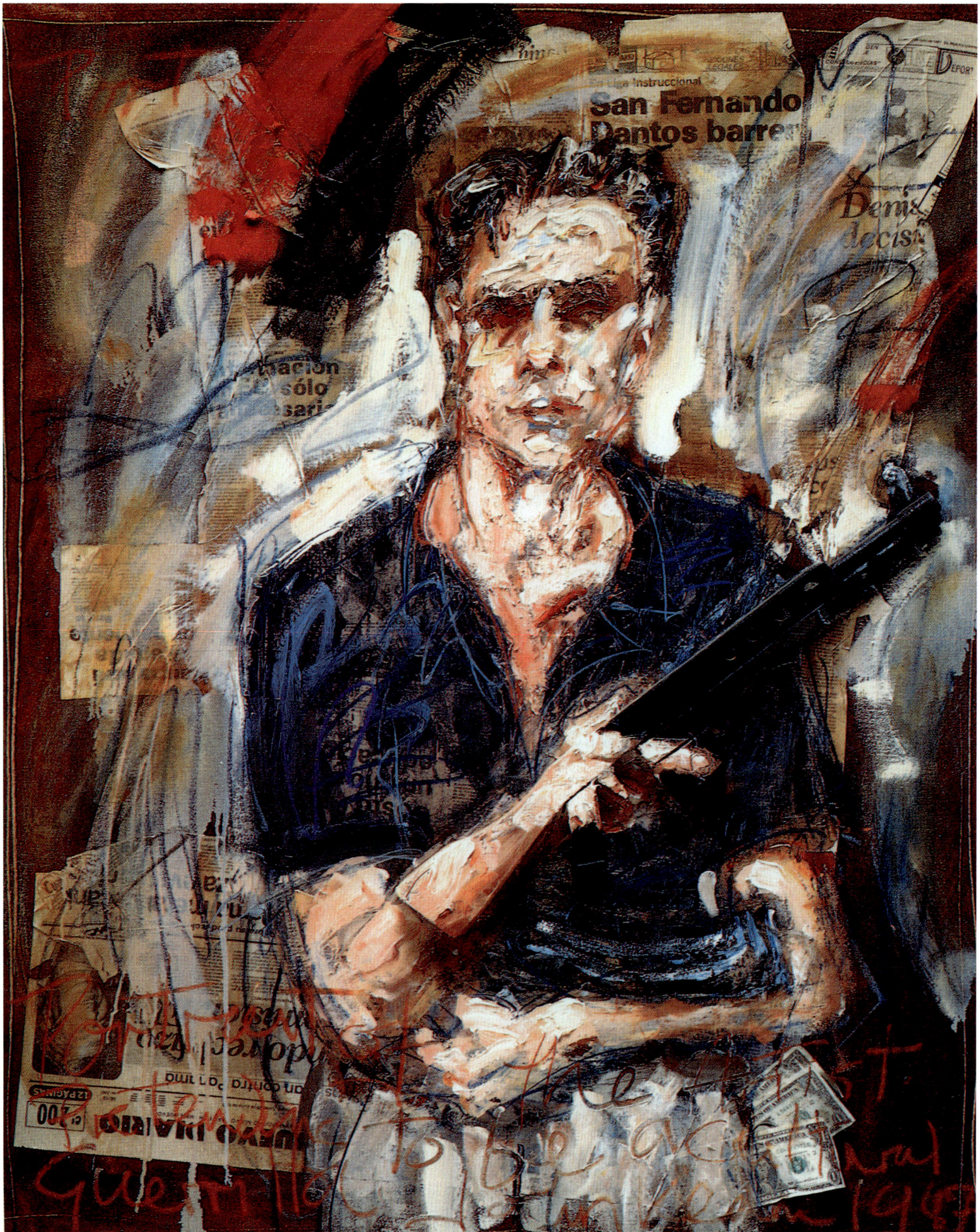
San Fernando

CHAPTER TWO

SELFIE

On one of my visits to the studio, the artist not only, unsurprisingly, answered the door but, more unexpectedly, also loomed large from the wall, watching us rather severely through thick black-framed spectacles above a cloudy white shirt.

Keane has turned his gaze on himself before. He holds a toy gun in the 1987 picture 'Portrait of the Artist Pretending to be a Cultural Guerilla', from his Nicaraguan series (see chapter four) and becomes the surrogate for another killer, President John F. Kennedy's assassin Lee Harvey Oswald, in 'Backyard Painting' (1997), a doctored version of the best-known photo of Oswald. He shoots satirically in his own direction as well in a North London dinner party picture—'Supping with the Devil' (1993)—where he takes a seat at the smug supper. There is even a Freudian (Lucian not Sigmund) nude: 'Latter-Day Church of the Bleeding Heart Liberal' (1993). In the recent *Fear* series (chapter four), he inserts himself, Zelig-like, into a chilling set of arrest pictures of enemies of Joseph Stalin who are doomed to be executed.

But this latest image—formally posed, alone, white-shirted, looking out front—was the closest I had seen to a Rembrandtian self-portrait, which seemed to be sceptically scrutinising the likenesses in progress on the other wall: Putin, Brooks and Murdoch.

ML: So there you are on the wall. When I was here last time, there was no sign of it, so where did that come from?

JK: It's a good question. I'm thinking of it as a parallel to the group of portraits I'm working on. I've got a title for a future exhibition—'Speaking Power to Truth', which reverses that phrase about 'speaking truth to power', which people seem to like using. But why a self-portrait? I think that, with a lot of stuff I do, I never forget that this is me commenting about that. There's a self-consciousness.

ML: In the way that you appear in the corner of the dinner party paintings?

JK: Yes, it's possibly also self-deprecating, in that it's saying: 'This is only me.'

ML: I just wonder if two things you had going on—being 60 and having to talk about yourself for this book—might they have triggered something?

JK: Possibly. I think inevitably you take stock, look back. And you're thinking about mortality, in the end. The older you get, it crops up from time to time. So reflection on self and life becomes more prominent.

ML: Also, which might have surprised Rembrandt and Van Gogh, there's the odd fact that almost everyone now takes self-portraits: the 'selfie'. And so the fact that you're painting from a projected photo of yourself, that's a sort of selfie-portrait?

JK: It is. The original image was taken on the computer and so it can't escape reference to the fact that selfies are ubiquitous. But a selfie is instant and almost disposable; whereas making a painting undermines that disposability. It's not something that can be erased, deleted.

ML: But it must be bizarre for an artist to see people now—especially young people—taking pictures of themselves all the time, photos of their food, whoever they meet and so on?

Portrait of the Artist Pretending to be a Cultural Guerilla, 1987
Oil and mixed media on canvas
119 x 94.5 cm / 47 x 37¼ in
Private Collection, UK

JK: Yes. It is a fascinating cultural shift towards this almost obsession with the self, which to many people in previous eras would have been frowned upon as being embarrassing and somehow unhealthy. But there has been a definite shift that has been facilitated by the digital revolution. Also people are much more — dare I say it? — shameless these days: sexting and all that stuff, that people are much more willing to share intimacy.

SIXTY YEARS BEFORE PAINTING HIS SELFIE-PORTRAIT, in a Britain where cameras were a rare and bulky luxury, John Granville Colpoys Keane was born, in 1954, in the Hertfordshire town of Harpenden.

It was a prosperous, conservative (and, in elections, solidly Conservative) place that incubated the sort of rigorously reactionary upper-middle class opinions that tend to be described by those advancing them as "no nonsense". To this day, it is common for the more reactionary letters to the *Daily Mail* or *Daily Telegraph* to have the town as their geographical sign-off. It also ranks high in articles in those newspapers listing the most well-off locations in the UK: average property prices are at least twice the national benchmark.

Long ago, invaders of Britain came and stayed there — there are Roman remains in the local Rothamsted Park — but, more recently, the most powerful inhabitants have been more likely to come and go every day. With London easily reachable by train, it is a dormitory town for the commuter community, although one of the most celebrated residents was chauffered to BBC TV studios: Eric Morecambe, probably Britain's most revered single comedian, lived there for most of his adult life and, during his TV shows with Ernie Wise, would sometimes suddenly shout "Harpenden!" as a cry of surprise.

More typically of the professions represented, the artist's father, Granville Keane, was a stockbroker, leaving the large Victorian house in Wordsworth Road — probably worth, these days, around as much as a small Rothko — to take the train to the City of London to make money into more money at Sheppard's (later Sheppard's & Chase and then swallowed by other concerns.)

Granville had been born in Ireland — which would remain both personally and professionally significant for his son — but, during his childhood, the family had emigrated to England, apparently fearing the suspicion and possibly worse that the developing 20th century was likely to bring in politically febrile Ireland to British landed gentry stock.

The senior Keane spent three and half years in Japanese prisoner-of-war camps during World War II, a conflict in which two of his brothers had been killed: biographical details that inevitably leap out flashing to viewers of John Keane's substantial production of art about war.

John's mother, Elaine Violet Meredith Doubble, had been significantly scarred as well by the conflagration of 1939–45. Her first husband — father of Keane's older half-brother — had been killed in Normandy.

The writer Michael Morpurgo, who was born too late to be conscripted in a war but has made conflict his frequent subject — in novels such as *War Horse* and *Private Peaceful* — has attributed his literary interest in the military to a sort of familial osmosis from his parents: his mother was mourning a brother who was killed in active service during the Second World War and his mother's first marriage had been ended by the separation imposed by the conflict.

Backyard Painting, 1997
Oil and collage on canvas
158 x 123 cm / 62¼ x 48½ in

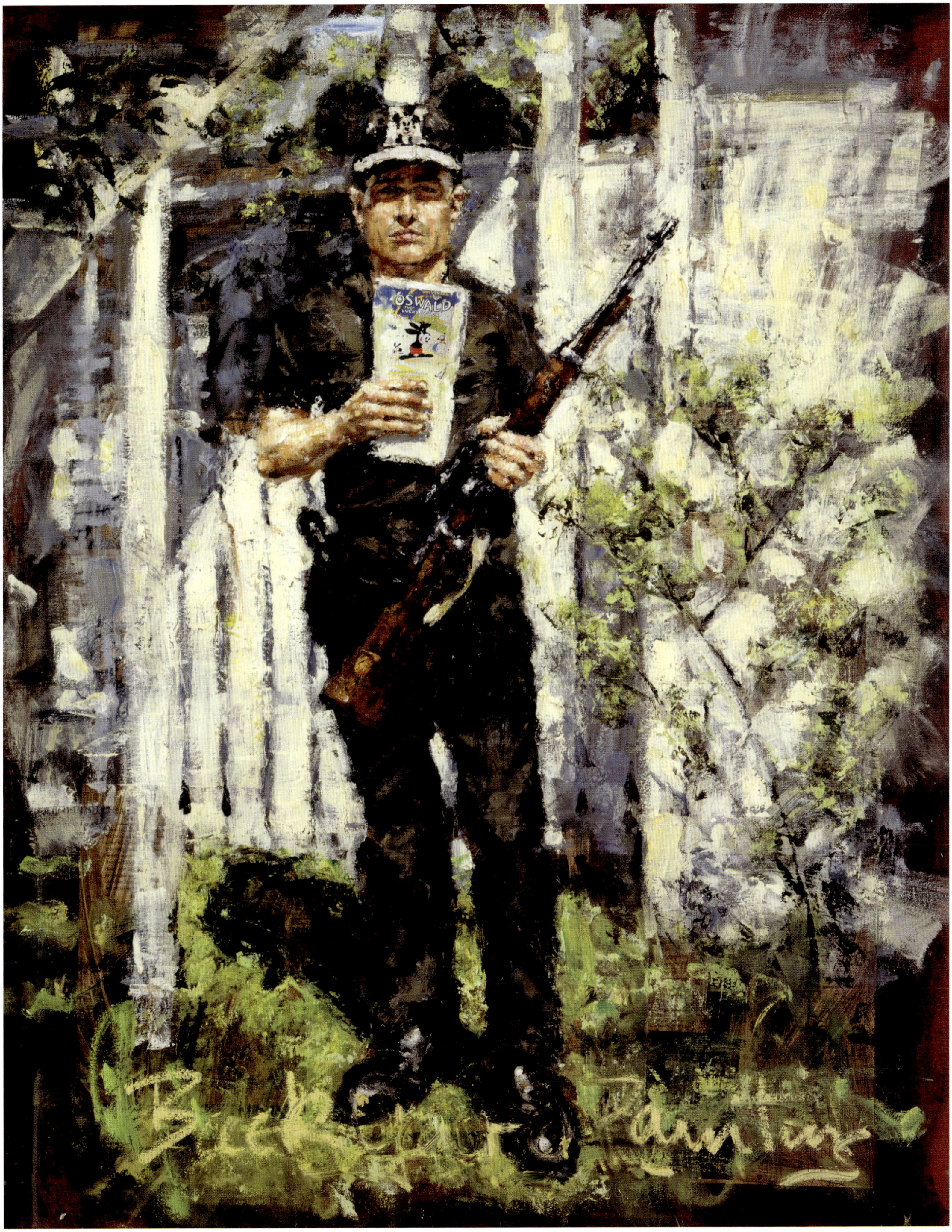
OSWALD

Starting work on this book soon after interviewing Morpurgo, it struck me that Keane has a very similar biographical and artistic arc: a post-war child who has obsessively explored soldiers and battles and whose parents both carried significant battle damage.

ML: Do you think there might be overlaps between you and Morpurgo in that?

JK: Mmm? A lot of what I grew up with was just part of the landscape. I didn't think about it at the time and it's only in retrospect, I suppose, that. . . .

ML: Yes, well that's what we're getting into: the deep sub-conscious.

JK: It doesn't feel from my point of view that it is significant. I suppose, if I'm on the couch. . . .

ML: But you are on the couch in this book. And it must be significant to your subject matter?

JK: I don't feel that consciously. And I went through a lot of things before I settled on war. But. . . .

ML: Well, I think we'll leave the possibility hanging.

On the morning that we were talking — 11-11-14 — a BBC radio phone-in, inviting listeners to share family experiences of military sacrifice and damage, had featured several children of war heroes and veterans saying that they had only understood what their parent went through second-hand from diaries or letters discovered posthumously because those most affected by the war were often reticent about discussing their experiences. John Keane recognises this phenomenon in his father.

JK: He referred to it, made jokes about it, anecdotes, comic characters, whatever. But the reality of it, he only mentioned once. He gave me a book, by an Australian, who had been in many of the same camps and their experiences matched. I would have been in my 20s by then and I read it and we talked about it. And that was the only time in my life I ever saw him cry. And what had prompted that was talking about an extraordinary act of mercy shown by one of the Korean guards, who had given him some medication when he was very sick. And that act of mercy for some reason greatly moved him.

ML: Did your mother talk more about the war?

JK: Yes. She talked about it. But, bless her, she was a bit batty and she talked about lots of things. Her first husband was in the Royal Ulster Rifles. And was on one of the gliders, just after D-Day. He was killed in Deauville by a random shell explosion. In fact, we went just a couple of years ago to visit his grave, when we were in Normandy.

ML: Was he talked about?

JK: Now and again. There was a photo of him in the house. And we were very close to his family in Northern Ireland. We'd go there or stay in a hotel with them somewhere.

As well as symbolically unifying Ireland — the Keane relatives in the South now matched by the Johnston clan of his mother's first husband — the marriage of Granville and Elaine produced, as well as their son John, two daughters. In the fashion of that class at that time, the girls — Clare and Patsy — were educated locally while the boys — John and Bruce — were sent away to board, first at Cheam preparatory school in Hampshire and then Wellington College in Berkshire.

ML: We see a lot at the moment—with David Cameron and George Osborne, for example—people apologising for being posh or having gone to public school? Have you suffered from that?

JK: Oh, yes. I'd always try to play it down: especially at art school. Yes, there was a kind of 'inverted snobbery', as it was called then. A bit more street-cred was more acceptable. I always had a slight embarrassment about it. If anything I try to conceal it. Because it undermines your artistic credibility somehow?

ML: And you were never tempted to send your own children to Wellington?

JK: Definitely not. I would never send a child away to school, having been sent away myself. It seems barbaric to me: having children and then sending them away for most of the year. I mean, I'm not saying there weren't benefits of being sent to Wellington. And one of them—to be honest—was being sent away.

ML: Really? Why?

JK: Well, it gave me an independence. To be honest, I wouldn't be doing what I am now if I'd been at home all the time. But the misery and homesickness and missing your family: I wouldn't inflict on anyone.

Although the English public schools are often seen as a feeder system for the higher reaches of the Establishment—and, at the time of writing, both Prime Minister Cameron and Archbishop Welby of Canterbury are Old Etonians—the elite teaching system also has a long history of affecting counter-radicalisation.

While Open Day brochures for prospective parents may play down the associations, the leading figures in the ring of Soviet double-agents known as the Cambridge Spies—Kim Philby, Guy Burgess, Donald Maclean and Anthony Blunt—were products respectively of the playing fields of Westminster School, Royal Naval College Dorset, Gresham's School in Norfolk and Marlborough.

Less dramatically—or, depending on your perspective, more—there is also a distinguished history of political-artistic apostasy. The most influential left-wing writer in modern English literature, George Orwell, attended both Wellington and Eton. Two of the leading English dramatists on the Left—David Hare and David Edgar, who wrote the catalogue preface for Keane's *Intelligent Design* show (chapter five)—are alumni of Lancing and Rugby. Francis Wheen, the leading radical English journalist of his generation, is another OE.

So it is tempting to attribute the persistent oppositional instinct in Keane's art to a reaction against what he saw in living room and classroom. But the artist demurs.

JK: I don't think that there was anything about Harpenden, Wellington or that quintessential middle-class background that I detested. I have to admit that I was actually pretty happy in my schools, although I hated being sent away each term. It was just that my horizons were broadened and so it obviously raises questions about what you have previously just accepted. . . . Also, because I was growing up in the 1960s and beginning to think for myself, I was quite aware of the changes in attitude that were going on. There may have been an element of reaction against public school but the more important thing was the atmosphere of dissidence and counter-culture. Rebellion was in the air.

In 1969, as a bright artistically-interested schoolboy of 15, Keane was an ideal viewer for Monty Python's *Flying Circus*, the BBC comedy series that began in that year. Although most fondly remembered for the laughter produced by John Cleese, Michael Palin, Graham Chapman, Terry Jones and Eric Idle—in verbal comedy such as The Dead Parrot Sketch and

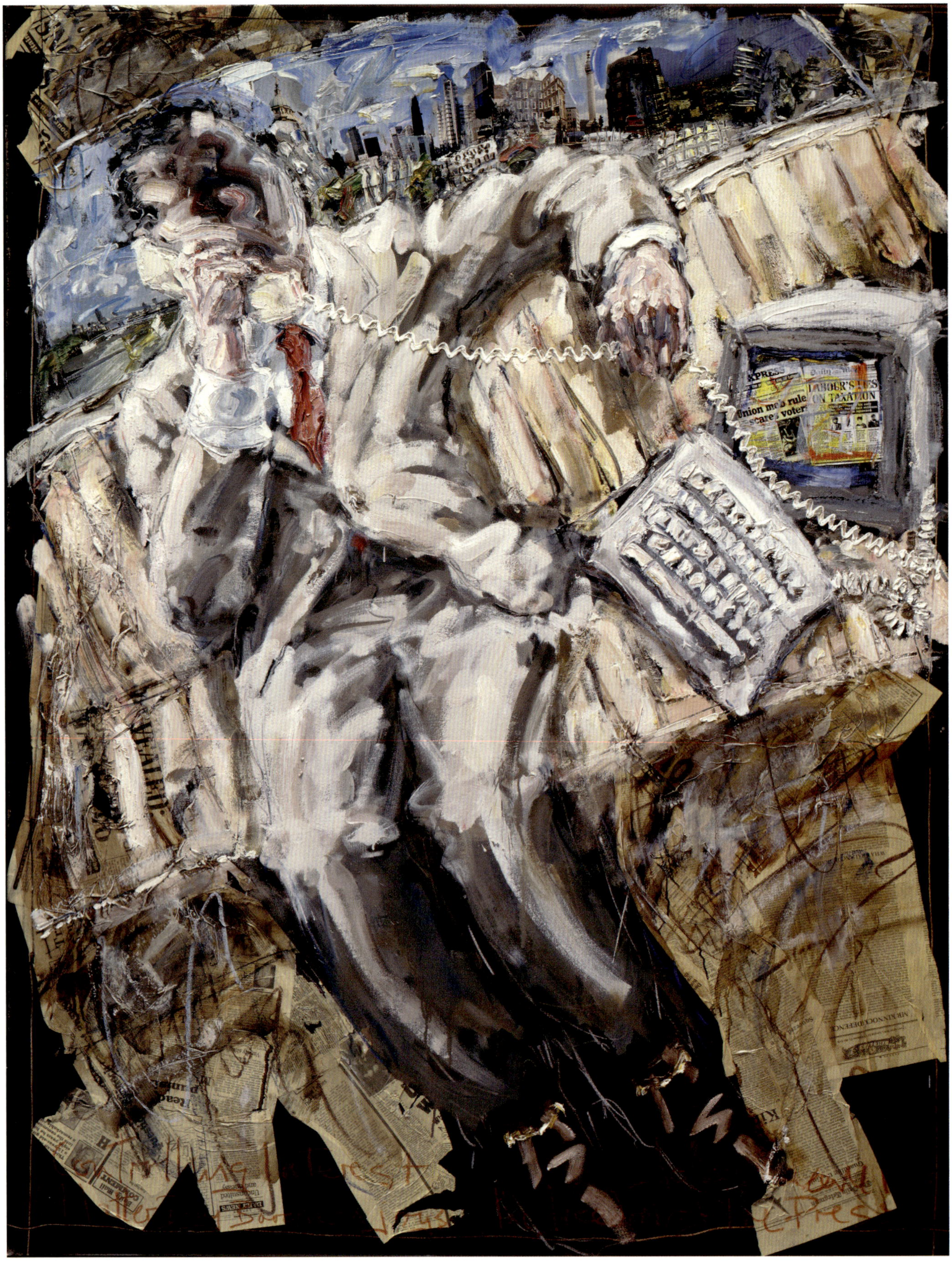

Controlling Interest
(a Latter Day Baron Enjoying the Freedom of the Press), 1987
Oil and mixed media on canvas
183 x 152 cm / 72 x 60 in
Collection: Harris Museum and Art Gallery

The Emperor's New Pose or Doing for d'Offay or The Importance of Being Important or
The Pot Calls the Kettle Black, 1985–86
Oil and mixed media including felt stolen from a Joseph Beuys installation
244 x 183 cm / 96 x 72 in.
Private Collection, UK

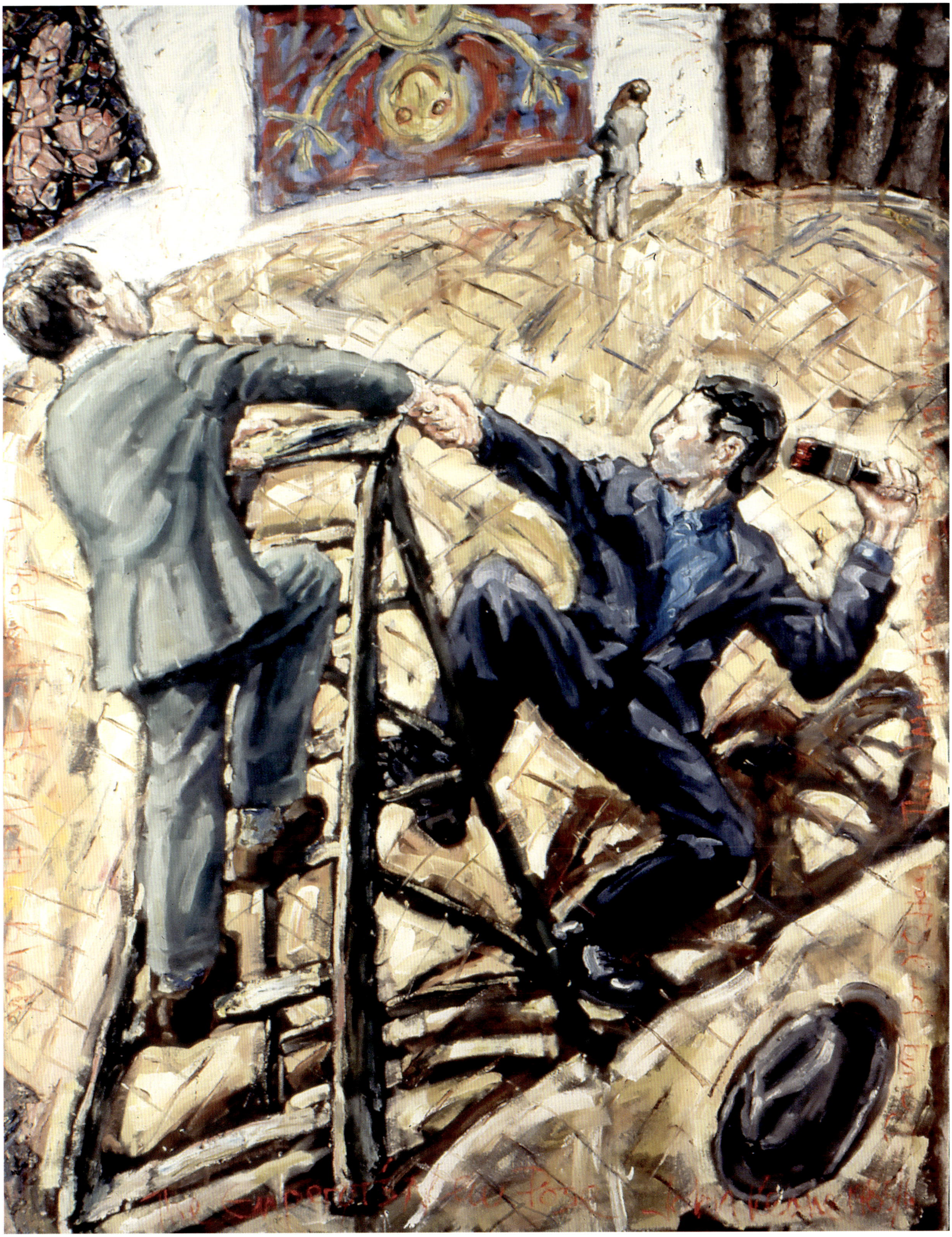

musical rudery including The Lumberjack Song—the series also gave an unusually large part to art. The American illustrator Terry Gilliam introduced surrealism to the British mainstream—a tip-off eagerly followed up by advertising agencies—through peculiar and rude animated cartoons that drew on influences including the European surrealists Rene Magritte and Salvador Dali and the American pop art star Andy Warhol.

Keane credits Monty Python as the biggest cultural influence of his adolescence. The popularity of the show led to the setting up of a surrealistic magazine at Wellington and Keane was asked to contribute drawings. Python also, via Gilliam's graphics, affected his artistic development.

ML: Who were the artists who first engaged you?

JK: Dali, I'm afraid. And Magritte, who I still rate.

ML: I remember a great flurry at the BBC, when Damien Hirst mentioned in an interview that he had sent childhood paintings to *Blue Peter* and *Vision On* and those types of shows. There was a search in the archives, as they would probably be worth quite a lot. Did you ever send anything in to Val Singleton or Tony Hart?

JK: No. No I never did.

ML: After the surrealists, who caught your eye?

JK: Then it was the abstract—Mondrian, Rothko. And Andy Warhol has always been there to some extent. I definitely had a pop art pastiche phase.

All biographers are in search of the smoking gun, the moment or fact from childhood that underlies the creative life. In the case of Keane, despite the subject's scepticism, I am convinced that smoke from the guns of the Second World War front has entered his imagination through parental osmosis. But, in our discussions about his childhood, I was also in search of the smoking pun.

In line with the frank editorialising of much of his work, Keane has never been one of those painters who vaguely label a work 'Composition XI' or 'Untitled'. But, beyond that decision, his namings favour jokes and word-play: 'The Emperor's New Pose' (1985–86), 'Controlling Interest' (1987) or, in his series inspired by the 1984 miners' strike in Britain, 'Face', a title neatly referring to both the coal-face and the portrait of one miner in the foreground.

ML: And your fascination with word-play. Can that be traced back to anything?

JK: I like jokes. And puns really make me laugh. I know John Cleese—was it?—once said that the first rule of comedy was no puns and the second was no puns. I entirely disagree. I love things with multiple meanings. Where it came from I'm not sure. Ah, suddenly something's come to mind. A story I wrote; I must have been 13 or 14 at school. We'd been given titles to choose from and the one I chose was 'Science has gone too far'. And I wrote a story about a rabbit who was called Science because he was so bright. And there was an animals' running race. And Science finds a pair of springs and attaches them to his feet. And, at the end, he gives one great bounce and goes right over the finishing tape and someone says: 'I think Science has gone too far!'

ML: And were you given a detention?

JK: No, it was read out in class and I remember a great chuckle at the end.

ML: Well, there you go. We've cracked it. A great Freudian [Sigmund, not Lucian] moment.

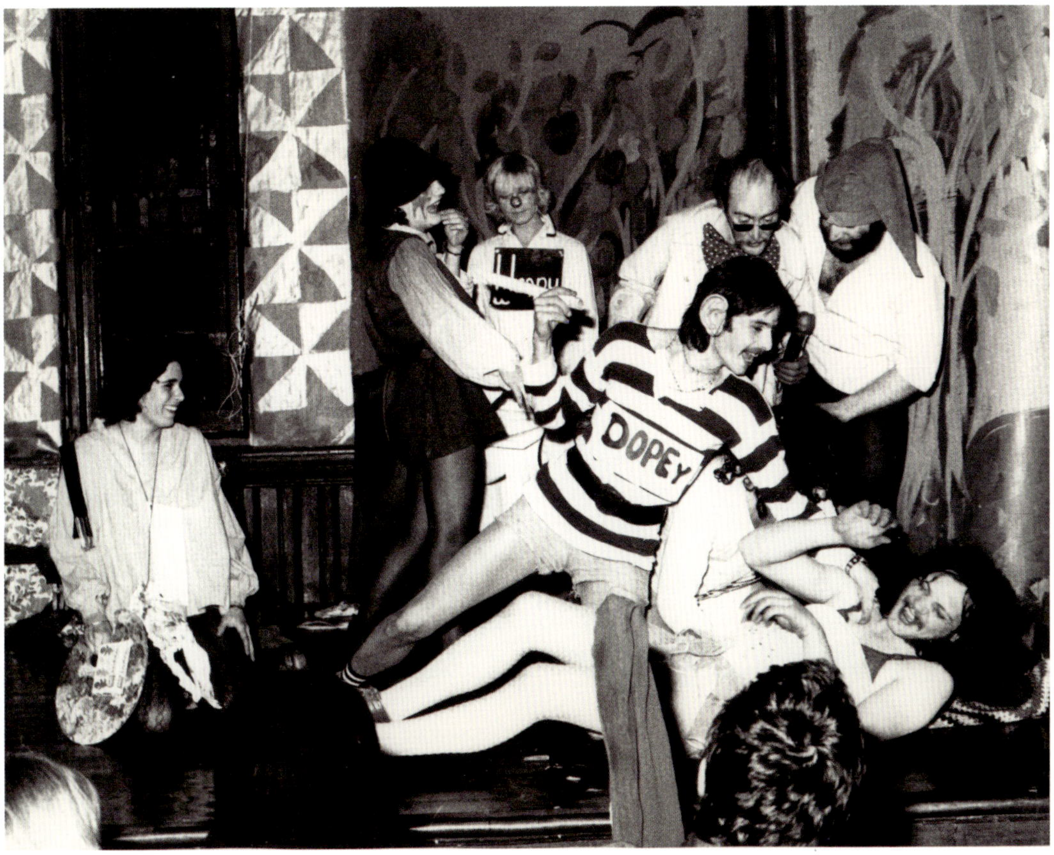

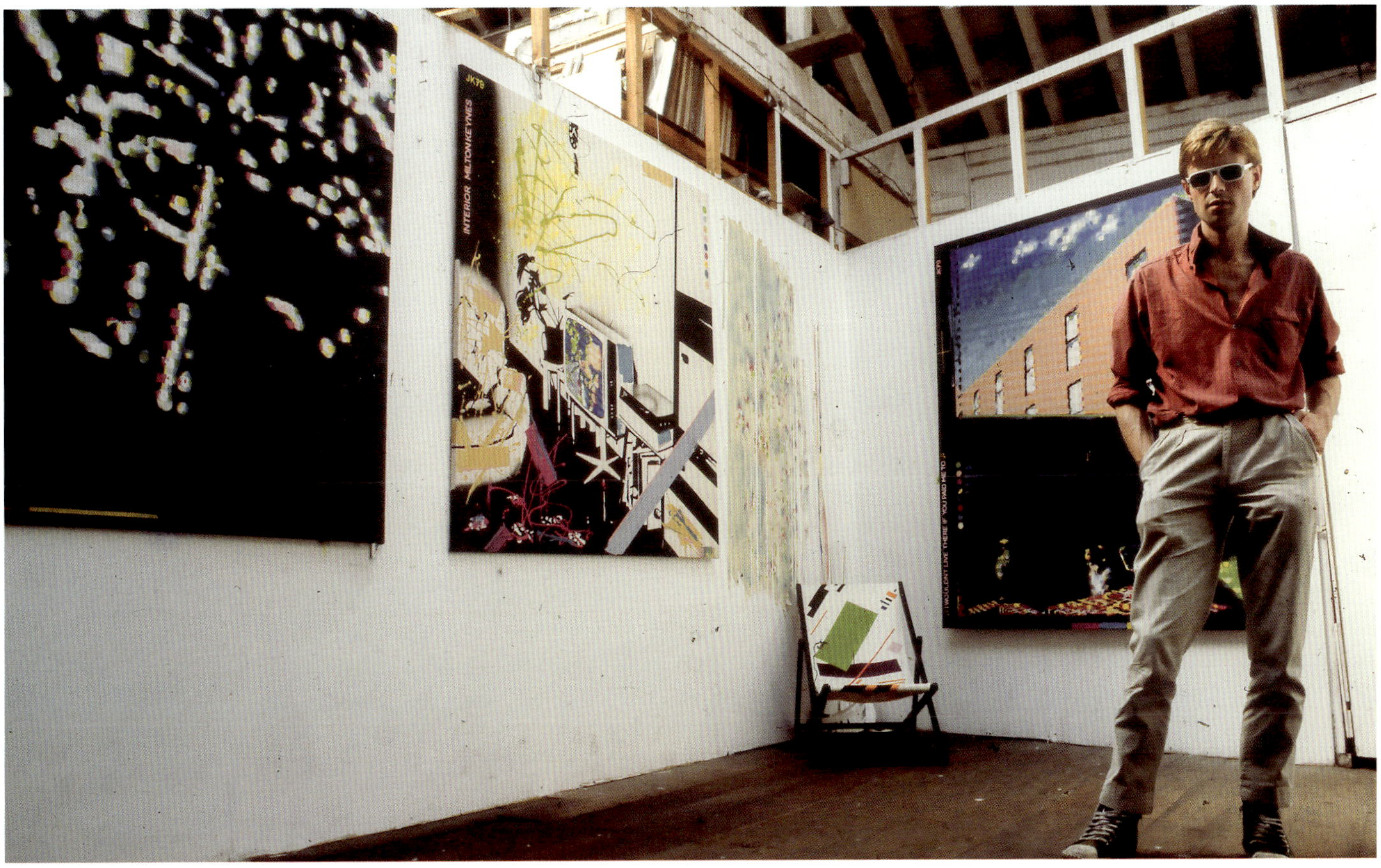

Camberwell School of Art Panto 1975, with John Keane as Dopey the Dwarf

John Keane in his Berry Street studio, Clerkenwell, London, 1978

The convention at Wellington was that the brighter sons were encouraged towards Oxbridge and the dimmer ones into the military. But Keane, against familial and educational precedent, was sure from the age of 15 that he wanted to be an artist, although a notably broad set of A level subjects—Maths, Physics, English, Art History—allowed his parents and teachers to hope that those plans could still be redrawn.

But the art teacher at Wellington, to whom Keane remains grateful for the mental pictorial history of which he still makes use, was encouraging, sending off for prospectuses, from which the 18-year-old student chose Camberwell in London, applied, was accepted and started in September 1972.

ARTISTS AND WRITERS HAVE PIECES OF LUCK—good and bad—from the slice of time they live through. Keane, who had the fortune to be at school during a period of counter-cultural revolution, was by chance at art college, from 1972–76, during a spell of exceptional political instability.

A lengthy miners' strike in 1973—more successful than its 1984 successor, which would become a subject for the artist—resulted in a three-day working week and regular black-outs of the domestic power supply. Anyone who was at school or college during this period possesses the weirdly 17th century memory of candle-wax dripping on to hands and foolscap while doing homework.

In 1974, there were spring and summer elections, until Labour leader Harold Wilson gained a sufficient majority over Conservative leader Edward Heath in the second poll.

But the mess went on. Extraordinarily, within two years, both the American President and the British Prime Minister were forced to resign despite not having lost an election. Richard Nixon vacated the White House voluntarily in order to avoid prosecution for his part in the Watergate scandal caused by surveillance and secret recording of political enemies; Wilson left office suddenly as well, an event attributed by some to dirty tricks by the security services but more likely due to the politician's diagnosis with the early stages of Alzheimer's. As a result, for a period in 1976 both Britain and America had unelected leaders: President Gerald Ford and Prime Minister James Callaghan, both of whom would lose the only general election they fought.

During this pre-digital era of art, Keane was able to go on painting and drawing by flame even during the power cuts but was otherwise largely unaffected by the legislative meltdowns. He was bemused when Marxist students attempted to reorganise the classes at Camberwell into communes rather than age-groups and is not even sure that he bothered to vote in the year of two ballots.

> JK: Art school was a complete upheaval after the background of public school. I can't really say that I enjoyed my time there. I was fairly disorientated and rather in turmoil. And art school was quite a disappointment to me. I'd expected it to be a vibrant, intellectual place and it was rather small-minded and vindictive. Most of the time, I was caught up in the growing pains of being away from home and having all kinds of unhappy relationships with women.

As the artist's father had a job that involved making money expand, his parents perhaps understandably panicked intermittently that their son had chosen a career path in which the cash supply was prone to contract catastrophically. This was before the present era in which, art teachers report, students read about Damien Hirst and Jeff Koons and see pictures as possible route to riches. At the end of the foundation year, the Keanes urged John towards graphic design, which was practical and even bankable, but he opted for the purity and possible poverty of fine art.

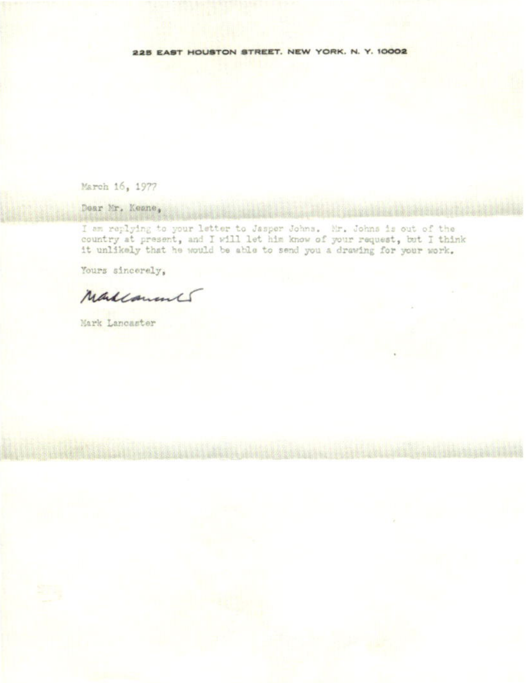

225 EAST HOUSTON STREET. NEW YORK. N. Y. 10002

March 16, 1977

Dear Mr. Keane,

I am replying to your letter to Jasper Johns. Mr. Johns is out of the country at present, and I will let him know of your request, but I think it unlikely that he would be able to send you a drawing for your work.

Yours sincerely,

Mark Lancaster

Letter from Jasper Johns, March, 1977

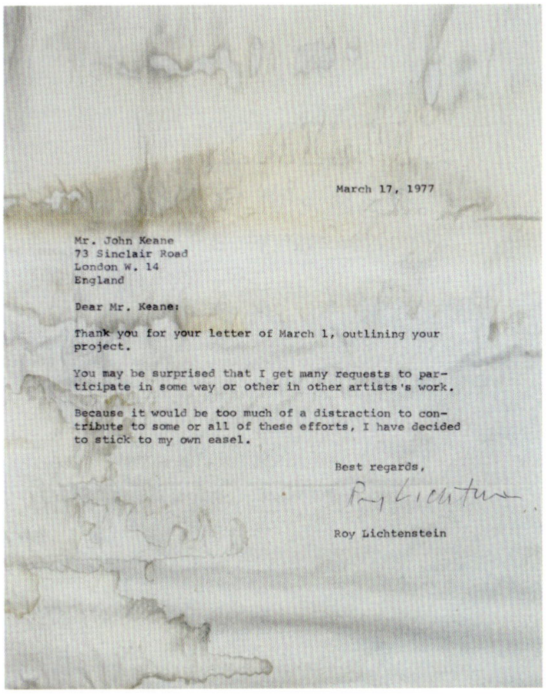

March 17, 1977

Mr. John Keane
73 Sinclair Road
London W. 14
England

Dear Mr. Keane:

Thank you for your letter of March 1, outlining your project.

You may be surprised that I get many requests to participate in some way or other in other artists's work.

Because it would be too much of a distraction to contribute to some or all of these efforts, I have decided to stick to my own easel.

Best regards,

Roy Lichtenstein

Letter from Roy Lichtenstein, March, 1977

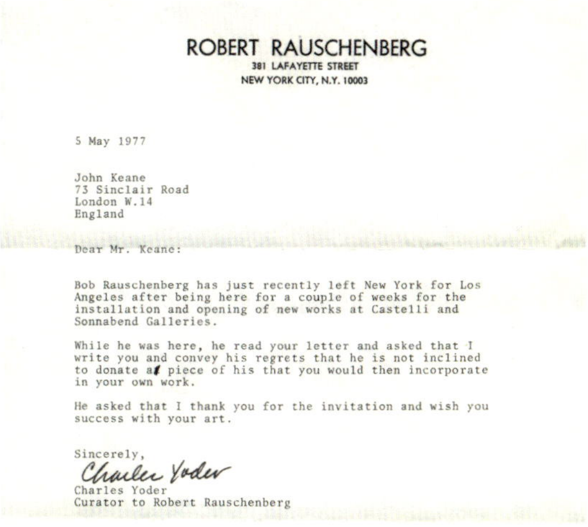

ROBERT RAUSCHENBERG
381 LAFAYETTE STREET
NEW YORK CITY, N.Y. 10003

5 May 1977

John Keane
73 Sinclair Road
London W.14
England

Dear Mr. Keane:

Bob Rauschenberg has just recently left New York for Los Angeles after being here for a couple of weeks for the installation and opening of new works at Castelli and Sonnabend Galleries.

While he was here, he read your letter and asked that I write you and convey his regrets that he is not inclined to donate a piece of his that you would then incorporate in your own work.

He asked that I thank you for the invitation and wish you success with your art.

Sincerely,

Charles Yoder
Curator to Robert Rauschenberg

Letter from Robert Rauschenberg, May, 1977

In cultural academia, there is often a tension between an orthodoxy taught on the course and the interests and instincts of some students — Keane was a victim of such a collision. The key teacher at Camberwell was Euan Uglow, in whose work figurative painting converged with complex geometric theories. The Uglovians and Keane, who was more interested in Warholian image-manipulation and photo-realism, were unsympathetic to each other, which was one reason that he graduated in 1976 with a 2:2 that he found hugely disillusioning.

Almost abandoning hope of his chosen career, he took a job as a clerk in the Inland Revenue Sorting Centre in Kew. Stubbornness and determination, though, are very present in his personality and, by 1977, he had set up a studio and begun to make pictures.

But there is also a shy and reticent streak in Keane and, possibly illustrating his lack of confidence, he started with a sort of karaoke form of art, in which he covered someone else's work. Writing to famous artists around the world asking for a piece of their work that he could incorporate in his own — a kind of celebrity ready-made — he got a big no from most big names, including the American painter Jasper Johns, but the Bulgarian-American artist Christo, whose work often involves constructing fences or "wrapping" landmarks in material, sent back five signed postcards that Keane incorporated in a collage.

Although, in the final chapter of this book, Keane is largely dismissive of his early pictures, some of his formative work still has a visual and cultural sting and anticipates concerns and even — in the manipulation of media images — working methods that remain part of his practice today.

The artistic and ideological sponsor of these apprentice pieces is obviously Warhol, to whom Keane, in one beginning picture, made a direct act of homage through repainting by hand a Warhol screen print. But, once he starts making his own Warholian paintings, it's striking that, possibly hinting at the way that his political conscience was developing, Keane tends to choose enemies of the American way rather than the embodiments of it — the Kennedys, Marilyn, Elvis, John Wayne — to whom the American pop artist was drawn.

Fidel Castro, whose Communist regime provoked America's Cold War anti-communist paranoia, makes waves with two French literary figures often name-checked in Monty Python in 'Jean-Paul Sartre and Simone de Beauvoir Speedboating with Fidel Castro' (1978).

The main face in 'Interference' (1979) is that of Patti Hearst, the American media heiress (her grandfather the model for Orson Welles' Citizen Kane) who, in what can be seen as a precursor in moneyed America to the successful young Muslims who now leave the West to become jihadists, became a member of the terrorist organisation the Symbionese Liberation Army, converting to their cause despite having been kidnapped by them.

In order to suggest media distortion and unreliability—a critique and technique that continue in his recent *Speaking Power to Truth* portraits—he placed strips of masking tape across the canvas and then ripped them off to suggest the flickering pixelated instability of a TV screen. A similar effect is achieved more efficiently in the recent pictures by working from digitally altered images. In the way that some movie directors discover on set that a new type of camera or lighting has finally given their films the look that they saw in their mind's eye, Keane can be seen as an artist who anticipated digital possibilities even when working with analogue tools.

Warholian but also recognisably Keanean, 'Monday Blues' (1979) is a school photo that no parent would want to be sent home. Its subject is another American rich girl who, like Hearst, turned herself into a public enemy. In a pre-Columbine time when gunfire still remained an unexpected sound in US schools, Brenda Spencer, at the start of a new week, shot several classmates dead. Asked by police why she did it, the mass-murderer replied "I don't like Mondays", a chilling phrase that caught the lyrical ear of Bob Geldof, who expanded it into a Number 1 song for The Boomtown Rats, and the artistic eye of John Keane, who used the same tape-rip method as for 'Interference' (1979) to make the image televisual and speculative. By coincidence, both the painting and the pop video for Geldof's song make repeated use of a motif of a TV set.

People made notorious by the media—and the people in the media who make them so—would recur in the artist's work over the next four decades. But it would be as a recorder of wars—home and foreign, declared and unofficial that he would make his most powerful mark as an artist.

CHAPTER THREE

HOME CONFLICTS

Although the period of American and British politics from 1989 to 2014 covers a quarter of a century and featured four US Presidents and five UK Prime Ministers, the years, in terms of foreign policy, can be viewed as a single continuous narrative.

Even the names scarcely change. As this curve of time began, George Herbert Walker Bush was in the White House, while William Jefferson Clinton, governor of Arkansas, was contemplating a bid, in 1992, to replace him there. Under his preferred democratic monicker of Bill, Clinton succeeded and (despite his problem with another Monica, the Lewinsky sex scandal) served eight years between the single term of the first President Bush and the two terms of the second: his son, President George Walker Bush. Hillary Rodham Clinton lost her chance to continue the domination of the Oval Office by two families when Barack Obama beat her in the 2008 Democratic party primaries, but the Clinton name remained a regular entry in the White House entry log because Hillary served as Secretary of State in the first Obama administration. And, as the 2016 American election approached, a third Bush—Jeb,

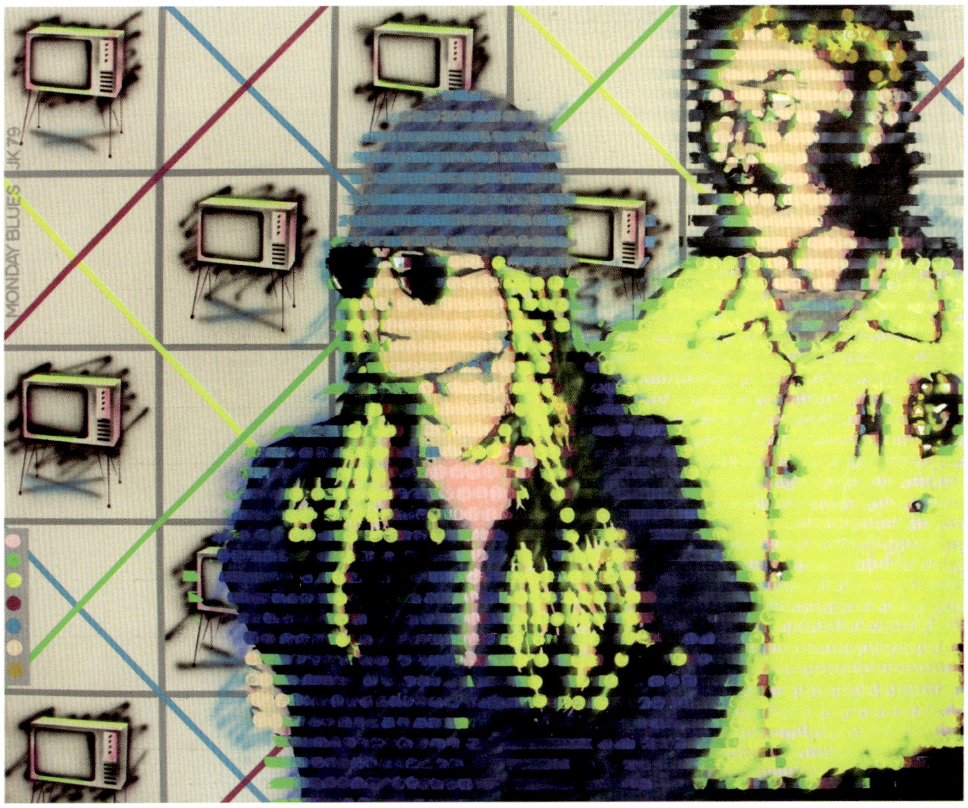

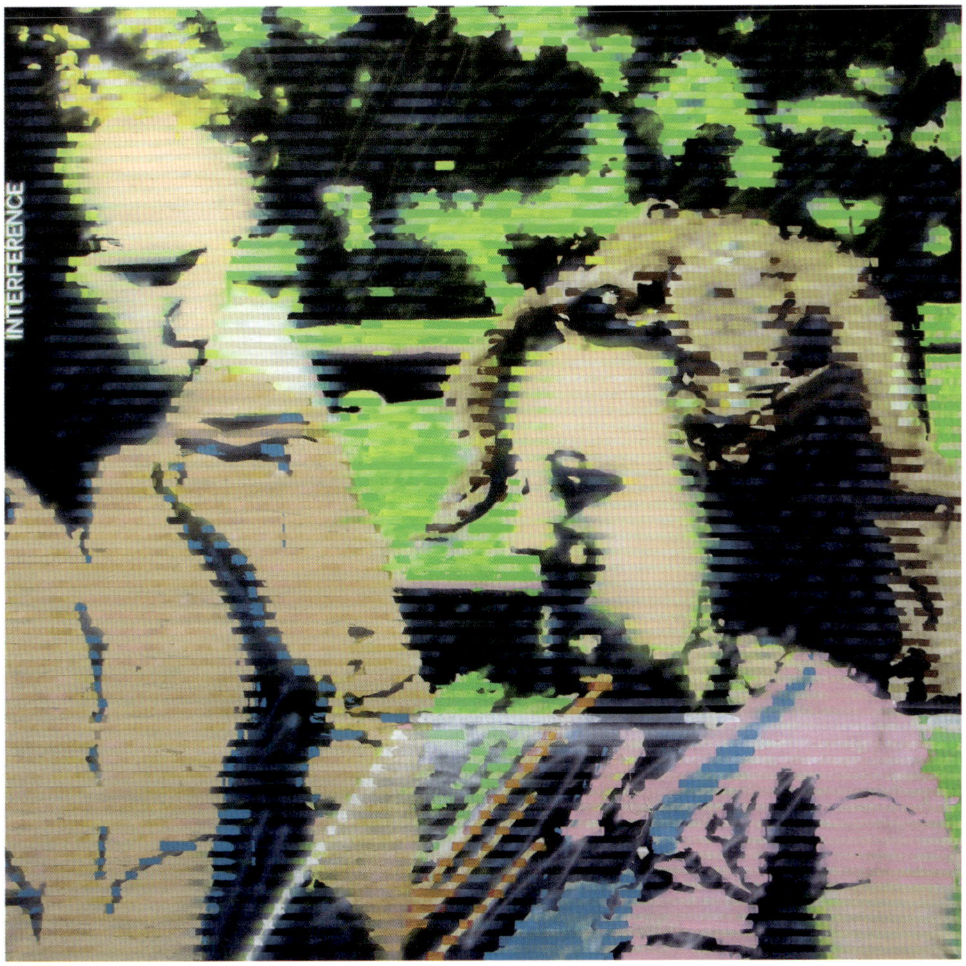

Monday Blues, 1979
PVA on canvas
152.5 x 183 cm / 60⅛ x 72⅛ in

Interference, 1979
PVA on canvas
152 x 152 cm / 60 x 60 in

brother of the 43rd President, son of the 41st—declared his candidacy, while Mrs Rodham Clinton spent more than 600 pages of her memoir *Hard Choices* carefully avoiding ruling out the possibility of making it another Bush-Clinton campaign race.

And this sense of continuity is not just nominal. The issues of home security and international relations that face the British Prime Minister chosen in 2015 and the American President elected in 2016 are the latest chapters of a story that began 25 years ago. The first President Bush, in the first Gulf War in 1990–1, removed Saddam Hussein from Kuwait, which he had invaded, but left him as President of Iraq, from where, in the Second Gulf War of 2003, the second President Bush, strongly backed by British Prime Minister Tony Blair, deposed him.

Landing a military jet on an aircraft carrier, George W. Bush declared "Mission accomplished", but a terrible game of consequences had begun. Resentment of the West—and especially the US and UK, who led the more invasive second war—fomented rhetoric and recruitment in the Middle East that violently energised the Islamist terrorist organisations, Al Quaeda, Hamas and, most recently, the grouping variously known as ISIS / ISIL / Islamic state.

These organisations prosecuted a new form of warfare in which enemy nations were invaded briefly but shatteringly by small numbers of soldiers who accepted certain death in the attempt: hijacking passenger jets and flying them into New York's World Trade Centre, Washington's Pentagon and a field in Pennsylvania on September 11, 2001; blowing up Underground trains and buses in London on July 7, 2005; and seizing and executing British and American hostages in Syria from 2013 onwards.

A feature of these attacks was a deliberate taunting quotation of visual imagery. The day now known in America as 9/11 was a parody of the aerial bombing raids that have been a favoured tactic of the American air force from Berlin to Vietnam to the two Gulf Wars. And the second President Bush's most controversial response to 9/11—locking up suspected terrorists without trial or appeal at a facility called Guantanamo Bay—was deliberately and brutally cartooned in the ISIS beheading videos, with their fuck-you gesture of dressing the men due to be executed in orange jumpsuits.

From President George Bush to candidate Jeb Bush—from Americans and Britons killing Iraqis in the desert to Syrians killing Americans and Britons on another patch of sand—this stretch of history is seamless and relentless and it has been tracked at every stage by the paintings of John Keane: from the role of official British war artist of the attack on Iraq, through pictures dealing with 9/11, 7/7, Guantanamo Bay and, now, the beheading pictures.

ML: Do you approach the subject of war essentially as a pacifist?

JK: Um, that's probably putting it too bluntly. I actually don't know if I'm a pacifist. Which is one reason I keep coming back to the subject.

ML: But we're the first generations for a long time to have been required neither to do national service nor to fight a war. And, in my experience, there's a spectrum among men from regret to relief. Where would you be?

JK: Oh, relief, absolutely. And that's one of the reasons the subject fascinates me—how appalling it would be to have to fight. What I keep coming back to is the question of how people are motivated to kill each other and what justifies that.

The consonance of UK / US foreign policy during the last quarter of a century is that all of the wars or attacks involve the Middle East. But there is an argument that one aspect of these dynamics — the ability of the British and Americans to overcome respective fears of another Suez or Vietnam and invade foreign nations — dates from several years earlier and that the work of this leading modern War artist also began there.

On 31 March, 1982, the Argentinian flag was planted on South Georgia, an uninhabited but British-owned rocky outcrop in the South Atlantic, in rather farcical circumstances by a gang of scrap-metal merchants from Buenos Aires. What felt at first like an adult rag-and-bone version of a student prank became a national crisis when, at dawn two days later, the Argentinian army took over South Georgia's populated neighbour, the Falkland Islands, where 2000 UK dependents lived. After three years as Prime Minister, and facing polling showing that she might struggle to be re-elected, Margaret Thatcher gambled on forcing an Argentinian back-down — or, if not, fighting to regain the islands — by sending a missile-armed naval "task-force". That word was one of several new coinages, including "yomp" for a long walk by soldiers, that the war popularised in British vocabulary.

For liberals of that period — including Keane — the Falklands conflict (never officially declared as a war) was politically infuriating — the bounce from Mrs Thatcher's victory was widely thought to have secured her second general election win in 1983 — but also ideologically confusing. It was not at all that they had expected their lives to be free of war but more that, when it came, they assumed a short and final armageddon: their generation, and those on either side, had given many sleepless nights and CND marches to the fear of nuclear conflagration.

But, instead of the long-anticipated Third World War that lasted seconds and left the white cliffs of Dover radio-active, what happened was a 74-day naval and land battle that was almost 18th century (when a previous stand-off between the countries had happened over the same land) except that the principal weapon was the exocet missile, the most lethal non-atomic armament of the time. Non-nuclear bombs, however, still killed efficiently: 649 Argentinian and 255 British troops and three Falkland islanders were killed in the fighting and hundreds of soldiers seriously and often disfiguringly injured.

27 at the time of the conflict, Keane remained as apolitically apathetic as he had been at art school but was radicalised by the "jingoism" (another newly popular term) of the public and — though it was hard to judge who encouraged whom — the press: after the *General Belgrano* was sunk by a British submarine with the loss of 323 Argentinians, *The Sun* newspaper's headline was *Gotcha!*

That contentious front page — which became symbolic of the inhumane sensationalism to which tabloid newspapers could stoop — is among the newsprint pasted to the canvas of 'Still Life (Insult to Injury)' (1984), in which the foregrounded still life items of a vase of flowers, a typewriter and a glass of whisky symbolise what would become a frequent theme in Keane's war work: the comfortable distance from which producers and consumers of the media watch and even enjoy conflict.

> JK: The Falklands pictures were a turning point from the rather detached and ironic stance I'd had towards my subject-matter and towards a more direct engagement. And I think that is what is important about this work — that it marked a change of attitude.

Penguins were understandably a common motif of Falklands coverage — *Guardian* cartoonist Steve Bell's 'If . . .' strip told the story of the war mainly from the marine birds' perspective — and a flock of them is depicted in the polymer PVA in 'The Individual in Relation to the Masses' (1982–83), one of the earliest works in the Falklands series, in which the much bigger penguins looming over a group of smaller ones may represent either politicians, the military or the media or some combination of these. Another painting, 'Nuclear Penguin

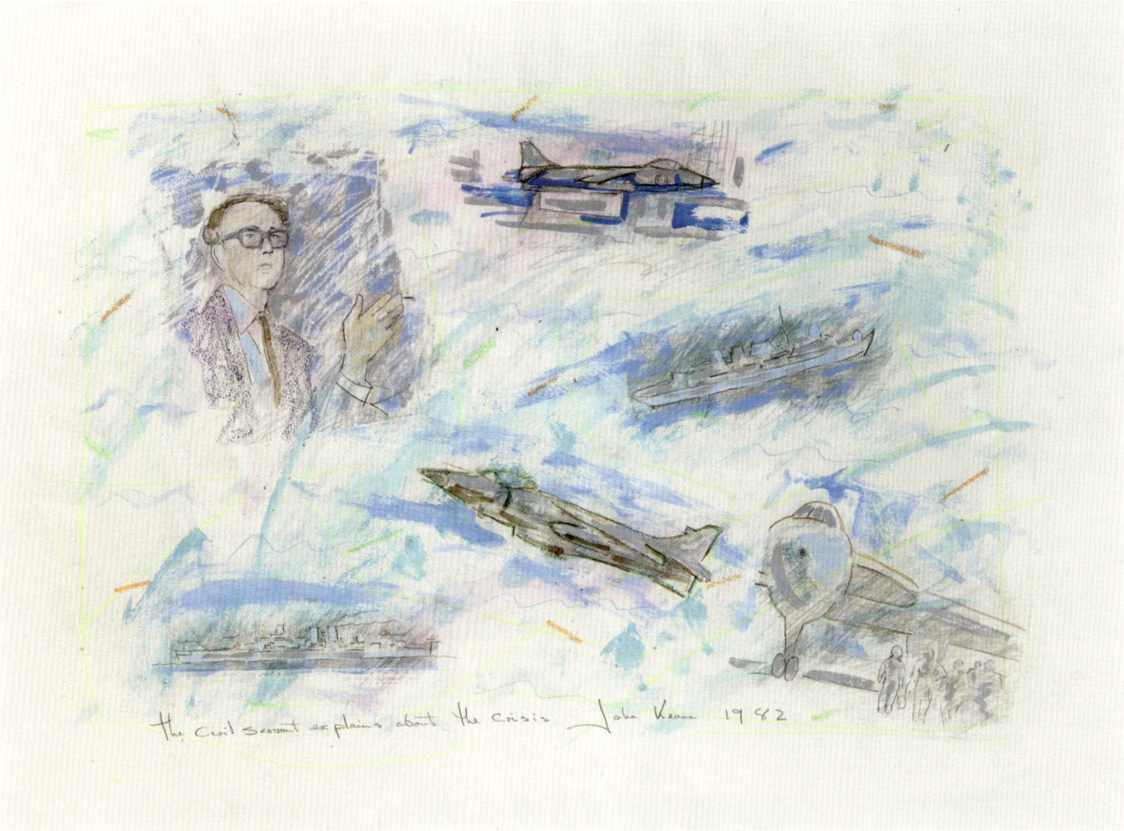

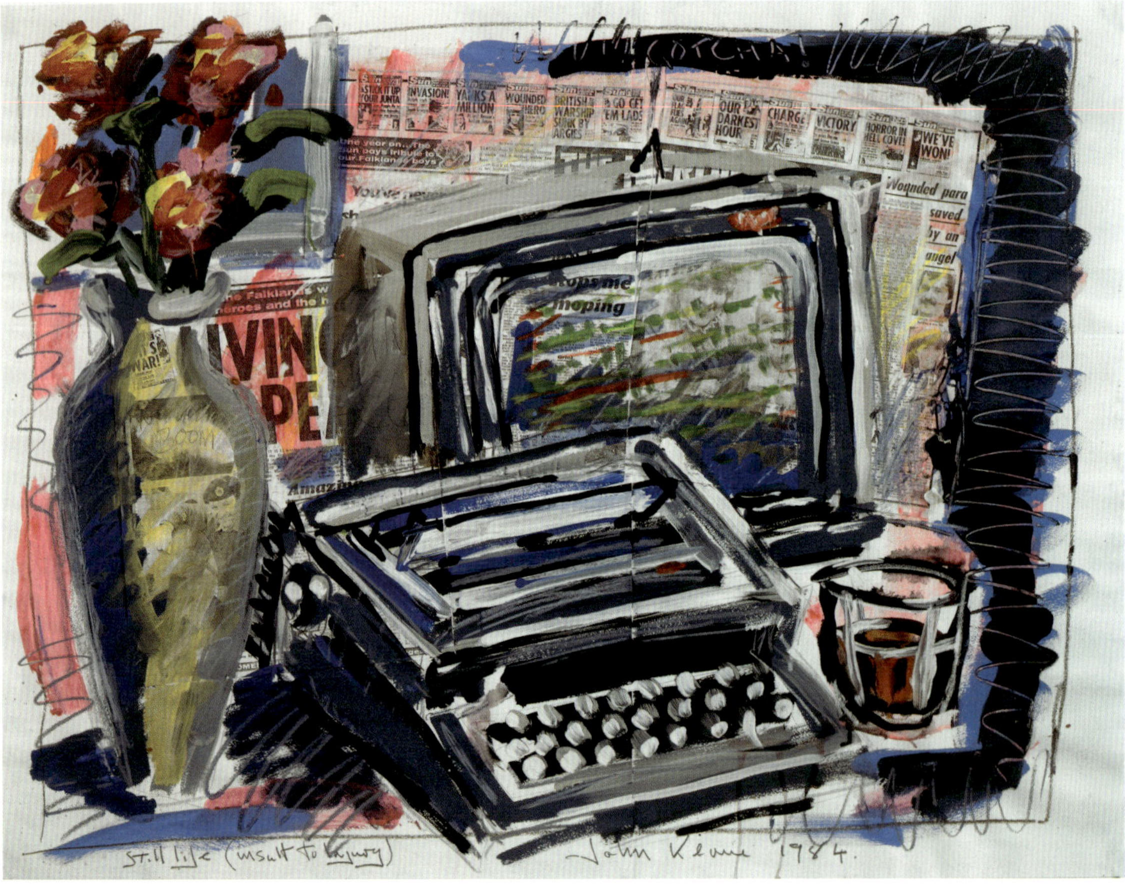

The Civil Servant Explains about the Crisis, 1982
PVA, crayon and phototransfer on paper
56 x 76 cm / 22 x 30 in

Still Life (Insult to Injury), 1984
PVA, crayon and collage on paper
76 x 99 cm / 31⅛ x 39 in

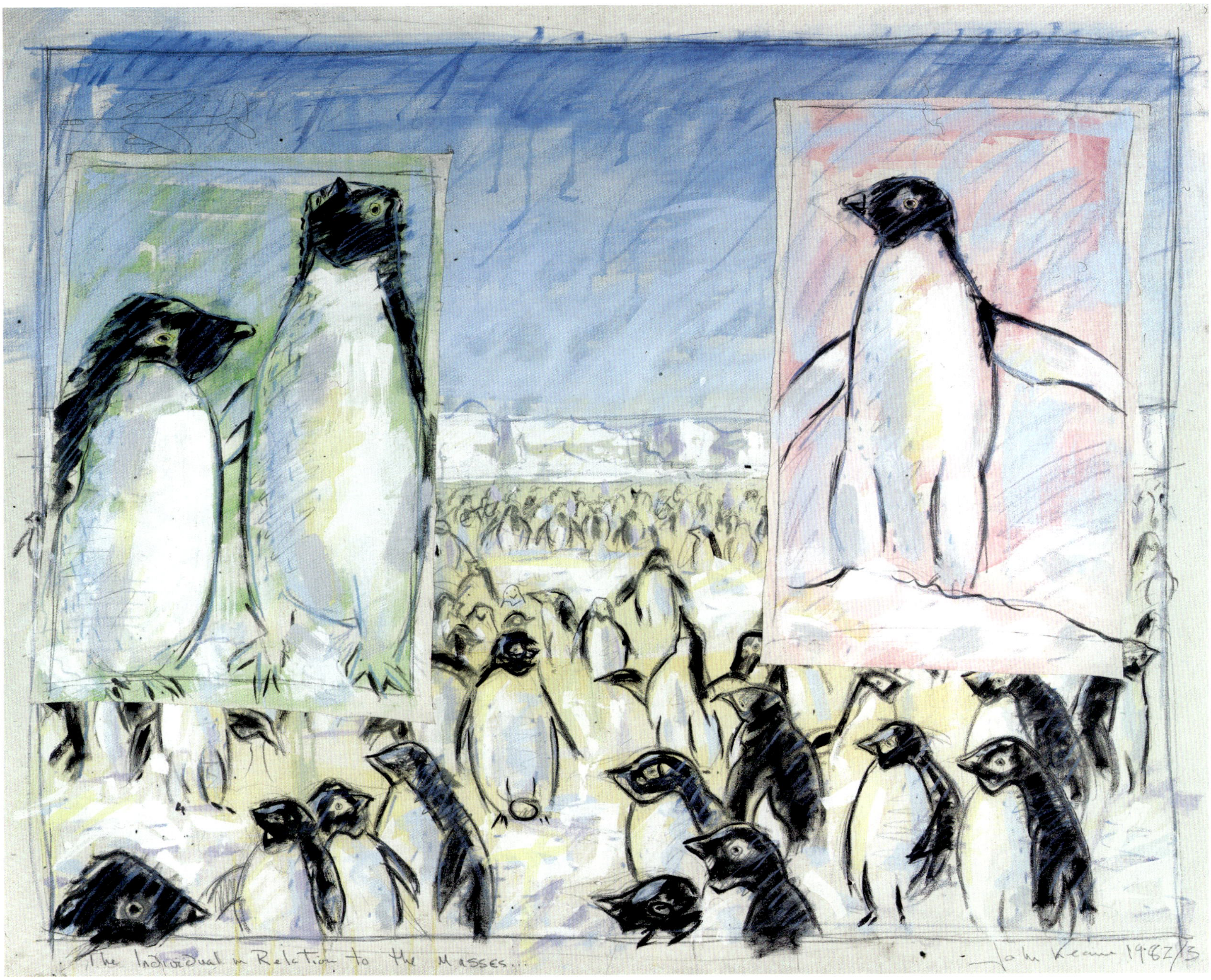

The Individual in Relation to the Masses, 1982/3
PVA on canvas
122 x 171 cm / 48⅛ x 67⅜ in
Collection: Leicestershire County Council

Family', suggests, as Bell's strips did, that a possible world war—which, some argued at the time, the Falklands scrap could theoretically set off—was being risked for a wild bird sanctuary that housed a few Brits whose presence was an historical anomaly.

Exhibited in a show called *War Efforts* at the Pentonville Gallery in London, these pictures accelerated Keane's career: two of them were bought for the Imperial War Museum collection and the artist was signed by Angela Flowers Gallery, as it then was, in Tottenham Mews in London. More than three decades later, he is still represented by Flowers, now run by Angela's son Matthew.

Two central aspects of Keane's artistic identity—journalistic subject-matter and reflection on media distortion of events—were established by these canvases. A third was soon to emerge: going to the source of the story.

ALTHOUGH THE FALKLANDS CONFLICT is sometimes given the shorthand 'Thatcher's War', the Prime Minister, during her three terms, fought two others, bloody but also undeclared, and on both of which Keane pictorially reported.

Northern Ireland was a home subject in two senses. Although it was a common view that Britain was not involved in a serious foreign policy crisis between Suez in 1956 and the Falklands 16 years later, the UK had been embroiled since 1969 in what most other cultures would have called a civil war, resulting from the despatch of British troops to subdue the violence between the Protestant and Catholic communities. However, although happening across the water from the rest of the UK, the conflict proved easily ignored and, by the 1980s, featured infrequently on British TV in drama, documentary or even news, unless an IRA (Irish Republican Army) bomb exploded in London or there was more than usual loss of life in Northern Ireland: such as the Remembrance Day massacre in Enniskillen in 1987.

But, far more than most people in what it was unwise in Ireland to call the "mainland", Keane had a reason to take interest, due to several pre-Troubles holidays in Newcastle, County Down.

JK: I think we had five or six summer holidays running in Northern Ireland in the 1960s.

ML: In the run-up to the Troubles?

JK: Absolutely. We stopped going in 1969, for that reason. And then we started going to Suffolk, which also had war connections because that was where my dad would play golf with his POW buddies.

ML: And, when you went back to do the Northern Ireland pictures, was any of it familiar from having been in childhood?

JK: Belfast, not particularly. Because we hadn't spent much time there. So yes and no. It was quite strange but there are a few familiar things that I remembered from back then.

His memories did inform one work in the Northern Irish project, which combines pastoral landscape with self-representation in the coastal idyll, 'Portrait of the Artist as a Small Boy' (1990) (chapter two), depicting a day from a Co. Down vacation. The title of another picture, 'Mournes', a rural Irish scene from before the fighting, pricks up the painter's alert ear for double meanings by ominously suggesting that the poetic placename will become a site of mourning.

Although his family had stopped going there because of the violence, Keane now went

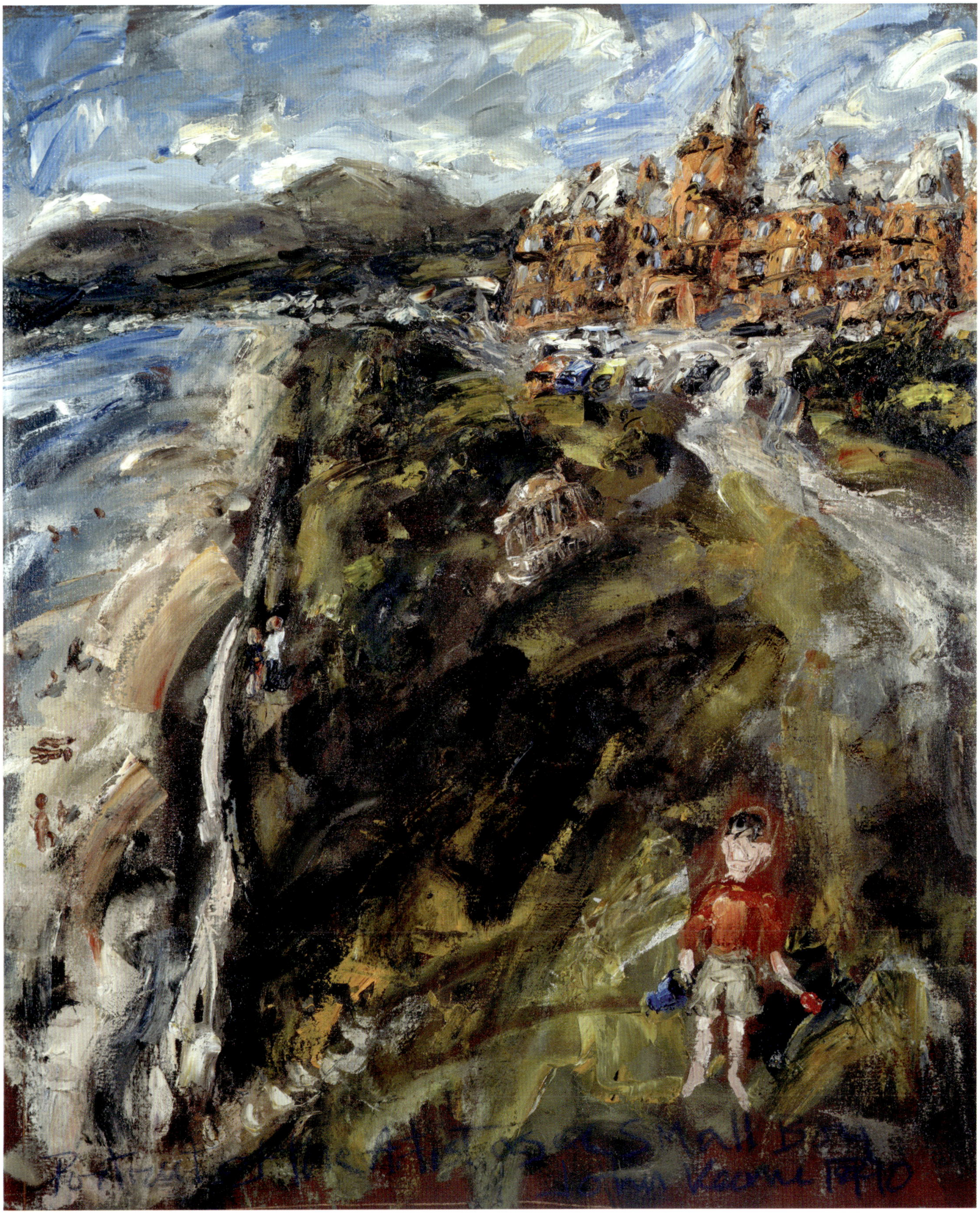

Portrait of the Artist as a Small Boy, 1990
Oil on canvas
76.5 x 61 cm / 30¼ x 24 in
Private Collection, UK

back because of it, staying with relatives in the summer of 1989, during a month in which a friend who worked for Ulster TV arranged interviews with supporters of the IRA and its political wing Sinn Fein and of the UDA (Ulster Defence Association), the loyalist paramilitaries who, by that time, seemed to many to be matching the savagery and fanaticism of their Republican rivals with the more famous set of triple terrorist initials.

With an electronic Olympus camera — in retrospect, a step towards his eventual preferred digital working methods — and notebook, the artist made an aural and visual sketchbook that informed the pictures included in the exhibition *The Other Cheek?*, seen at Flowers East in March 1990 and then, in a war art version of coal to Newcastle, toured to Belfast by the Arts Council the following year.

The title came from a phrase — "What do you expect us to do, turn the other cheek?" — that was used to him by representatives of all the warring parties to explain why they were unable to stop the bloodshed. It was horribly fitting that the words came from the Bible, which, although the hostilities involved two Christian denominations, was one of the points of opposition between the sides: the Unionist preacher-leader, the Rev. Ian Paisley, would refer to his side in sermons as "Bible Christians", with the deliberate inference that many elements of Catholic reverence were not in the book.

Adding a question mark to the show's title, *The Other Cheek?* places a dead Republican victim of a sectarian ambush on the left side of the canvas and a Loyalist casualty on the right, with a soldier kneeling over a dead comrade inbetween. As in the Falklands pictures, real newsprint is glued to the canvas and painted over.

An intriguing feature of *The Other Cheek?* series is the presence as realism of an effect that Magritte often used surrealistically: a painting within a painting. The Troubles tradition of mutually-abusive murals on the gables ends of buildings — a rare literal example of war art — means that a portrait of IRA paramilitaries and of the Unionist hero "King Billy" (King William III of England) occur naturalistically within Keane's illustration of Belfast life. In 'Brick Wall' (1989), the Royalist-Loyalist image is alone and enlarged in a painting with a name that literally describes the rough red architecture of Belfast estates but also keenly puns on the suggestion that dialogue or negotiation between the communities were, as the vernacular has it, as profitable as talking to a brick wall.

Although Keane is now equivocal about much of his early work (chapter seven), the Belfast pictures certainly work effectively as visual journalism which, a quarter of a century later, serve as a powerful historical record of what Northern Ireland was like at that time. 'March of History' (1989) catches the sinister vividness of a pipe-and-drum march by a loyalist Orange lodge, the flashes of their sacred colour now weirdly previewing its significance in Keane's recent pictures relating to a religious-political conflict in the Middle East. 'Peace Giant' (1989) shows a towering army observation post above a road in Armagh, adding a hint of a demon's eye to the observation post at the top to make it resemble an ogre from fairytale.

And, with the wisdom of hindsight, the Belfast pictures now look forward to the artist's paintings of the Palestinian territories (chapter four) and to his first official portrait, which would feature Dr Mo Mowlam, one of the politicians who finally brought the two sides in Northern Ireland to a sort of peace (chapter five).

By the time that ceasefire and power-sharing agreement were achieved, Margaret Thatcher was out of office but, as she spent her final time in Downing Street before being forced to resign by her party in November 1991, John Keane was making good one omission from his chronicling

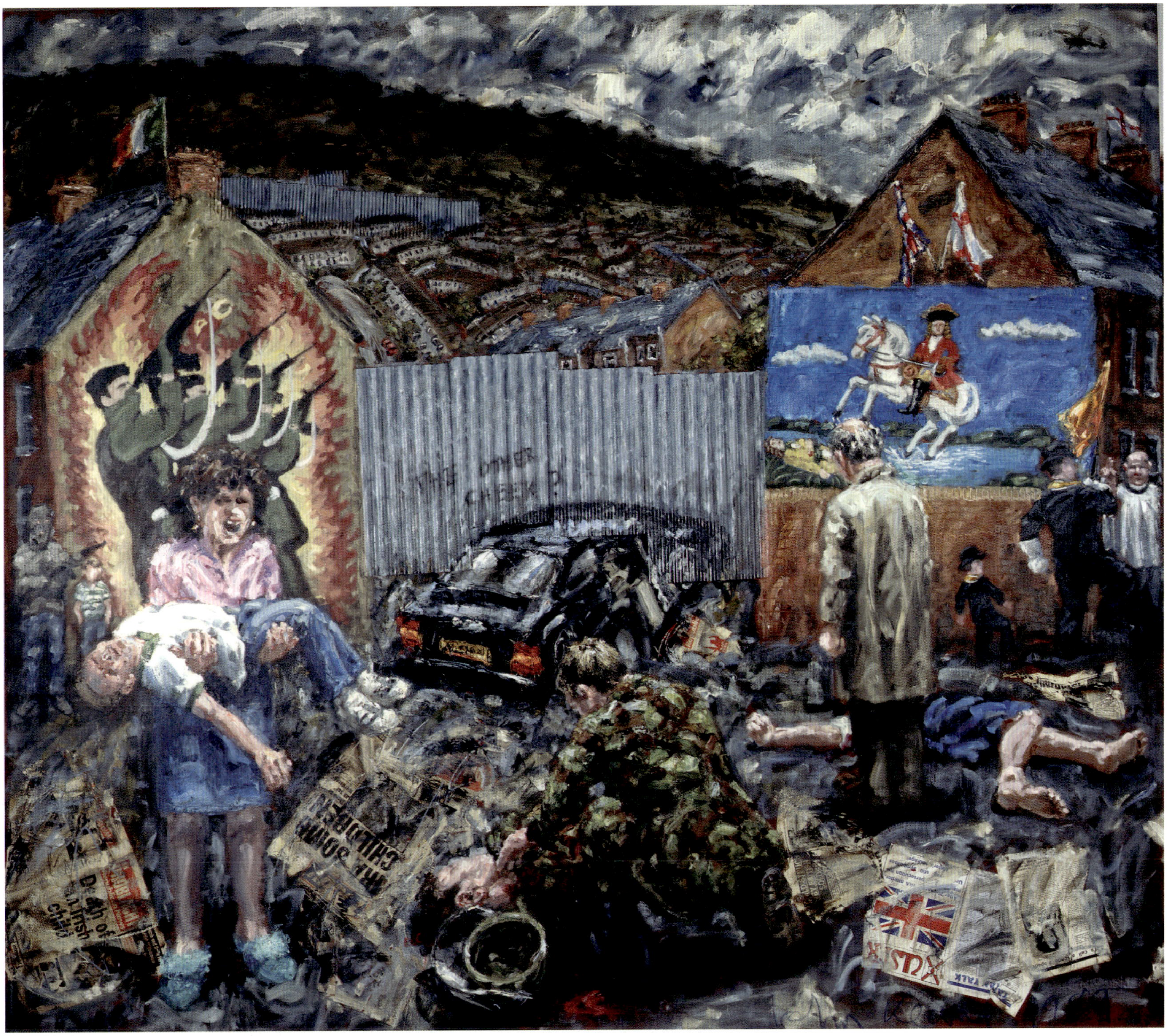

The Other Cheek?, 1989
oil and mixed media on canvas
224 x 274 cm / 96 x 107 in
Collection: Ulster Museum

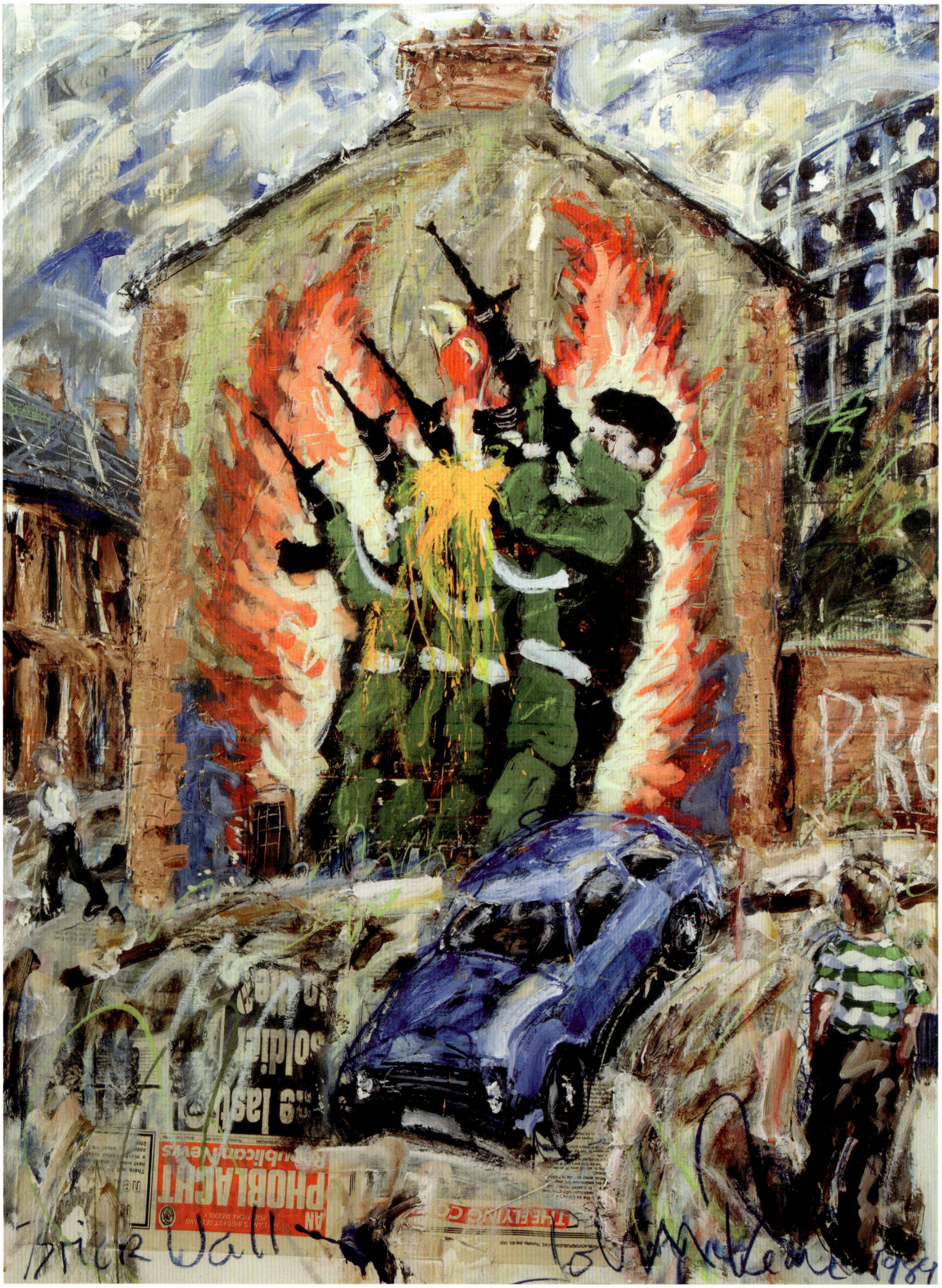

Brick Wall, 1989
PVA and collage on paper
115 x 85 cm / 45¼ x 33½ in
Collection: Jorgen and Beatrice Larsen

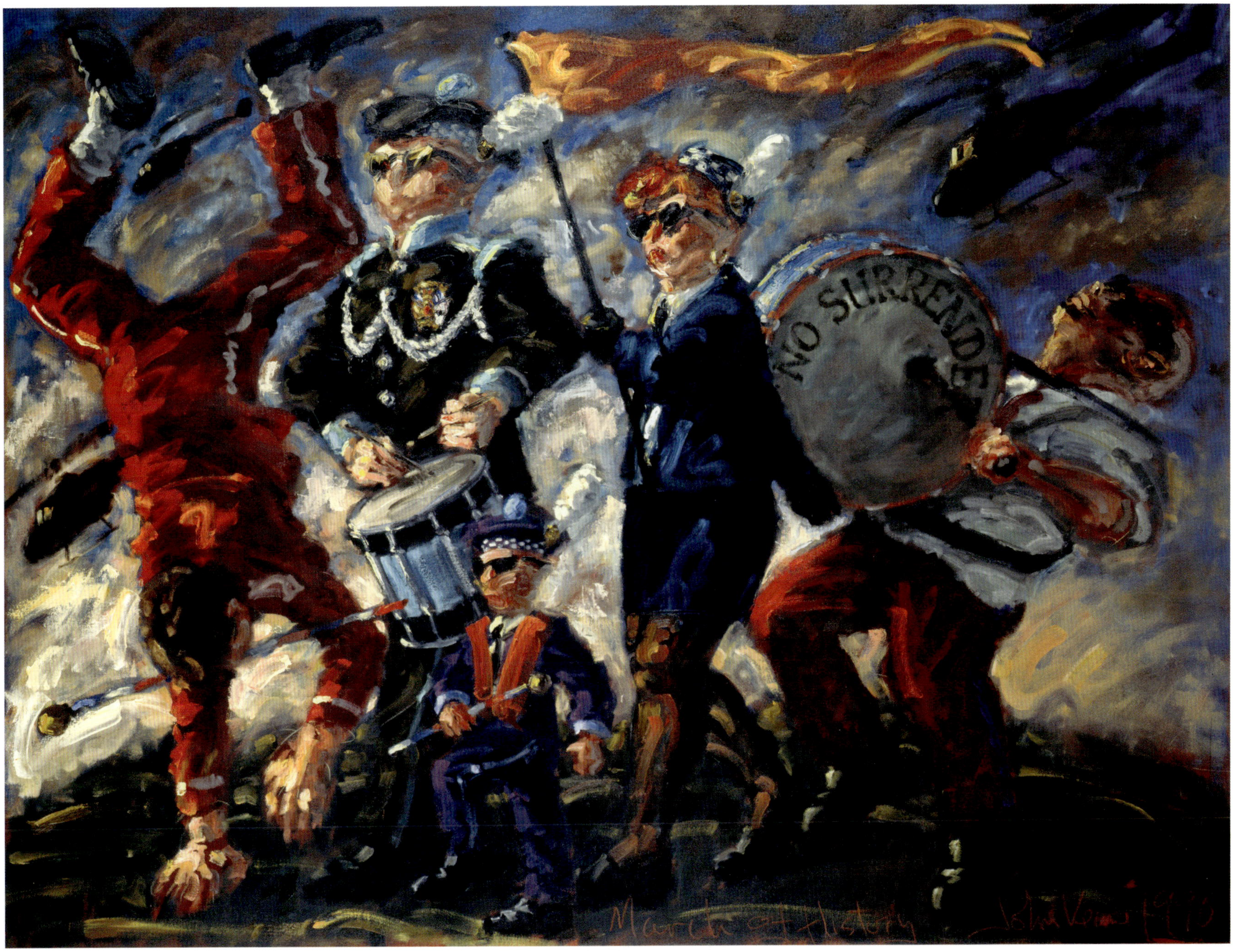

March of History, 1989
Oil on canvas
175 x 226 cm / 69 x 89 in
Private Collection, UK

of the Thatcher era. Despite responding to two of Thatcher's clashes with ideological opponents—in the South Atlantic and in Ulster—there had been no direct representation of the third: the 1984 miners' strike.

> JK: It's a fair point. I might have been expected to deal with it. It seems a natural subject. But, for whatever reason, I didn't feel particularly involved in it at the time.

Encouraged by the success of a predecessor's industrial action in causing power cuts a decade earlier at places including Camberwell College of Art, National Union of Mineworkers president Arthur Scargill called his men out. But, while the previous strike had become known as the 'winter of discontent', Scargill unwisely struck close to summer, when demand for power is inevitably less, was out-manoeuvered by the Prime Minister and the National Coal Board, and lost. The PM and the NCB, however, were helped by some startlingly fierce policing of picket-lines.

Some of the bitterest clashes had happened at the Ollerton Colliery in Nottinghamshire, which had become a show-case for strike-breaking, kept open throughout by the Union of Democratic Miners (UDM), a moderate keep-working alternative to the traditionally confrontational NUM.

In 1990, Keane was invited by Nottinghamshire County Council to observe work at Ollerton for a show that would inaugurate the city's new Angel Row Gallery: the result of the commission was *Cloth-Caps and Hang-Gliding*, which opened in April 1991.

Between *The Other Cheek?* and *Cloth Caps and Hang-Gliding*, there is an evolution of method, with the medium of most paintings in the latter series being the relatively conventional oil on canvas rather than the previous PVA and wax crayon on backgrounds thickened by Fleet Street's leftovers. The tutelary influence on this set often seems to be less Andy Warhol than Joseph Wright of Derby, the great 18th century social realist and painter of the Industrial Revolution.

> JK: The Ollerton work is deliberately much more direct than before. They're much more to do with observation and recording in a literal way. I felt that the subject demanded it. It's not a modern, ironic thing that these men are doing.

There is, though, one striking link of image with the previous exhibition: the huge electricity pylon in 'Fossil Fuel (1)' (1990) chimes with the massive surveillance gantry in the Belfast picture 'Peace Giant' (1989), although, in this case it is an icon of peace-time, although the miner crouched in the tunnel at the bottom of the image has to endure something like the conditions of a soldier in the trenches in order to make this stick figure work. And, 'Canteen' (1990), with what now seems another flash forward of orange working clothes, showing two coal-diggers enjoying mugs of tea and a fry-up after a shift, includes a collage use of a tabloid paper that is, for once, literal rather than metaphorical: one of the men is holding the publication although, in another of this artist's intermittent digs at print journalism, the miner seems to have been distracted by something more interesting.

Peace Giant, 1989
Oil and mixed media on canvas
228.5 x 157.5 cm / 90 x 62 in
Collection: National Army Museum

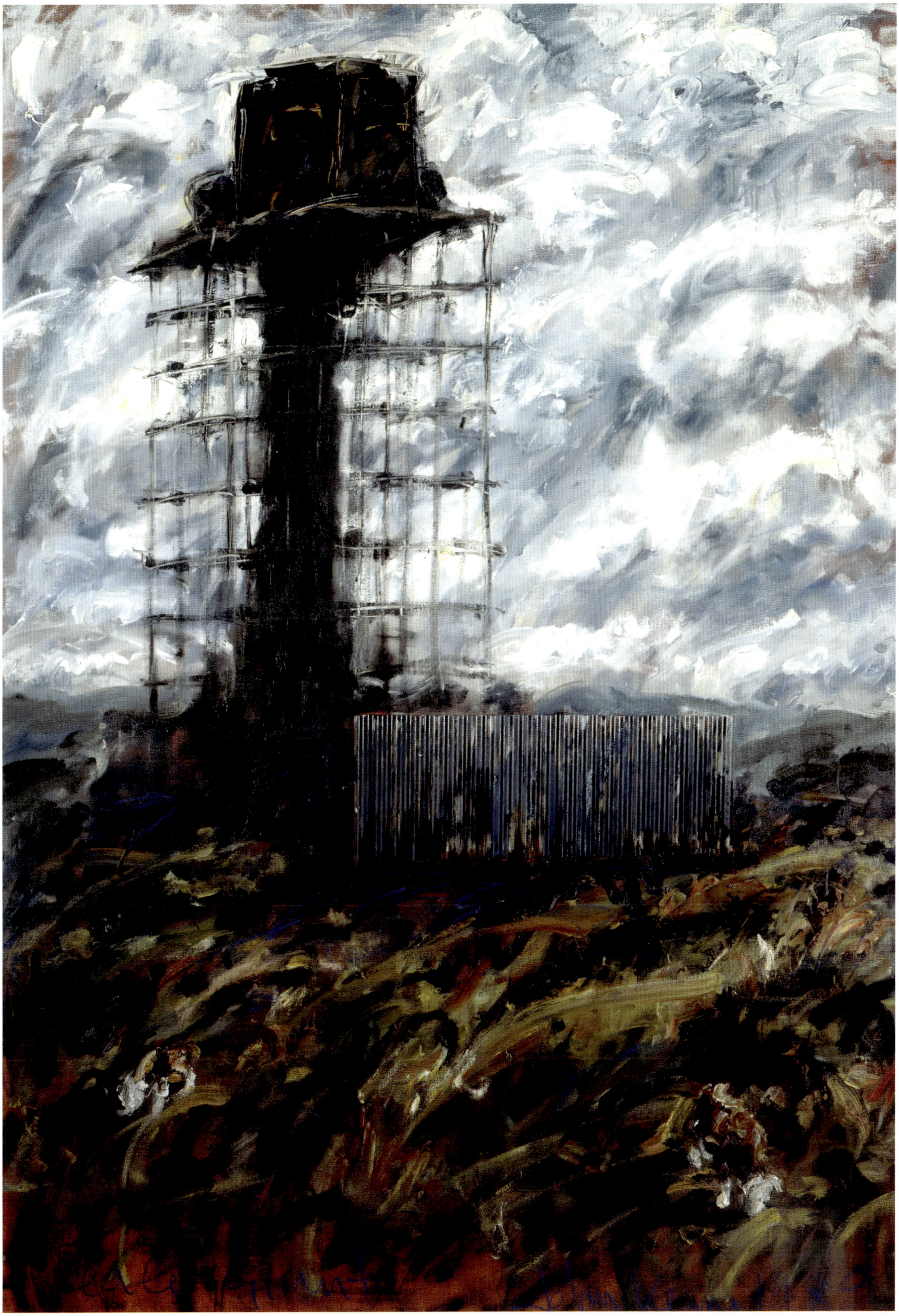

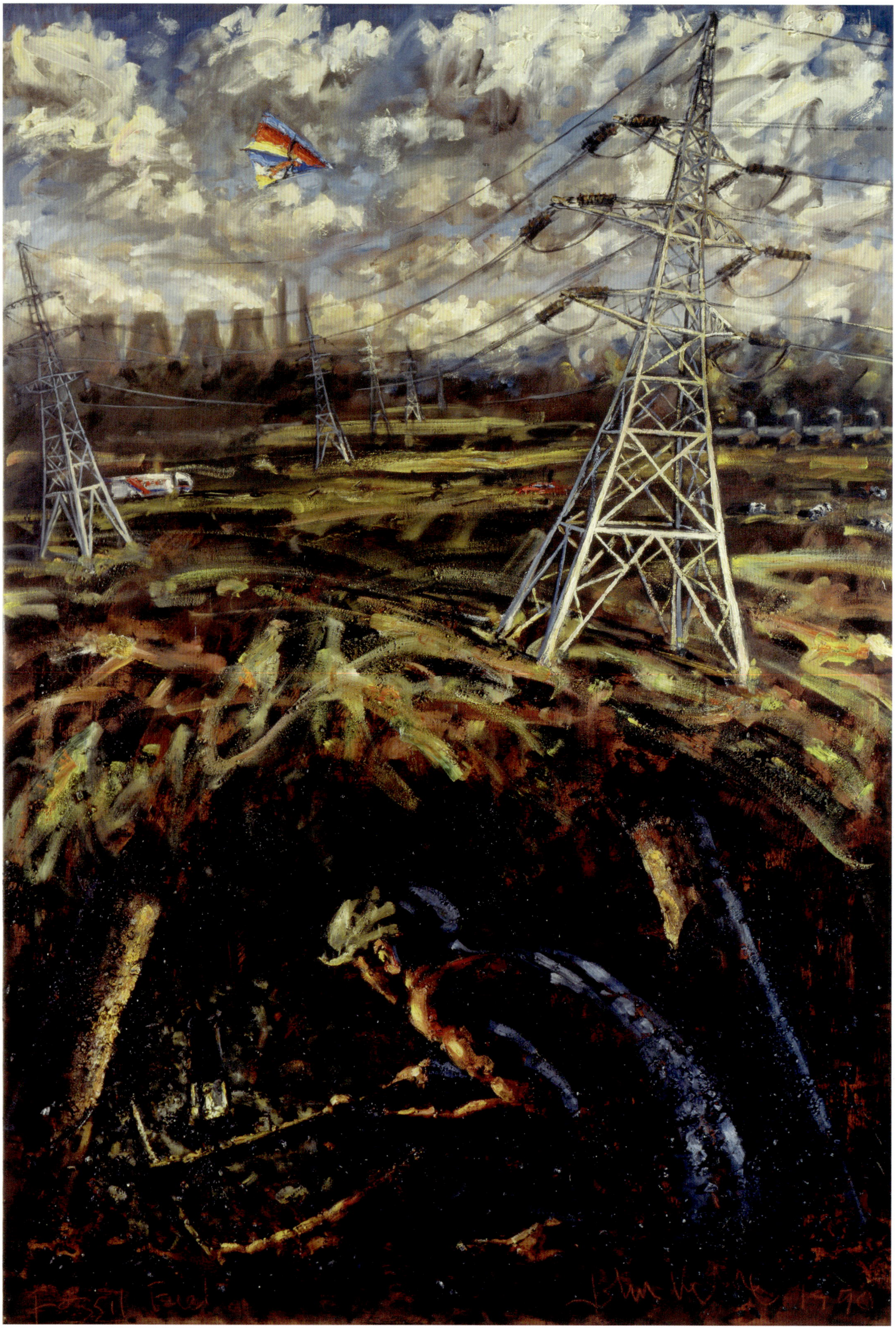
Fossil Fuel

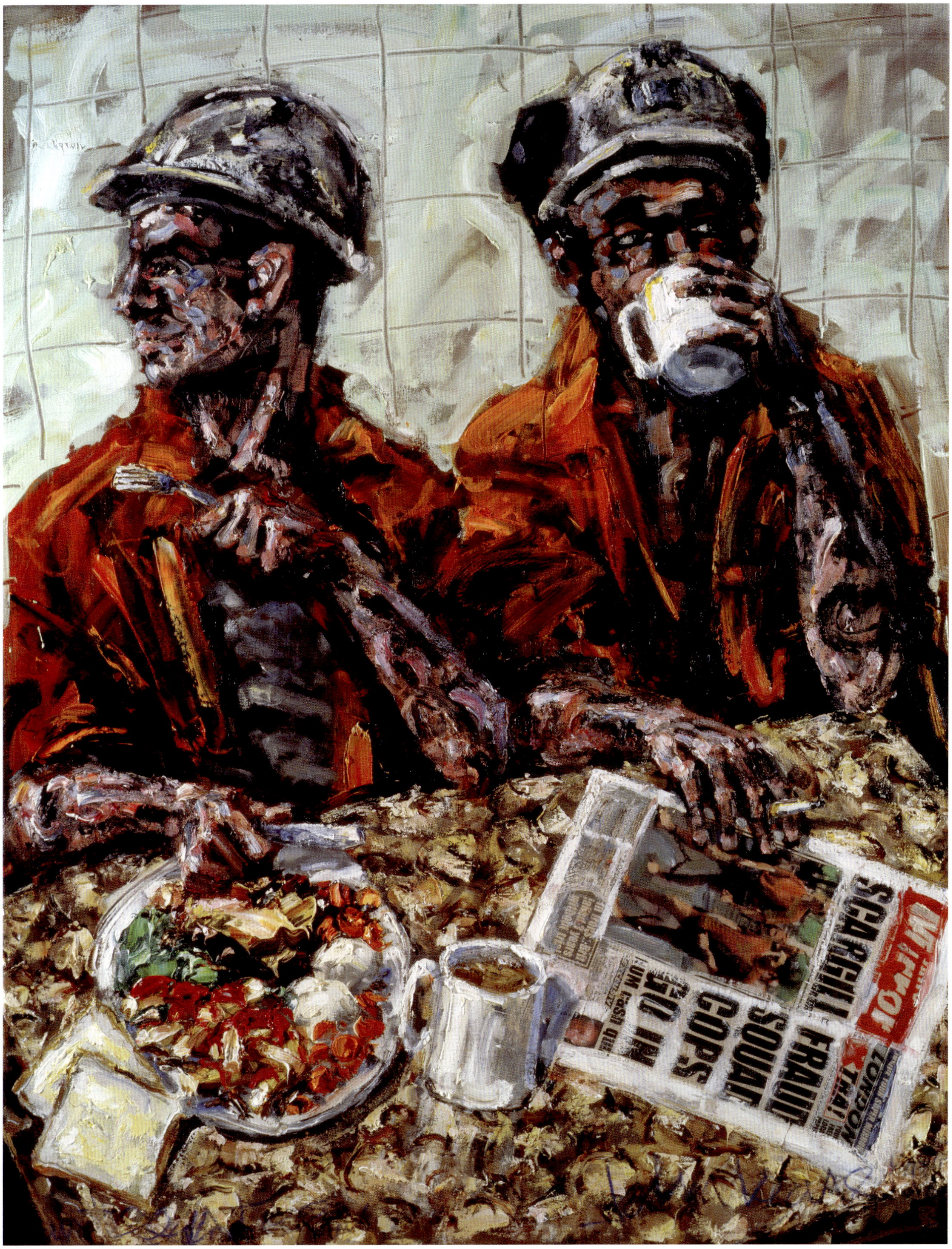

Fossil Fuel, 1990
Oil and coal on canvas
259 x 175 cm / 102 x 69 in

Canteen, 1990
Oil and collage on canvas
133 x 102 cm / 52½ x 40¼ in

By the time Keane went underground, the miners' strike was six years in the past but a serendipitous connection was provided by the copy of the *Daily Mirror* the miner was not quite reading when Keane was doing his research: the front-page splash is a story (later discredited) alleging financial misdealing by President Scargill. The media, regular gallery-goers to Keane shows note, are still trying to script-write political life.

During the year that Keane was working on this seam of material, Margaret Thatcher, to her visible tearful shock when leaving Number 10, came to share with many British miners the experience of redundancy. While fighting the leadership challenge from Michael Heseltine, which eventually led to John Major replacing her as Conservative Prime Minister, Thatcher and her supporters had argued that it was unwise—and even pseudo-unconstitutional—to unseat a PM at a time when military action against Iraq's invasion of Kuwait was threatened.

The tactic failed. But the war that Major fought in Thatcher's place would provide Keane with the most important job of his career.

PRESIDENT SADDAM HUSSEIN OF IRAQ was a notable collector of modern art, though only in a somewhat specialised sense: he commissioned and displayed massive pictures and statues of himself, which were raised and hung around the country, making the capital Baghdad in particular a sort of architectural precursor of the Facebook page.

The event that would make Saddam (as he was generally first-named, like Madonna) a subject for John Keane began on August 2, 1990, when he ordered tanks and aircrafts into Iraq's neighbour, Kuwait, a comparatively tiny state but massively attractive financially (and crucial to the West) because of its underground ocean of oil.

Although the West's outrage was framed where possible as a defence of demoracy, this position was complicated by that fact that Kuwait was a dictatorship. It was therefore widely believed that the West was essentially defending its petrol pumps, aviation fuel and central heating, although this could be dismissed as a wholly reprehensible motive only by those who lived in solar-powered houses and bicycled to work and holidays. But a sharply-targeted chant from Washington anti-war protestors—"Hell, no, we won't go! We won't die for Texaco!"—unsettled politicians. In one of his sharpest double-entendres, one of Keane's Gulf pictures is called 'Oil Painting' (1991), referring to both the artistic medium and the prize that the two sides contested.

Another concern—post-Vietnam paranoia about starting wars on the behalf of other nations—is reported to have led President George H.W. Bush to "wobble" about a military response but Prime Minister Margaret Thatcher, emboldened to foreign intervention by her Falklands success, encouraged him to put together an international task-force—'Operation Desert Shield'—that gathered in Western-friendly Saudi Arabia, warning that, unless Iraq met a United Nations deadline to leave Kuwait by January 15, 1991, its troops would be forcibly removed. The collaboration was truly global—including supportive UN votes from Russia and logistical assistance from Egypt—and this would later prove a crucial distinction from the more narrowly US–UK focus of the Second Gulf War.

The horrors of conflict are historically progressive. The homicidal novelty in the Falklands conflict had been Exocet missiles; in Kuwait, it was, for the coalition troops, the prospect of chemical weapons, which Saddam was believed already to have used against dissident Iraqis and the Kurds, and, for the Iraqis, the threat of targeted missiles that were supposed to be able to turn corners in order to hit the right target. During failed peace negotiations, the US Secretary of State, James A. Baker, is said to have shown the Iraqi delegation simulated pictures of the kind of carnage that American weapons could achieve.

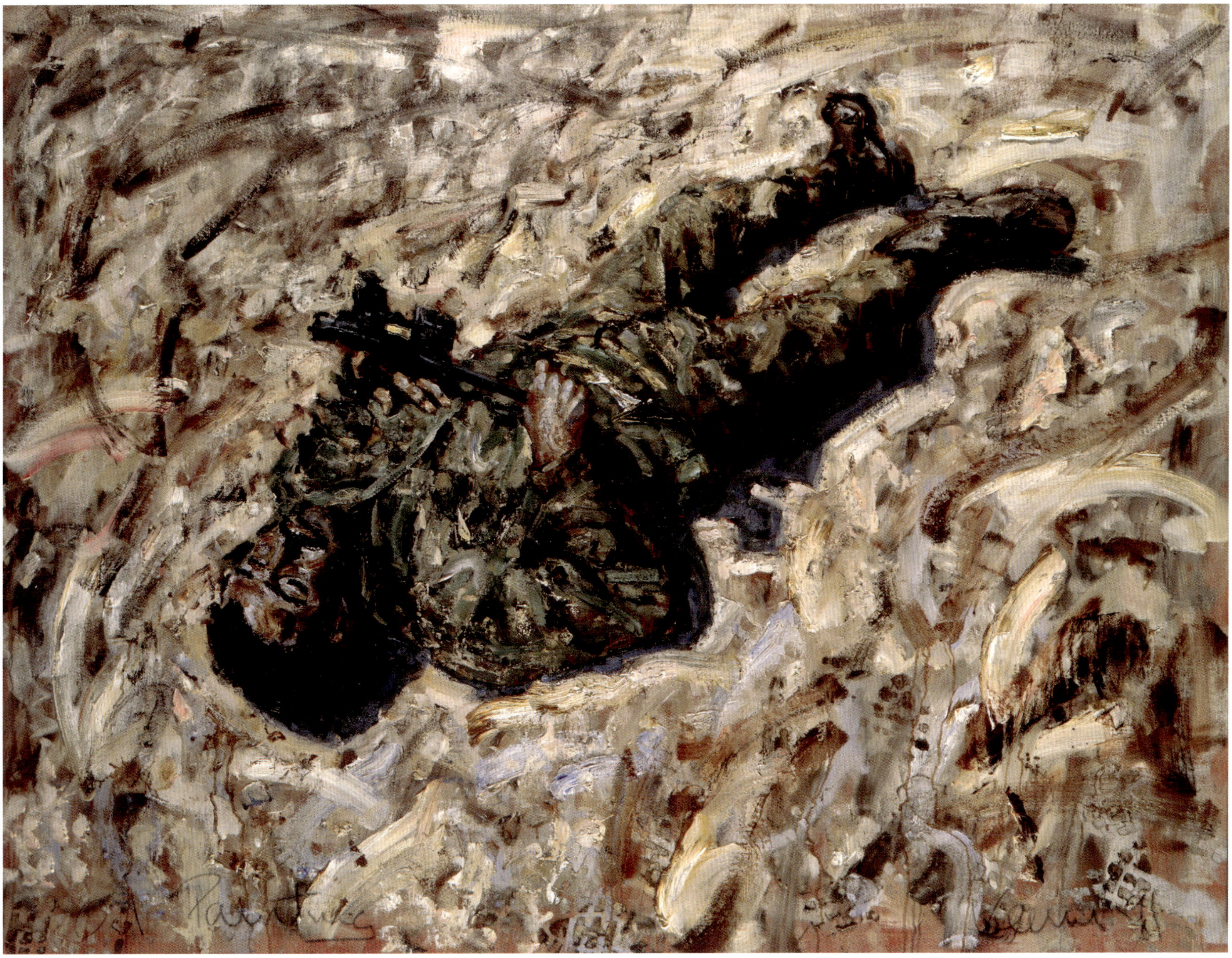

Oil Painting (Dead Iraqi With Toy Gun), 1991
Oil on canvas
132.5 x 173 cm / 52¼ x 68 in

It is a measure of the diplomatic and media pessimism about the possibility of a Saddam back-down that, as early as August 1990, when Thatcher was still Prime Minister and Keane was painting coal-mines, Britain's leading gallery for military pictures was already making battle plans. The artist found a flashing light on his answerphone, a technological innovation of the time.

> JK: There was a message from Angela Weight at the Imperial War Museum. She said something like: 'How do you fancy being a chemical warfare victim?' And I thought: you probably don't get asked this kind of thing twice so I accepted straight away.

With the First Gulf War now safely in the history books, time has largely erased the sense of how febrile and frightened the atmosphere was in the UK at this time. There were reports, almost certainly false, that conscription papers had been printed for fighting-age males, ready for an expected lengthy and escalating war in the Middle East. The American media reported on industrious stitching and shipping of "body bags" to the region for the victims of the expected chemical armageddon. Getting married in September 1990, as the countdown to invasion began, I distinctly remember, standing outside the 13th century church in Middle England, having a flash of how the "last summer" of 1914 might have felt in England.

But, if Keane would have good reason to worry about going, it was the Ministry of Defence who seemed more paranoid about his trip. The MOD refused to give insurance to him, although this had been a standard part of the package for other war artists. A private policy would have cost a third of his IWM commission fee and it was only when *The Guardian* newspaper agreed to cover the premiums that the trip became plausible. Oddly, once on assignment, Keane discovered that David Cobb of the Royal Society of Marine Artists, hired by the Royal Navy to record events in watercolours, had been accepted and insured without question. So the assumption must be that a background check on Keane—revealing membership of CND and the Labour Party and artist travels to Belfast and Nicaragua (chapter four)—had created specific opposition to his presence.

On its own terms, however, the MOD was right to be concerned about the sort of images that Keane might bring back. Although the Bayeux Tapestry can be viewed as a variety of war art, the tradition is generally held to have begun with the French artist Constantin Guys, who, during the Crimean War in 1855, filed wood-block engravings of battle-scenes to the *Illustrated London News*.

Subsequently, the genre filled two purposes: basic reportage in the period before the invention or easy portability of cameras and propagandistic tableaux to sustain morale or celebrate triumph back home. During the First World War in particular, the latter ambition was subverted by British war artists such as Paul Nash and C.R.W. Nevinson, whose images of trench warfare unsparingly put the pain into paint.

In the Second World War, 40 official artists were salaried to the War Office, including Eric Ravilious, who died in a military plane crash. Because this global fight, unlike the previous one, involved a British home front and a struggle for national survival, there was to some extent a return to the idea of war pictures as public uplift, such as Henry Moore's moving sketches of Londoners using Underground stations as emergency air-raid shelters.

By 1991, the official British artist in the Gulf was ideologically suspicious of any rabble-rousing role for battle canvases, while the role of visual recorder was widely perceived to have been ceded to TV: one of the beneficiaries of the conflict would be CNN, the Atlanta-based 24-hour cable news service, which would make this the first war to be fought on live television.

Keane, however, found the new uncertainty about both the journalistic and indoctrinating purposes of war art invigorating.

> JK: Obviously you can't deny that the electronic media played a role in that war that superseded all previous wars, took on a new dimension. But the direction that they were going was a totally different direction—fulfilling a role that has to do with conveying information for tonight's news or tomorrow's breakfast table. In a way, I was liberated by that. I could try to redefine what being a war artist was. I didn't see my role as perhaps a previous generation of war artists had. I didn't have to merely record what had happened and I had no obligations to produce propaganda. In fact, I could address such questions as the political constraints on the other media. I saw myself as being outside all that.

Yet, if the artist did not regard himself as being in competition with the visual news media, they proved suspicious of him. His kit-bag for the Gulf mission contained a Camcorder—another step towards the eventual found visual basis of all his work—and a notebook. Journalists and art critics who retained a romantic image of the military artist hunched over an easel illuminated by the rocket's white glare felt that Keane was somehow cheating.

> JK: For me, the camera is serving simply as a sketchbook of an instantaneous kind. Given that I want to make paintings—and paintings are essentially a reflective form, not an observational method, although they may contain elements of that—photography is simply the most practical way of recording information I may want to use later . . . a way of having information available to make a subsequent painting which is to do with the memory of that situation and having been in that situation.

Because of his delay in securing insurance, by the time Keane reached the Gulf, the defensive Operation Desert Shield in Saudi Arabia had become, due to Saddam's failure to comply with the UN ultimatum, the offensive Operation Desert Storm, with aerial bombing of Baghdad and Iraqi forces in Kuwait and preparations for a ground offensive to reclaim the invaded emirate.

The artist flew first to an RAF compound in Dhahran, Saudi Arabia, and then to Bahrain, where bomber pilots and navigators, in a rare alcoholic oasis in an otherwise dry war, shared beers at night with the media in a latter-day version of a scene from the work of Graham Greene or Ernest Hemingway. From there, Keane travelled to the sands of Saudi, where the main mass of ground troops was gathered.

As would become the norm in future wars, military media management favoured the concept of "embedding", in which journalists were attached to a part of the army or navy, offering greater safety and protection than the Vietnam way of heading off in a jeep with a local fixer but also, to the advantage of the forces, allowing greater control of what they saw. Keane was given the choice of attachment to an army Forward Transmission Unit (FTU) or being helicoptered to a ship in the Gulf.

The artist had been badly spooked by a chemical attack alert during a desert exercise: due to the MOD's reluctance to accreditate him, he had missed the protective suit training given to the media, resulting in a panic self-deprecatingly recorded in 'Ecstasy of Fumbling (Portrait of

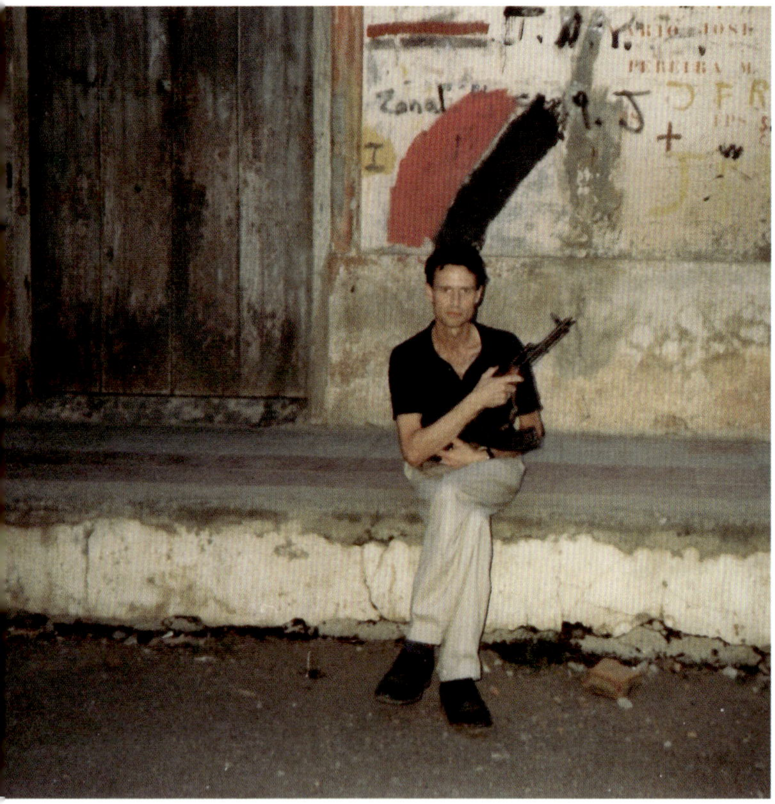

John Keane in Nicaragua, 1987

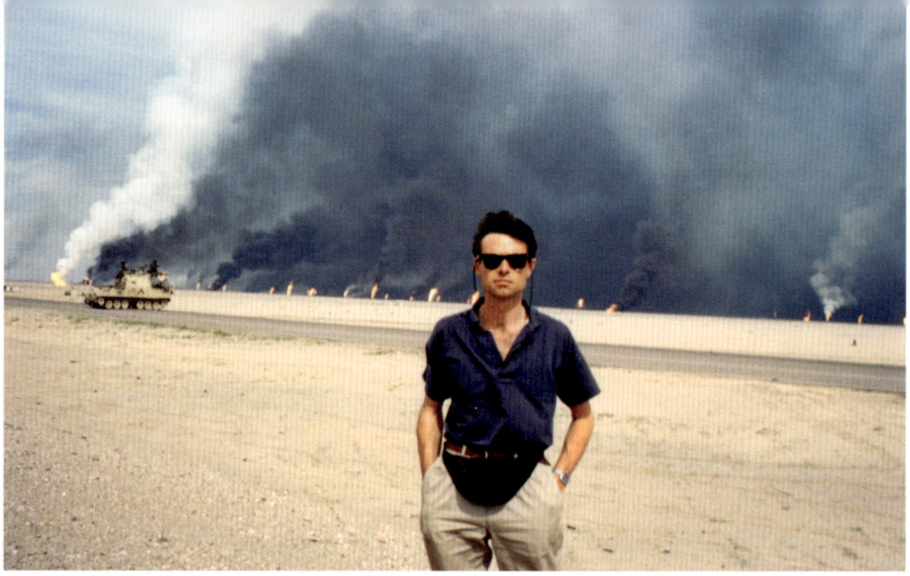

John Keane in Kuwait oli fields, 1991

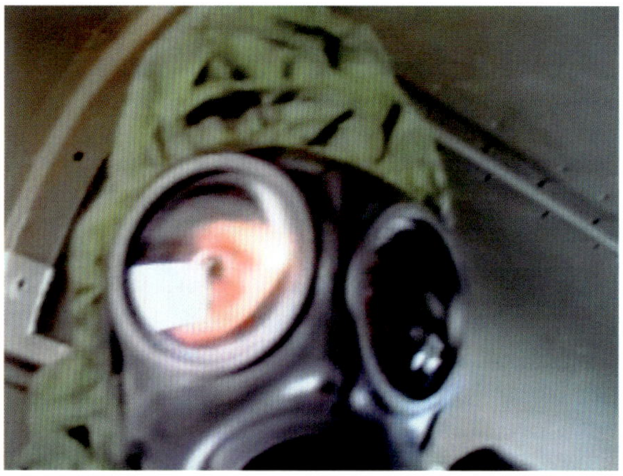

John Keane, gas alert, Saudi Arabia, 1991

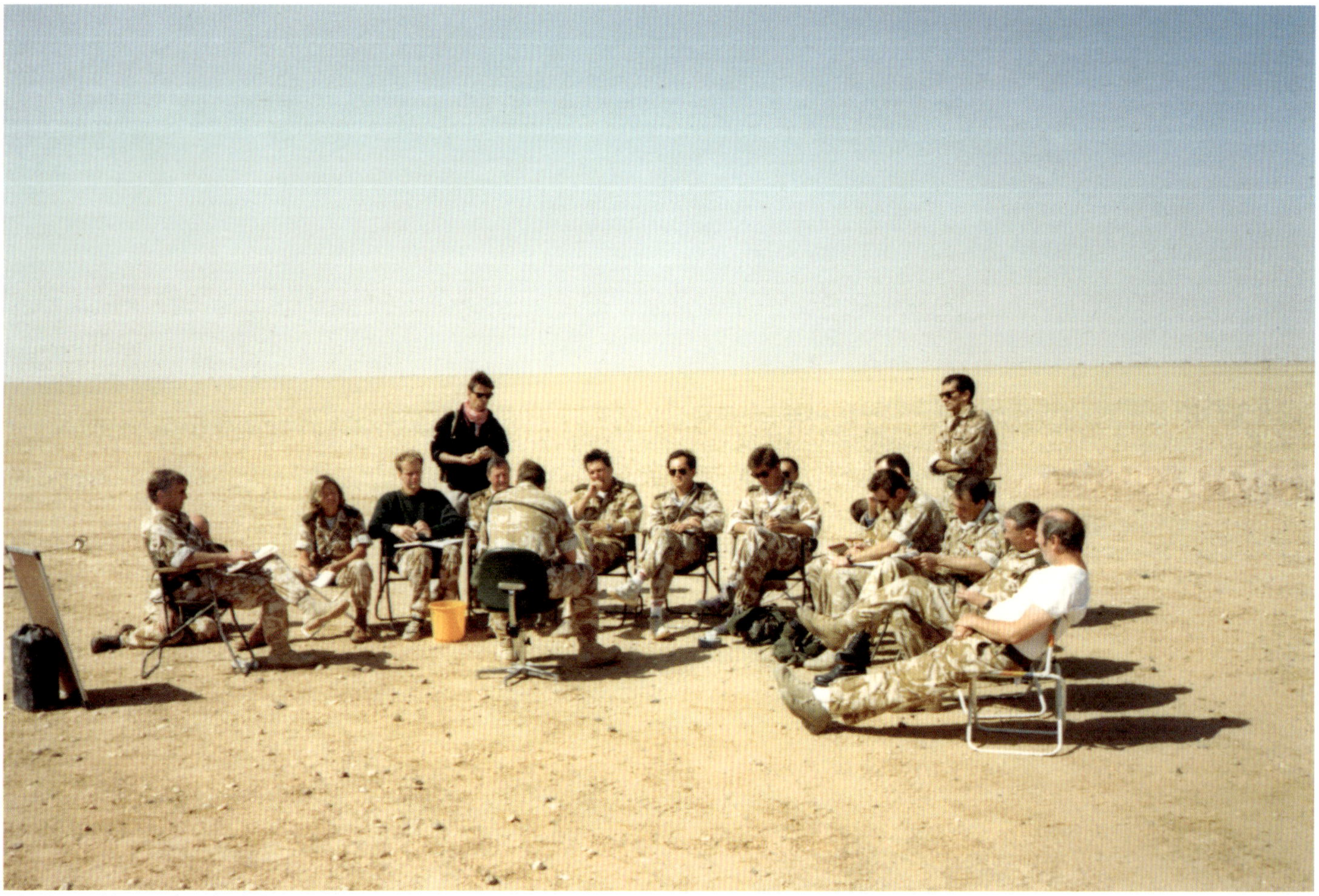

John Keane with journalists, Saudi desert, 1991

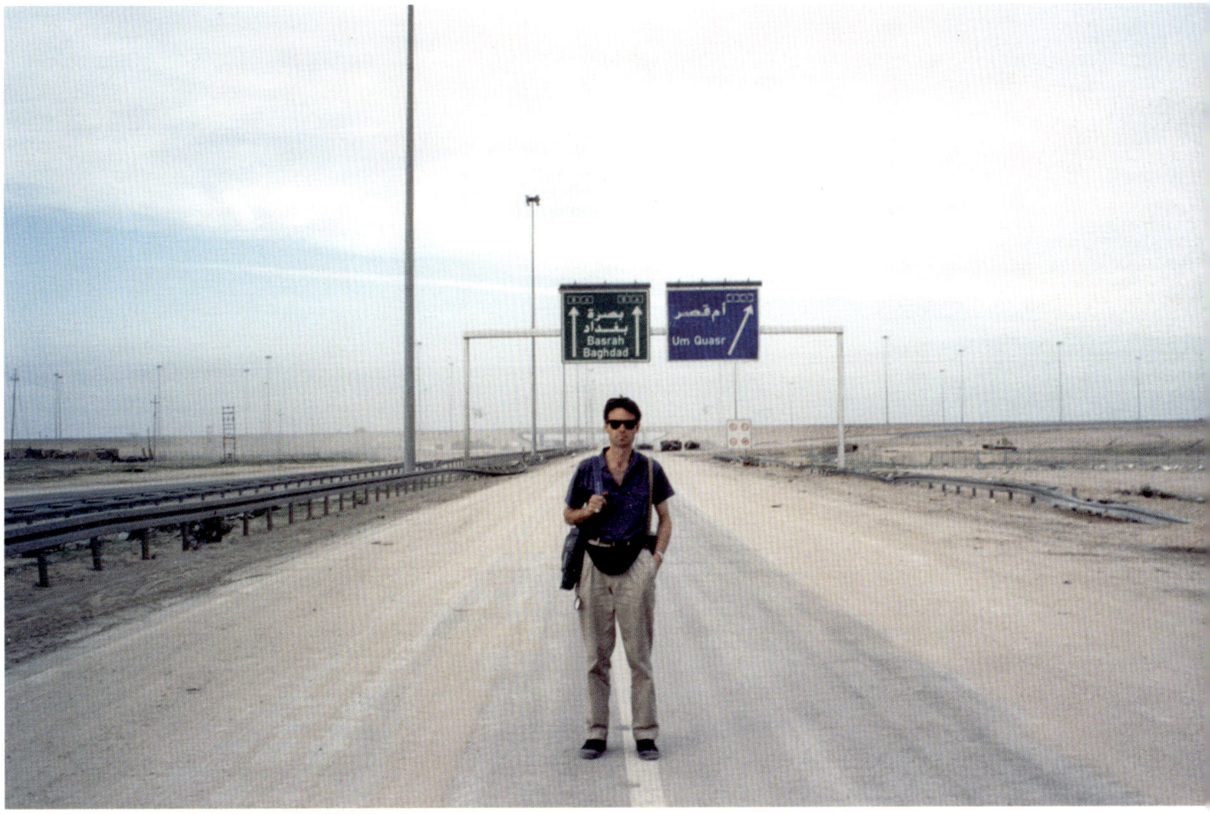

John Keane, Basra Road, 1991

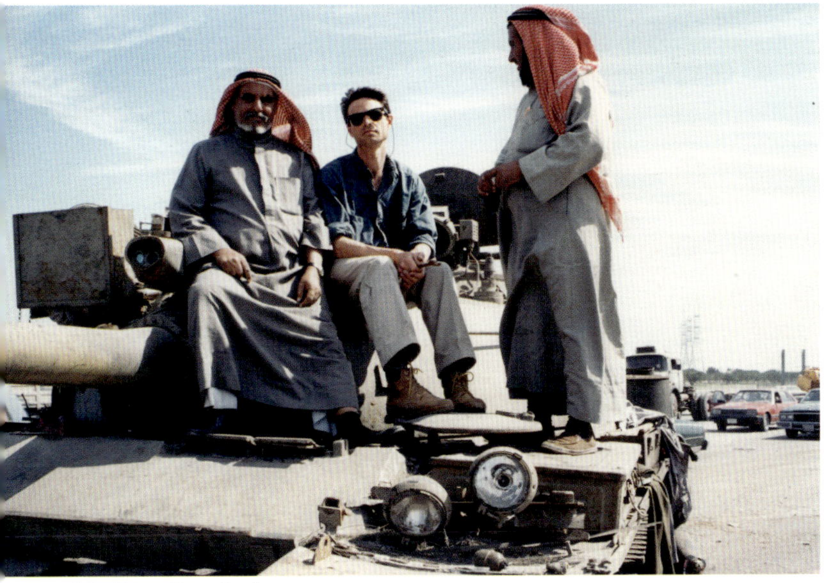
John Keane, Basra Road, 1991

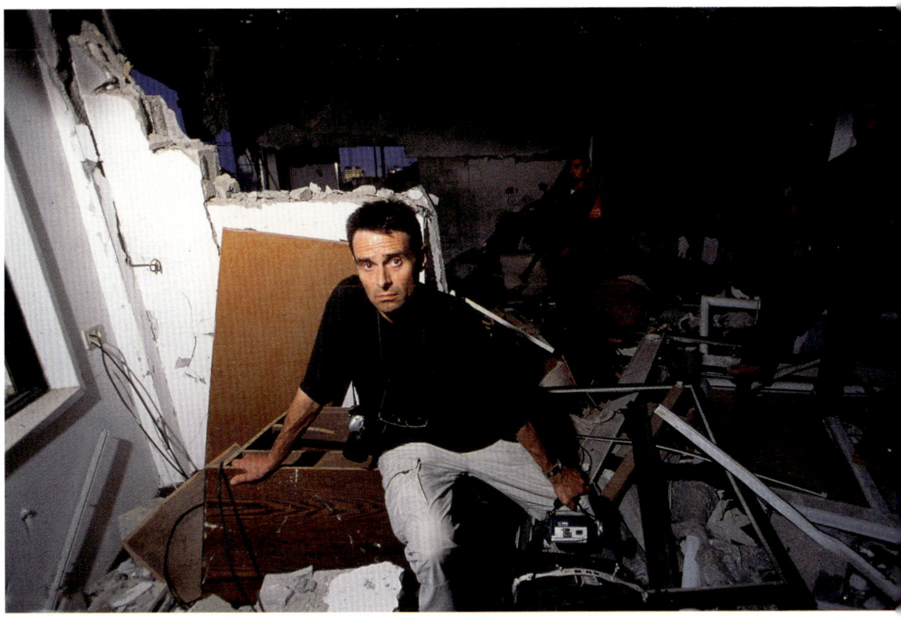
John Keane, Yasser Arafat's office, Gaza City, 2002 © Paul Hackett

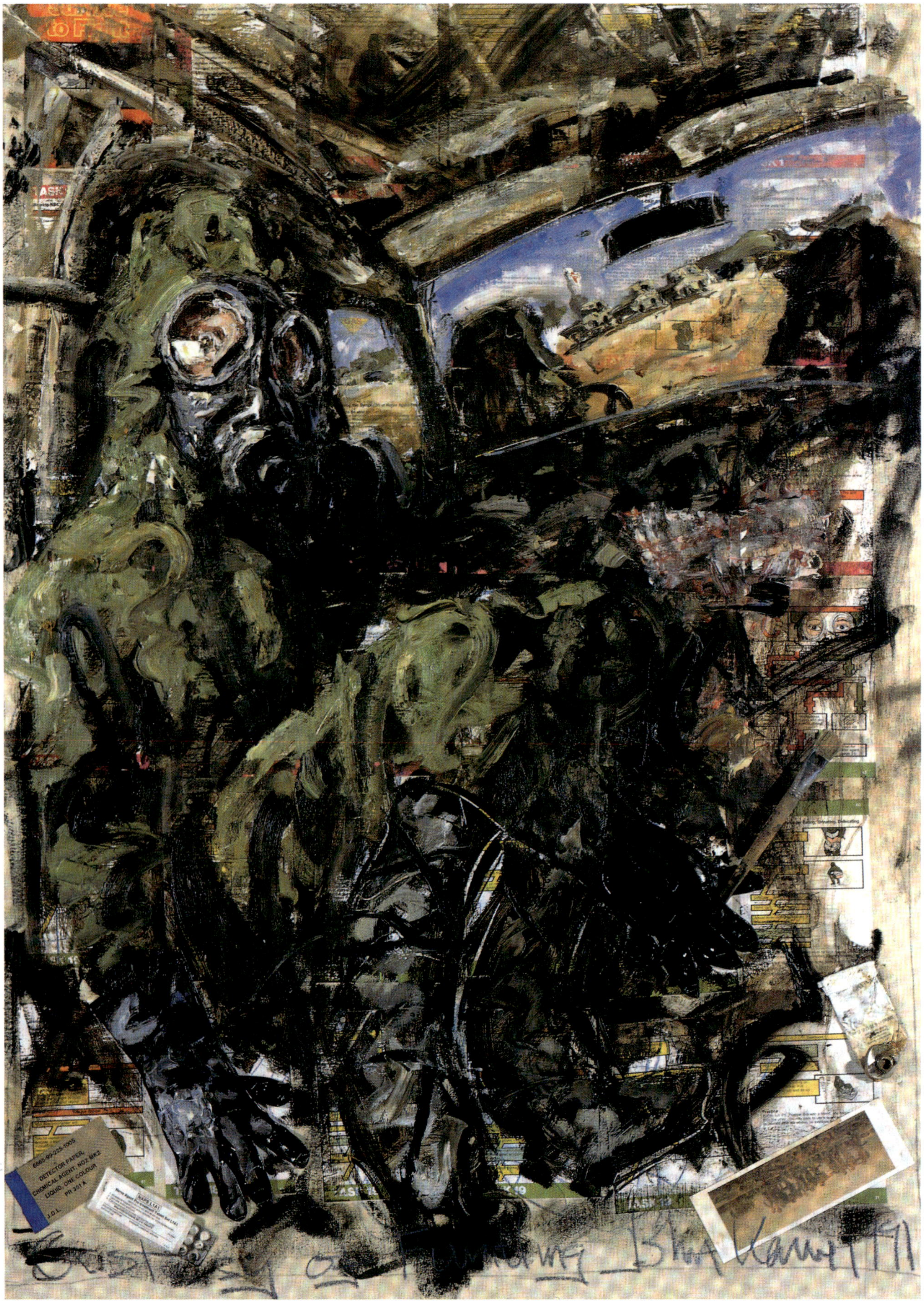

Ecstasy of Fumbling (Portrait of the artist in a Gas Alert), 1991
Oil and collage on canvas
152.5 x 107 cm / 60 x 42¼ in
Collection: National Army Museum

the Artist in a Gas Alert)' (1991). Accordingly, the artist chose to go to sea. But, as the supreme commander, General Norman Schwarzkopf, made the opposite strategic call of fighting with boots rather than boats, the official British chronicler spent the conflict watching unneeded doctors on hospital ships smoking and playing cards.

The First Gulf War lasted 100 hours until the Iraqi surrender and became a rout in which most of Saddam's unhappily conscripted soldiers rapidly retreated, heading northwards on the road to Basra, a border town between Iraq and Kuwait. Coalition Apache helicopters easily picked off the fleeing vehicles, creating scenes of charred corpses sitting in blackened trucks. With Kuwait already liberated, the first President Bush was worried about accusations of disproportionate savagery towards a defeated people and called a ceasefire, ending plans, as revealed in General Schwarzkopf's memoirs, to advance to Baghdad and depose Saddam. Many in America questioned this clemency, including, which would turn out to have extensive geopolitical consequences, the second President Bush.

So, by default, Keane became a post-war artist, traveling with the press pack to inspect the aftermath of the bombing of Kuwait City and the Basra Road. 'Scenes on the Road to Hell (1)' (1991) focuses on abandoning refugees and abandoned vehicles on that violently-freed freeway. In a continuation of his previous style, many of the surfaces are collages of thematically relevant material: sand, ashes, dollar bills, pages from the Koran and, in the case of 'Looking for Evidence (Shadows and Doubts in the Palace of Torture)' (1991), a reproduction of a photo of a young girl.

The building featured is a Kuwaiti police barracks, converted from a Royal Palace, that was rumoured to have been used as a torture chamber during the Iraqi occupation, and which Keane visited with two print journalists. Seeing the portrait on the floor, he photographed the photo and incorporated it in his painting, touched by the poignancy that it was impossible to know who the mystery figure was: might she be a victim, witness or the child of a torturer? So, back in London, he was surprised to see the abandoned snap reproduced on the front of a newspaper supplement, introducing a long article describing the girl's life and the circumstances that had apparently brought her to the torture chamber. Startled by this feat of research and recreation, the artist included the torn-out report among his mixed media as a tribute to the interpretative diligence of the print media.

Keane himself was suspected — although easily exonerated — of fictionalising reality in what became the most celebrated of his Gulf War works, except, admittedly, among the corporate enforcers of Walt Disney Inc.

'Mickey Mouse at the Front' (1991) is a large, surreal seascape. Barbed wire curves around the coast at Kuwait City, its skyscrapers rising in the distance. A shopping trolley, stacked with missiles that look like cucumbers grown in radioactive soil, runs over the Kuwaiti flag. And — the image which was, as lawyers say, 'complained of' — a maniacally smiling Mickey Mouse perches on some kind of plinth, which is surrounded by twists of shit. A palm, its trunk broken and buckled, bows down to the ground, like a thirsty camel. In 'Legacy' (1991), the most famous rodent in showbiz watches from his throne as Kuwait City burns and a soldier corrals a line of locals.

In general, Keane's Gulf pictures are relatively less polemical than the rest of his dispatches from military and political conflicts. This is partly because, except on the grounds of total pacifism, it was much harder to argue against than, for example, the Second Gulf War: in this case, a genuinely multi-national force was responding to an act of aggression against another sovereign nation and, for all the horrors of the Basra road, the West, unlike 12 years later,

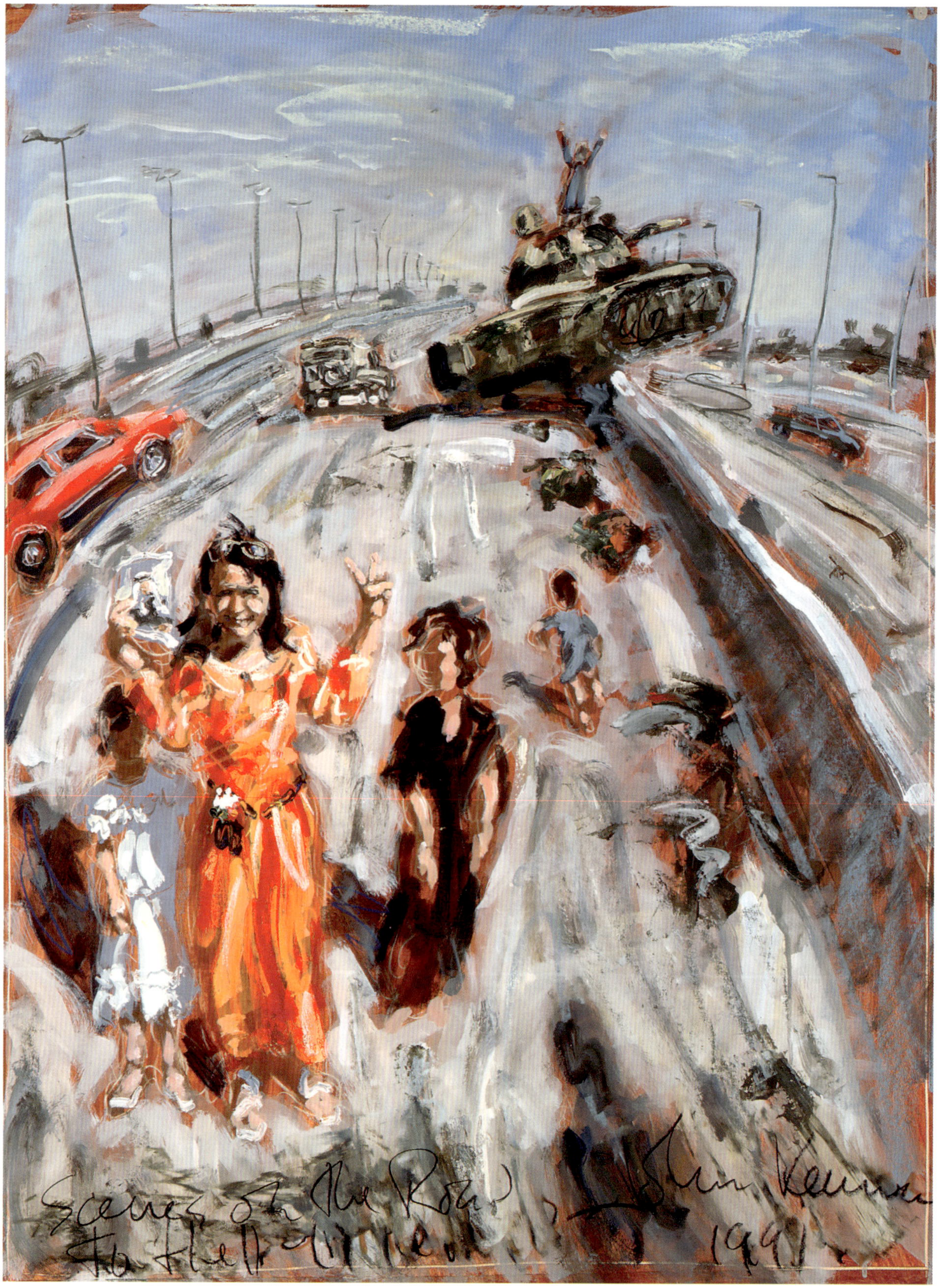

Scenes on the Road to Hell I, 1991
PVA on paper
114 x 84.5 cm / 44⅞ x 33¼ in
Collection: Imperial War Museum

Scenes on the Road to Hell III, 1991
Mixed media on paper
114 x 84.5 cm / 45 x 33¼ in

Scenes on the Road to Hell VI, 1991
Mixed media and PVA on paper
114 x 84.5 cm / 45 x 33¼ in
Collection: William Corbett Winder

Scenes on the Road to Hell IV, 1991
Mixed media on paper
114 x 84.5 cm / 45 x 33¼ in

Scenes on the Road to Hell V, 1991
Mixed media on paper
114 x 84.5 cm / 44⅞ x 33¼ in
Collection: Herbert Art Gallery and Museum

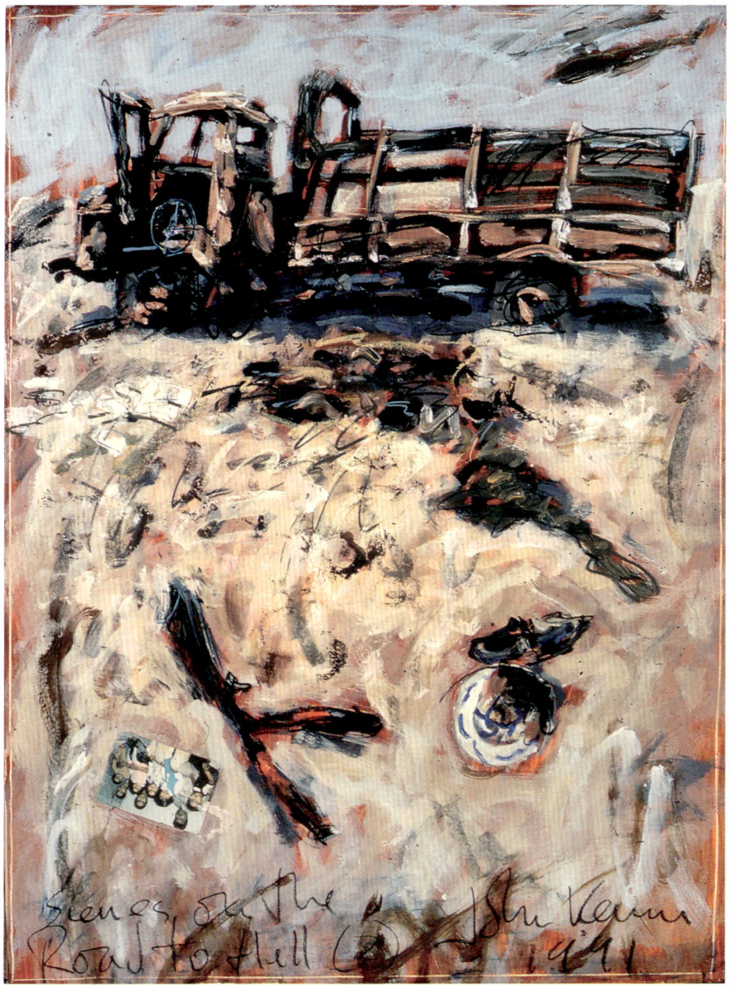
Scenes on the
Road to Hell
John Keane
1991

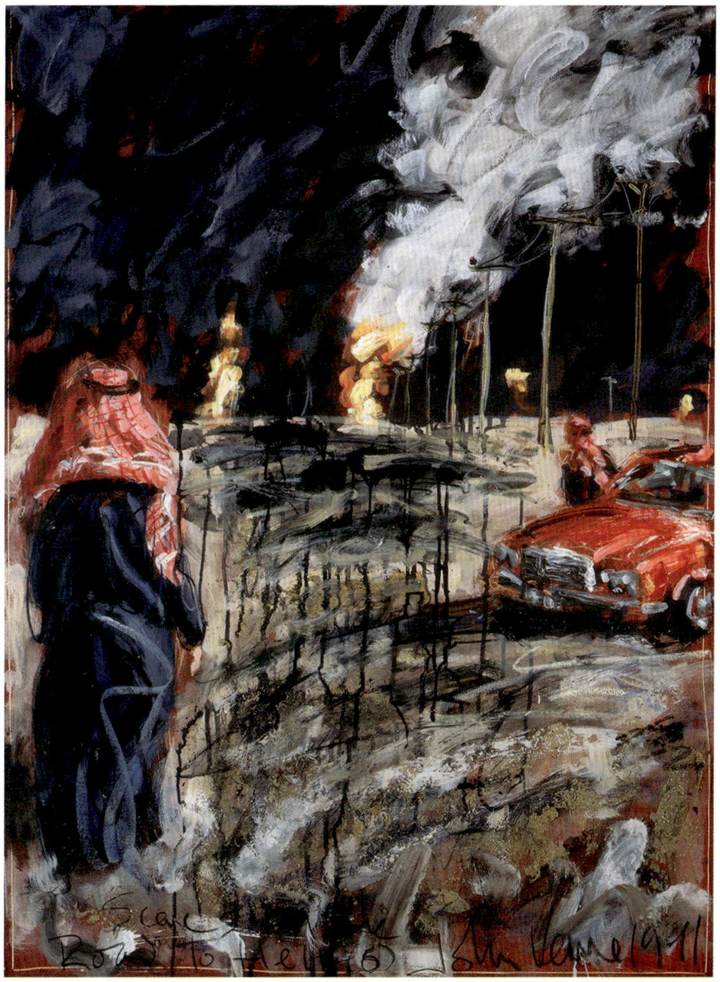
John Keane 1991

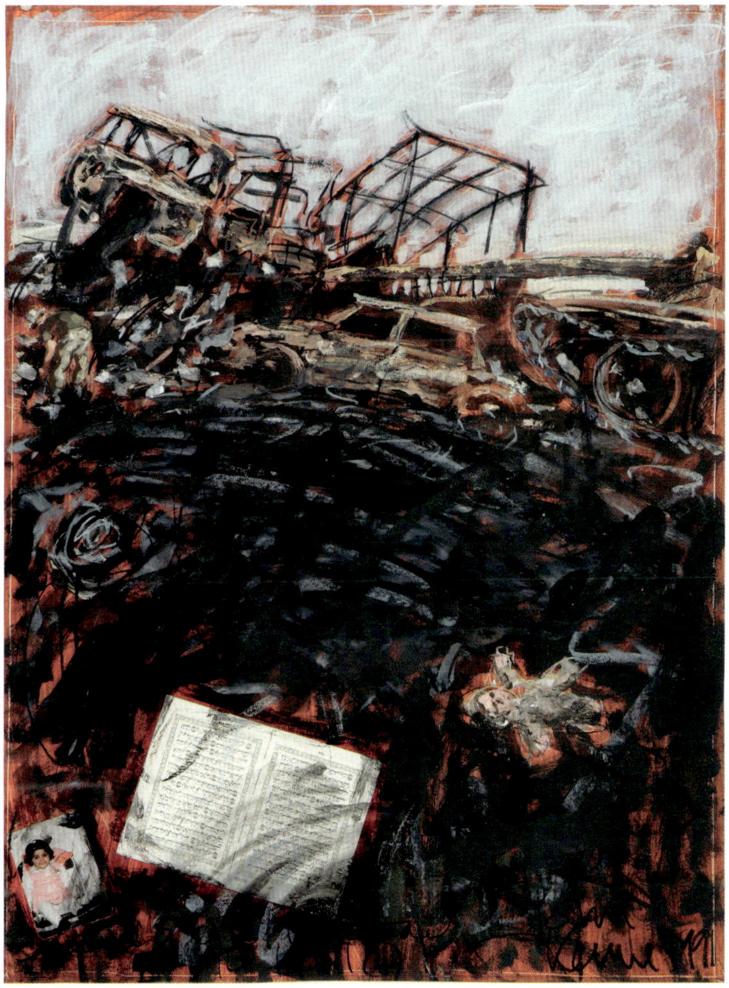
Keane 1991

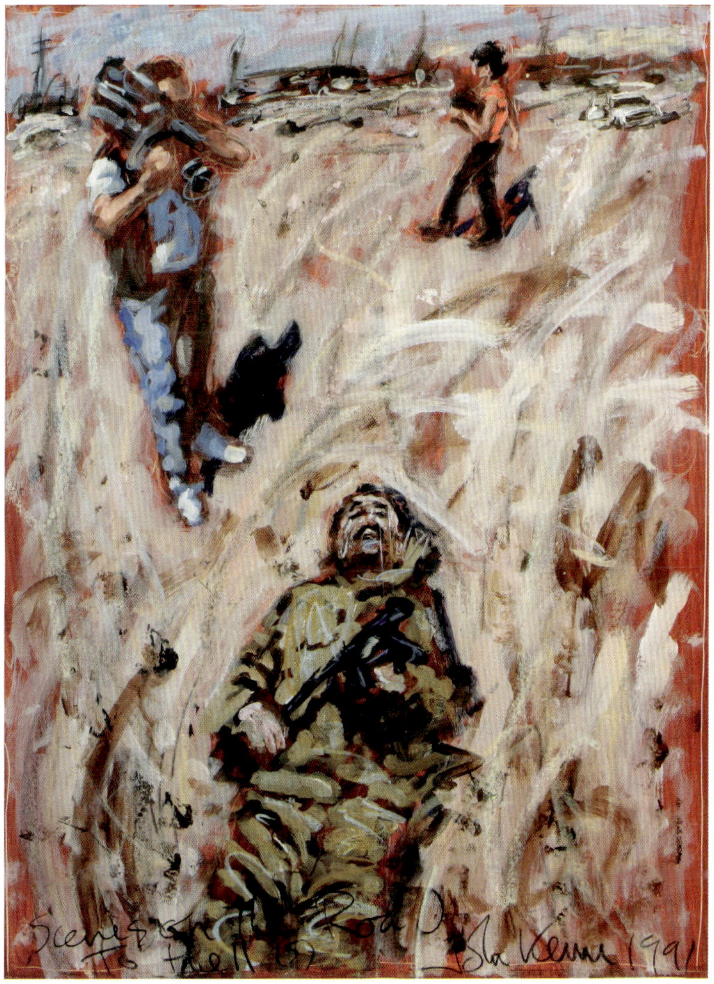
John Keane 1991

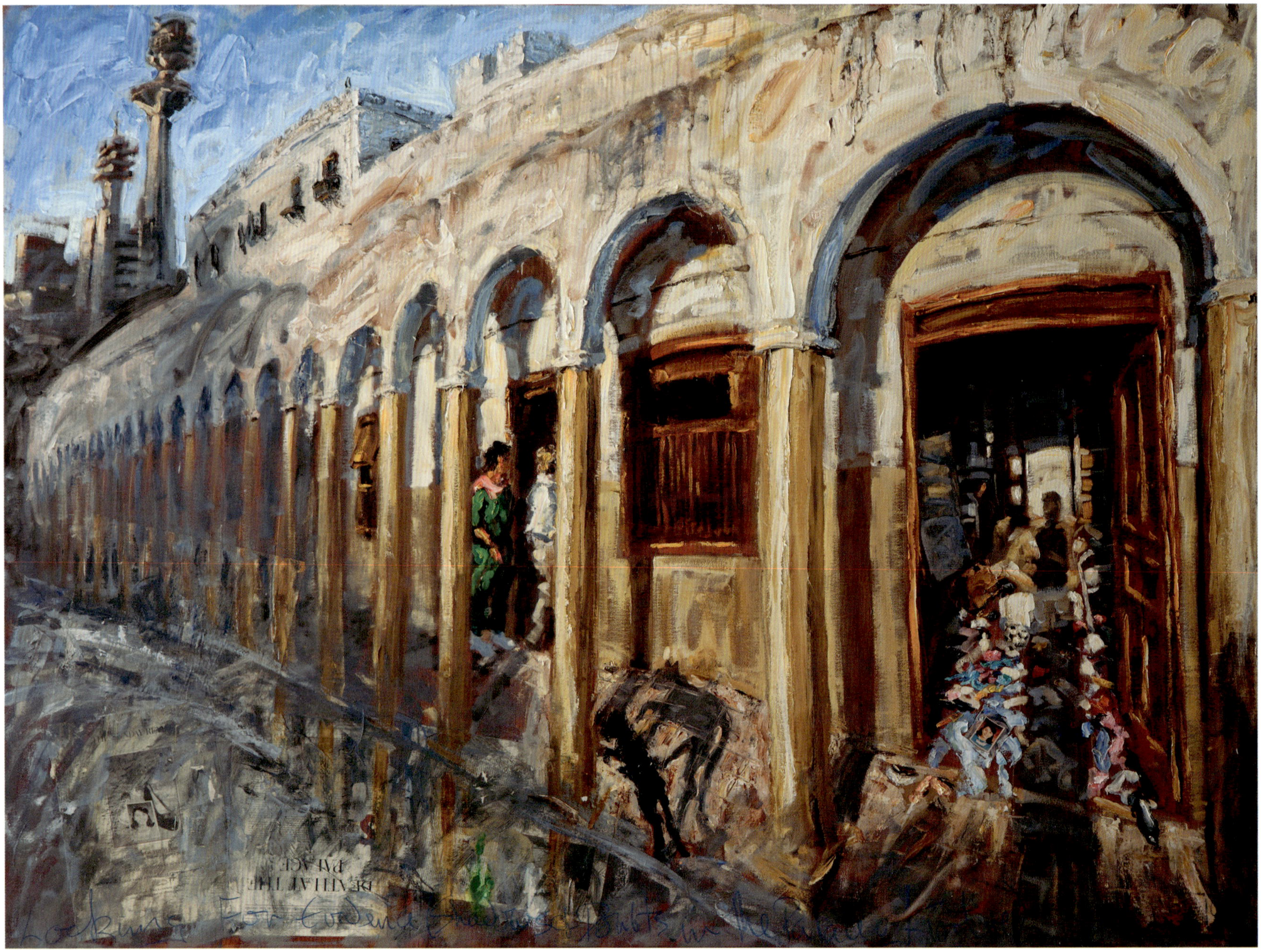

Looking for Evidence (Shadows and Doubts in the Palace of Torture), 1991
Oil and collage on canvas
174 x 231 cm / 68½ x 91 in

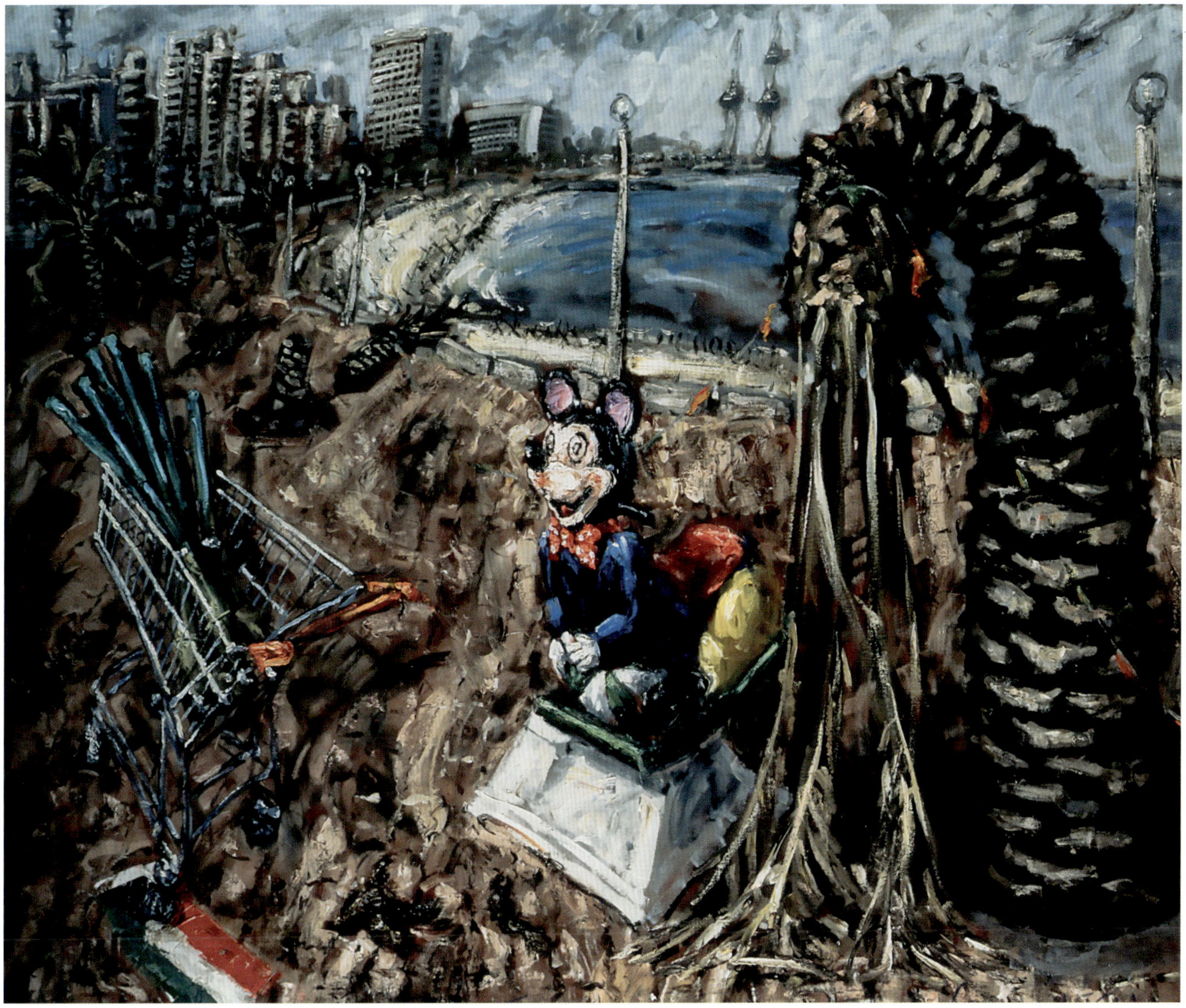

Mickey Mouse at the Front, 1991
Oil on canvas
173 x 198 cm / 68 x 78 in
Collection: Imperial War Museum

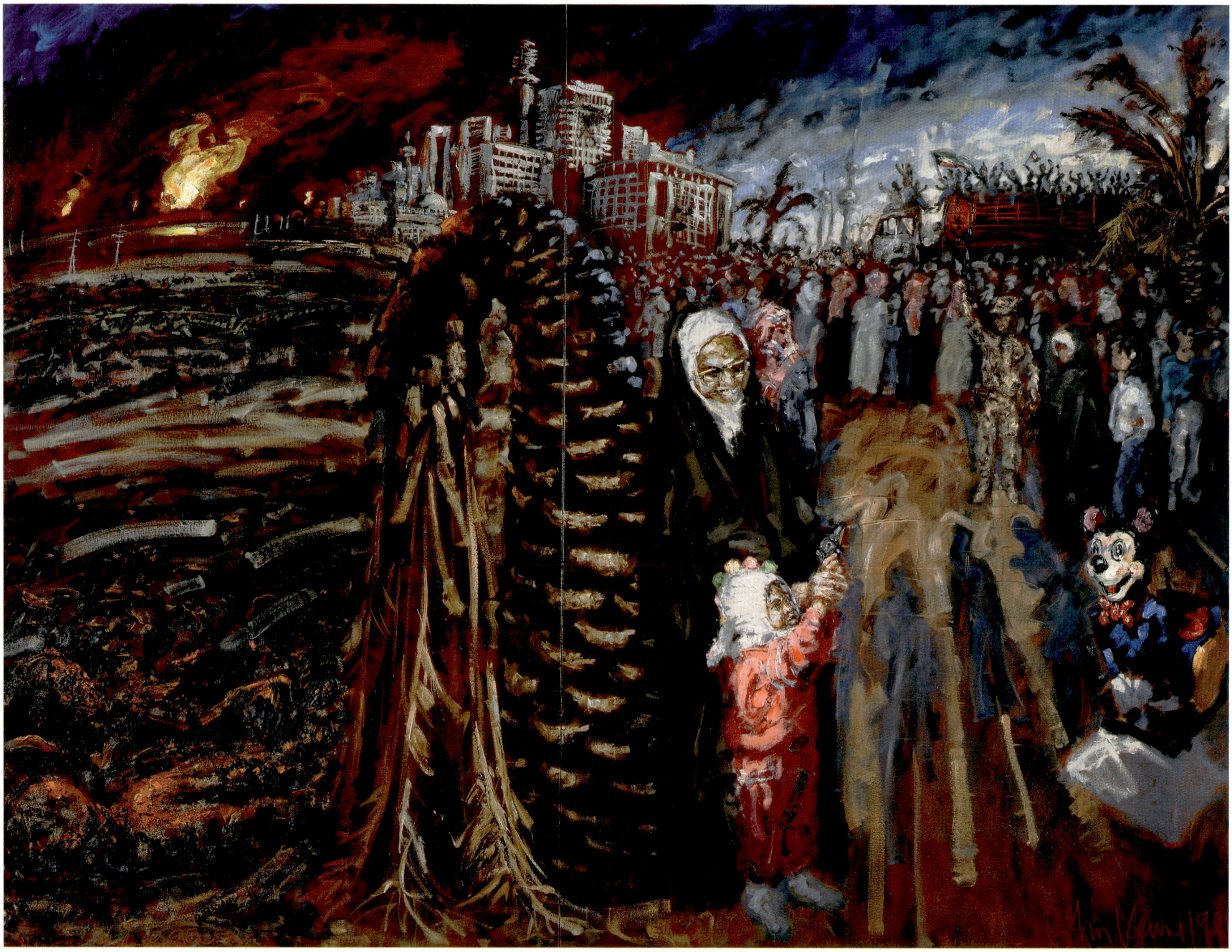

Legacy, 1991
Oil on canvas
229 x 297 cm / 90 x 117 in

deliberately stopped short of regime-change in Iraq. It would be hard to phrase the placards to carry in a march against this war. This may be why some of the images — such as the chaotic 'Ashes to Ashes' (1991) — come closer to abstraction, avoiding any hint of editorial comment.

The Mickey Mouse pictures, though, were all too easy to read, or at least some newspapers thought that they were. The controversy that engulfed the artist was partly due to the mistaken belief that Keane had subversively imposed an image of American cultural power on the site of the coalition victory. In fact, it was an extraordinary objet trouvé. On his last morning in the Kuwaiti capital, he had visited a supermarket that had been used as an armoury by the invaders: a trolley had become a weapons carrier and an amusement arcade, including a rocking toy of Mickey Mouse for children, had been commandeered as a latrine. Hence, as with the paintings of paintings in Belfast, the image was the opposite of surrealism.

In January 1992, as the opening of the *Gulf* exhibition at the Imperial War Museum approached, Keane gave an interview to the *London Evening Standard,* which reproduced some images, including 'Mickey Mouse at the Front', interpreting it, and by extension the whole show, as anti-war. The phone began to ring in first the artist's Hackney studio and then his Highbury flat. Possibly helped by the fact that he sounded posher than tabloids would expect a bad-boy artist to be, he was able to pretend to be someone else and told reporters that the controversial painter was away.

Saying nothing is an understandable and often sensible short-term tactic in such situations but it does not prevent others from having their say and may encourage them to do so. Next day's papers quoted the father of one of the British soldiers killed in the conflict as finding the painting "depraved", while the Armed Forces minister, Archie Hamilton, charged Keane with trivialising the events. But the harshest bombardment came, typically from *The Sun*, in words that may have helped to guide Keane's hand in his later twisted portraits of the paper's owner, Rupert Murdoch. Under the headline 'Black Art' was one of the few art reviews in the publication's history.

> The paintings of the Gulf War show Mickey Mouse sitting on a lavatory
> amid the destruction of Kuwait.
> Families of dead soldiers are outraged at the sneer at their sacrifice.
> We share their revulsion.
> The painter, John Keane, was sent to the Gulf War as an official war artist.
> He is entitled to his opinions about the war.
> But, feeling as he did, why did he accept the commission?
> Just for the money?

A report on the news pages correctly stated the fee — £10,000 — that Keane had been paid by the IWM, although a museum that included numerous bloody and despairing depictions of war on its walls and in its archives would surely have been surprised at the idea that an artist who failed to see any jingoistic pictures should hand back the commission fee. *The Sun* had also mispresented the reason for the Disney character's squatting perch: it seems unlikely that the designers of the children's toy intended him to be defecating. Once the mistake had been made, the littered faeces might have been taken as circumstantial support — the message that Keane's detractors inferred — America (Mickey Mouse) shitting on Kuwait was actually the reverse: Iraqis had literally shat on a symbol of the US.

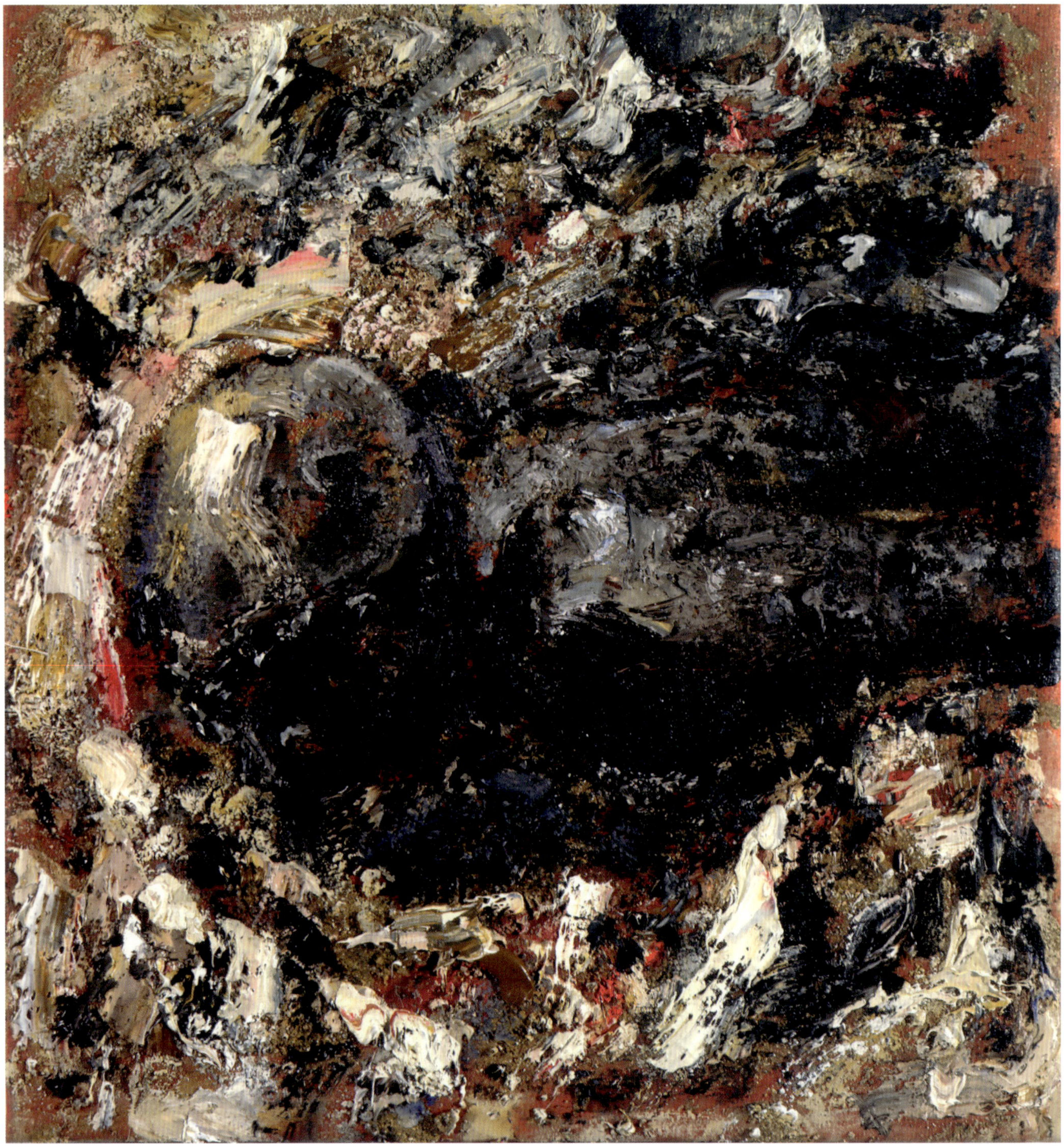

Ashes to Ashes I, 1991
Oil and sand on canvas
72 x 66 cm / 28½ x 26 in
Collection: Matthew and Emily Flowers

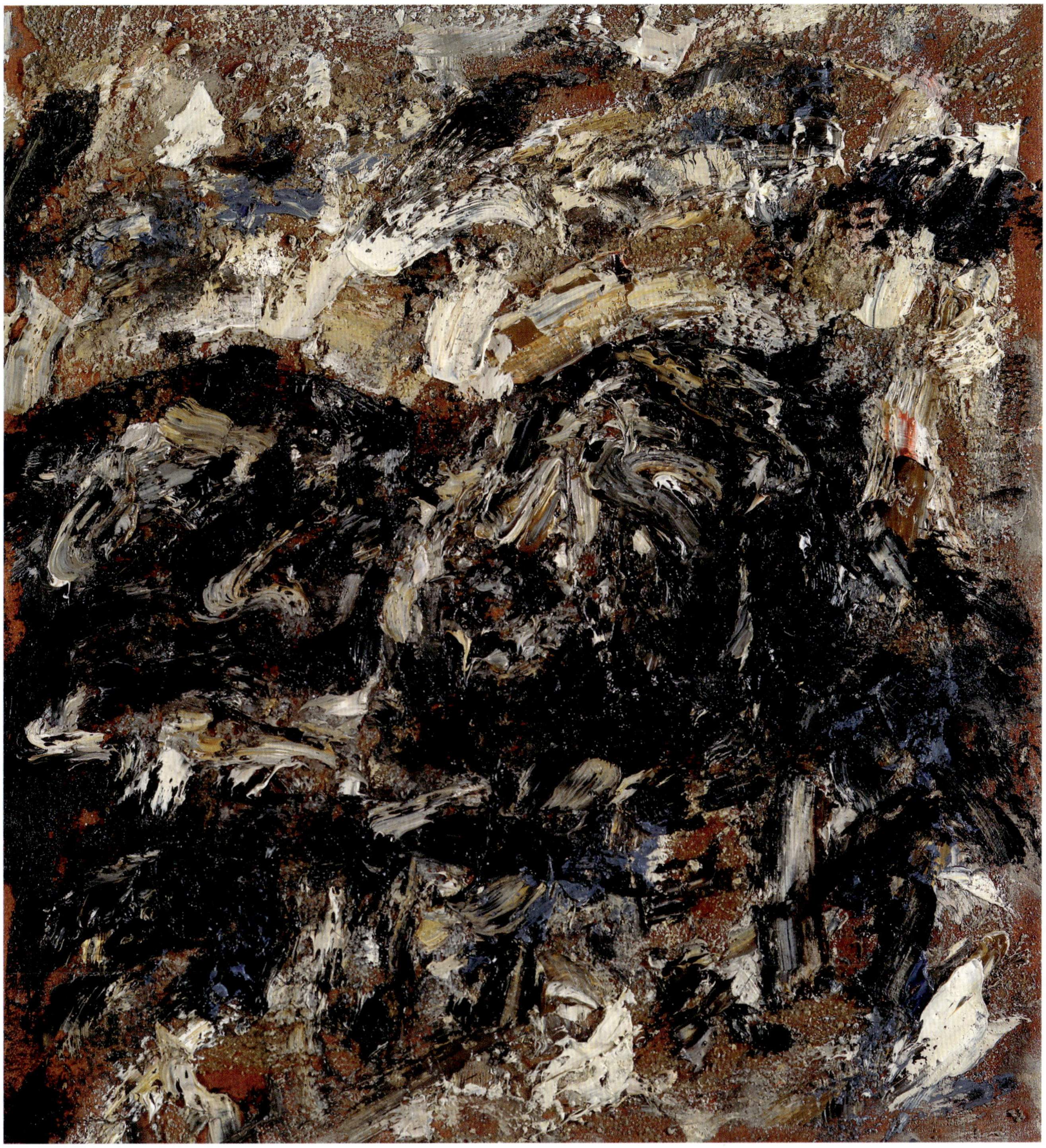

Ashes to Ashes II, 1991
Oil and sand on canvas
72 x 66 cm / 28½ x 26 in
Private Collection, UK

JK: I was thinking of the American influence on Kuwait . . . or the 'Mickey Mouse defences of the Iraqis against an invasion from the sea that never came. But, above all, it was just a startling image that I had witnessed in that arcade.

Disney briefly considered suing over the unauthorised use of the image but ultimately let the image hang. But the works had touched another — prophetic — sensitivity. As Western culture has discovered — most horribly in the deaths resulting from cartoons published first by the Danish magazine *Jyllands-Posten* and more recently *Charlie Hebdo* of France — the most sensitive sects of Islam impose a blasphemy taboo that is unusual in being so specifically visual: due to the belief that the physical appearance of the Prophet Mohammed, held to be unknown and unknowable, must never be shown.

Keane had not depicted the most sacred figure in Islam but he had used, in a border of 'Alien Landscape' (1991), 34 pages from the Koran which, in another startling found image, he had discovered scattered on the Basra road. With the novelist Salman Rushdie under a *fatwa* (or religious death sentence, later rescinded) from Iran after being accused of anti-Islamic blasphemy in his book *The Satanic Verses*, the Imperial War Museum was nervous of protests at Keane's appropriation of the holy book and decided to exclude 'Alien Landscape' from the show. During the exhibition's UK tour, both that painting and one of the *Road to Hell* pictures were removed from public view, although they were hung in a closed booth.

By contrast, the curtain had lifted on John Keane, who was now one of Britain's better-known — and, to some including *The Sun*, notorious — younger artists.

In the 25-year cycle of violent revenge described at the start of this chapter, the First Gulf War led to 9/11 and then — through a presidential son apparently determined to finish his

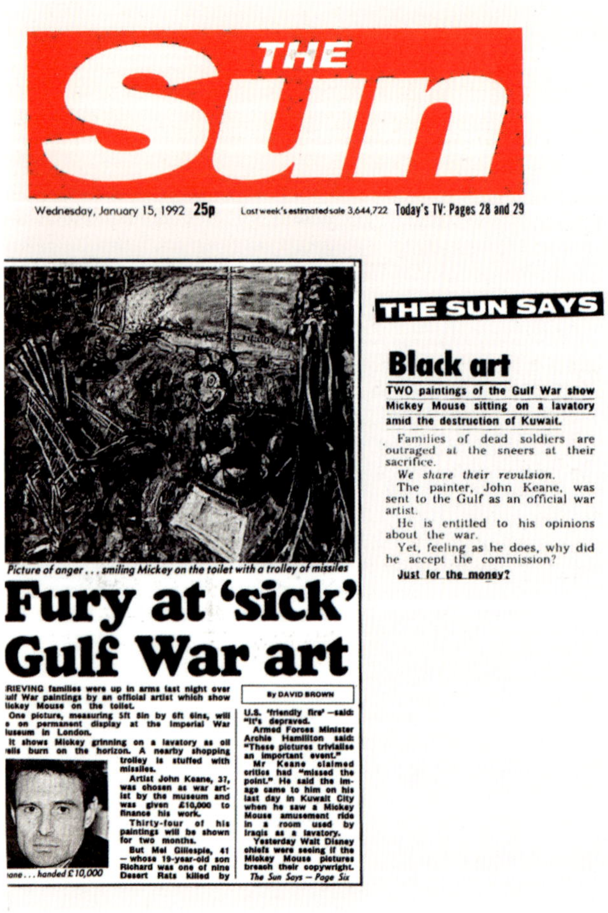

THE Sun

Wednesday, January 15, 1992 25p Last week's estimated sale 3,644,722 Today's TV: Pages 28 and 29

Picture of anger . . . smiling Mickey on the toilet with a trolley of missiles

Fury at 'sick' Gulf War art

By DAVID BROWN

RIEVING families were up in arms last night over ulf War paintings by an official artist which show lickey Mouse on the toilet.

One picture, measuring 5ft 8in by 6ft 6ins, will e on permanent display at the Imperial War luseum in London.

It shows Mickey grinning on a lavatory as oil ells burn on the horizon. A nearby shopping trolley is stuffed with missiles.

Artist John Keane, 37, was chosen as war artist by the museum and was given £10,000 to finance his work.

Thirty-four of his paintings will be shown for two months.

But Mel Gillespie, 41 — whose 19-year-old son Richard was one of nine Desert Rats killed by U.S. 'friendly fire' — said: "It's depraved."

Armed Forces Minister Archie Hamilton said: "These pictures trivialise an important event."

Mr Keane claimed critics had "missed the point." He said the image came to him on his last day in Kuwait City when he saw a Mickey Mouse amusement ride in a room used by Iraqis as a lavatory.

Yesterday Walt Disney chiefs were seeing if the Mickey Mouse pictures breach their copywright.

The Sun Says — Page Six

ane . . . handed £10,000

THE SUN SAYS

Black art

TWO paintings of the Gulf War show Mickey Mouse sitting on a lavatory amid the destruction of Kuwait.

Families of dead soldiers are outraged at the sneers at their sacrifice.

We share their revulsion.

The painter, John Keane, was sent to the Gulf as an official war artist.

He is entitled to his opinions about the war.

Yet, feeling as he does, why did he accept the commission?

Just for the money?

The Sun, Wednesday, January 15, 1992

Alien Landscape, 1991
Oil and collage on canvas
210 x 173 cm / 82¾ x 68 in

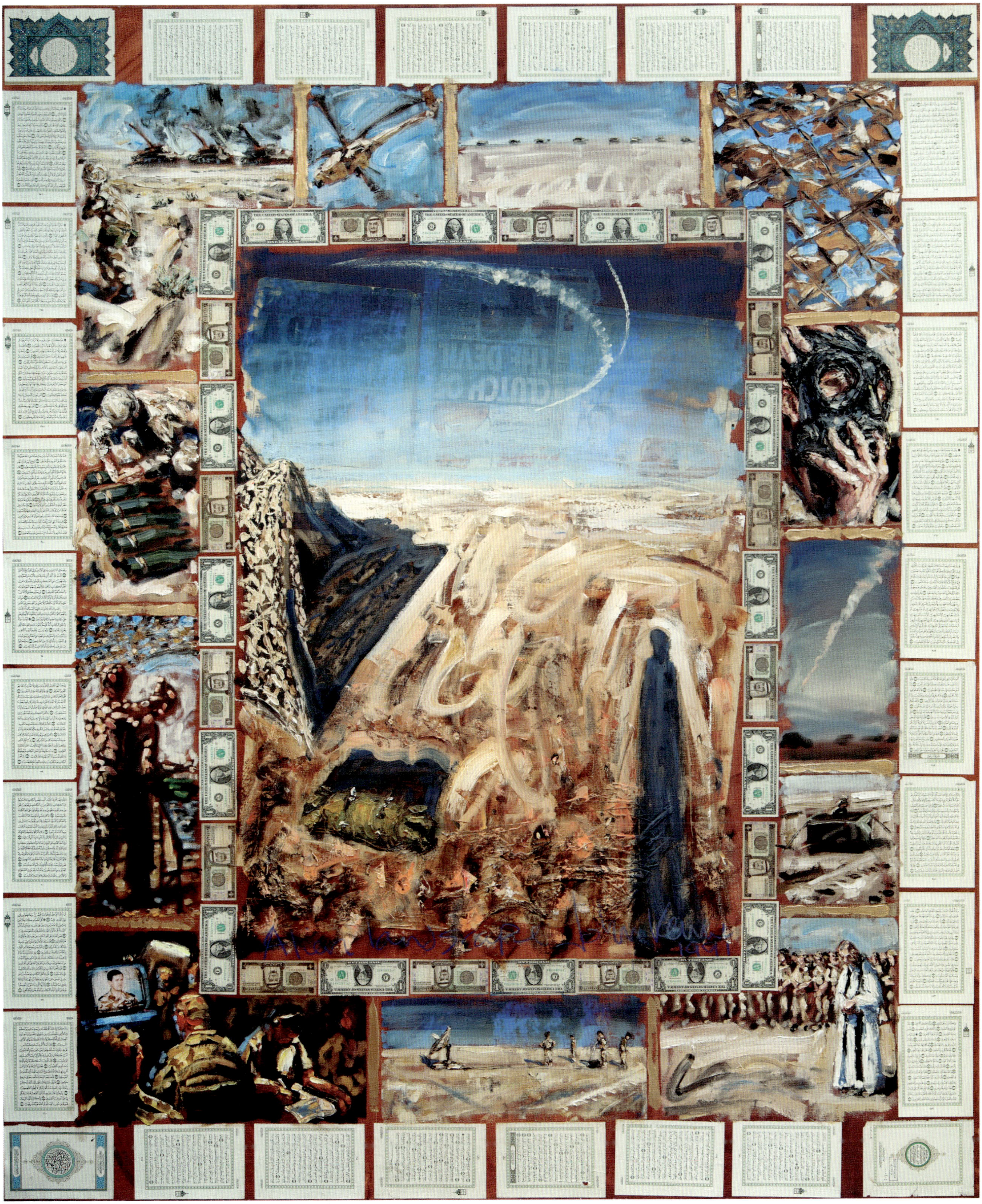

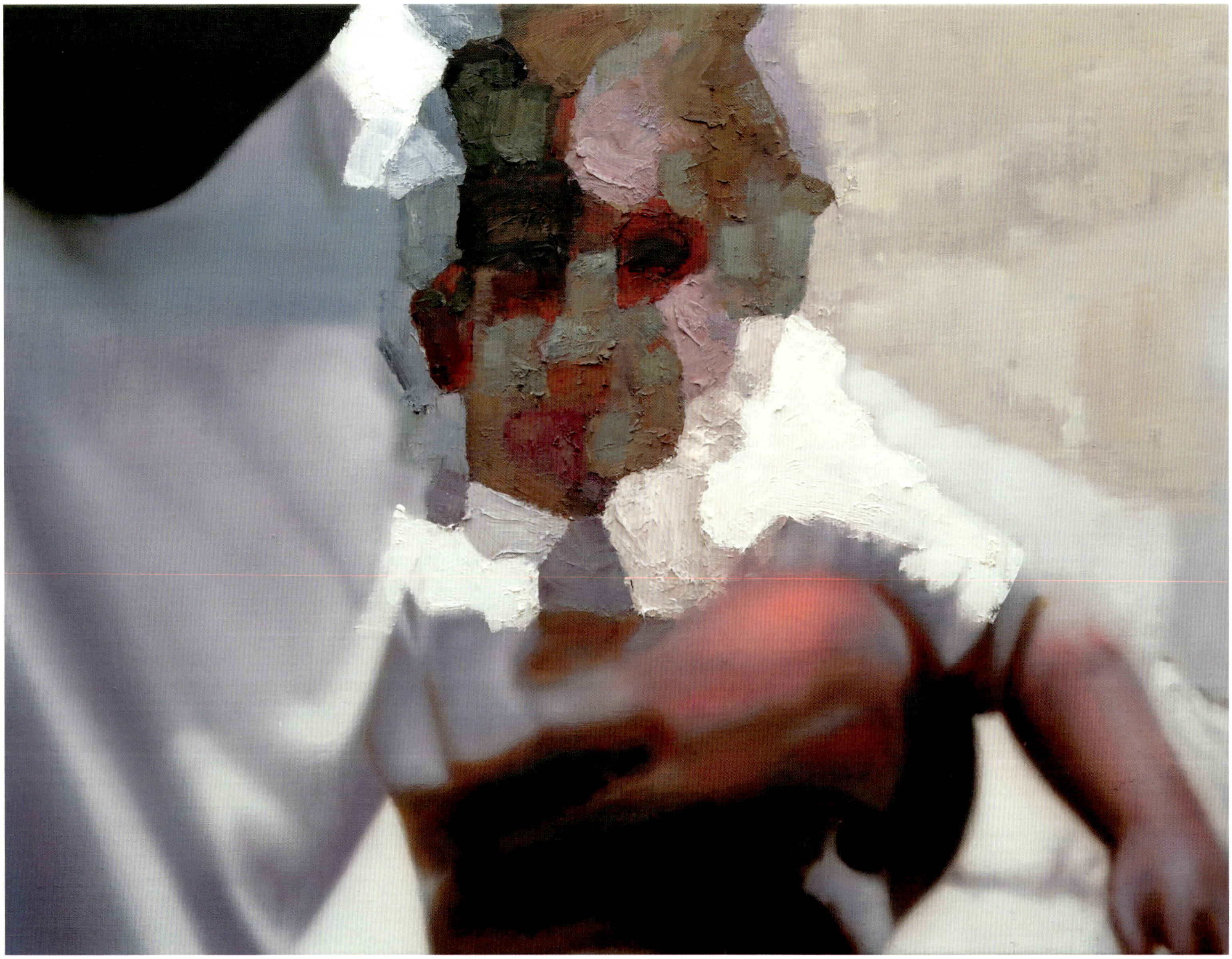

Love You to Bits, 2008
Oil on linen
85 x 110 cm / 33½ x 43½ in

father's work — to the Second Gulf War and to 7/7, all reflected in the increasing references in Keane's work to Western aggression and religious fundamentalism: in 'Love you to Bits' (2008), a still from a suicide video made by one of the London bombers, holding his child as he speaks to the camera, is pixelated with paint.

A year before the transport attacks in the British capital, a sense of this developing historical continuum was already apparent in a mini-retrospective, *Back to Fundamentals*, in the late winter of 2004. The selection stretched from greatest hits of the past, including 'Mickey Mouse at the Front' and 'Murphy's Law, Enniskillen' (1989) to two post-9/11 works. In 'Bad Faith' (2002), Jesus Christ turns into Al Qaeda supremo Osama Bin Laden on a mock-up of the Turin Shroud, believed by some Christians to have been Christ's burial shroud. 'Modernism and Martyrdom' shows some of the desperate would-be escapees falling from the World Trade Centre. Fundamentalism was now at the base of so much.

ML: And — again, your love of puns — you take a John Major phrase 'back to basics' and the idea of fundamentalism, now very current.

JK: Yes. Well, as I say modestly [laughs], if you look back at my work over the years, you will discern a remarkable prescience. There is a sort of 'I told you so' — the financial crash, religious fundamentalism, Rupert Murdoch. The things I have banged on about and returned to — such as the workings of financial institutions — have proved to be quite good choices, although I say so.

But the pivot of this period of history was the Guantanamo Bay detention facility, part of America's revenge for 9/11 which in turn provoked Islamist retaliations in London, the Syrian desert and Paris.

Because of the number of conflicts at home and abroad that he has covered, it's easy to see Keane as a sort of painterly equivalent of a news photographer: an artist-journalist, whose work offers detailed reportage of the tensions of the more than a third of a century during which he has worked.

This editorial emphasis can result in his aesthetic decisions — perspective, colour, the manipulation of paint — being under-considered. But his work of the last decade has been dominated by one particular shade of paint — orange.

With a catalogue preface by the Nobel Prize-winning playwright and political polemicist Harold Pinter, describing Guantanamo Bay as a "concentration camp", the 17 paintings exhibited as *Guantanamerica* at Flowers in 2006 digitally misshape photos of the orange jump-suited detainees without trial to create abstracted shapes that variously evoke the Rorschach psychological test, which invites interpretation of ink-blots, blood stains, cartoon monsters and another pun on the name of the substance crucial to the work of artists and of industrial economies: eight images called *Oil Interference* (2006).

JK: One of the things that did intrigue me with my love of wordplay and so on was 'oil interference.' With oil on water, you get patterns . . .

ML: Which you see on the asphalt at petrol stations: some extraordinary patterns.

JK: Yes. Those rainbows. But I also liked the other [political] meaning of oil interference. But it was really just playing around on a computer with colour and colour-saturation and separation. And suddenly finding you were getting almost these oil interference patterns on the surface.

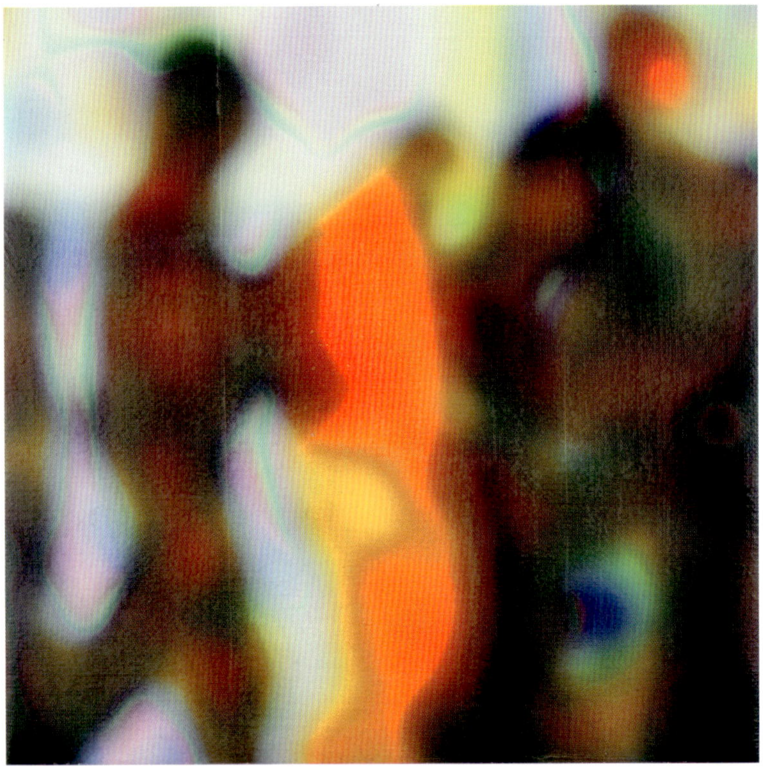

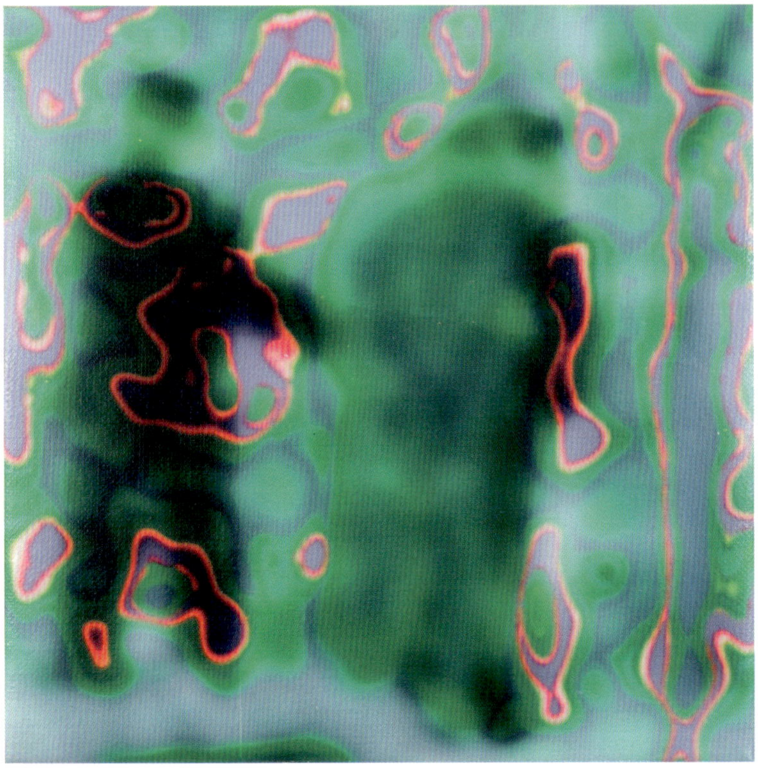

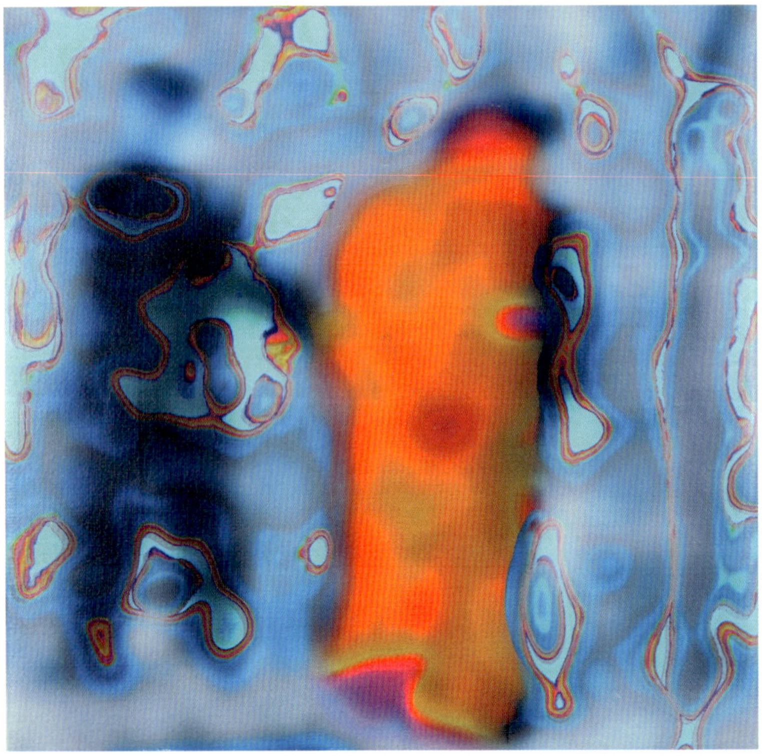

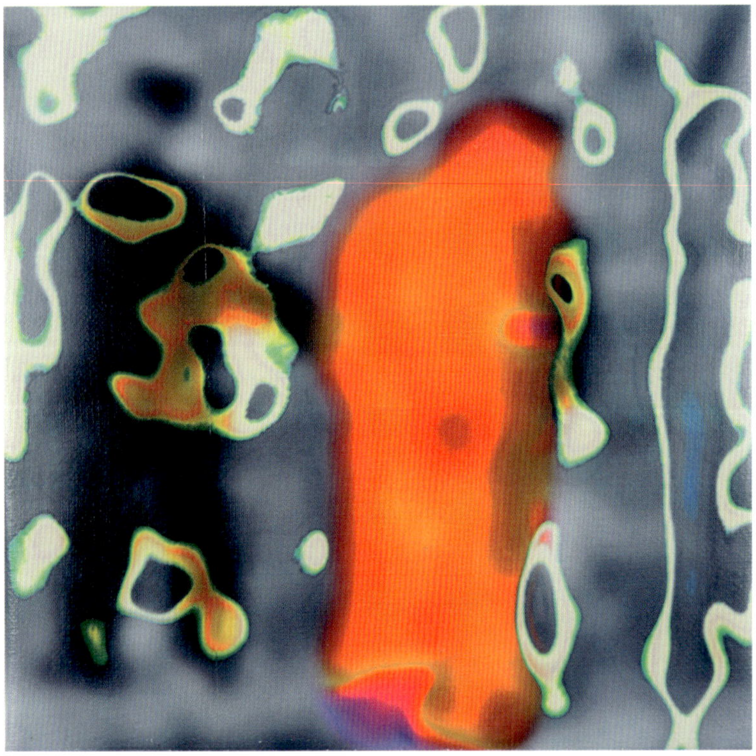

Oil Interference Patterns #1, 2006
Inkjet transfer and acrylic on jute
35 x 35 cm / 14 x 14 in
Private Collection, UK

Oil Interference Patterns #5, 2006
Inkjet transfer and acrylic on jute
35 x 35 cm / 14 x 14 in
Collection: Nick Taylor

Oil Interference Patterns #3, 2006
Inkjet transfer and acrylic on jute
35 x 35 cm / 14 x 14 in

Oil Interference Patterns #4, 2006
Inkjet transfer and acrylic on jute
35 x 35 cm / 14 x 14 in
Collection: Matthew and Emily Flowers

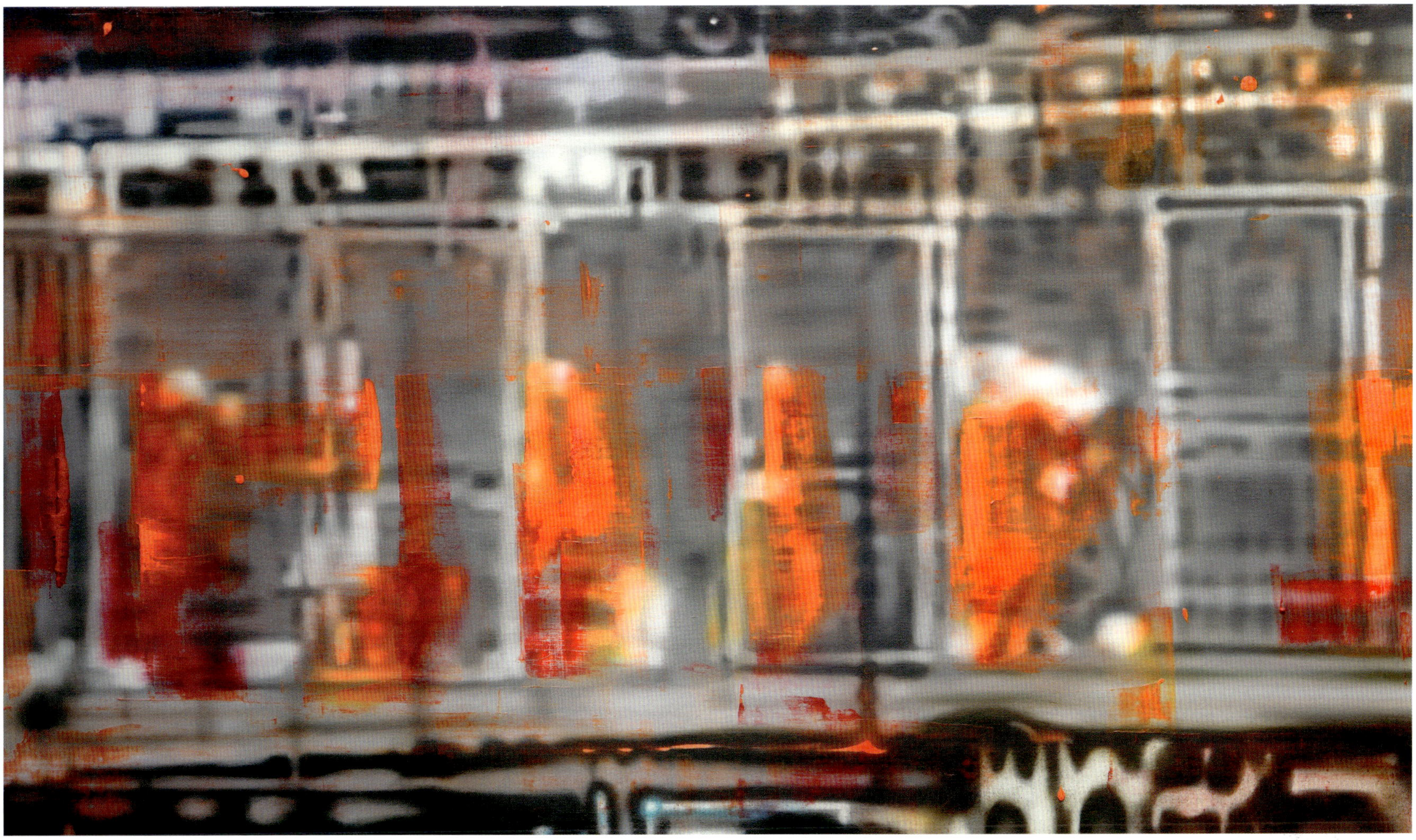

Guantanamerica, 2005
Oil and acrylic on linen
117 x 198 cm / 46 x 78 in
Collection: Nick Taylor

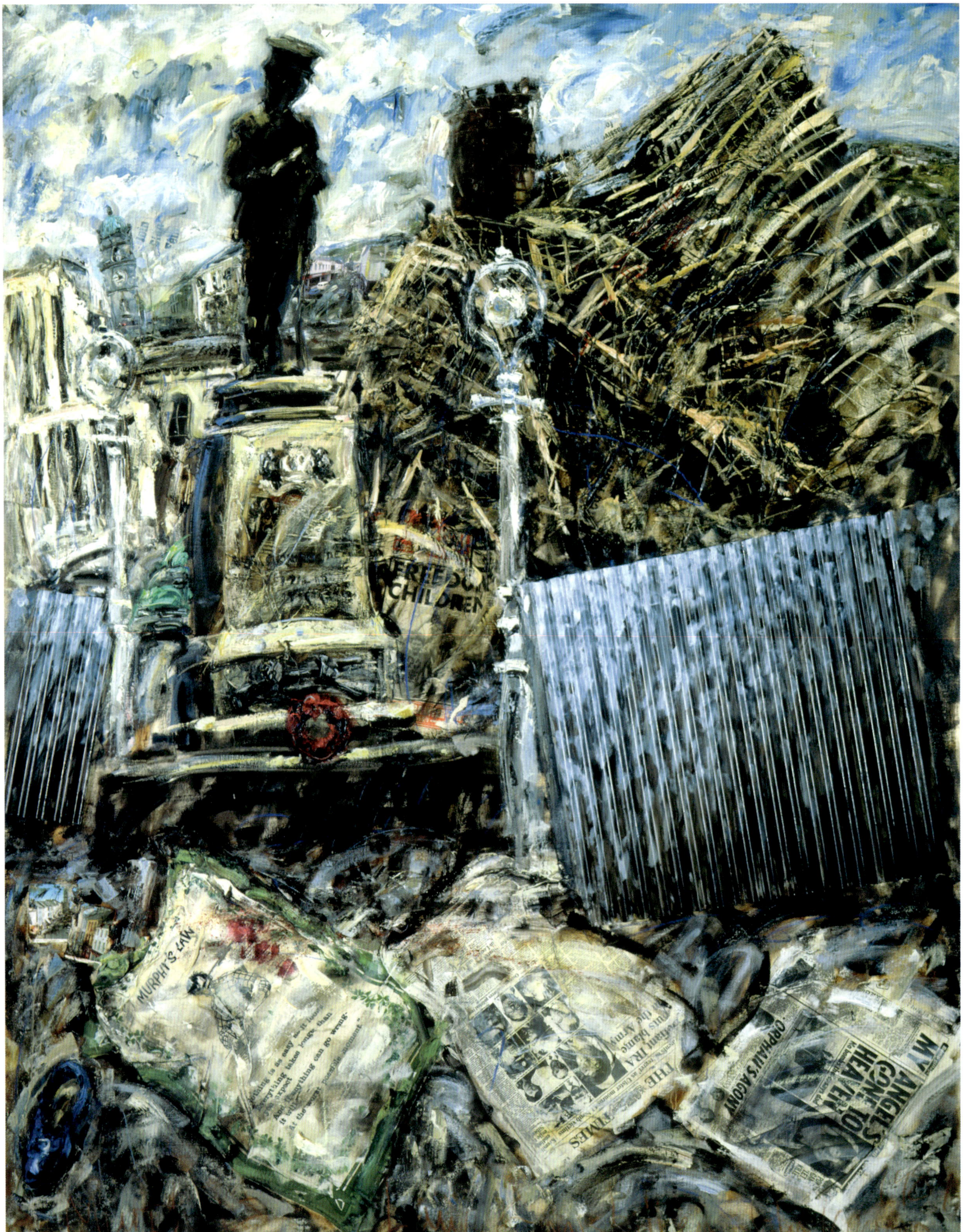
MURPHY'S LAW
ORPHAN'S AGONY
MY ANGELS GONE TO HEAVEN

ML: And also it's like cells under a microscope?

JK: Yes, it is. The meanings and intentions are there but also the simple sensual appearance of things is important.

From Belfast—through the Falklands and the Gulf—to Guantanamo, Keane has explored the wars across the water in which his home nation had a considerable—and sometimes controlling—interest. But he has also depicted countries and situations to which most Britons turned a blinder eye.

CHAPTER FOUR
FOREIGN CONFLICTS

IN THE SUMMER OF 2014, JUST AFTER STARTING WORK ON THIS BOOK, I went, for journalistic purposes, to Enniskillen in Northern Ireland. The town is mainly connected in memory and on Google with the day in 1987 when 11 people were killed by an IRA bomb at a Remembrance Day service: a massacre depicted in Keane's 1989 picture 'Murphy's Law, Enniskillen' (chapter 3), in which rubble is piled above abandoned newspapers in the gutter.

Subsequently, the place has aimed to offer more positive alternatives to search engines and one of these is the annual Beckett International Festival, performing and exploring the plays, books and films of the Irish-French winner of the Nobel Prize in Literature, who went to school in Enniskillen.

As a group of journalists was driven up into the hills of County Fermanagh to watch at an abandoned church a cross-cultural collaboration—*Catastrophe*, Samuel Beckett's dramatic sketch dedicated to the then jailed playwright Vaclav Havel, later first President of the Czech Republic—I witnessed another multi-national alliance so striking that I had to check with locals on the coach that it had really been there.

The marching season, in my mind because of Keane's work on the subject, had just started and, as we went through villages and housing estates, flags outside houses and on lampposts flapped tribal affiliations: the Union Flag of the loyalists and the Republicans' tricolour. But, in places that identified as Irish, the nationalist emblem alternated with, or was tied to, the colours of the Palestinians, while, in locations that considered themselves British, the favours of Israel were used to the same parallel purpose.

As a journalist during the 'Troubles', I had observed visual and verbal links between the Catholic and Palestinian communities, whose perception of military and religious oppression had obvious overlaps. The other doubling, though, was new to me. But, it was explained, in the sort of tit-for-tat response to what the other side was doing that has been a reflex of Northern Ireland's sectarian divide, Unionists had reacted to Republican sympathy for the Palestinians by twinning the Protestants of Ulster with the Israelis: a community violently hated by its

Murphy's Law, Enniskillen, 1989
Oil and mixed media on canvas
223.5 x 173 cm / 88 x 68 in
Private Collection, UK

neighbours and dependent for survival on a geographically separate state (the UK, the US) that was seen recently to have weakened in its historical support.

The situations also echo each other in the work of John Keane. A decade and a half after the Northern Irish pictures in *The Other Cheek?*, the artist exhibited *The Inconvenience of History*, a series of paintings prompted by a visit—with the relief and development agency Christian Aid—to Israel and the Occupied Palestinian Territories. In one of the acts that triggered international concern about disproportionate response by Israel, the Israel Defense Forces (IDF) had recently entered and levelled the Jenin Refugee Camp on the West Bank, claiming that the settlement harboured terrorists, from the Hamas and Islamic Jihad organisations, who were launching regular rocket and suicide-bomb attacks on Israel.

ML: This is another set of pictures that begins with an air ticket?

JK: Christian Aid got in touch in 2002—there was a lot going on: suicide bombs and Jenin being flattened. I was approached and asked if I wanted to go with a Relief Assessment Group that works with Christian Aid's partners in Israel and Palestine. And, of course, I said: 'Yes. Absolutely.' It felt like one of those things—like before I went to Northern Ireland—that seemed to have been with us so long that you no longer think about them.

Keane made two trips to the region. The first, a preliminary recce of ten days, followed the assault on Jenin and coincided with the siege at the Church of the Nativity in Bethlehem, where, as part of the same IDF action, forces laid siege to the biblically-resonant building for several weeks after suspected Palestinian militants had taken refuge there. The charity subsequently arranged a tailored trip for Keane, during which he collected images and notes that led to 'The Inconvenience of History', which, after being seen at the London Institute Gallery in early 2004, travelled to Belfast.

Keane also filmed a 30-minute documentary that was screened by BBC4.

ML: Even though you had experience as a war artist, were you apprehensive?

JK: Yes. Because it was quite tense. But it was fascinating: the Middle East and the Holy Land have such a grip on us because of our cultural heritage. They're almost in our DNA regardless of whether you're religious. All the names—Bethlehem, Jerusalem, Armageddon—are so familiar and yet it feels so foreign. It's a place steeped in mythology and yet real people are also living and dying there. So there are many layers of interest. It's probably one of the most intense trips I've made.

There is a crisply photo-realistic quality to the images inspired by this trip, a consequence of the artist's increasing use of digital location photographs but also, in this particular series, by a technological benefit of the artist's position at that time as Visiting Research Fellow at Camberwell College of Arts. The college's inkjet printer allowed Keane to reproduce a photo on viscose (a wood-pulp fabric) and then paint on top. The result, in a picture such as 'Ismael' (2003), which shows an old man in front of an Israeli settlement apartment block, is an almost

Ismael, 2003
oil and inkjet on viscose on linen
126 x 84.5 cm / 49¾ x 33¼ in

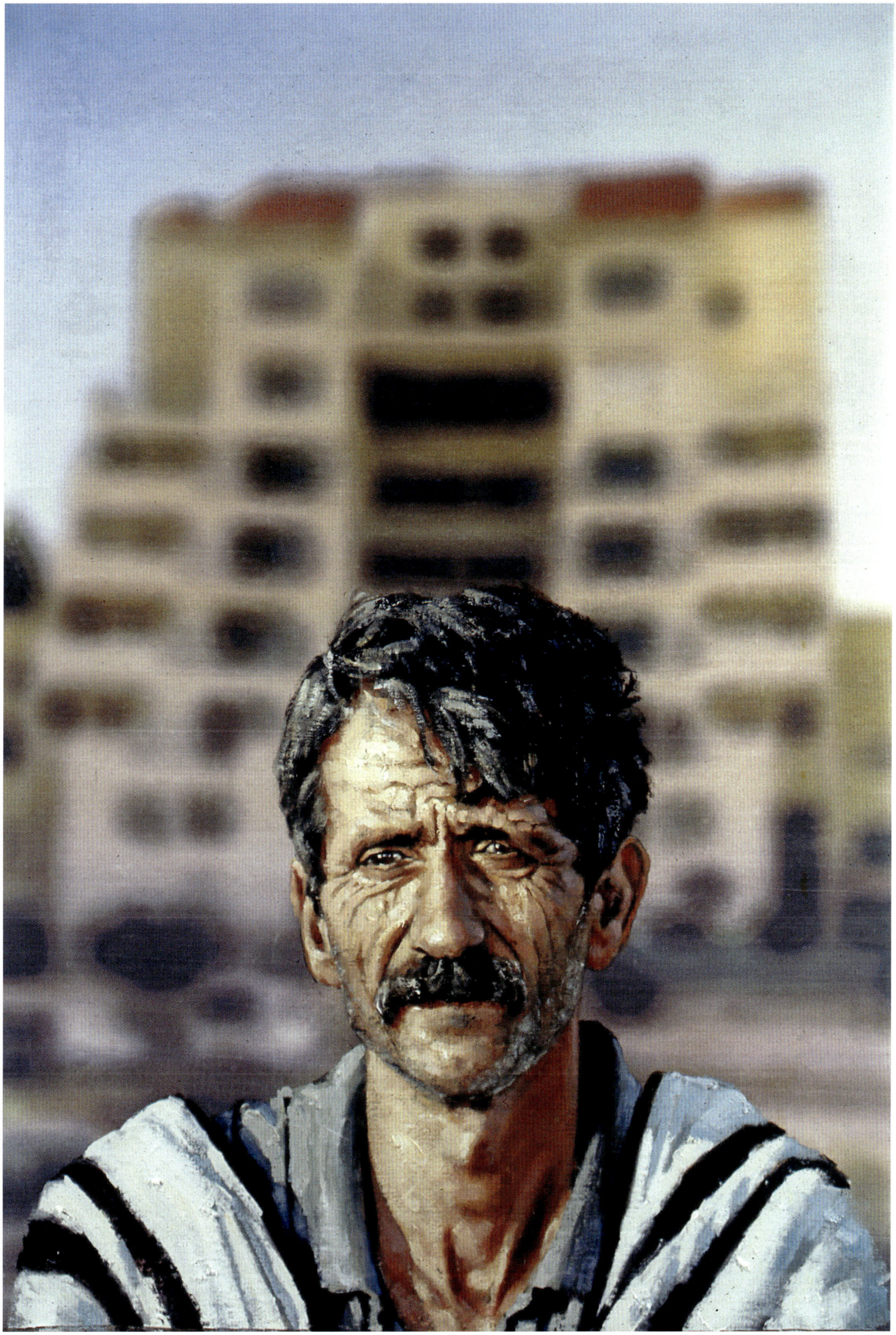

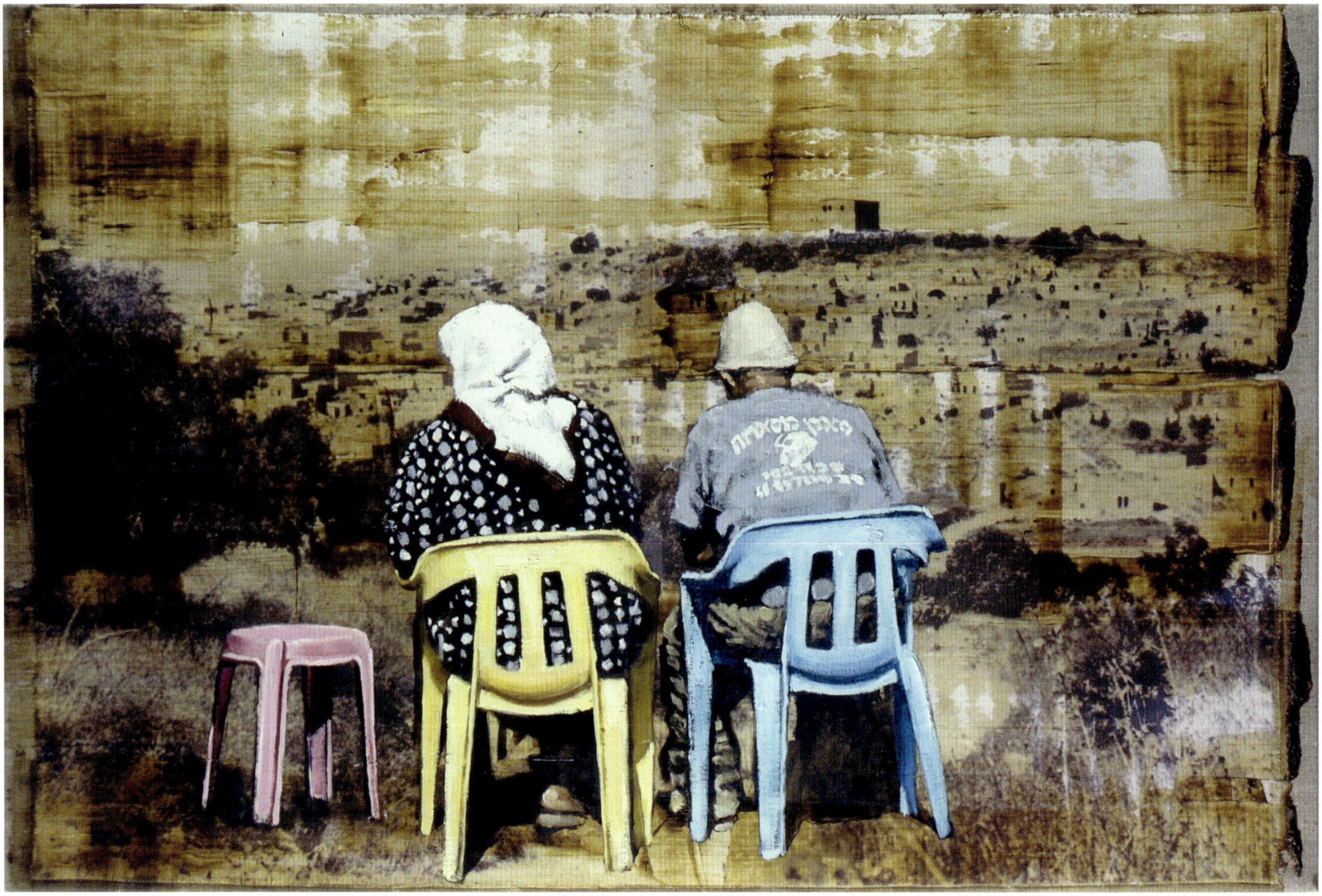

The Inconvenience of History I, 2003
Oil and inkjet on viscose on linen
81 x 122 cm / 32 x 48 in
Private Collection, UK

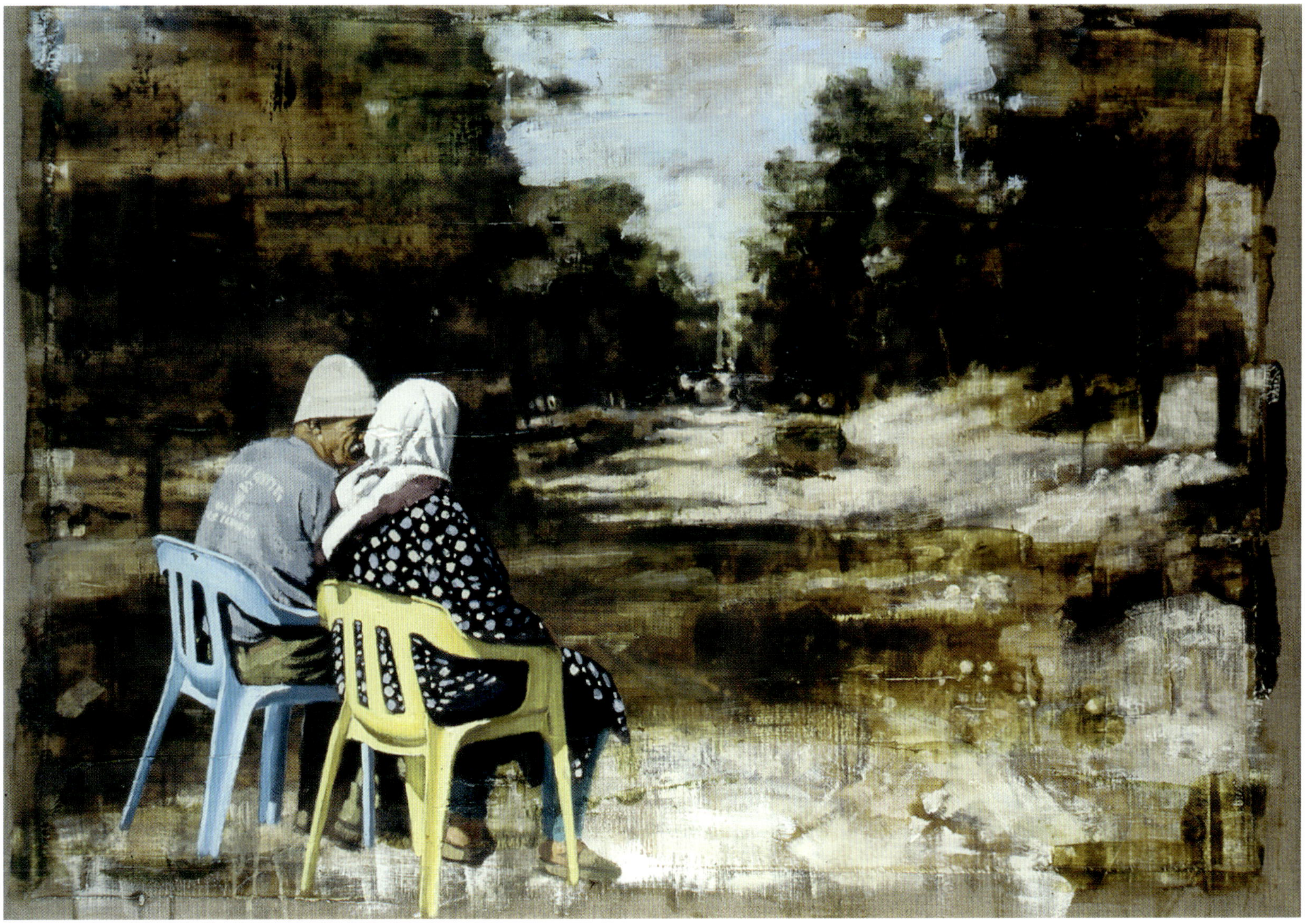

The Inconvenience of History II, 2003
Oil and inkjet on viscose on linen
86 x 122 cm / 34 x 48 in

three-dimensional sense of depth and levels in the image. But another feature of this series is that images that look too striking or symbolic to be true actually prove to be the truth.

In a pair of pictures that share the title of the exhibition, an elderly Palestinian couple sit in locations that could have been used to film *Jesus of Nazareth*, except for the incongruous plastic cafe chairs — lurid blue and yellow beside a pink stool — that support them. In another doubled image, 'School of the Innocent I. Jenin' and 'School of the Innocent II. Jenin' (both 2002), cartoonish wall paintings of a schoolboy, in one of which he holds a giant pencil in the 'present arms!' position like a gun, are bordered by martyrdom photos and riddled with bullet holes. And 'Hopeless in Gaza II (Nativity)' (2003) shows a child cradled between his Middle Eastern parents in what looks like a pointed modernisation of a classical representation of the baby Jesus. A sceptic — or Israeli government information minister — might think that these scenarios are — to borrow the title word — convenient. But they are not.

ML: These are found images?

JK: Yes, the 'School of the Innocent' pictures were painted from images I photographed that I found on the side of a door. It was in Jenin, I think. And the martyrdom photos were all over the walls. So the idea of contrasting this with a boy who was about 12 and had clearly been martyred — holding a pencil and holding a gun.

ML: And 'Hopeless in Gaza II (Nativity)' has extraordinary religious and artistic resonance but that's also a found image?

JK: Absolutely. Yes, it's a found image from a newspaper. And the image has an almost Biblical sense.

ML: And unlike most artistic Nativity scenes, the features are racially correct.

In much of his recent work, as discussed later in this chapter, Keane plays with trick images and the impact of subjectivity on interpretation. But, in the case of *The Inconvenience of History*, we can usually believe what we're seeing, however unlikely it seems. For instance, we are alert to a possible joke in 'The Office of Yasser Arafat' (2003) as the title for a scene that might come from the brochure for a luxury hotel: sand and lapping sea glimpsed through the canopy of what looks like a beach bar. But, as the BBC4 film testifies, this really was what the HQ of the late PLO leader looked like.

But, even though an image or fact is objectively accurate, there can still be subjectivity in the decision to choose or use it.

ML: When you go to the Middle East or to Ireland, where in effect there are civil wars — I realise that objectivity is a complex idea but do you aim for any kind of journalistic objectivity?

JK: If I put my hand on my heart, my sympathies would be with the Republicans in Ireland and the Palestinians in the Middle East. But I think I do also want to ask difficult questions. I don't want to be a propagandist. So, for example, there's this painting 'Moment'. I thought I couldn't go to this area and not address the question of the suicide bomber. I went to a cafe in leafy Jerusalem, where a suicide

Hopeless in Gaza II (Nativity), 2003
Oil and photocopy on linen
162 x 137 cm / 63¾ x 54 in

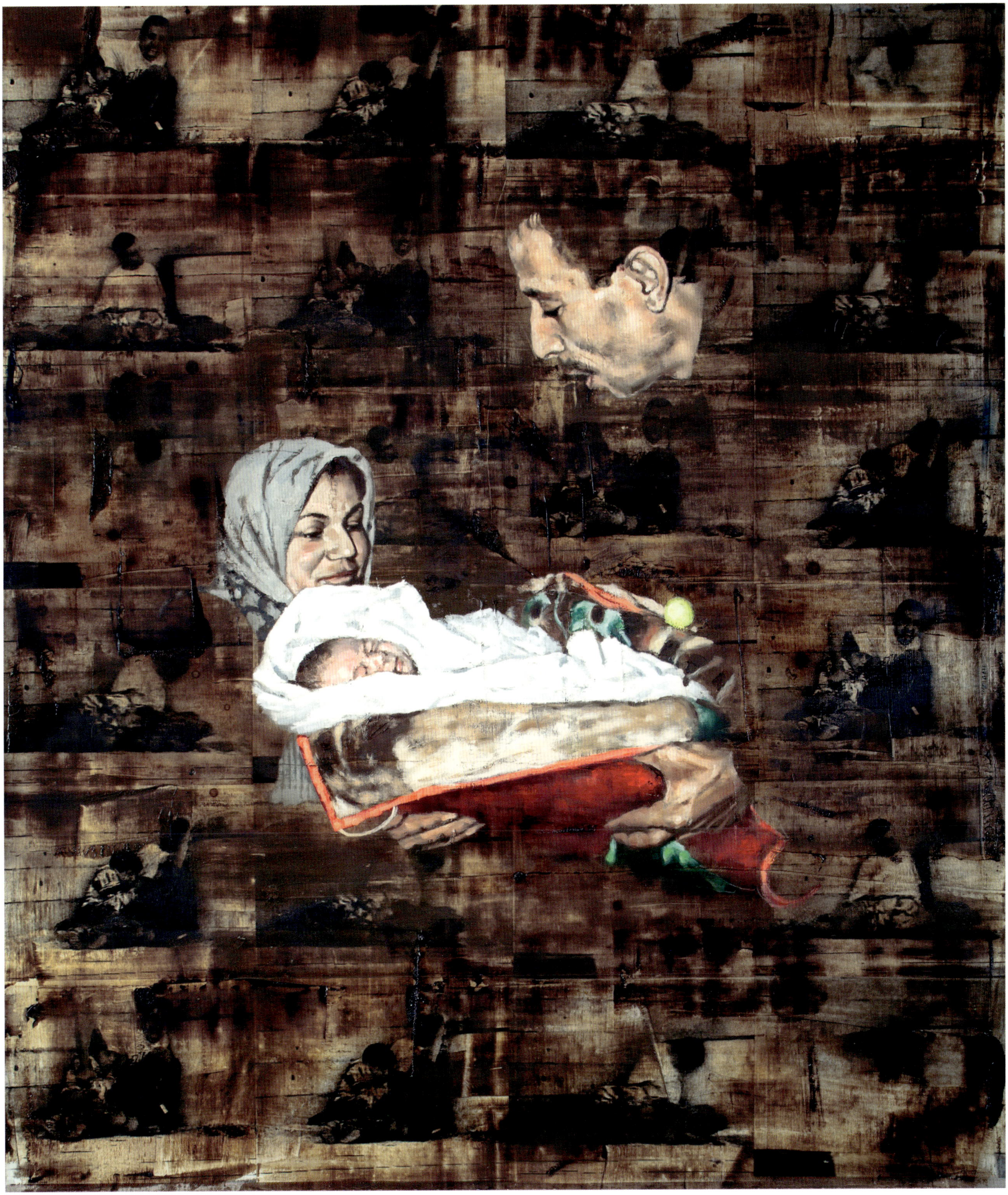

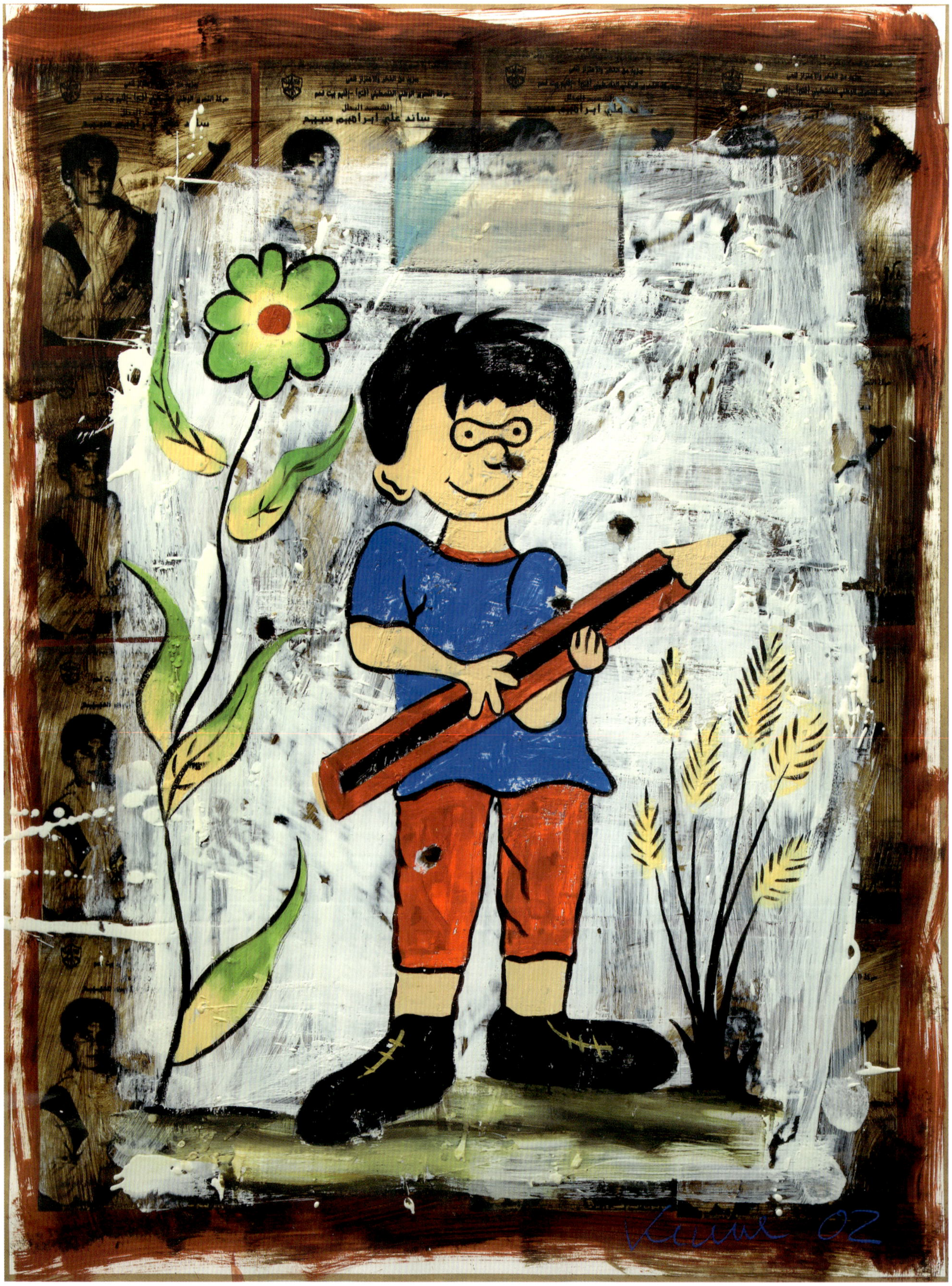

School of the Innocents I, Jenin, 2002
Oil, beeswax and photocopies on paper
115 x 84 cm / 45¼ x 33¼ in

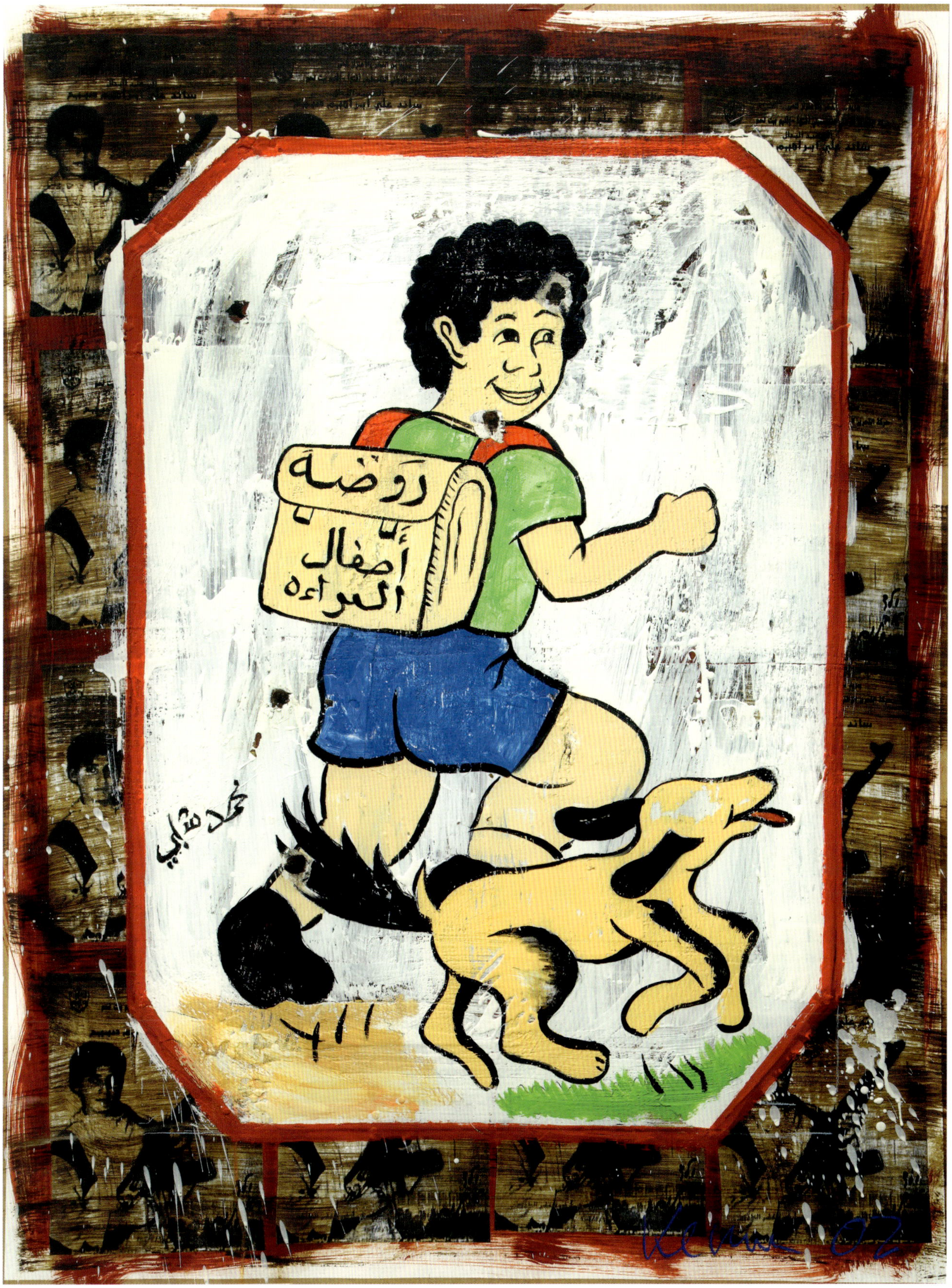

School of the Innocents II, Jenin, 2002
Oil, beeswax and photocopies on paper
115 x 84 cm / 45¼ x 33¼ in

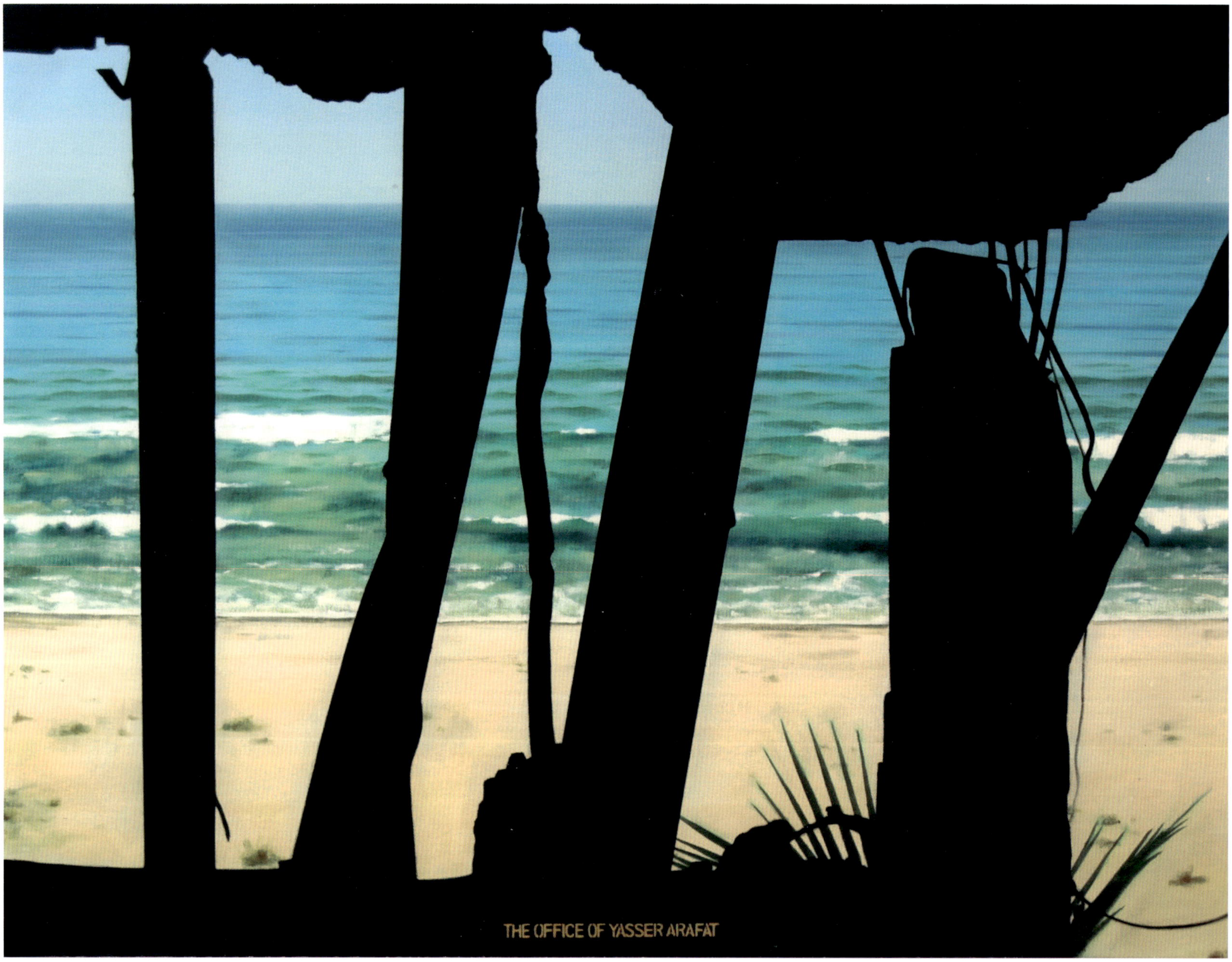

The Office of Yasser Arafat, 2003
Oil and gold leaf on canvas
142 x 183 cm / 56 x 72 in

bombing had happened a few months before. It was frequented by young liberals with cappuccinos. Very European in that sense. And by chance, when we were filming there, there was a guy who had survived the explosion. And again by chance I came across a newspaper photo of a Palestinian painting of a suicide bombing, which was intended as a heroic depiction of the act. So I took that as my starting point and with the computer enlarged it and then inserted images of the 11 victims, almost subliminally, in order to undermine it. Even if I know where my sympathies lie there are questions about aims and means.

Generally considered one of the greatest novelists not to have been awarded the Nobel Prize in Literature, the English writer Graham Greene (1904–1991) gives his name directly to the work from one of Keane's worldwide excursions—his 1995 exhibition, *Graham Greene and the Jungle of Human Dilemma*—but he is the presiding spirit of all the artist's foreign projects.

Very unusually for a fiction writer, the majority of Greene's books are set outside the country in which he was born. Believing that writing comes as much from the feet as the hands, he went to Mexico for *The Power and the Glory* (1940) and the travel book *The Lawless Roads* (1938), found fiction in Sierra Leone for *The Heart of the Matter* (1948) and, at the age of 80, non-fiction in Panama for the journal *Getting to Know the General*.

Keane's Mexican visit was at first personal rather than journalistic—he was accompanying on holiday his then girlfriend, now wife, the TV producer Rosemary McGowan—but, when Keane read *The Lawless Roads* and realised that his itinerary almost exactly matched the author's, the trip led to the set of pictures displayed, at Flowers East in 1995, as *Graham Greene and the Jungle of Human Dilemma.*

In the decade before his name-check in the Mexican exhibition, Greene had also had a curious involvement in Keane's exploration of Nicaragua, which led to the 1988 exhibition *Bee-Keeping in the War Zone*.

During the 1980s, Nicaragua became a symbolic point of contention between the Left and Right in Britain and (to the extent that paranoia about Communism allowed there to be a Left there) in America.

This was because, in July 1979, the country had undergone the most significant socialist revolution since Cuba two decades before, when the corrupt and repressive but pro-Western dictatorship of President Anastasio Somoza Debayle was overthrown by the Frente Sandinista de Liberación Nacional (FSLN), which became known colloquially in both Nicaragua and North and West London as "the Sandinistas", named for Augusto Sandino, who had led guerilla resistance during the American occupation in the 1930s.

Although the Americans had long been back in Washington, Nicaragua remained part of their broad definition of the "backyard", as politicians cosily described the nation's sphere of interest. After Ronald Reagan became President in 1980, he channelled millions of dollars to the Contra rebels who now opposed the Sandinistas and, when aid was blocked by the Democratic-controlled Congress, allowed his aide Colonel Oliver North to set up a secret operation which illegally sold arms to Iran (infuriating, with future consequences, President Saddam Hussein of Iraq) and sent the profits to the Contras. When exposed, the so-called "Iran-Contra" affair intermittently over-shadowed and even threatened the administrations of Reagan and George H.W. Bush.

In Britain, where the recently-elected Margaret Thatcher agreed with Reagan on Nicaragua, as on most matters, allegiance to the Sandinistas and the Contras divided on Left and Right lines and, as had happened in the Spanish Civil War, writers and artists took sides. Salman Rushdie went to the country and wrote an admiring travelogue, *The Jaguar Smile*, while the dramatist Harold Pinter spoke at rallies and benefits and hosted the Nicaraguan President Daniel Ortega at his Holland Park home. From his exile in Antibes, Graham Greene wrote pro-Ortega letters and pieces.

Right-wing writers, including the novelist Piers Paul Read, published articles critical of the Socialist government and especially the left-wing politicisation of the theoretically neutral Catholic Church. He and Pinter were near-neighbours and, in a symbolic moment, the playwright once called out, when they passed each other in the street, in his direct but not necessarily unfriendly manner: "Piers, you know fuck all about Nicaragua."

Keane's views were usually closer to Pinter's—as shown by the playwright's fiery preface to the *Guantanamerica* catalogue—and, in 1987, their concern with Nicaragua overlapped.

> JK: The country had become a kind of focal point of world history—one of those proxy wars that was representative of the Cold War era, where US influence and Soviet influence were vying. And, after overthrowing a brutal regime, an attempt was being made to reconstruct the country along socialist lines, which was of interest to me. In the end, I felt it was a conflict I could get my mind around. I understood the issues, whereas Afghanistan or the Iran-Iraq War, or whatever, would have been much more difficult to comprehend.

The Nicaragua Solidarity Campaign in London arranged (somewhat loosely, it proved) for the artist to spend six weeks there in the summer of 1987. It was during this visit that he developed the working methods that, allowing for improvements in photographic technology, continued on all subsequent travel projects: collection of photos, written notes and found materials on location, which became the basis for paintings and works on paper once home in the studio.

More unusually, once the Nicaraguan images were completed, Keane used the camera to photograph them and then posted transparencies to Graham Greene in Antibes, asking if he might provide an introduction for the catalogue. With impeccable politeness, the writer declined, citing his pressing need to write more fiction before death, and disappointed the artist further by failing to send back the images. A further exchange of letters, in 1988, contained an elegant but possibly startling explanation.

> I am desolated that I didn't realise you wished to have the photographs back.
> I was discussing them with a friend abroad, who very much wanted to see them, and I posted them to him. I am afraid abroad in this case was Russia.
> I am writing to try and recover them but the posts both ways are very hazardous.

There is a tantalising possibility that the other man was the third man. The title of Greene's most enduring movie script, *The Third Man*, became associated with Kim Philby when he was suspected of having been the next most significant figure in the Burgess and Maclean spy ring. Although initially exonerated, Philby later came under further suspicion and fled to Russia, where he lived as a VIP guest of the Communist government until his death. Greene was himself an ex-spy and friend of Philby—an inspiration for Greene's espionage novel *The Human Factor* (1978)—and they remained in touch, through visits and phone calls, during one of which, it seems highly likely, they talked about the Nicaraguan pictures of John Keane.

Though they have no direct connection with the novelist, there is also a Greenian political and reportorial sensibility behind the products of another of the artist's foreign projects: the ten works related to Guatemala that were shown at Flowers East in 1992 under the title *Burden of Paradise*.

But, though Greene was less in the picture, there is a Pinter link. In 1991, his Gulf year, Keane had been invited to join the playwright and other showbiz socialists, including the actresses Charlotte Cornwell and Julie Christie, as a member of the Association of Artists for Guatemala (AAG).

The populous Central American state had experienced a Sandinista-like people's revolution in 1944, with the new government implementing socialist policies including the reclamation of land owned by foreign corporations, such as United Fruit Company from America. This raspberry from Guatemala to the US provoked the CIA to overthrow a regime that they considered a "beachhead for Soviet expansion" and replace it with a conservative, pro-Washington administration. The minimum wage and collective ownership were replaced by economic inequality so severe that, at the time of Keane's visit, it was estimated that 87 per cent of the nation lived below the poverty line. A form of *apartheid* was also in operation, with the suppression and even genocide of the majority Mayan Indian population by the 'Ladino' ruling class of mixed-race *mestizos*.

Such human rights abuses and economic inequality persuaded AAG to send a fact-finding visit to the country, with Keane invited to be among the delegates. Although Keane is sometimes seen as a partisan left-wing artist, his excursion-related work—in the Gulf, Nottingham, Belfast and even the Middle East—expresses far more nuance and confusion than, say, a Pinter political poem. But, in the case of Guatemala, the artist admits to being on-side.

> JK: Yes. After working with the idea of the artist as outsider, it was interesting to be involved in something you believe is a good thing, are more actively committed to. Through what I do, I am obviously trying to influence people—I always have a line, however woolly that may be—but to actively align yourself with a cause, it was interesting to do that.

Created across a period of eight years, the Guatemalan, Nicaraguan and Mexican pictures may differ in their strength of political identification, but there is an artistic continuity, with most of the works at this stage created through combinations of PVA, crayon, and collaged found objects and substances (litter, beeswax) on paper or wood, although, in the later pieces, the increasing use of oil paint and 'oil sticks' (a sort of oil paint crayon) hint at the direction in which Keane's painting was heading.

An unofficial triptych could be formed with a picture selected from each series: 'The Ruin of Managua Cathedral Sits Uneasily in the Plaza de la Revolucion on the Fault-Line. The Hotel and the Bank of America Look On' (1987); 'El Basuero' (1992), and 'Zapatista Jungle' (1995).

The first picture, with a 27-word title expansive even by Keane's standards scrawled in red crayon across the bottom of the canvas, shows a pointed but actual architectural opposition in the Nicaraguan capital: the centre of Catholic worship, built with blind faith on a fault-line and destroyed in a 1972 earthquake, overlooked by the luxury hotel that is always an uneasy presence in the developing world, and the financial powerhouse of the former American overlords.

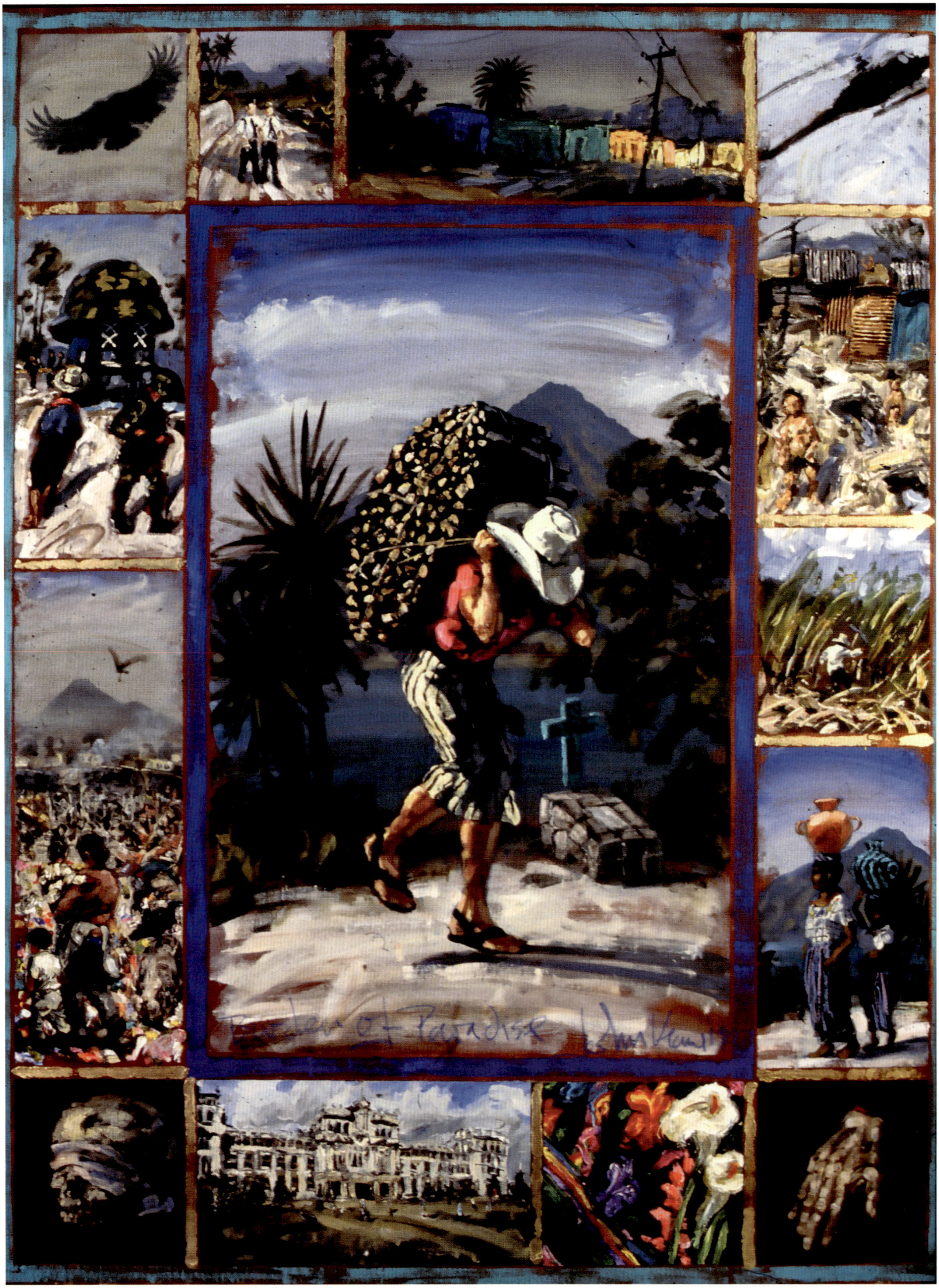
of Paradise

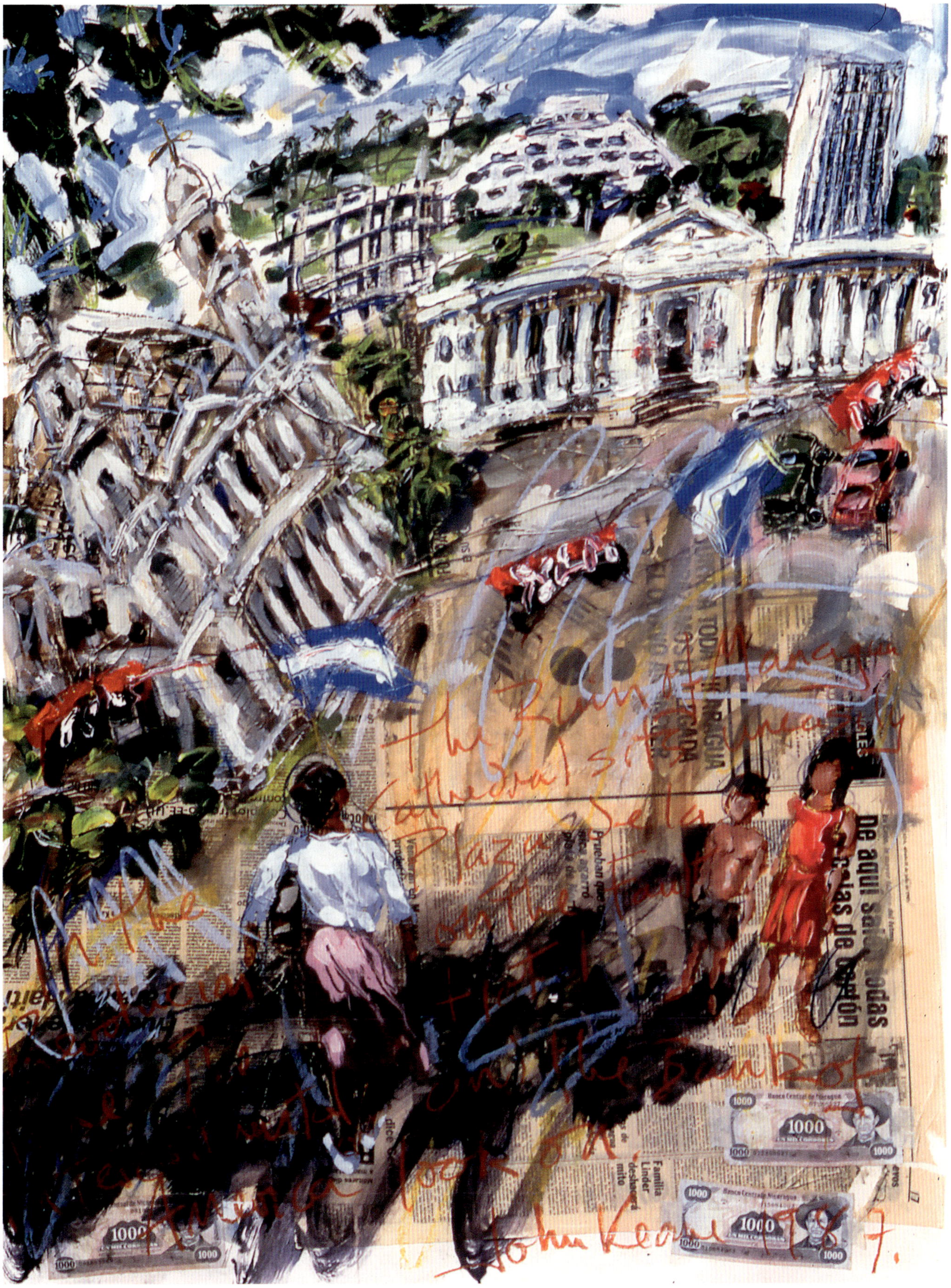

Burden of Paradise, 1992
Oil on canvas
230 x 173 cm / 90½ x 68 in
Private Collection, UK

The Ruin of Managua Cathedral sits uneasily in the Plaza de la Revolution on the Fault Line. The Hotel Intercontinental & the Bank of America look on, 1987
PVA and mixed media on paper
184 x 83 cm / 72½ x 32⅝ in
Private Collection, UK

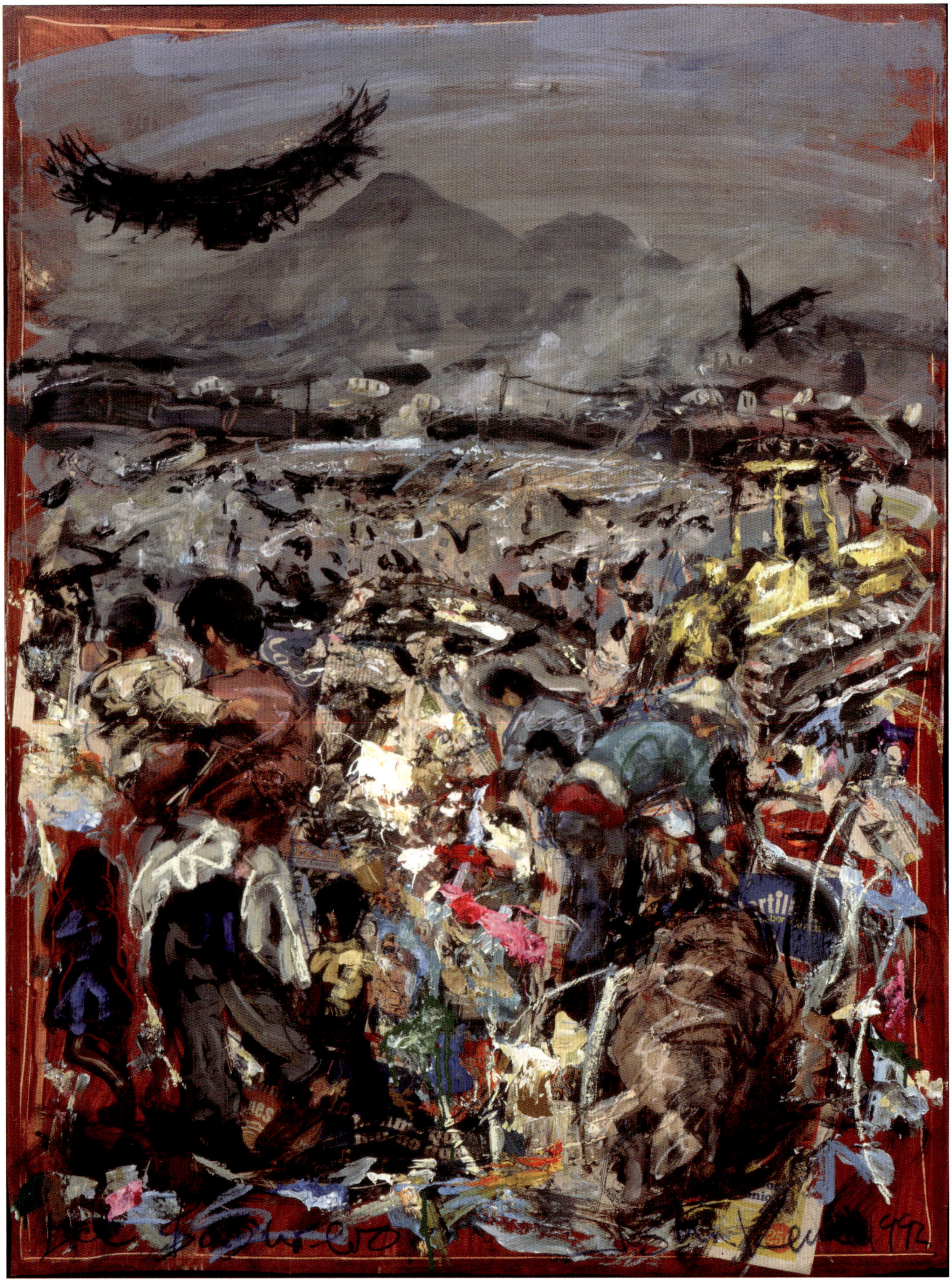

El Basurero, 1992
PVA and Mixed media on paper
114 x 84 cm / 44⅞ x 33⅛ in

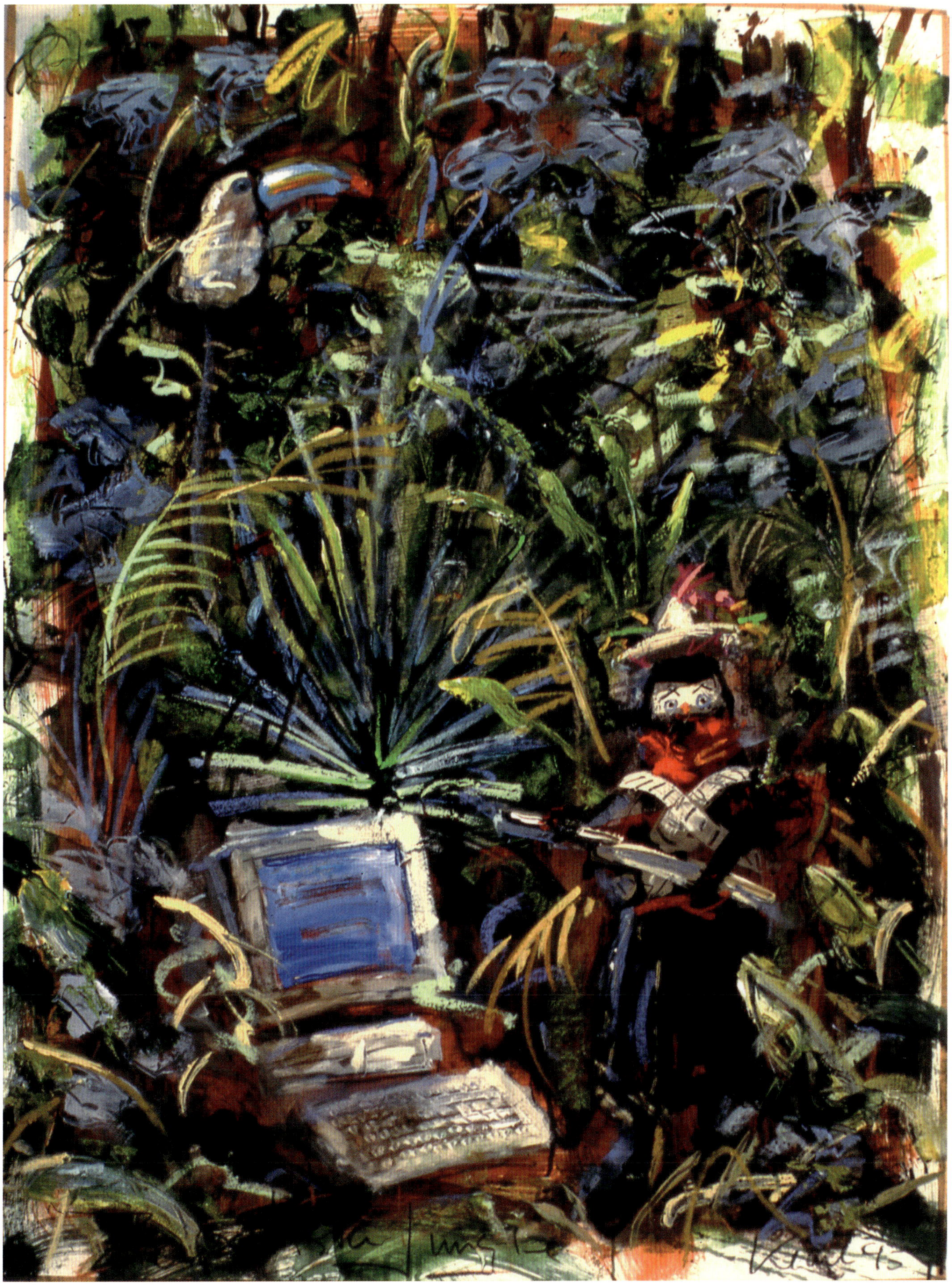

Zapatista Jungle, 1995
PVA and mixed media on paper
114.5 x 84 cm / 45¼ x 33¼ in
Private Collection, UK

In the Guatemalan middle image, piled paint and stuck-on objects create a rubbish dump, on which a vulture perches, with another above, and a young boy, by implication one of the super-poor who scavenge the left-overs of the super-rich, tramps through the mess.

The mess of tropical foliage in the forest is suggested through similar stylistic devices in the Mexican picture, with the vulture replaced by a toucan with a vividly-striped beak. Into this ancient landscape intrude two contemporary still life objects: an early computer terminal suggests the interventions of either writers, financial dealers or, a phenomenon that was beginning at this time, for the spread of terrorist or revolutionary rhetoric by the Zapatistas, guerillas who opposed the 1994 signing of the North American Free Trade Agreement, which made the nation an economic ally of Canada and (most contentiously) the US Keane's painting includes a doll of Subcomandante Marcos, the pseudonym and fictional persona used by the leading Zapatista propagandist.

With an eye for both comedy and tragedy, the Nicaragua-Guatemala-Mexico pictures are distinctly Greenian but also, by his criteria at that time, very Keanian.

The name of the patron saint of the artist's foreign pictures is obliquely present in the inspiration for the working trip that came after the Mexican pictures. In the late '90s, Keane had met a director of Greenpeace, the environmental campaign group.

JK: And I didn't hear from him for ages and then he told me they had a ship going to the Amazon as part of an anti-logging campaign.

ML: Partly because—as a war artist—you were seen as the sort of painter who went on things?

JK: Yes. I'd done that. I'd been on expeditions and trips. I think I may have met him in connection with the Nicaragua pictures. I was desperate to go to the Amazon.

The pictures shown at Flowers East in 2001 as *Saving the Bloody Planet* include an unusual designation of working surface: 'Oil on illegal wood'. The rainforests of the Amazon are threatened by both government sanctioned logging and freelance clearings by mercenaries serving the international timber market. So one of the six pictures painted on a slice of stolen trunk, 'Souvenir 4 (Vanishing Point)' (2001), its subtitle featuring another sharp word-turn, makes the point through both the image—a ravaged wood of truncated amputee trunks—and its canvas.

Less politically, some of the other works project an Attenboroughian sense of wonder at the beauty of water, sky, foliage, birds and butterflies. By now working mainly in oil, Keane also employs frequent mirroring and reflection effects. In 'Lepidoptery, Symmetry, Mimicry, Verisimilitude and Art' (2001), a butterfly with identical wings divides an image of a tree-lined river that itself seems to be in two identical halves. In 'Bank (1)' (2001), the red Greenpeace ship splits another perfectly doubled image.

ML: Do you have a a sense when traveling of what the finished artwork will be?

JK: Sometimes. But then it can be completely wrong when you get back to the studio.

ML: And the Rorschach Blot is behind some of these images as well?

JK: Yes. This evolutionary facility we have to survive by recognising patterns. If you see something in the forest that might be a threat, we are attuned to seeing these things. Certainly, in terms of appearance, symmetry is very important.

ML: The butterfly and the boat on the river are, in effect, mirror paintings?

JK: Yes, it's invoking those very still days you get on the Amazon sometimes. And also the Rorschach idea of the blot and I literally folded these paintings over—and also playing with the idea of symmetry on a butterfly's wing. But, yes, it was taking your canvas and folding it over and getting blobs. It was just enjoying that process and seeing where it led.

ML: Would you ever use real butterflies as Damien Hirst did?

JK: I've thought about that because of them already being dead. Actually I've got something here. [crosses studio] Look at this butterfly—it is an extraordinary thing; I bought it online. But would I? Well, I can't now because Damien has done it. The Amazon trip was the first time I'd had a digital camera and so I was excited by those possibilities.

ML: And were you Hockneyesque in immediately being excited by the technological potential?

JK: It was really exciting. Because it was such a stimulating environment and an almost pristine area of the planet is awe-inspiring.

ML: But also digital technology means you can take as many images as you want?

JK: Yes, you get very profligate because you can fire off as many images as you want.

Although most of Keane's exhibitions introduce a new country or concern, he acknowledged the connection of *Intelligent Design*, his show at Flowers in 2008, to earlier work with the own-up sub-title 'More Paintings About War and Religion'. Butterflies, blotches and doubled images recur.

JK: Yes, I was dealing again with perception and seeing what you want to see: Darwin's face in a butterfly and so on. . . .

ML: Which is like those newspaper stories about Koranic inscriptions in an aubergine or the face of Mother Teresa in a tea-cake?

JK: Yes, taking on all that. But, looking back, I can see the connection now between Intelligent Design and the Kennedy portrait on the 'floorboards' which I wouldn't have realised at the time. It's about belief systems: the recognition of something that you really want to see or are conditioned to. And I think in these paintings, it was about the eye in the butterfly wings: seeing a butterfly with an almost photo-realist eye-spot in its wing. Hang on, Charles Darwin, how does this work? And it really made me think about the process of evolution and perception. And I read up about it and realised that there was a logic to this: it was the butterflies who most resembled a threat [from the eye] who would be least predated. Therefore, the less realistic ones would get eaten; the more realistic ones would frighten off predators. And so you end up with this almost photo-realistic bird's eye on a butterfly's wing. And so I thought about how this related to seeing something that wasn't there and our belief systems. And how, in religion, you see things that reinforce your belief systems. The face of Jesus on the Shroud of Turin and so on.

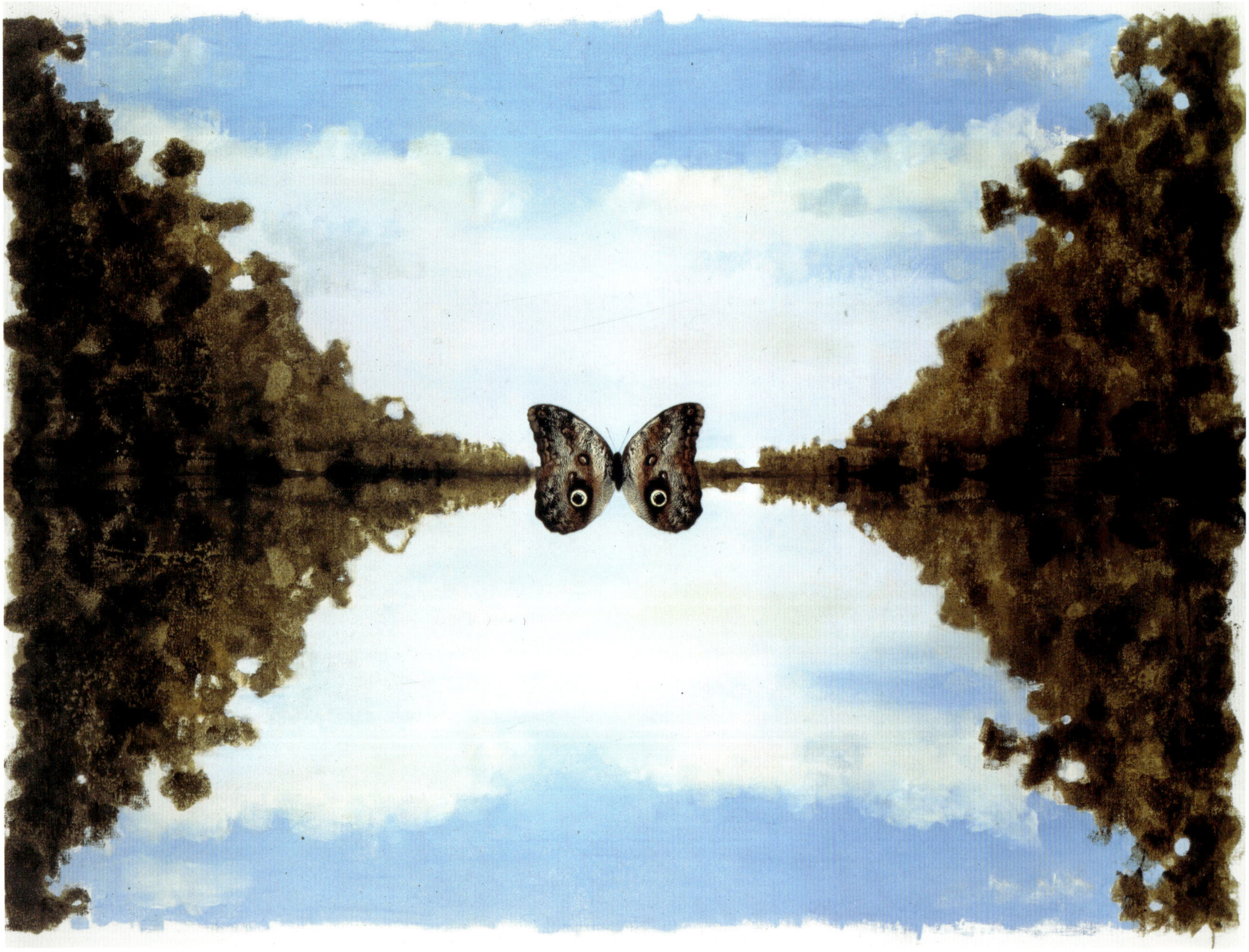

Lepidoptery, Symmetry, Mimicry, Verisimilitude & Art, 2001
Oil and silkscreen on canvas
158 x 209 cm / 62¼ x 82¼ in
Collection: Tim and Lisa Kring

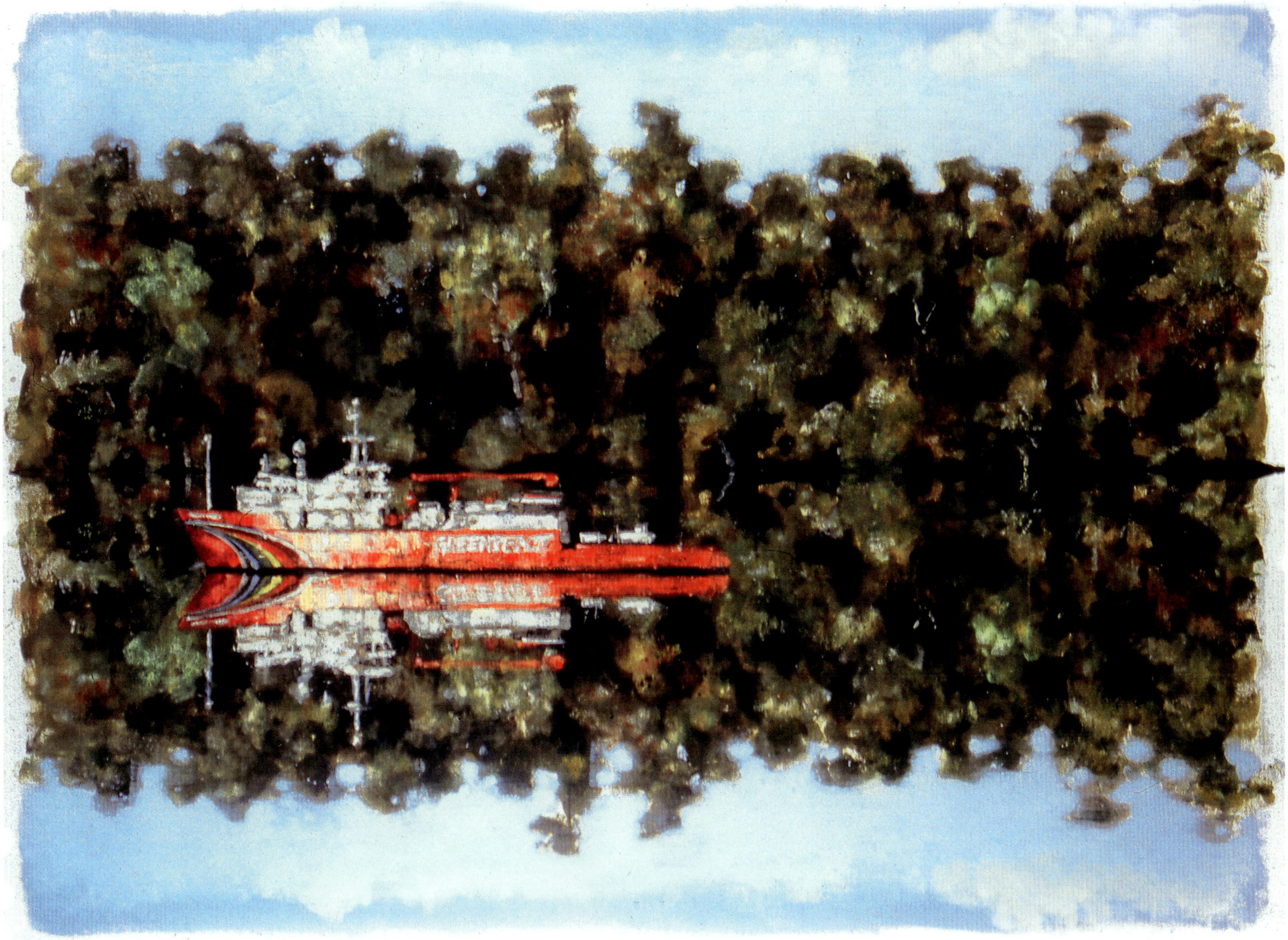

Bank (1), 2001
Oil on canvas
158 x 209 cm / 62¼ x 82¼ in
Private Collection, UK

ML: Whereas Warhol was a Catholic artist, you're not but there is a lot of it in your work for some reason: crucifixions, true crosses, Graham Greene.

JK: Yes, I know. I'm a fervent atheist. But I'm interested in religion, although from the perspective of a sceptic.

In the nicest possible sense, the charity Christian Aid seemed to associate John Keane with trouble and, four years after facilitating the artist's Middle Eastern trip, they offered him another holiday in hell—or, more accurately, a recovering hell as, at the time of Keane's visit in 2006, the former Portuguese colony in Southern Africa was approaching five years of peace after the 27-year civil war that followed the foundation of an independent republic in 1975.

JK: I'd never really done anything about Africa. The Middle East and Central America, obviously, but Africa had somehow not come up. But the opportunity to travel somewhere always interests me.

ML: Which—we talked about this before—but it's very Graham Greenian: the idea that the artist must go in search of subject matter?

JK: Well, yes. That's absolutely true. I went and they organised a group exhibition, a touring show. They wanted to highlight the effect of conflict on children.

The resulting touring group show—*Children in Conflict*—opened at the Wolverhampton Art Gallery in 2007 and included seven works by Keane, created, as had now become his standard practice, from mediating, through computers and paint digital, photographic images captured on location, although, in this case, with the variation that he painted on jute, the plant-based sacking that is a standard material in Africa, rather than his preferred working surface of linen.

JK: We went to a very remote part in the south west on the border with Zambia. And I did find Africa culturally very difficult. Say in the Middle East, it's very easy because there are so many cultural references we can relate to that are part of our own heritage. Africa is very different and there's also much less to look at: it's shot through with either hideous new buildings or dilapidated old ones or nothing at all. Visually, there's not much to excite.

Lacking inspiration in architecture and landscape, he focused to powerful effect on the people. The titles of the Angolan paintings contain some of the artist's bleakest word-play. In 'Arsenal' (2007), three young boys who look to be single-figure ages (although even a child of ten would have reached a quarter of life expectancy in Angola at that time) stand in front of a cratered wall. Two of them are holding a contraption made from poles, wires and tin cans, which, to the viewer who has no benefit of captions or conversations with the artist, could either be a toy or an improvised mine-sweeping device; it was, he told me, a plaything.

One of these children in conflict is wearing a replica football shirt that bears the name of the English Premiership club Arsenal, although we suspect that the garment is cheap and fake—a replica replica- shirt—because the colours on the strip are inaccurate. And, in an Angolan context, the team name sparks connections with weaponry rather than sport: any pitch on which this trio tried to have a kickabout would likely have arsenal under the surface. To poignant effect, the Angolan boy is actually reclaiming the word for its original meaning: the North London club had its origins in the South of the capital in the late 19th century as Woolwich Arsenal, a works football team founded by staff at the armaments factory, the Royal Woolwich Arsenal.

Another picture with a heart-breakingly punning title — 'Mine' (2007) — shows a mother, two young children hooked to her hips in the touchingly trusting body-language of young children, looking out at parched wasteland, the drought-brown colour of which contrasts with the rich red of her traditional African cloth skirt. The painting's title combines both the proud possessive that is part of the parental vocabulary in every culture — "That one's mine", one mother will say to another as their children play — with the murderous explosives that are hidden under the burned earth.

The diptych 'Brother 1' and 'Brother 2' (both 2007) looks like a matching pair — similar faces of adult African men placed in an oval framed by swathes of patterned fabric — but there is a striking reason that each man has a separate portrait. They, the catalogue notes explain, are Luis and Amaral Samacumbi, brothers who served as child soldiers — one of the most notorious aspects of the Angolan civil war — although on opposite sides, having been commandeered by the rebel UNITA and government MPLA forces respectively. At the war's end, in 2004, they were reunited, reconciled and discovered that they had once participated in the same battle. Keane discovered the story because one of the brothers, who ran an aid agency in the capital Luanda, was the local fixer for his trip. The fabrics used to frame the portraits were a gesture to African tradition — resembling nods to native cloth in the work of British artists Yinka Shonibare, Sokari Douglas Camp and Grayson Perry — but also led Keane in a non-conventional direction.

JK: One of my ways in to the subject was through the fabric, designing and playing with the idea of making African fabrics, eventually creating a cloth using the repeated pattern of mine victims and land mines. And then — purely by chance — Nicole Farhi made some shirts from my patterns and they were sold to raise money for the charity. I really enjoyed making those: it's another interesting thing you can do on a computer.

One group of Keane's "away" pictures are unusual in that, although representing a specific foreign setting, they are informed by neither travel nor contemporary news images. Instead, a sort of time-travel — through archive footage — was behind the work collected as *Fear* at Flowers Gallery in Shoreditch in 2013.

The artist read a book about Joseph Stalin's purges of Russian society in the 1930s, when hundreds of thousands of officials, artists and citizens were accused of dissidence or other departures from Socialist norms, found guilty in "show trials" and executed. Stalin's fearsome secret police, the NKVD, followed the custom of other law enforcement officials in taking a mug-shot of the arrested. It struck Keane that these were portraits of people who knew that they were going to be killed.

JK: I was fascinated by this extreme example of a culture where fear becomes the prime motivating factor of human behaviour, and the intrinsic irony of this in a society that aspires to a Utopia, where the greatest good should predominate for the greatest number of people. At this time no one, from the top of the Bolshevik hierarchy to the humble factory worker, was safe from denunciation as either saboteur or political deviant. Anyone who fell foul of authority could expect a bullet in the back of the head.

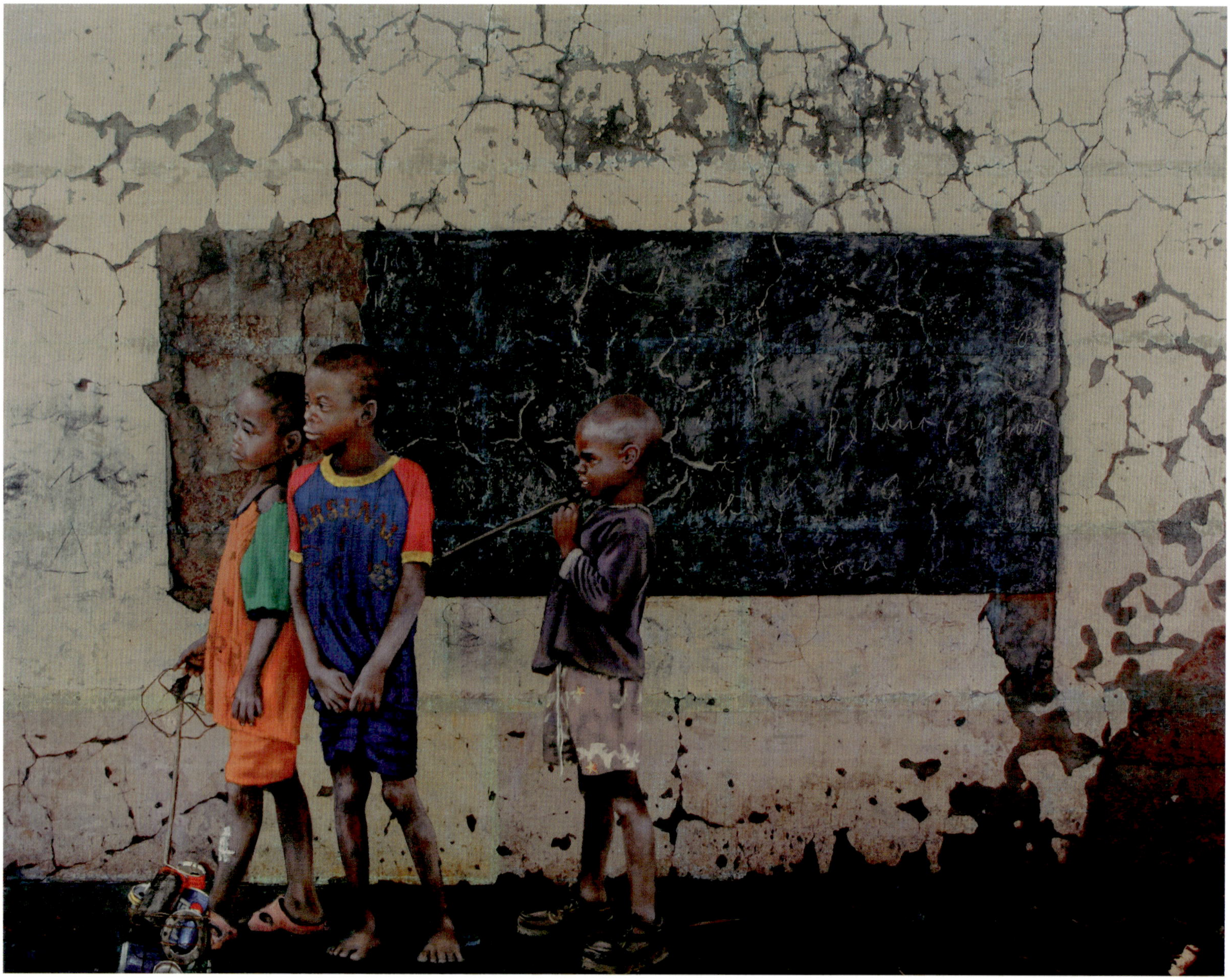

Arsenal, 2007
Oil and inkjet transfer on jute
154 x 195 cm / 60¾ x 77 in
Collection: Exceed Trust

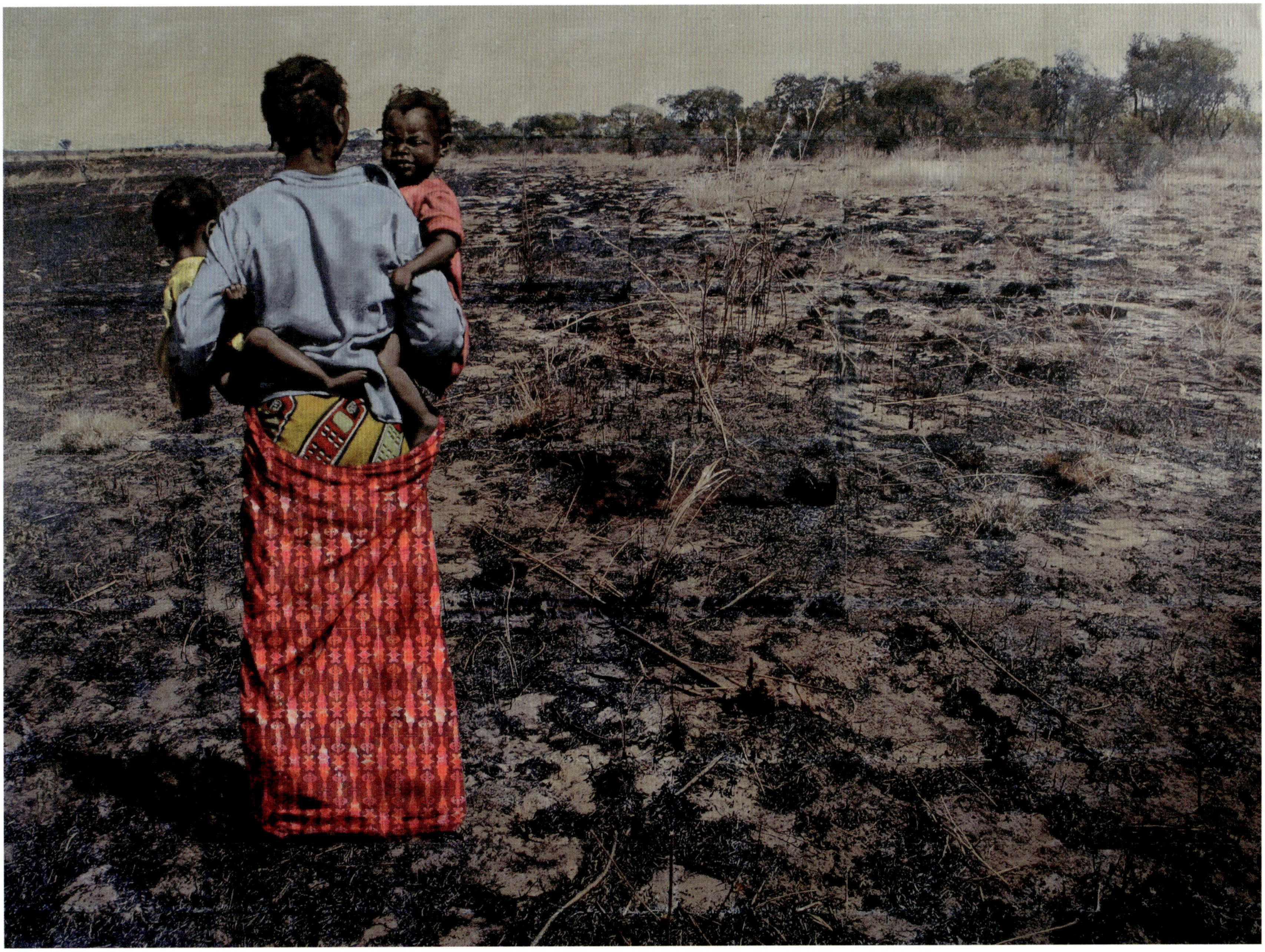

Mine, 2007
Oil and inkjet transfer on jute
178.5 x 238 cm / 70½ x 93¾ in

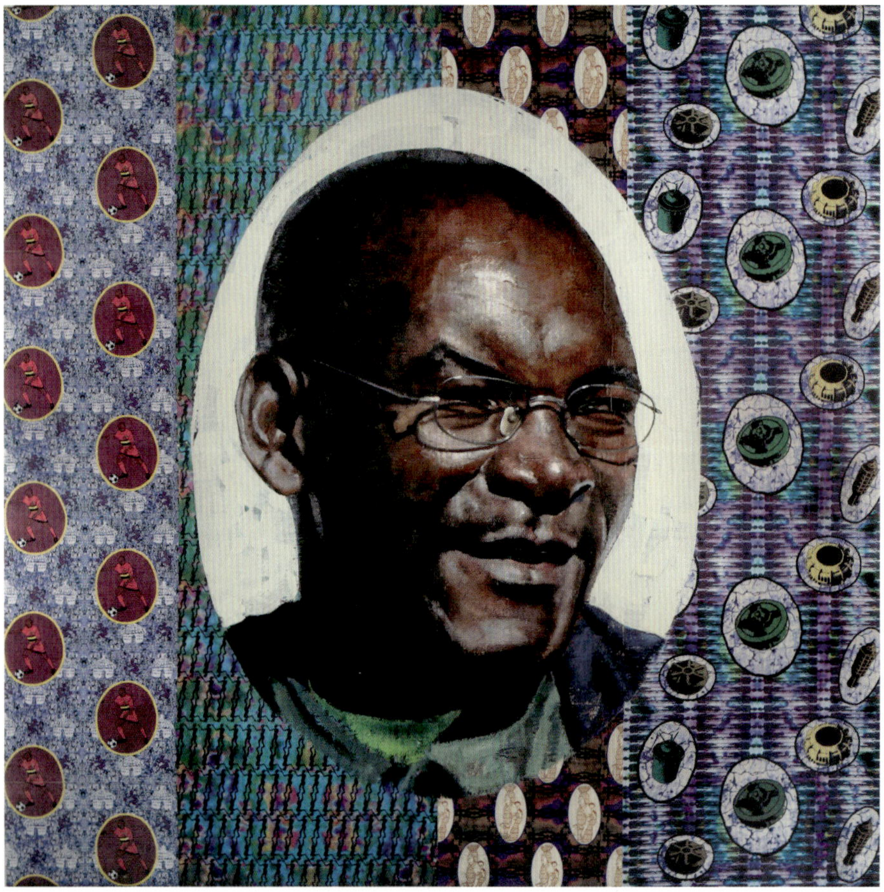

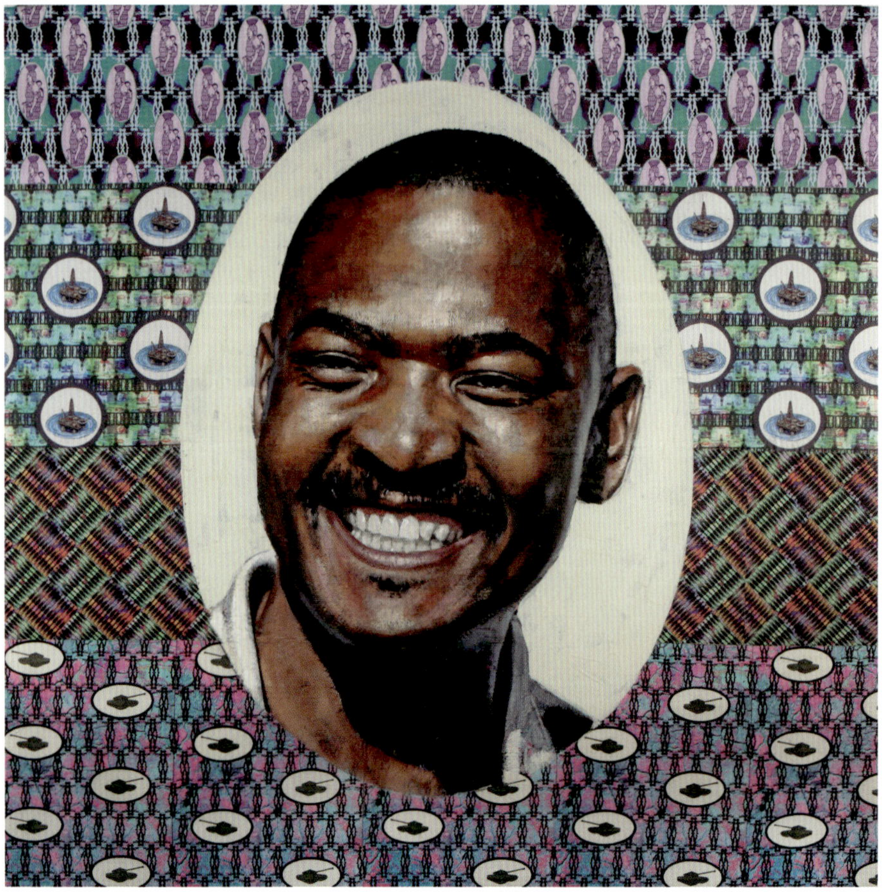

Brother (1), 2007
Oil, Beeswax and inkjet transfer on jute
131 x 131 cm / 51¾ x 51¾ in

Brother (2), 2007
Oil, Beeswax and inkjet transfer on jute
131 x 131 cm / 51¾ x 51¾ in

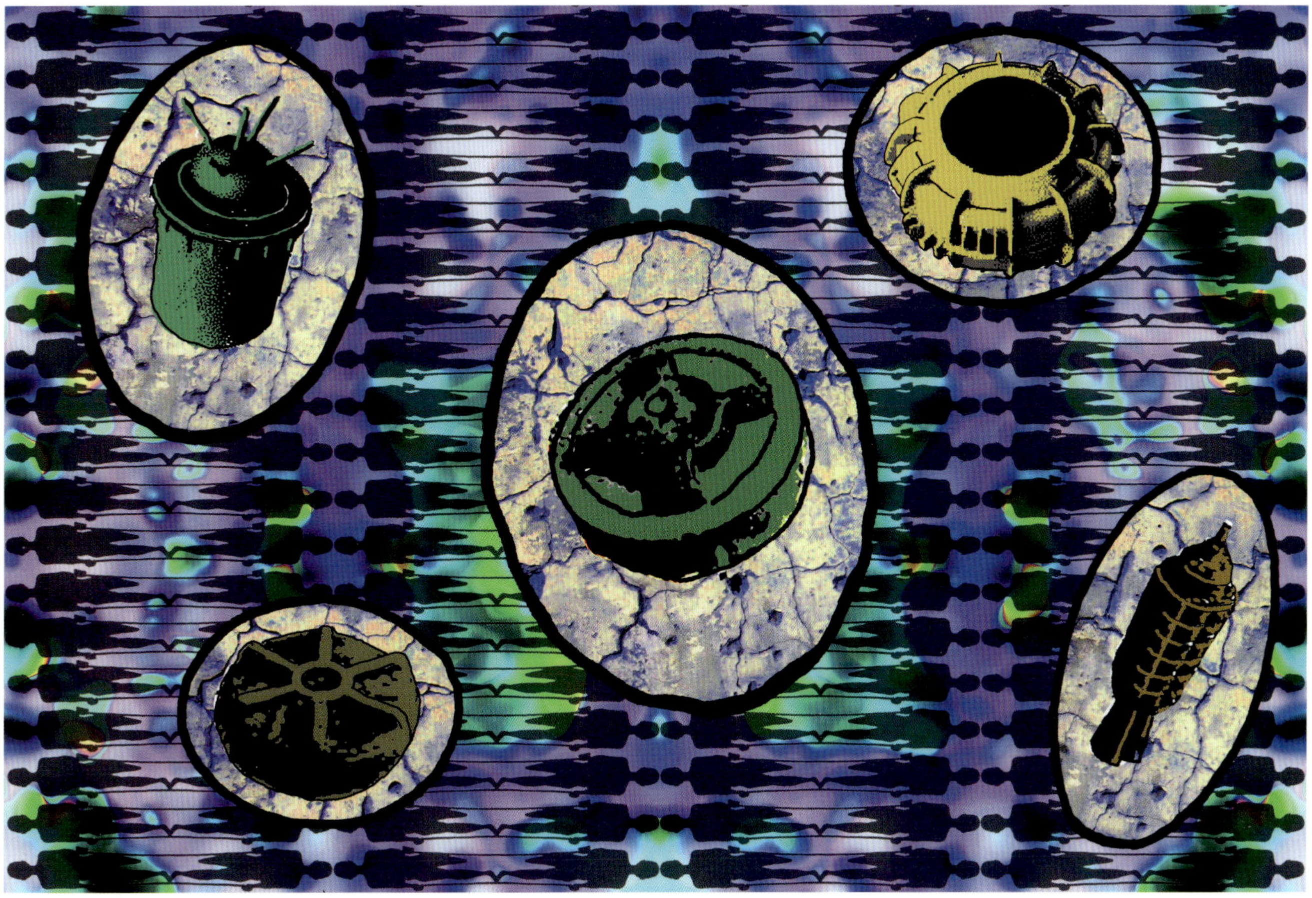

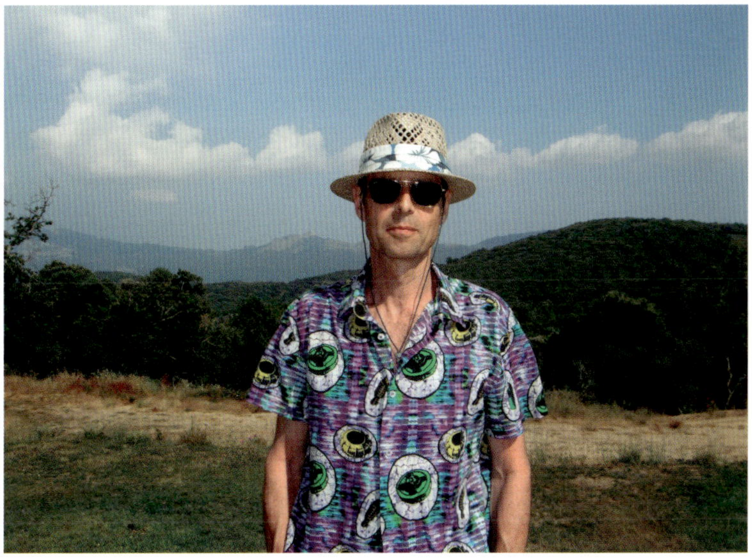

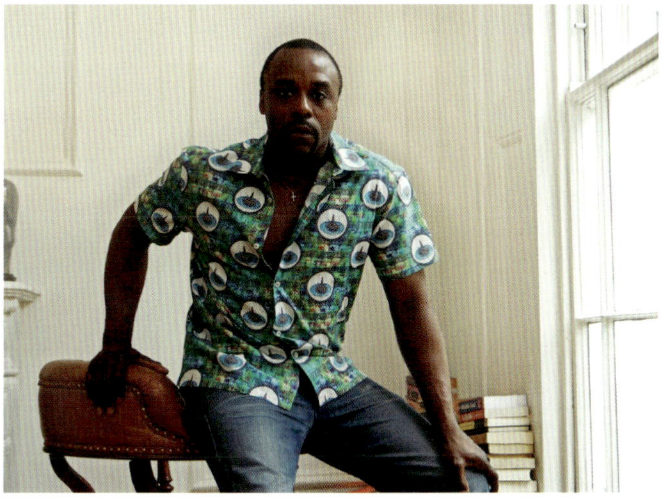

Angola inspired fabric by John Keane used in shirts designed by
Nicole Farhi; shirts modeled by John Keane and Ariyen Baka

That extremity of human emotion — the knowledge that a terrible and violent death is unavoidable — connects the *Fear* series to two other Keane themes: the people on the roof of the WTC on 9/11 and the hostages kneeling in the desert beside their black-clad executioner. More broadly, the quarter-century cycle of violence between West and East featured in Keane's work from *Gulf* to 'Jump' (2015) can be attributed to mutual fear of the beliefs and lifestyles of the other side.

The triggering visual material had dictated that orange would be the governing colour of the images dealing with Guantanamo Bay and Syria, and, through the same process, grimy black and white is the palette of the *Fear* paintings, which are based on the NKVD arrest photos and screen-grabs from period documentaries.

> JK: I was particularly drawn to the image of Grigory Zinoviev, who at one time, as Lenin's second in command played a leading role in the Bolshevik revolution, and as such could take much responsibility for the terror machine to which he ultimately fell victim, along, of course, with countless others.

In a seminar as part of his duties as Artist in Residence at St Andrews, Keane, in 2014, expressed the hope that, although standing as a rare depiction of the far past in his work, *Fear* might have a more contemporary resonance as well.

> JK: Whilst these paintings refer to a specific and extraordinarily terrifying moment in modern history, I hope they allude also to that universal human emotion of fear that can so often determine human behaviour in all walks of life whether it relates to community, corporation, religion, state — maybe even university.

Definitely recognisable as modern were a sub-set of paintings that introduced a contrasting burst of colour to the *Fear* galleries. These were inspired by the Putin regime's treatment of members of the Russian female rock group Pussy Riot — a name that caused visible and audible discomfort to some British and American news presenters during the span of the story — after they staged an impromptu performance in Moscow's Cathedral of Christ the Saviour to protest at the increasingly repressive tendencies of the government. Interrupted by church security, they turned the events into an online music video, called 'Punk Prayer — Mother of God, Chase Putin Away!', a title that may have sounded less clunky in Russian. After the video went viral, the musicians were arrested, subjected to a show trial with obvious historical precedents and imprisoned.

Keane's paintings on the subject contain a smart artistic opposition — faded icons on the church walls playing against the shocking brightness of the pop video — and add another dimension to his impressive portfolio of ideological collisions around the world.

And the man least likely to have Pussy Riot on his iPod, President Putin, would also feature in pictures that, in the second half of his career so far, showed a new face of Keane's creativity.

Jump, 2015
Oil on linen
200 x 200 cm / 78¾ x 78¾ in

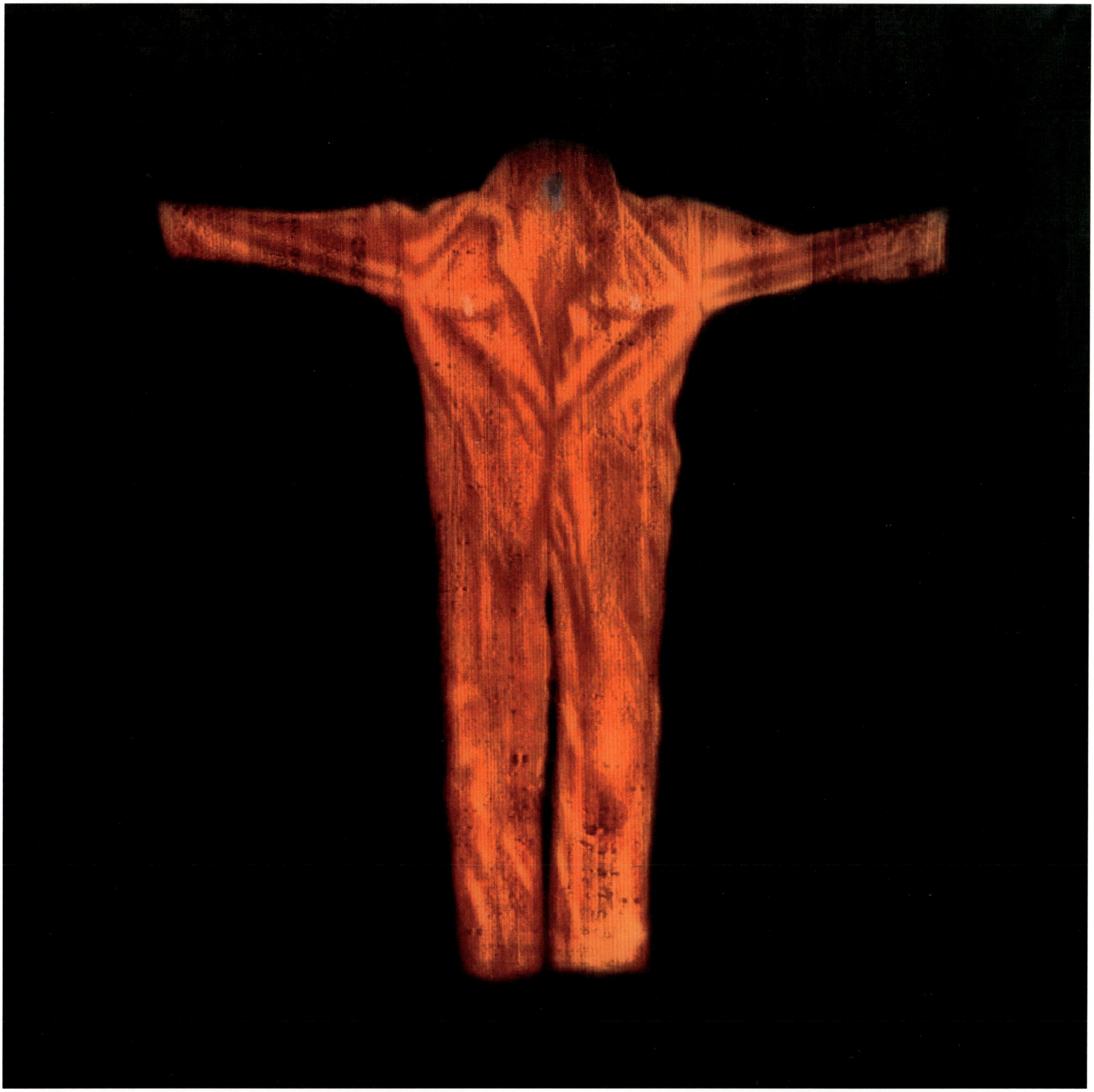

CHAPTER FIVE

THE INTERNATIONAL PORTRAIT GALLERY

A joke popular with newspapers and publishers consists of a heading followed by a page deliberately left empty. In the autobiography of a footballer, such a satirical blank might come under the chapter title 'What The Average Club Owner Knows About The Game" while a Labour or Liberal Democrat manifesto might play the same trick below the words 'Conservative Policies To End the Wealth Gap'.

And, twenty years ago, when I was writing *Conflicts of Interest*, a previous book about John Keane, the gag might have involved the promise of a section that dealt with: 'Portraits of the Rich and Famous'.

But, two decades on, he has been active enough in this genre for a whole chapter to be allocated. His list of famous faces divides neatly between paintings that were commissioned and those that might be described as uncalled-for. The former includes two leading British political figures for the National Portrait Gallery and a controversial hanging in the Council Chamber of the BBC. Among the latter are the mucked-about studies of Murdoch, Putin and Rebekah Brooks that were taking shape in the studio during the period of our interviews.

ML: When we talked 20 years ago, you were very uncertain about the whole idea of portraits but, since then, you've done a huge number?

JK: Yes, I know. I'm probably as surprised as you. The commissioned portraits came from an approach from Charles Saumarez Smith, when he was running the National Portrait Gallery.

Among the jobs of the director of the NPG is to scout potential new portrait-painters. Saumarez Smith had been to see Keane's 1997 show at Flowers East — *Truth, Lies and Super-8* — which expanded a new strand of biographical painting that seemed to follow naturally from the walk-on part given to the novelist Graham Greene in Keane's Mexican paintings of the mid-90s (chapter 4).

Historical characters who figured in the subsequent exhibition included the Marxist revolutionary Leon Trotsky in 'Art & Revolution' (1995) and two images of the assassinated pacifist Mahatma Gandhi, one of them 'Struggle With Truth' (1996), in which the Indian thinker is shown composing a letter to Adolph Hitler requesting the end of the Second World War. The killing of President John F. Kennedy in November 1963 features in a sequence of 11 paintings, several of them treating details from the Super-8 tourist video shot by Abraham Zapruder which, though this seems increasingly astonishing in an era of permanent news, is the only official record of Kennedy's death.

ML: In the Lee Harvey Oswald paintings, it's your face or Mickey Mouse rather than LHO?

JK: Yes. You remember all that stuff about whether it's a fake portrait and the shadow is wrong and so on.

ML: And, although you insist you're not a portrait painter, the individual face at this stage of your career was more and prominent?

JK: Yes, certainly individual images crop up more and more. The Gandhi ones come out of going to a museum in — I forget which Indian town. There's a rather pathetic letter in the museum from Gandhi to Adolph Hitler pleading with him to stop the war.

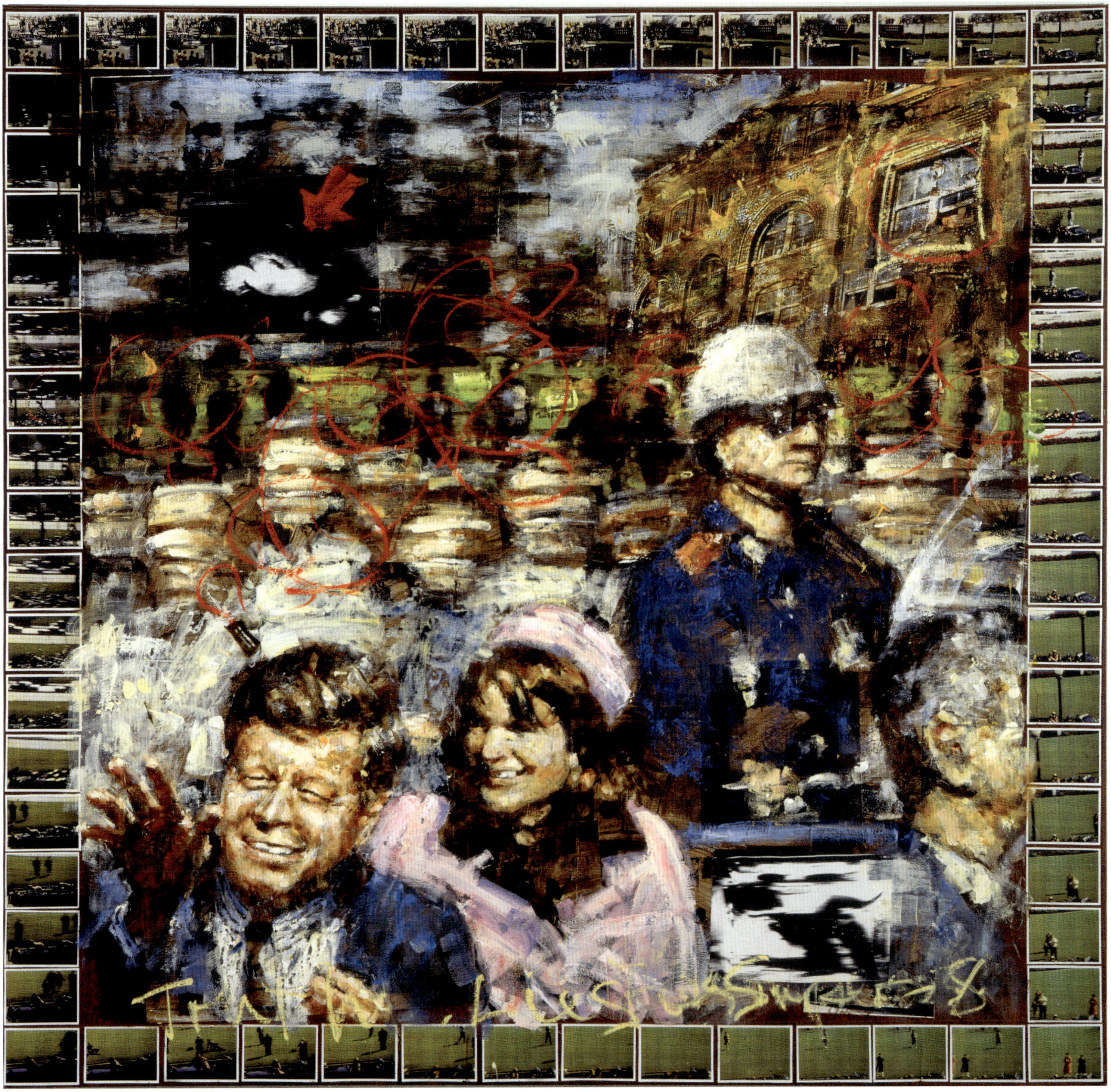

Truth, Lies and Super-8, 1997
Oil and collage on canvas
244 x 249 cm / 96 x 98 in
Private Collection, USA

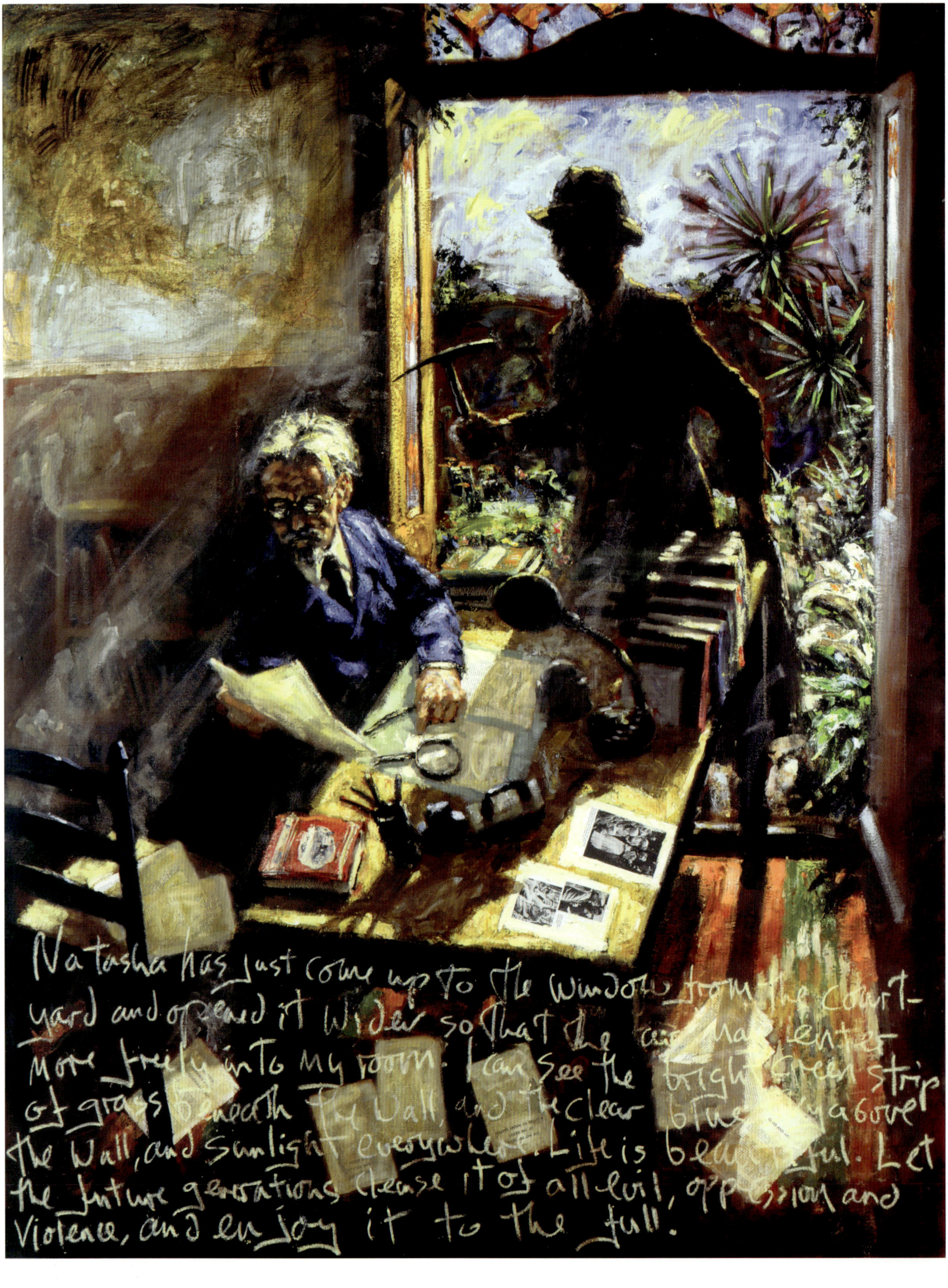
Natasha has just come up to the window from the court-
yard and opened it wider so that the air may enter
more freely into my room. I can see the bright green strip
of grass beneath the wall, and the clear blue sky above
the wall, and sunlight everywhere. Life is beautiful. Let
the future generations cleanse it of all evil, oppression and
violence, and enjoy it to the full!

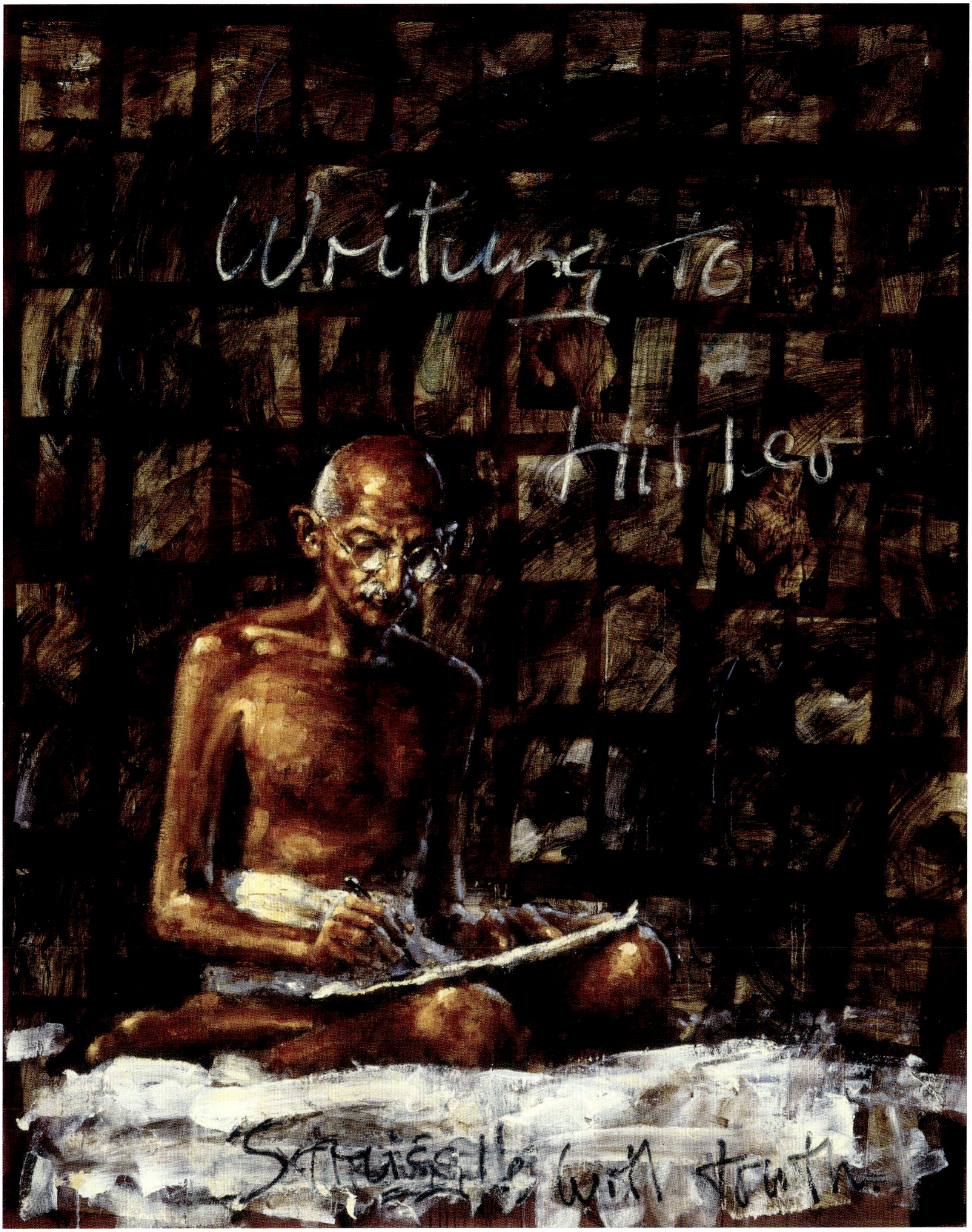

Art & Revolution (Part 1), 1995
Oil and collage on canvas
255 x 194 cm / 100¼ x 76½ in
Collection: Sarah Ingham

Struggle with Truth, 1996
Oil and collage on canvas
209 x 163 cm / 82¼ x 64¼ in
Private Collection, UK

The face of the murdered John F. Kennedy is painted as well, within a chalk oval of the sort that police used to draw around bullet holes, in the startlingly-titled: 'Painting of President Kennedy on floorboards from the Texas School Book Depository' (1997).

ML: It is genuinely on wood from the building Lee Harvey Oswald was in?

JK: What do you think?

ML: I think it isn't.

JK: Mmm. I don't know if I'm going to tell you.

ML: You have to tell me because I'm your biographer.

JK: Of course, it bloody isn't. But that's the point. It's about believing what you're told, like a relic of the true cross.

ML: I think the writer Evelyn Waugh claimed that, if you put together every supposed relic of the cross on which Christ died, the crucifix would be miles high and miles wide?

JK: Yes, that's exactly what I was thinking of.

ML: So your Kennedy image is a sort of icon, a religious relic?

JK: Yes, although a piss-take of one.

It was these pictures of dead legends that led Charles Saumarez Smith to wonder about asking Keane to immortalise some living ones. His first suggested sitter was the American film director James Ivory who, with his collaborators Ismail Merchant and Ruth Prawer Jhabvala, had created a powerful franchise of superior literary adaptations including *A Room With a View* and *The Remains of the Day.* But, before Keane could even be mentioned, Ivory made clear that he already had a preferred interpreter and the director's portrait for the NPG was done by the American artist-writer Don Bachardy.

This was 1997 and Tony Blair had just been elected to the first of what would turn out to be three terms as Labour Prime Minister. The NPG tried to put Blair and Keane on the same ticket but Lord Derry Irvine, the young Prime Minister's fixer, took a long view of the process and no deal was fixed. As it turned out, there was no official NPG painting of Blair until 2013 (when it was done by Alastair Adams) and, by that stage, Keane would not have been a candidate for the job, being among those liberals who believed, after the Iraq War, that Blair should be hung not in the National Portrait Gallery but at the War Crimes Tribunal in the Hague. But the former Prime Minister's smug-shot has featured in Keane's collection of uncalled-for portraits.

JK: I'm relieved, in retrospect, that doing Blair for the NPG didn't come off.

ML: Because you wouldn't want to be associated with him?

JK: Yes. Absolutely.

The Secretary of State for Northern Ireland in Blair's first cabinet was the gallery's third candidate to be captured by Keane. Dr. Marjorie Mowlam (1949–2005), the vivacious and abrasive Labour MP for the North-East seat of Redcar, had won public sympathy and

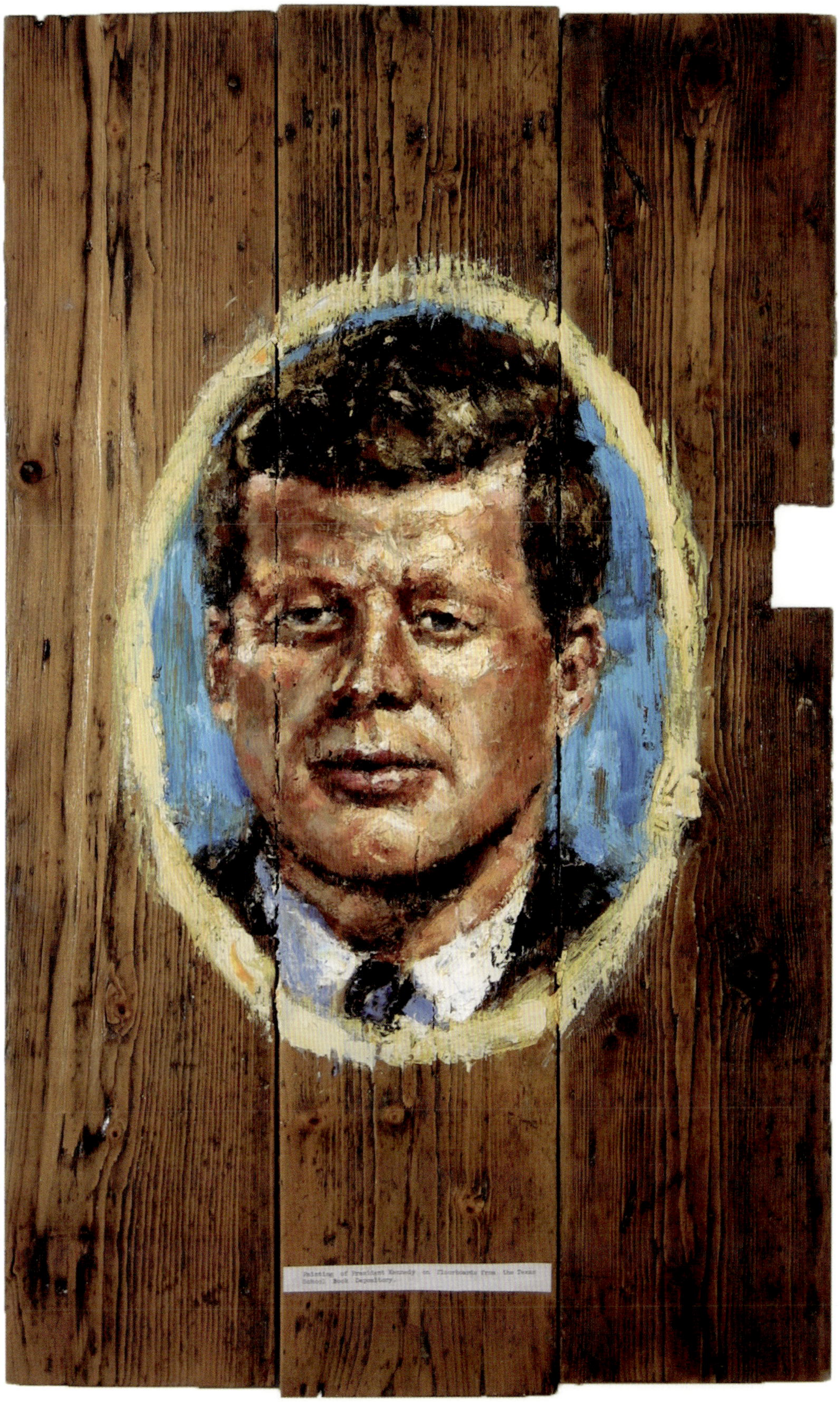

Painting of President Kennedy on Floorboards from the Texas School Book Depository, 1997
Oil on wood
81.5 x 49 cm / 32 x 19¼ in

popularity for fighting the 1997 general election and taking on the gruelling Northern Ireland role in government despite recent surgery, chemotherapy, and radiotherapy for a brain tumour. The hair loss caused by her treatments was covered by a wig, which she would reportedly whip off to ease (or distract from) the tension during the talks between Republicans and Unionists that led to the Good Friday Agreement in 1998, setting out a framework for peace and devolved government in Northern Ireland.

But, though the Troubles were suspended, their legacy scuppered Keane's original commission. The NPG wanted a group portrait of the quartet most involved in the settlement: Mowlam, Gerry Adams of Sinn Fein, the Ulster Unionist leader David Trimble and John Hulme, who led the SDLP. Initially, all four parties agreed and Keane recorded interviews with Adams and Hulme for a TV documentary following the project. But, as tensions developed between the former warring sides over the make-up of the new government, Trimble ruled himself out of the foursome for the foreseeable future.

Saumarez Smith suggested doing Mowlam alone, which proved to be a smart call for posterity, as the politician was dead within four years, the tumour apparently having been (although she had kept this from Blair and the public) incurable. The pairing of artist and subject instantly proved simpatico. Keane already knew Mowlam slightly and she had some interest in art, as her husband, Jon Norton, was a banker turned painter: a professional transition which, as Keane points out, rarely occurs the other way round.

JK: She came to the studio, briefly. She wasn't someone who liked sitting around much. I don't like having people hanging around when I'm trying to work. So it suited both of us that she just nipped in for a quick chat and a photographic session. She came back once more briefly.

ML: She had a reputation for mucking around. Did she do it with you?

JK: Oh, yes. The phone rang during the sitting and she answered it in this grand voice: 'The studio of John Keane!'

ML: With portraits, the media and public often make a big deal of whether the person or their admirers like it. Does that consideration matter to you?

JK: I've always wanted people to like things. I think Mo came here when it was still on the wall and she liked it. Although she did say publicly once that it was "crap". But I think that was just Mo being mischievous.

ML: And the unforgiving eye in portraits—do you have to fight the temptation to be kind to people?

JK: Actually, no. What I'm looking for is what is human in someone. I'm selecting from photographic images I've made and the ones I choose tend to be the warmer ones and that's what interests me.

Unveiled in 2001, the picture presents Mowlam in a pink jacket against a cross-hatched background of yellows, browns and greens. Her appearance suggests strength and intelligence but also vulnerability, her post-chemo hair grown back thinner and wispier. She looks humorous and human, two qualities that she possessed to a degree unusual in a professional politician. Although no-one knew how close the picture would be to becoming her memorial, it freezes the politician as she is most widely remembered, partly because the actress Julie Walters portrayed the Mowlam of the same period in a BAFTA-award winning performance in the Channel 4 biopic *Mo*.

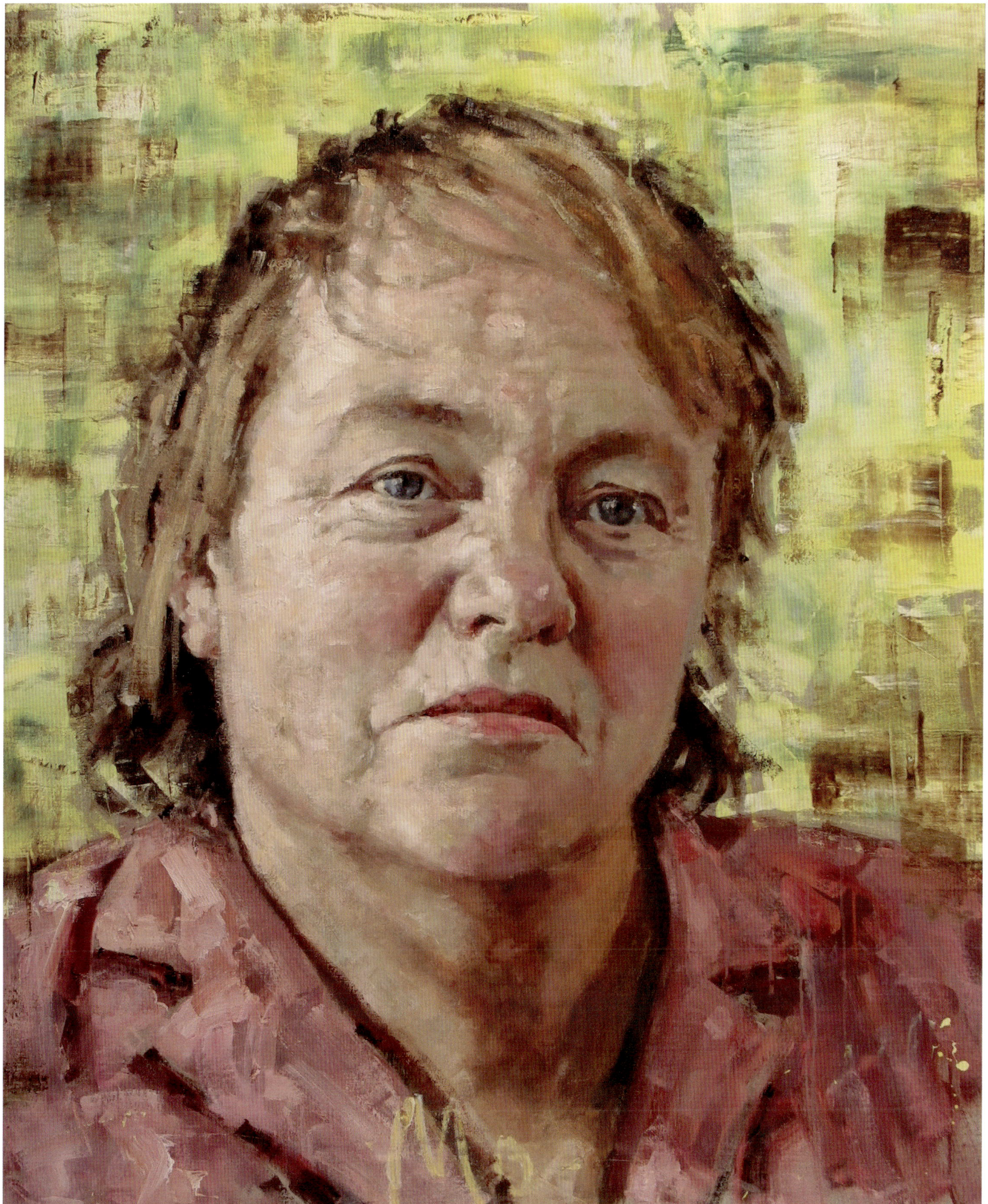

Mo Mowlam, 1999-2001
Oil on canvas
152 x 122 cm / 60 x 40 in
Collection: National Portrait Gallery

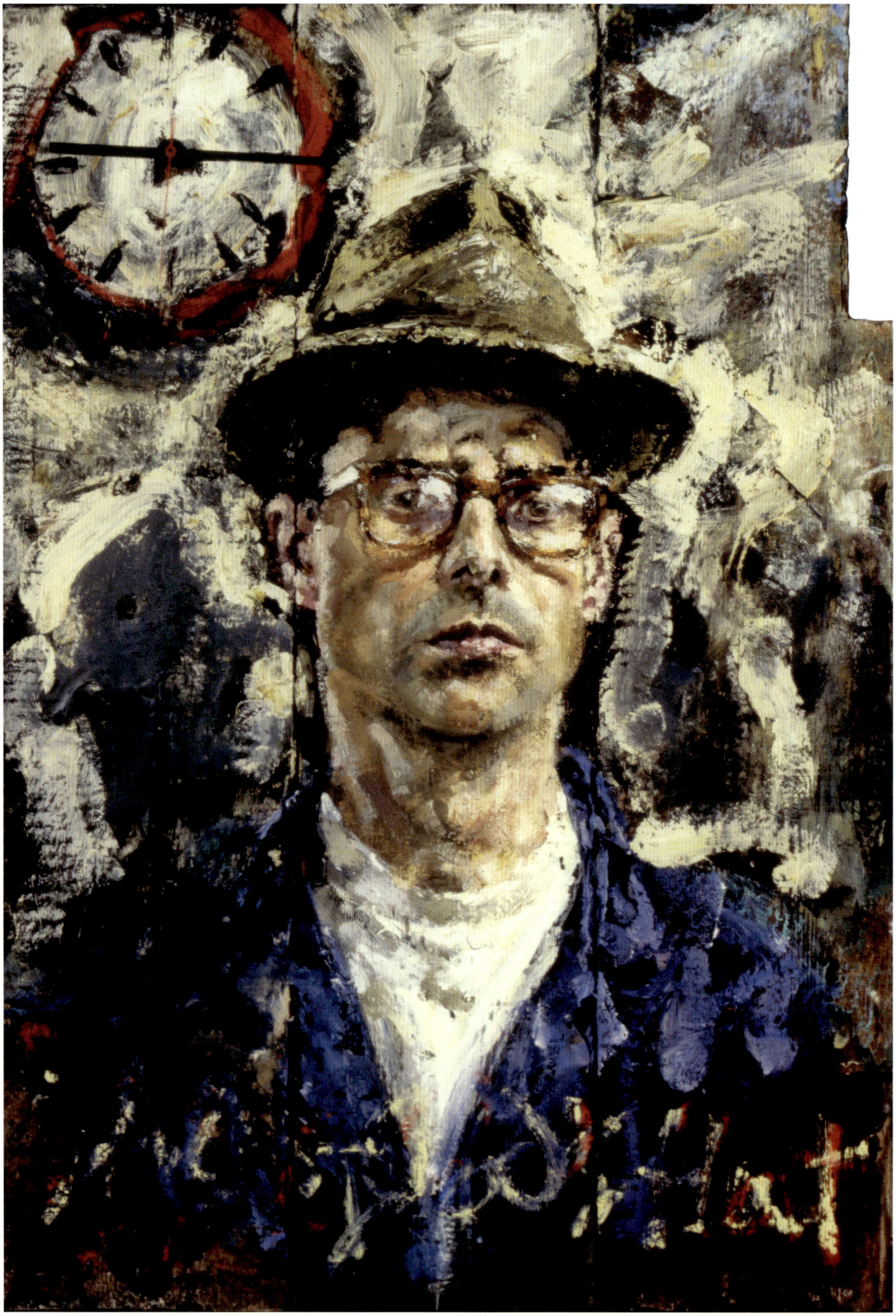

Time Left / Right Time (Dad's Hat), 1996
Oil and electric clock on board
77 x 52 cm / 30¼ x 20½ in
Collection: John and Rosemary Reuters

The NPG was clearly pleased because Keane was soon commissioned to paint the trade unionist Bill Morris, who became Baron Morris of Handsworth in honour of a career in which he became the first black leader of a British Union: serving as General Secretary of the Transport and General Workers Union from 1992 to 2003.

The Mowlam and Morris paintings show a change in the artist's approach to portraits. The politician is represented in traditional oil on canvas (although painted from photos) but the workers' representative employs oil painted on to cotton printed with an inkjet image of Transport House, the London union HQ.

JK: What you're trying to get is how they present themselves physically, how they occupy space.

In that respect, the former boss of the TGWU goes low-key. Some of the ennobled have chosen to be painted in their peer's robes but Lord Morris turned up at the studio in an open-necked shirt and sports jacket and so seems to transmit strength, pride in his unlikely rise to prominence but no sense of grandeur or arrogance.

A third official portrait was for the BBC, although done in sensitive circumstances. After the departure of a director general, the Corporation has a tradition of commissioning a painting to hang in gallery of former DGs, beginning with the BBC's creator Lord Reith, that lines the walls of the Council Chamber in Broadcasting House in London, where the most important management meetings are held. However, the 13th holder of the post, Greg Dyke, had left that room in unhappy circumstances in 2004, when effectively forced to resign after four years in office during the fall-out from a row between the BBC and the Blair government over a disputed report on Radio 4's *Today* programme about the dossier the administration had published to justify the invasion of Iraq.

Because of the circumstances in which he had left, Dyke was ambivalent about being hung in the Council Chamber but was eventually persuaded and, as with Mowlam, Keane captures aspects of both pugnacity and vulnerability: a bruiser who had himself been unexpectedly bruised. As it turned out, this will be the last BBC DG painting, not as a critique of Keane's work but because a combination of budget cuts and the post-job circumstances of subsequent holders — Mark Thompson left quickly for America after his term, George Entwistle went quickly home after 54 days — made the practice impracticable for the Corporation.

Other institutions, though, preserve the tradition of putting revered employees on the wall after they go out of the door and Keane was hired to paint Kofi Annan for the United Nations, when he ended his term as general secretary; current affairs presenter Jon Snow for the broadcaster Channel 4; and film producer Lord David Putnam to mark his service to the Open University as Chancellor. And the artist remains available for other face work.

JK: Not only did I enjoy it artistically, but don't let's play this aspect down: the good thing about a commission is that you know you're going to be paid, whereas, with most work, you do it and hope to sell it later.

Accidentally, but strikingly, his first three major public portraits were all of outsiders who overcame conservative assumptions about who could get such jobs done. Not only did Morris overcome the racial barrier in the labour movement but Mowlam was the first woman to

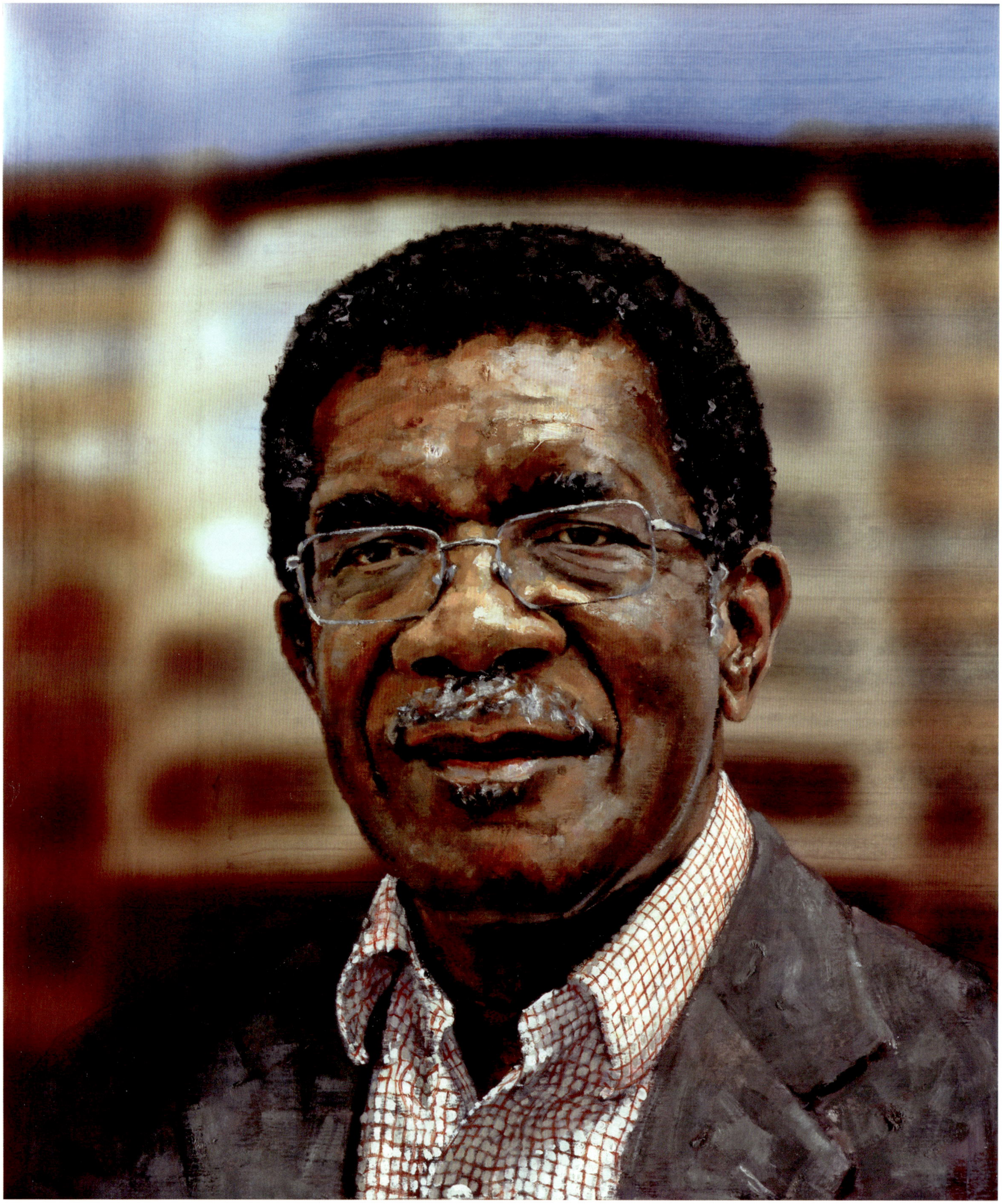

Bill Morris, 2005
Oil and inkjet on linen
115 x 96 cm / 45¼ x 37⅞ in
Collection: National Portrait Gallery

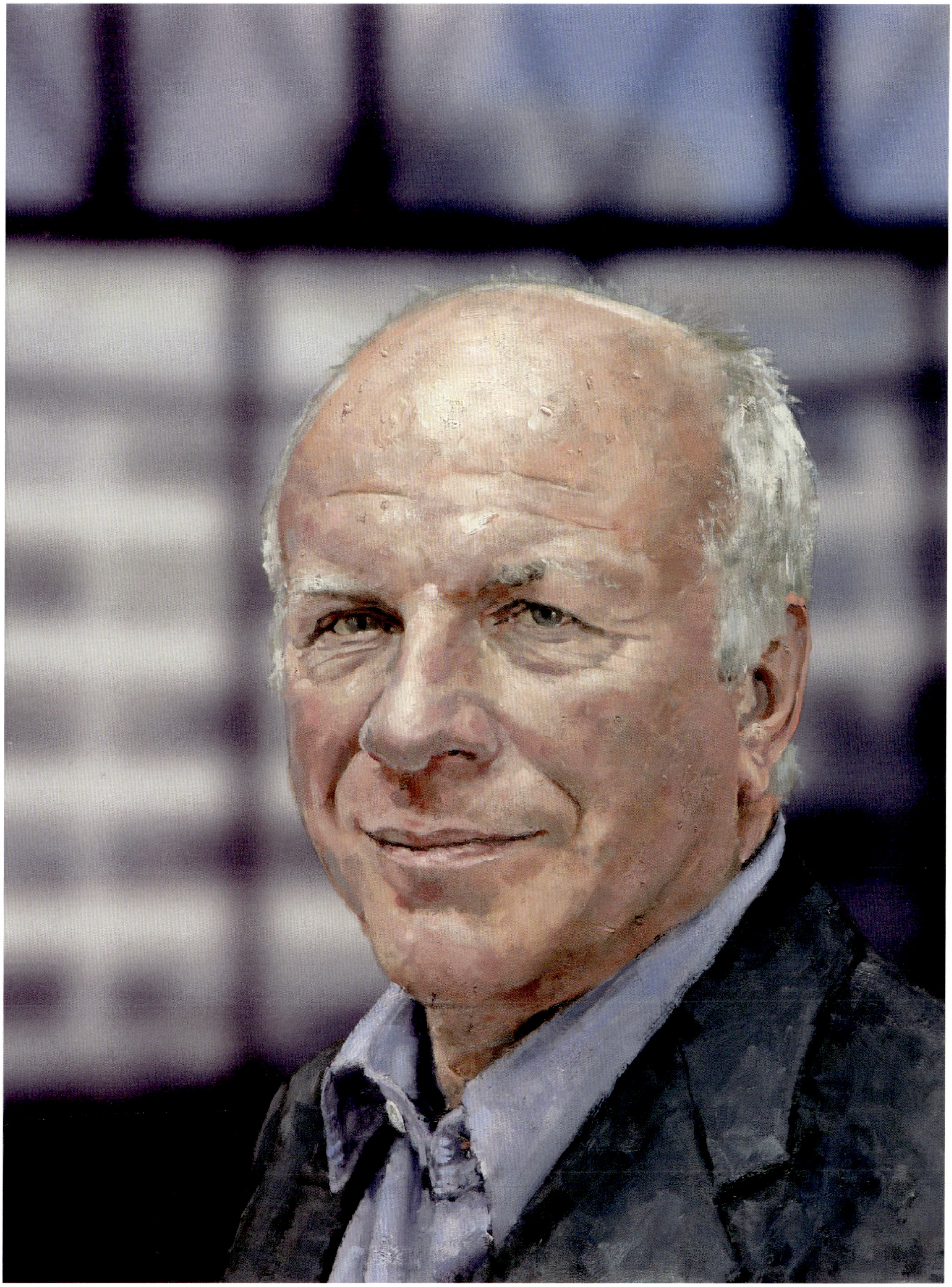

Greg Dyke, 2005
Oil and inkjet on linen
116.5 x 87 cm / 46 x 34¼ in
Collection: BBC

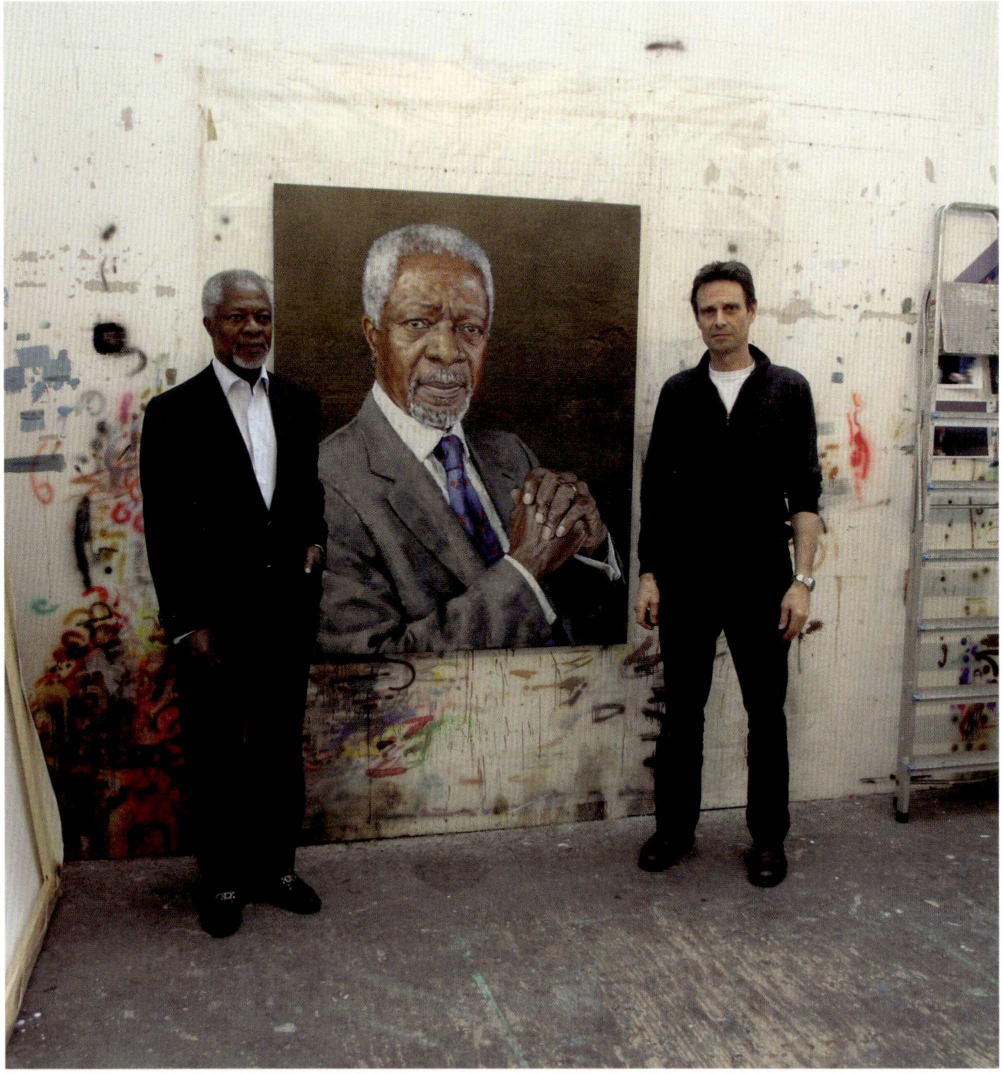

John Keane with Kofi Annan

represent Northern Ireland in cabinet and Dyke was the first leader who did have at least one of two establishment feathers — Oxbridge education or Army service — in his background.

His non-commissioned pictures of the living, though, have tended to feature rather more questionable role-models.

Created in the period leading up to his Mowlam-Morris-Dyke portraits, the paintings and prints in *Making a Killing*, a show at the Flowers East gallery in the year 2000, contained the faces of a trio who in two cases — media tycoon Rupert Murdoch and art tycoon Charles Saatchi — were unlikely and in the other — the late Diana, Princess of Wales — tragically unavailable to sit for the artist.

The fruit of Keane's increasing use of news video as a source, three sequences of a dozen portraits each — 'Porridge (Blinking Charles)', 'Blinking Rupert' and 'Blinking Diana' (all 1999) — track the progress of the involuntary opening and closing of the subjects' eyes during a screen appearance.

At a certain point in each series, the blink completely seals the lids and this offers different meanings in each case: Saatchi's eyes, so confident about the art that should be shown and

Kofi Annan, 2009
Oil on canvas
141 x 114 cm / 55¾ x 45 in
Collection: United Nations

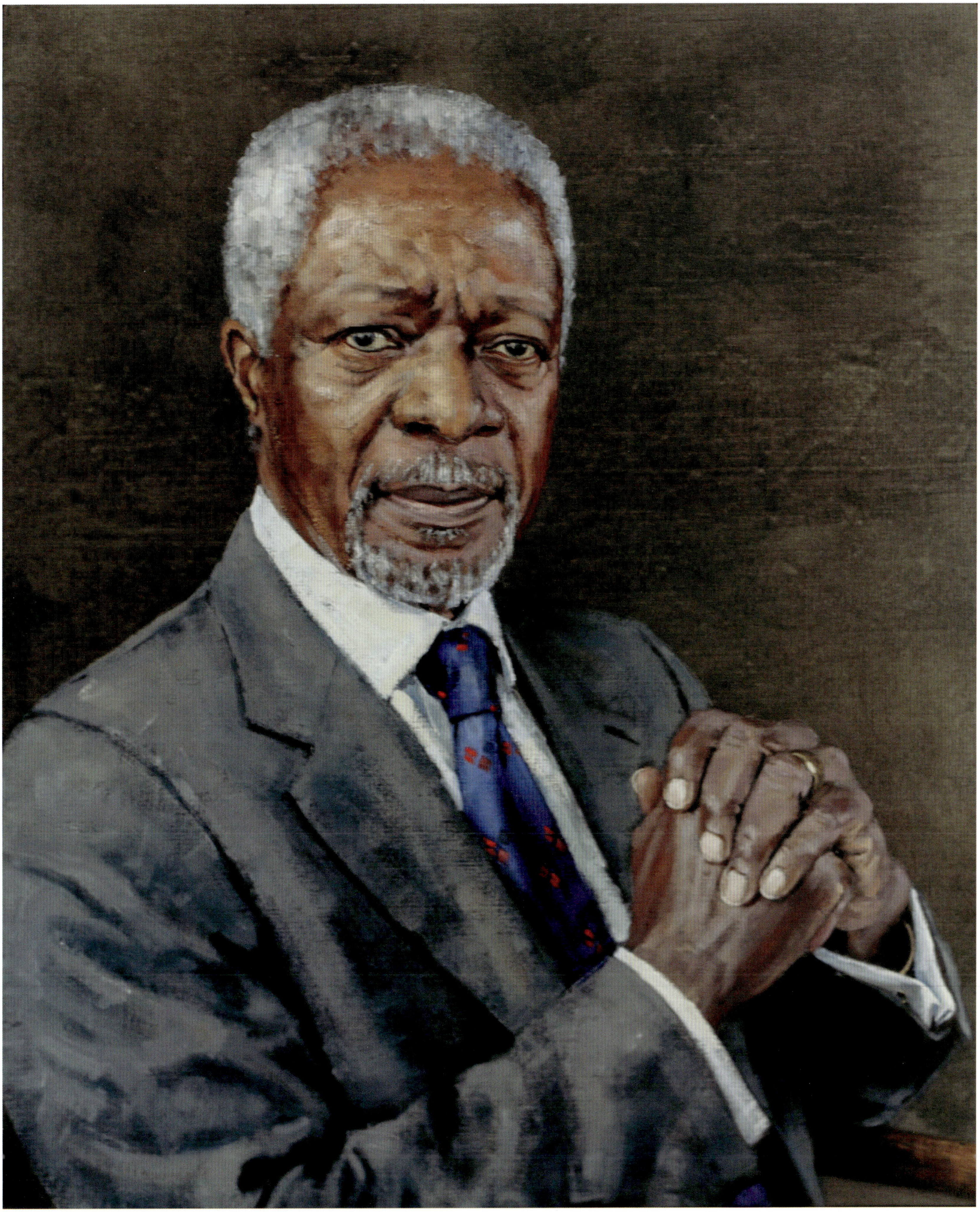

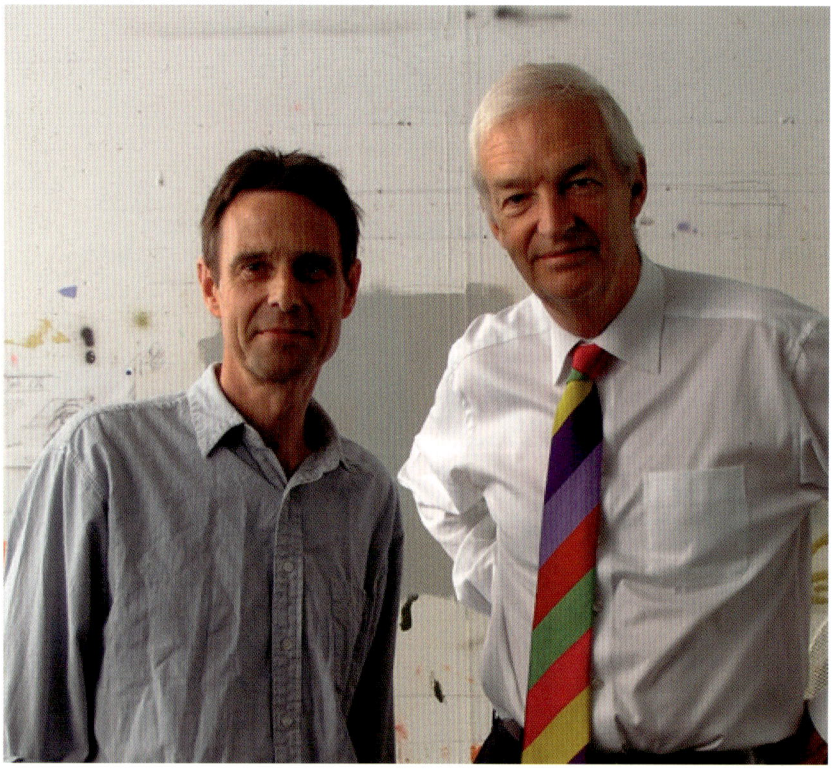

John Keane with Jon Snow

sold, are momentarily blinded; Murdoch might be taken to be averting his gaze from what some of his newspapers do; while, most poignantly, Diana might be dead, as, by the time of the picture, she had been for two years.

The serial presentation of these portraits—in lines with tiny variations—brings strongly to mind the premier artist of celebrity power:

ML: Andy Warhol feels in the background of these because Diana would clearly have been his Marilyn now?

JK: Yes. Glamour doesn't interest me as it did him but he was a great painter and I would acknowledge any debt to him.

ML: I'm thinking also of the way you arrange the frames in sequences?

JK: Yes. I don't think it's deliberate or conscious but clearly there is a debt.

A diptych of Diana and Murdoch is called 'A Bigger Killing' (1999), not necessarily suggesting that the media killed the princess—she might have survived the chase with French photographers if the driver of her car had not been drunk—but drawing attention to the amount of money that journalism made out of her in life and in death. But we, the public, are not excused from culpability: a series of collages of blurry, all-purpose crowds represents the killing curiosity that the media feed.

Murdoch would not have sat for Keane and we might also assume that he would not have stood for the treatment he receives but I had heard word that the artist is unexpectedly represented in a private collection in California:

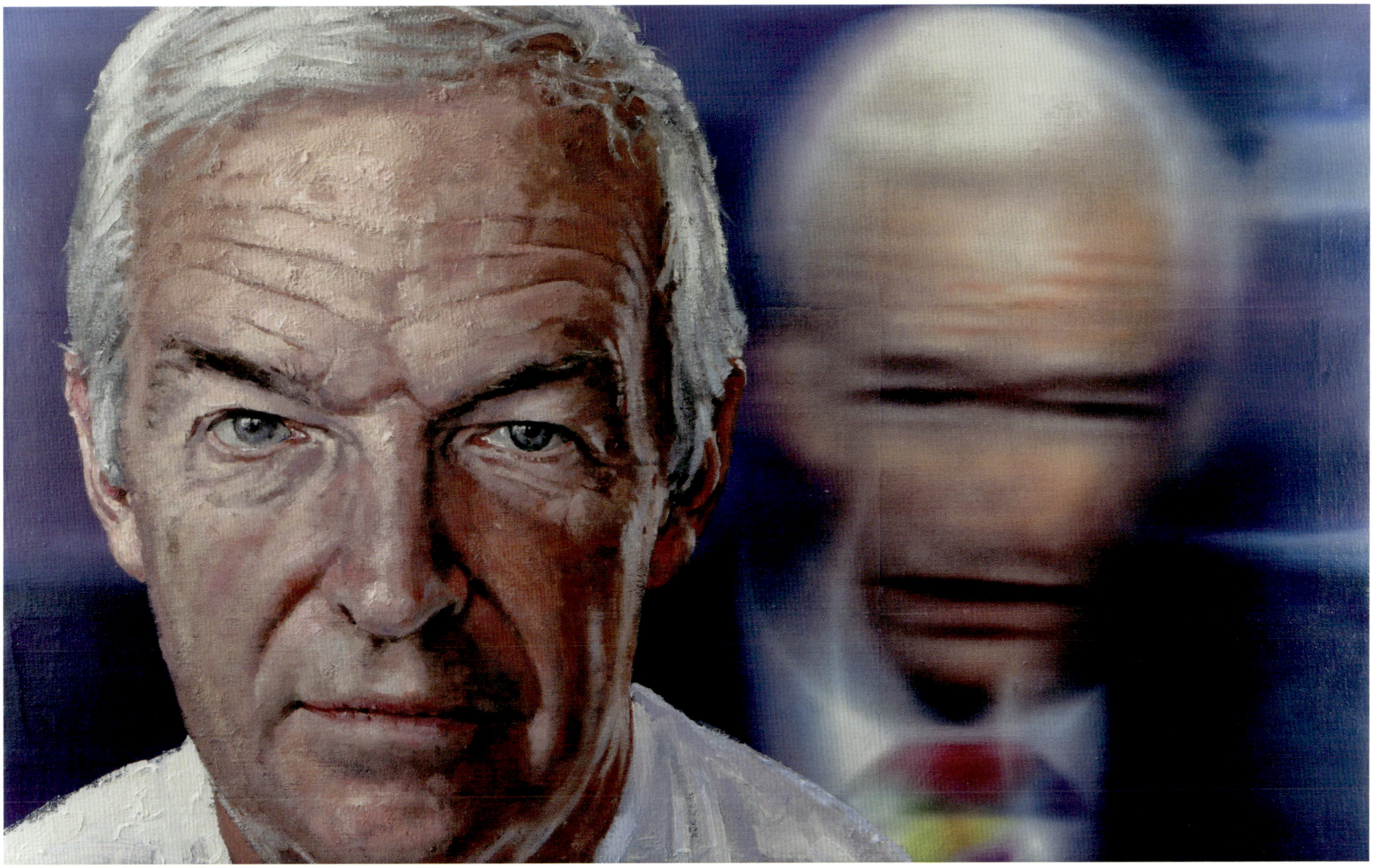

Jon Snow, 2009
Oil and inkjet on canvas
79 x 125 cm / 31¼ x 49¼ in
Collection: Jon Snow

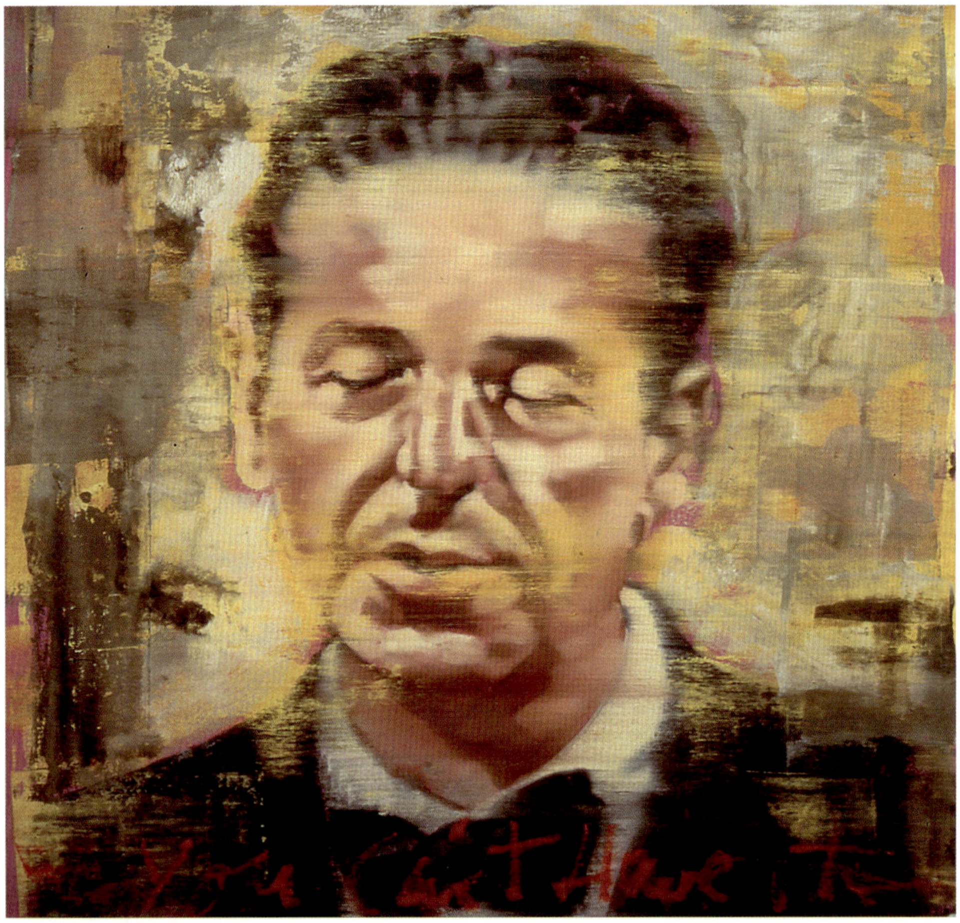

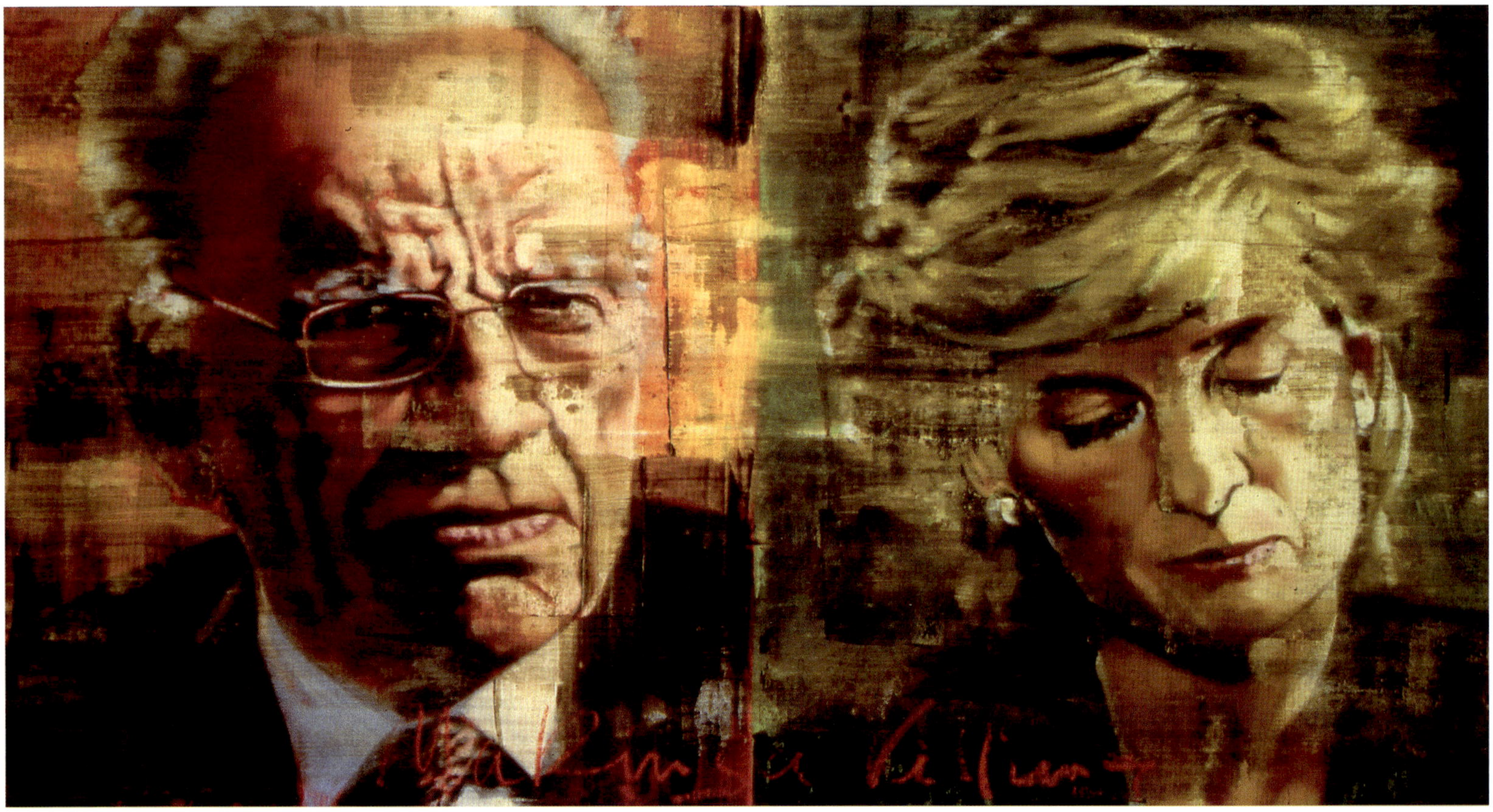

Secrets + Public Relations, 2000
Oil on canvas
86.5 x 86.5 cm / 34 x 34 in

A Bigger Killing, 1999
Oil on canvas
90 x 168 cm /35½ x 66¼ in

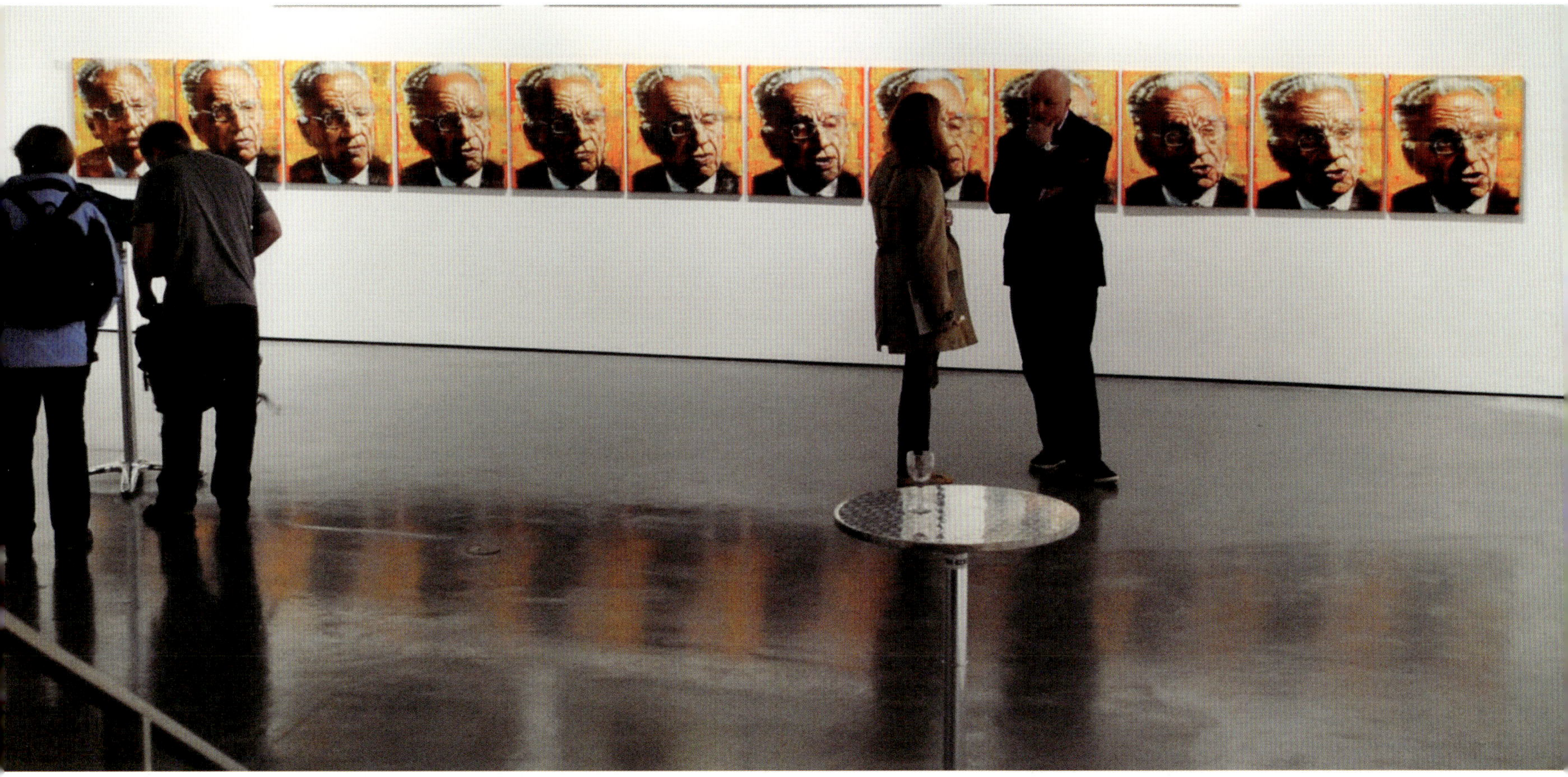

Blinking Rupert, 1999
Installation view, Mall Galleries, London

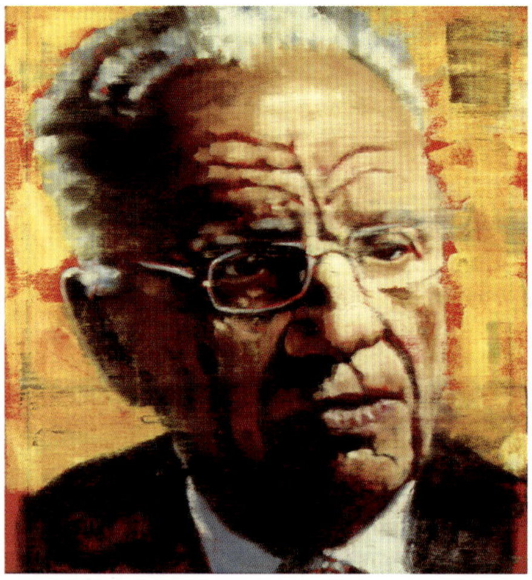
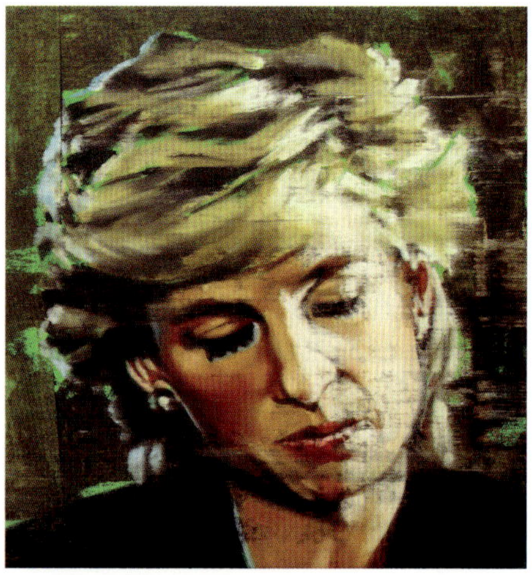
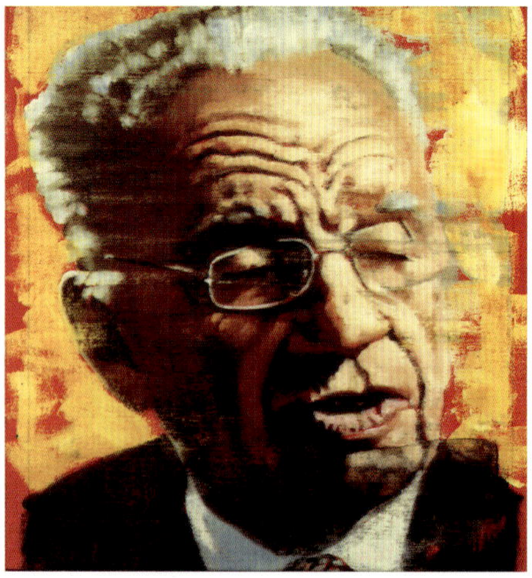
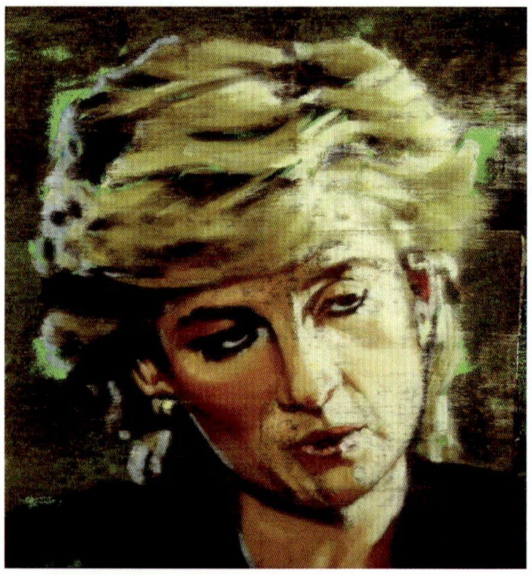
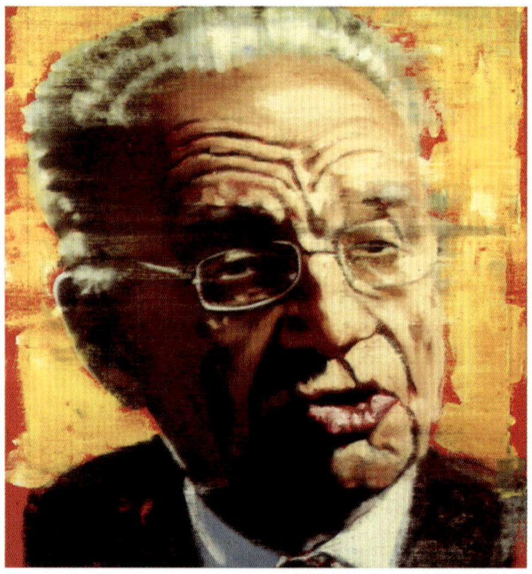
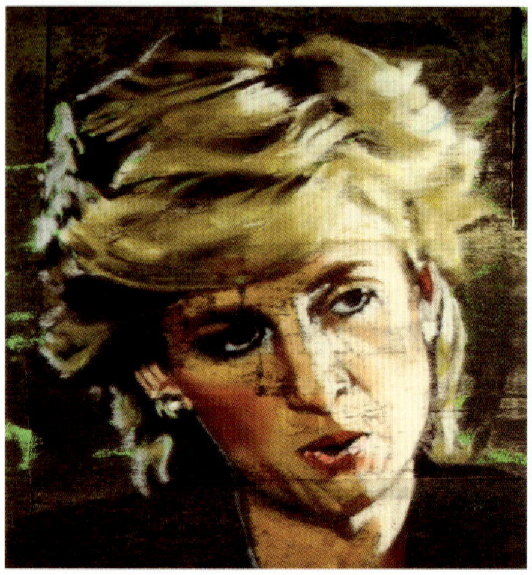
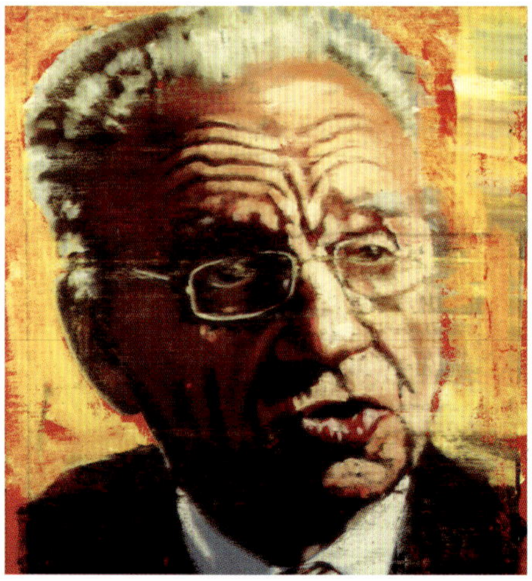
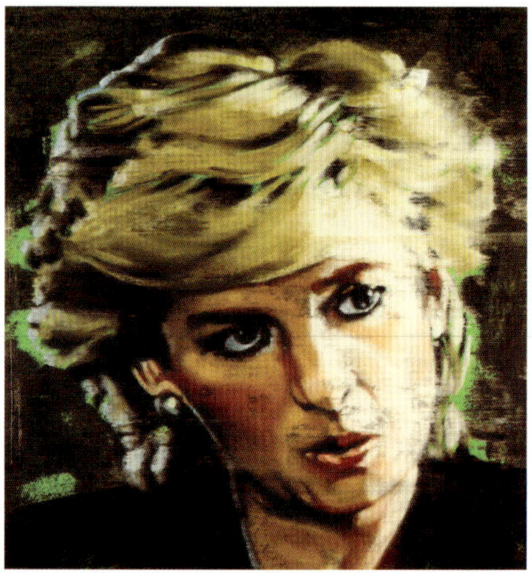

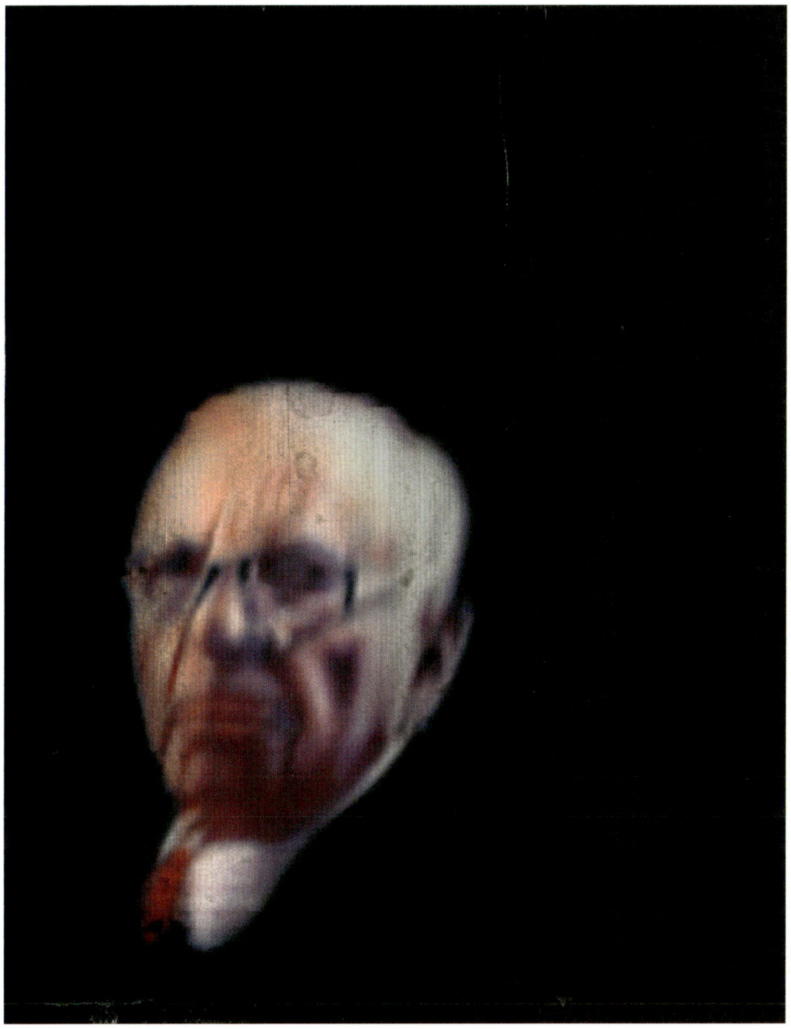

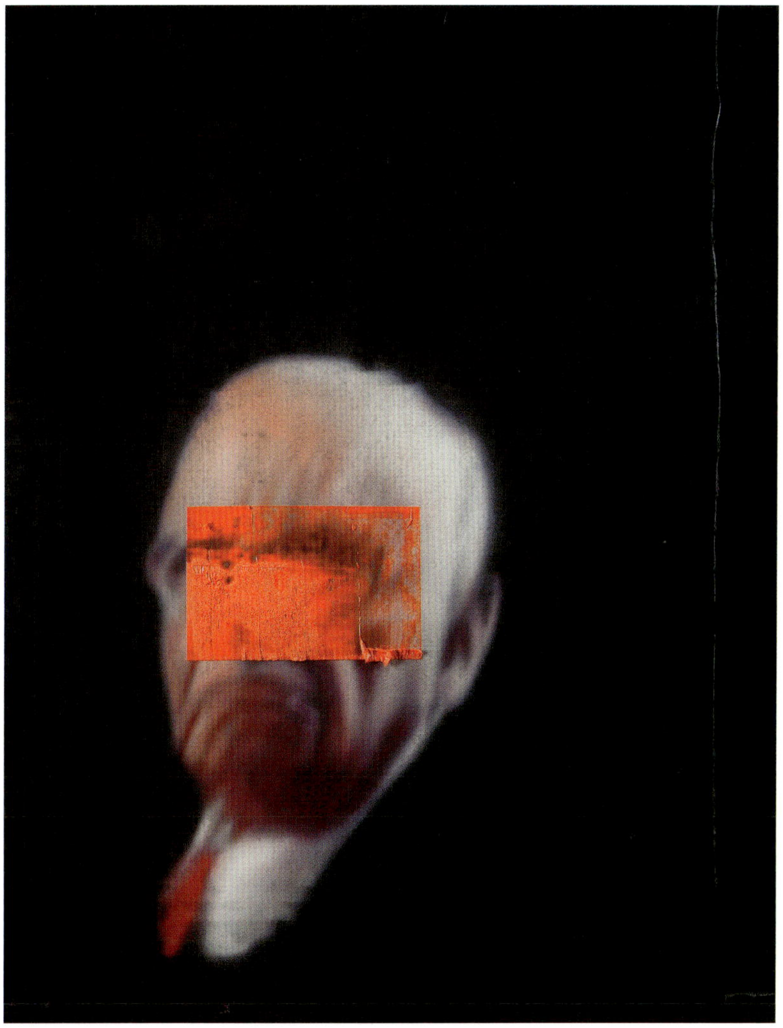

Blinking Rupert, 1999 (12 panels, 4 illustrated)
Blinking Diana, 1999 (12 panels, 4 illustrated)
all: oil on canvas
Each panel 66 x 61 cm / 26 x 24 in

Smear Test I, 2014
Oil on linen
121 x 91 cm / 47⅝ x 35⅞ in
Private Collection, UK

Smear Test II, 2014
Oil on linen
121 x 91 cm / 47⅝ x 35⅞ in

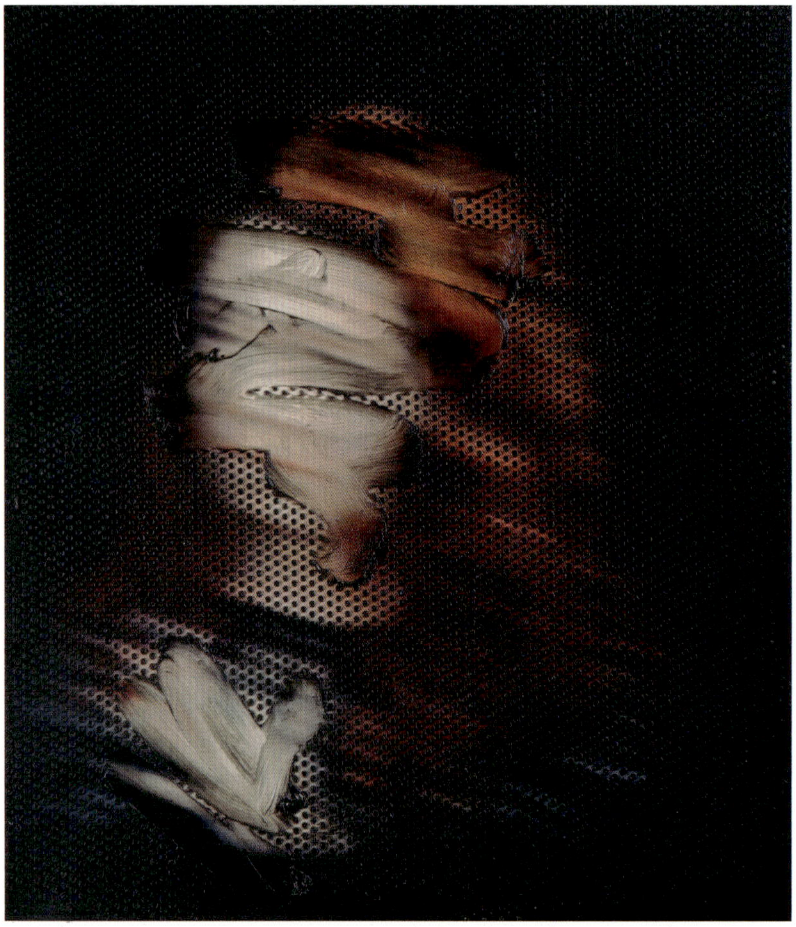

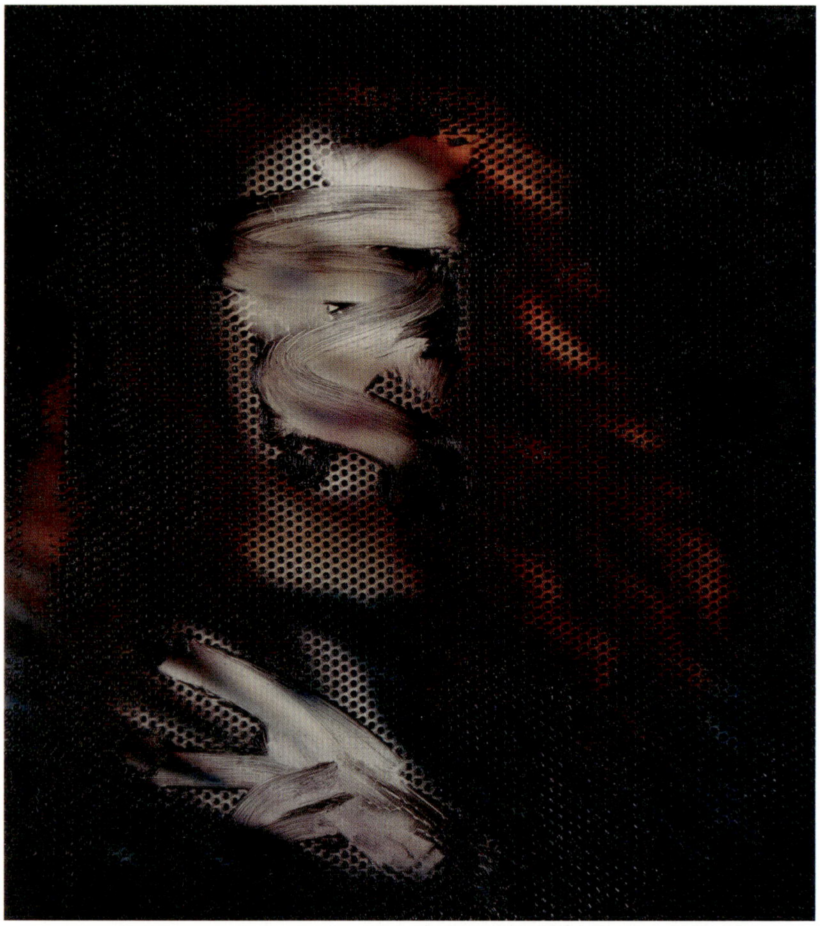

Pictures of Innocence I, 2014
Oil on linen
76 x 66 cm / 29⅞ x 26 in

Pictures of Innocence II, 2014
Oil on linen
76 x 66 cm / 29⅞ x 26 in

ML: There's a rumour that Rupert actually owns one of your pictures of him?

JK: He bought one, not from that series but, when Flowers had a gallery in Los Angeles, there was a show, around 1999, that had some early Murdochs. And an image was sent to Fox and a van was sent round—the painting had to be sent to him—and then a cheque came back. It was a fait accompli by the time I heard about it.

ML: In that area, I've always wondered with artists: do you have any veto over who buys?

JK: Well, I suppose I could refuse.

ML: And have you ever vetoed a sale?

JK: Well, I've always told Matthew Flowers that I'll never sell anything to Charles Saatchi.

ML: So Saatchi is another of your *bêtes noires*?

JK: I think he's everyone's now. It's the nature of the art world that it's susceptible to influence by anyone who has the money. I do have a debt to Saatchi in a way because in the days when he had that big space in Boundary Road, that was the first time I ever encountered Kiefer, for example. But anyone who is able to exercise that degree of influence is bound to cause resentment if you are not the beneficiary.

ML: And, if this principle were tested by him making an offer for something, you would stick to it?

JK: I don't know. I haven't thought about it. Anyway, his influence has waned and he has been replaced by people of even greater wealth and influence.

ML: Such as Roman Abramovich?

JK: Yes. Again, I've been out-spoken on this. But the art-world has become a currency for the super-rich. It's become a commodity through which people with ridiculous amounts of money can process, launder and maintain their fortunes.

Fifteen years after the *Making a Killing* series, Rupert Murdoch was up against the wall again. The phone-hacking scandal that led to the closure of the *News of the World*—and gave the media baron "the humblest day of my life" and a custard pie from a clown in front of a parliamentary committee—had made him a subject for Keane again, along with his ex-employee Rebekah Brooks—tried but acquitted on phone-hacking charges—and Vladimir Putin, the post-Soviet hardman who has created a post-Soviet Russia in which it is probably sensible for his opponents to assume that, at the very least, their calls are being listened to.

We stood in front of this rogues' gallery in progress.

JK: With all of these, it's about finding a photo that works.

ML: So let's go back to basics: you choose a photograph on the computer?

JK: Yes. I trawl the Internet for still images of the person or screen-grabs. Then I might play around with it, separate it from the background, for example.

ML: Or blurring or pixelating?

JK: Exactly. Then, with the aid of a digital projector, I put it on to the canvas and then draw it and then paint it, using an air-brush. I spent some of my 20s, working in the Kings Road, air-brushing duvets for rock stars, so it's interesting that I've come back to that. What you end up with is a more deadpan, flatter, depersonalised paint surface.

ML: And, with your love of word-play, is there any significance in the fact that 'airbrushing' is a pejorative term for making people look better than they are but you're reversing that process.

JK: No. [Laughs] Actually, I hadn't thought of that. In fact, with digital technology, airbrushing is an obsolete way of touching up a photograph. It's all Photoshop now. Although, in fact, you do have an 'airbrush' option on Photoshop. Everything I do now starts out on a screen and I'm very attracted to that process.

ML: But someone like David Hockney has actually created images using iPads or other new technology. You're not tempted by that?

JK: I haven't got into that. Anything I do on the screen carries with it the intention of becoming a physical product made with paint.

ML: So, for example, you have aggressively smeared out the middle of the face of Rebekah Brooks? A sort of pixelation, like newspapers have to do after Leveson?

JK: Yes, it's all that process of obscuring and obfuscation. I've used a kind of dot template of squeegee paint, which alludes to a half-tone newspaper print. And then I went over that with a brush with no paint on it.

ML: During our conversations, you've used the word 'painterly', a great deal, which is a word that only painters use. What does it mean to you?

JK: Good question. What I suppose it means immediately is that you think of the substance of an image. If you are making an image with paint, you are trying to make that substance somehow take on the quality of whatever you are depicting. And you can play around with how realistic you want it to be or whatever. But often what's enjoyable in looking at a painting is the tension between the image and the substance it's made of. It's enjoying the medium.

ML: Because a portrait of Murdoch or Brooks or Putin would, in the end, be pointless as photo-realism?

JK: Well, yes. Because, even though I'm starting out on a screen, I never forget that, in the end, it is going to be a painted surface. Because I've spanned the pre-digital age to the digital age, all the experience I've picked up from working with paint I can bring to bear on the screen.

ML: So you are heading towards some sort of portraits exhibition?

JK: Er, yes. Although I never like to think of them as portraits. I know I do a lot of portraits now but I never ever think of myself as a portrait artist.

ML: But there has been quite a shift towards the individual face in your work?

JK: Yes. I suppose there has. It's not a conscious decision, but just where you find yourself drifting. There hasn't been a plan.

As his next artistic departure would prove.

CHAPTER SIX

DRAMATIC ART

THERE IS A TRADITION OF ARTISTS—FROM DEGAS TO DAVID HOCKNEY—being lured from the studio to visualise theatre or dance shows. This happened once to John Keane when, in 1993, the director Lou Stein asked him to paint some backdrops for *Salsa Celestina*, a piece of Latin American music-theatre at the Watford Palace Theatre. The show stopped in Hertfordshire, as did the artist's ambitions to be a set designer: he was disappointed with the end result.

However, more than a decade later, between 2006 and 2012, Keane collaborated in two performance projects, in which his involvement went far beyond providing images for the actors to stand behind.

The first of these began—tragically but appropriately—in a theatre. On October 23, 2002, a performance of the Russian musical *Nord-Ost* was playing at the Dubrovka Theatre (which translates into English as 'House of Culture') in Moscow when the stage and auditorium were stormed by terrorists from Chechnya in the Northern Caucasus, a rebel province which the Russian government had first lost and then reclaimed during two civil wars.

Because the musical was attracting big crowds, the attack secured 800 hostages, whom the 40 gunmen and gunwomen held for 57 hours, while threatening to blow up the building unless President Putin's troops withdrew from the territory that the terrorists considered as the Chechen Republic. By pumping hospital anaesthetic gas into the theatre, Russian Special Forces aimed to disable the terrorists and storm the building, which they did, killing all the assailants. However, in a horrendous example of collateral damage and the law of unintended consequences, 129 of the theatre-goers also died, mainly from the effects of the sedative.

In an early example of terrorists using digital technology to broadcast their attacks—a tactic that reached its current apotheosis of horror in the IS beheading videos that inform Keane's 'Jump' and 'Distillation of Terror' series—the Chechens transmitted from inside the theatre to feed a story reported around the world to an audience that included John Keane.

> JK: The seed came in 2002, when I was in the middle of the Palestinian series. And I remember hearing about it on the radio. But I thought then: this is an interesting event and I may want to use it as subject matter. A year later, I watched a documentary on TV. The thing that really started it off was this idea of art and life—a group of people going to the theatre to see a musical, which they think of as an escape or diversion. The musical was set in the Second World War and there was a scene with a bunch of guys in military uniform. And, in the middle of this, another guy walks on stage, also apparently in military uniform and fires a weapon into the ceiling. And there was this moment of not knowing whether it was part of the performance or not. And they suddenly knew that this wasn't art, it was life, and a war happening thousands of miles away was suddenly in the theatre with them.

In some of the earlier paintings, titles were scrawled on the canvases in chalk or white paint and that system is mirrored in the *57 Hours in the House of Culture* series, although, in this case, the sentences are found words, taken from the sub-titles on the stills of the frames that Keane had screen-grabbed from the TV documentary.

> JK: When I was choosing images, the words somehow added a poignancy and they became titles that I incorporated in the paintings.

Some of these translated phrases include 'Suddenly, a girl walked into the auditorium'—showing one of the moments of blurring between performance and war—and: 'But now they seemed beyond caring', where the words run across a picture of some of the hostages in their stalls seats and carry the upsetting double-sense that either the prisoners might have lost their will to live or / and that the captors have abandoned all compassion.

If orange would be the governing colour of Keane's later work on the subject of Islamist terrorism, the dominant shades here are red—theatre seating and spilled blood—and black: the latter especially in the echo between two types of disguise: the balaclavas of the male hostage-takers—in 'I swear to Allah, we desire death more than you want life' (2004)—and the hijab, the facial modesty cloth worn by the women among the group, in 'Our women, children and old folk are dying' (2004).

The paintings in *57 Hours in the House of Culture* are a powerful combination of reportage and commentary which, in the deliberate emphases and redactions imposed on the found video images by Keane's brush, are one of the strongest examples of his reclamation of the role of the painter in a digital culture.

But, for their creator, something was missing—or, at least, might be added. For the first time in his career, Keane felt an instinct to take the images out of the gallery and into a cultural space that has only three walls.

ML: What led you to think of a performance spin-off?

JK: While I was doing the paintings, I'd been to see a couple of the Robert Wilson / Tom Waits collaborations at the Barbican and I thought: there's something unique and special about live performance that you can't replicate in any other art-form. And, while making the paintings, I thought: this could become something.

ML: And it also adds a third level because these Russian people in a theatre watching a performance are now themselves in a performance that is being watched?

JK: Of course. All that depth and resonance that comes from reintroducing it to the theatre. And I had no idea where to start because I have no theatrical connections. So I fired off e-mails to Artangel and so on but they said it wasn't for them. Although Michael Morris at Artangel did suggest trying the National Theatre Studio and Lucy Jones from there got back to me and wanted to talk about it.

ML: And you were offering yourself as—what?—The visual designer?

JK: Yes, all of that. But also as the hub of the collaboration, choosing the people I wanted to work with. As for the composer, I knew I didn't want, as it were, Andrew Lloyd-Webber but nor did I want Harrison Birtwistle.

After abortive talks with various musicians, Pete Wyer, a classical and jazz composer, was mooted and the artist found that their ideas meshed. And, after the National sent him a selection of plays by potential dramatists, Keane chose Bryony Lavery, whose psychological drama *Frozen* had recently been a London and Broadway success. Lavery suggested bringing in her friend "Lloydy", who turned out to be Phylidda Lloyd, a director whose CV is unusual in encompassing populist mega-hits (the stage and movie musical *Mamma Mia*) as well as Shakespeare and new plays.

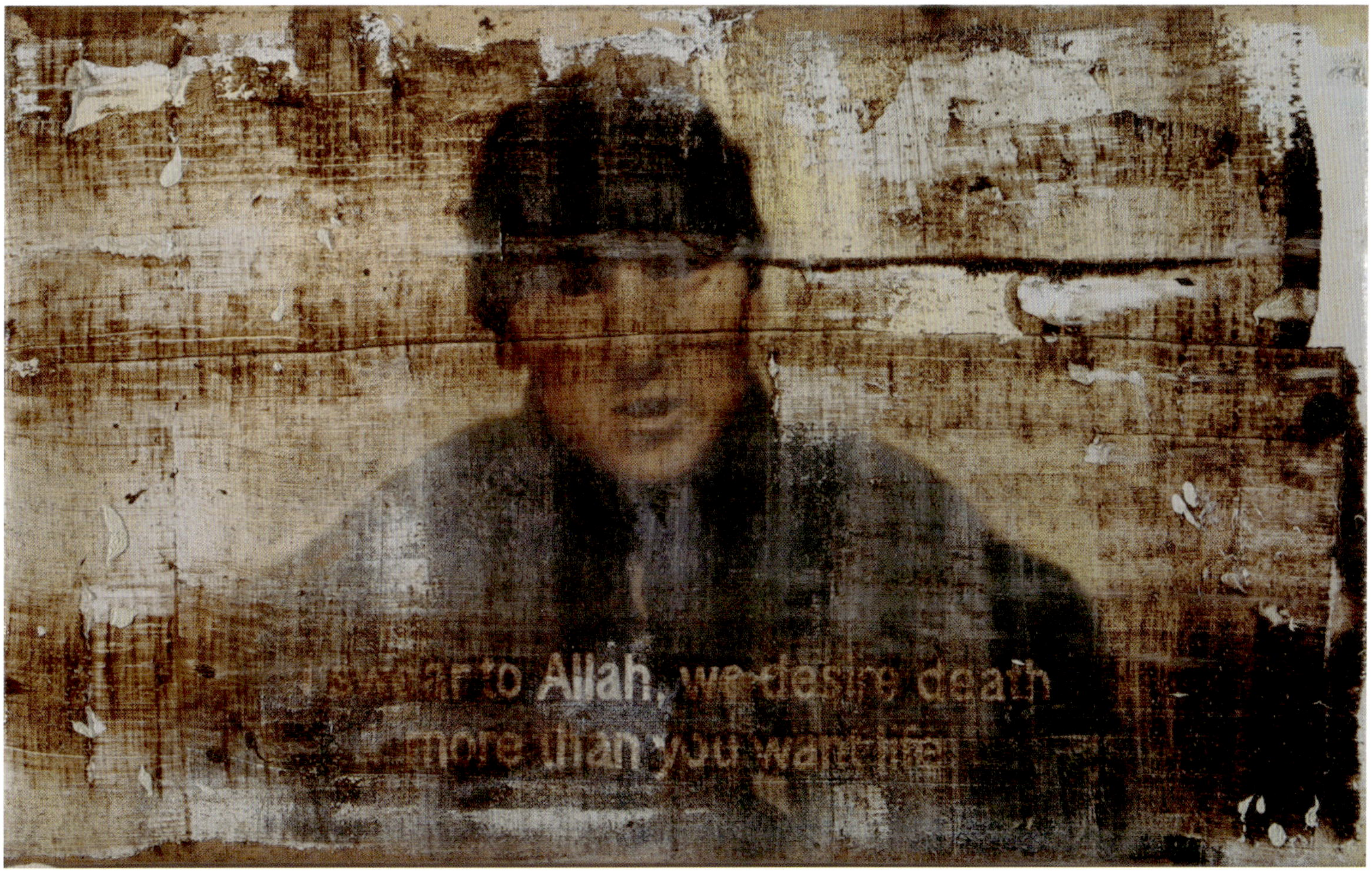

I swear to Allah, we desire death more than you want life, 2004
Oil on jute
51 x 82 cm / 20¼ x 32 in

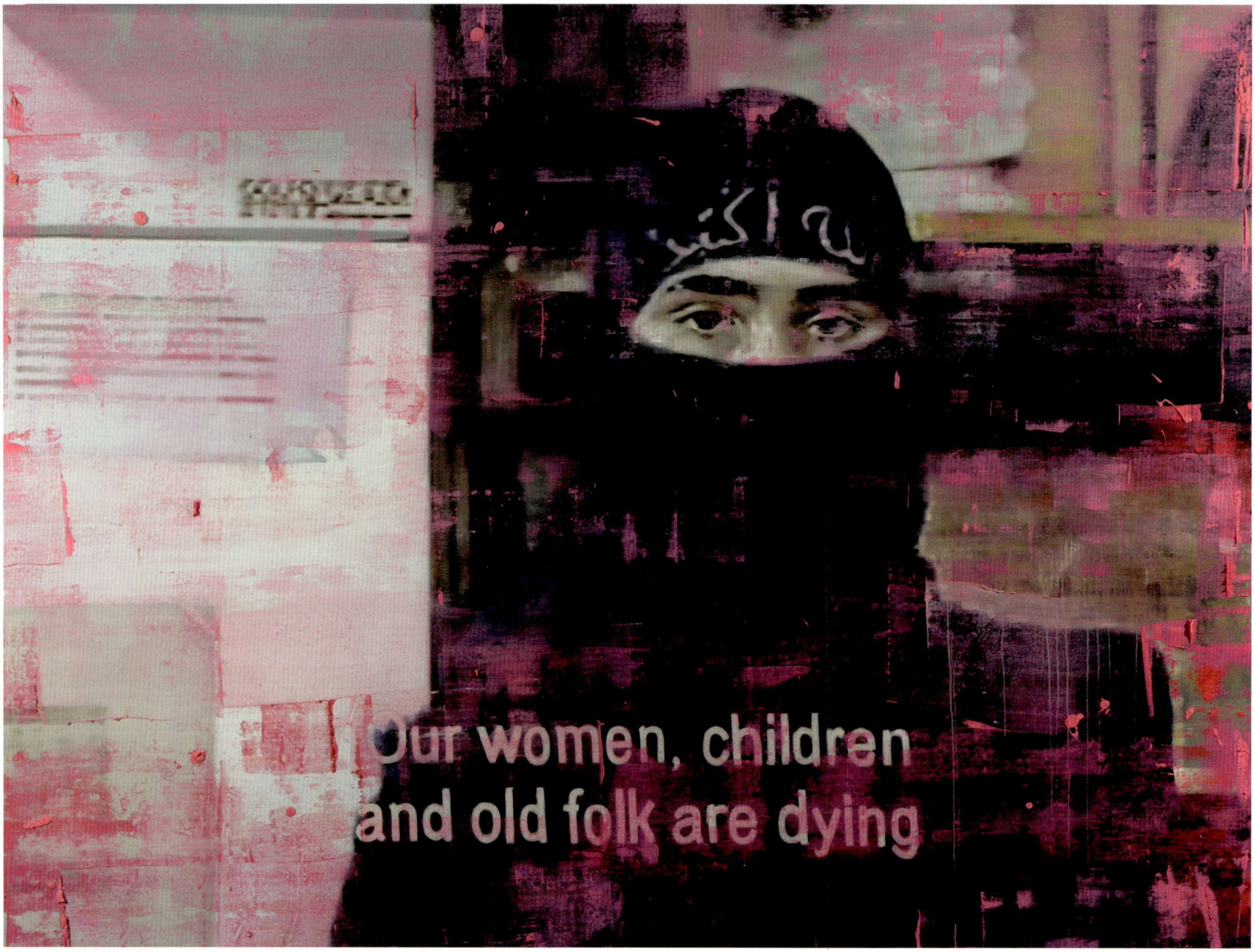

Our Women, Children and Old Folk are Dying, 2004
Oil on linen
212 x 282 cm / 83½ x 111 in
Collection: Nick Taylor

The National Theatre Studio exists to allow projects to be developed without the pressure or expectation of an imminent production. The Wyer-Lavery-Lloyd-Keane *57 Hours* was given two workshops, in 2008 and 2010, with the latter sessions captured in a video diary. From that record, it can be seen that the show featured intriguing use of video and still images (Keane) and inventive playing with theatrical convention that expands the artist's initial fascination with the collision of actuality and theatricality: taking their seats, the audience for *57 Hours* would be confronted, as in one of Magritte's pictures of receding repeat images, by the backs of ranks of theatre-goers who, in performance, would suddenly turn round and sing or speak. The libretto makes use of verbatim speech from documentary footage and interviews, anticipating, in that respect, Alecky Blythe's and Adam Cork's *London Road,* a later product of the NT Studio workshops, which became a commercial and critical hit.

The work-in-progress video ends with Phyllida Lloyd announcing: 'We're ready to do a production now.' But, despite her confidence and considerable influence, it didn't happen. The project ended with a presentation of extracts to Sir Nicholas Hytner, the National's artistic director, and, prompted by the musical element, John Berry, who held the equivalent position at English National Opera.

JK: We were really pleased with how it went; there was a real buzz about it. But then Nick Hytner said: 'It's not really for the National, is it, because it's an opera.' And John Berry said: 'Well, it's not really an opera.' So who knows?

ML: Is it dead now?

JK: Look, the last conversation I had was with the Brighton Festival after I did that thing last year [*Canticles,* see below] and we had a conversation in September 2013, in which they said it was too late for 2014 but we should think about 2015. And we exchanged a few e-mails but then the line went completely dead, which is bizarre and now he won't answer e-mails. Pete is in New York and thinks he might find some interest there.

It's a real disappointment because I really think there was something in it. And everyone was very positive about it except those who were in a position to commission it. It's a difficult business and because it's not my field it's hard to follow through.

Some consolation for the disappointment of the performance version of *57 Hours in the House of Culture* came from another theatrical commission, although — paradoxically — it would prompt Keane's one significant attempt at video installation.

At intervals between 1947 and 1974, the composer Benjamin Britten (1913–76) wrote five 'Canticles', a traditional form of church music, usually set to Biblical verses, although Britten was broader in his sources. For example, the third canticle, 'Still Falls the Rain' (1954), was based on a poem by Dame Edith Sitwell (1887–1964), written in 1940, at the start of the bombing raids during the Second World War.

In 2013, as a project for the Brighton Festival, the Aldeburgh Music Festival and the Royal Opera House, theatre director Neil Bartlett and lighting designer Paule Constable collaborated on a piece of musical theatre based around this Britten quintet. One practitioner from another medium — art, dance, lighting — was assigned to work on each piece, with Keane allocated the third Canticle, Bartlett explained in a programme note, because humankind's frequent recourse to war had been such a key theme of his work. Bartlett had assumed that the artist would produce paintings or stage sets but Keane saw a different possibility:

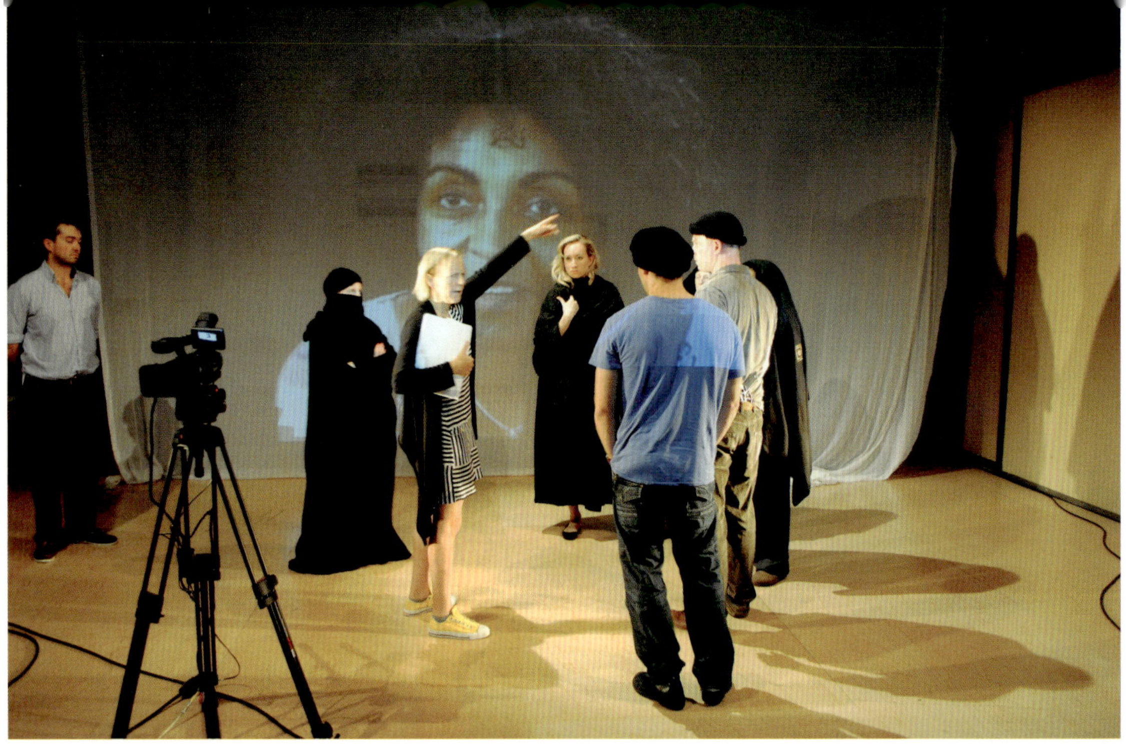

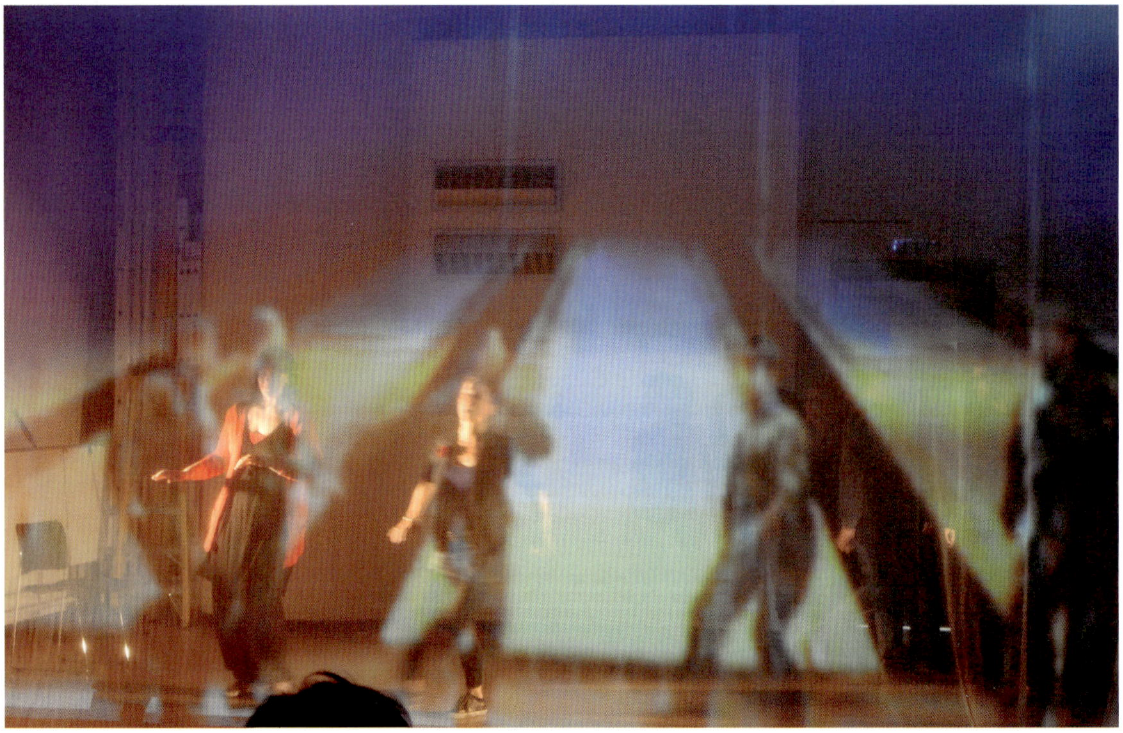

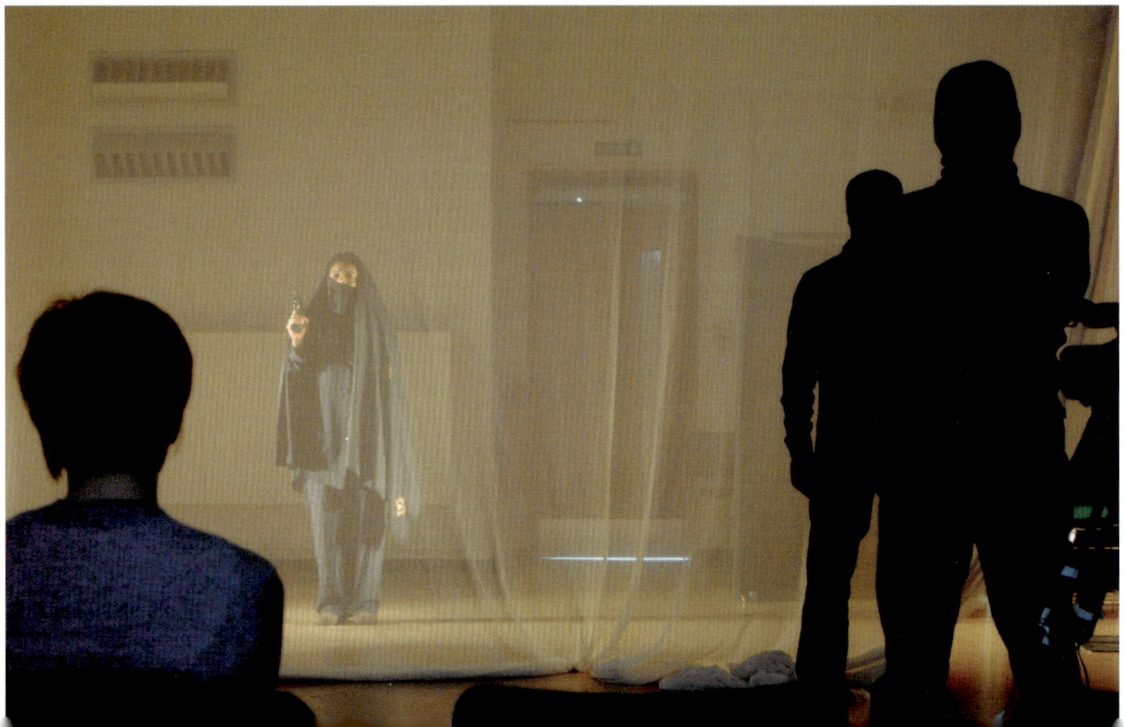

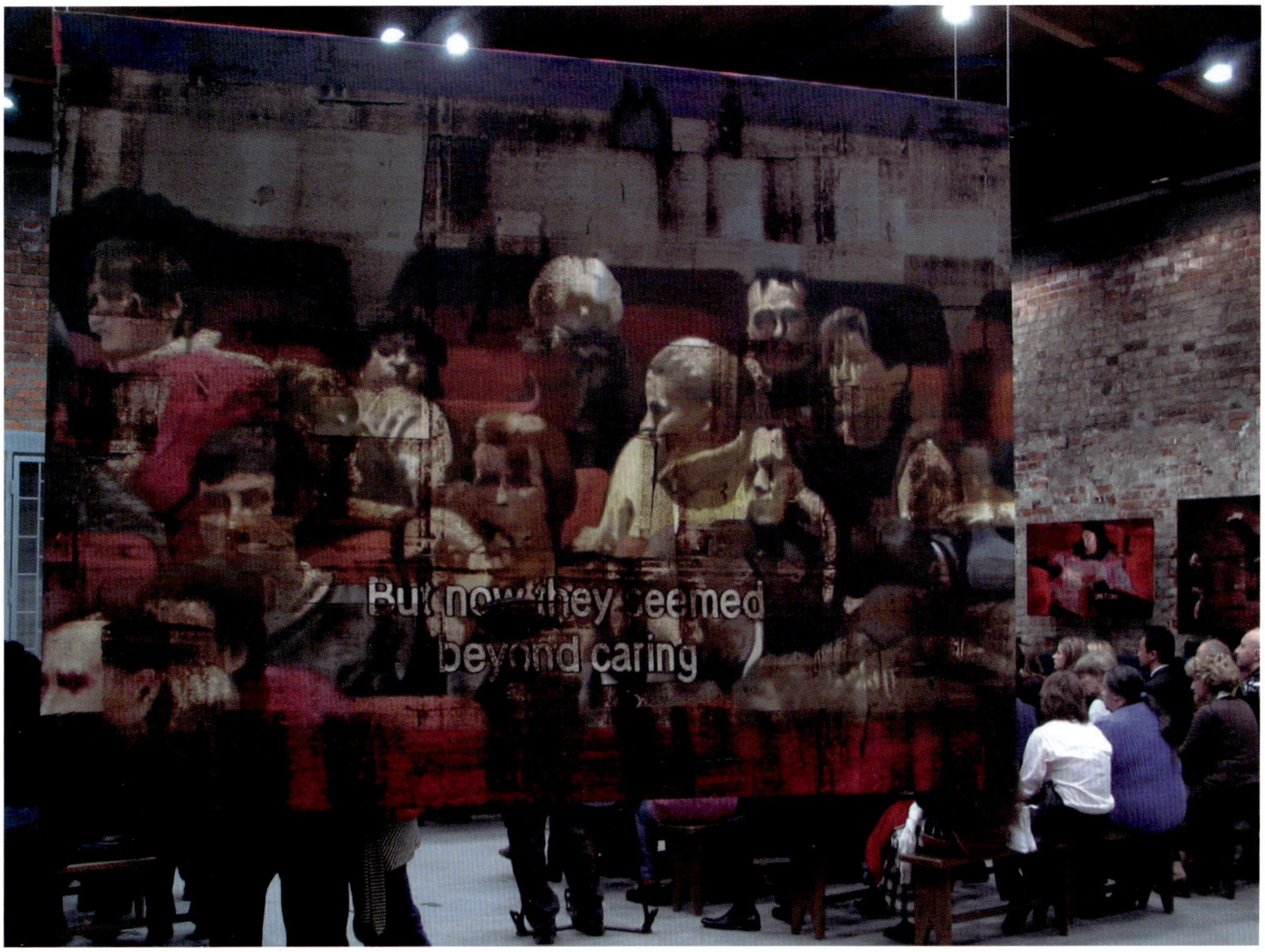

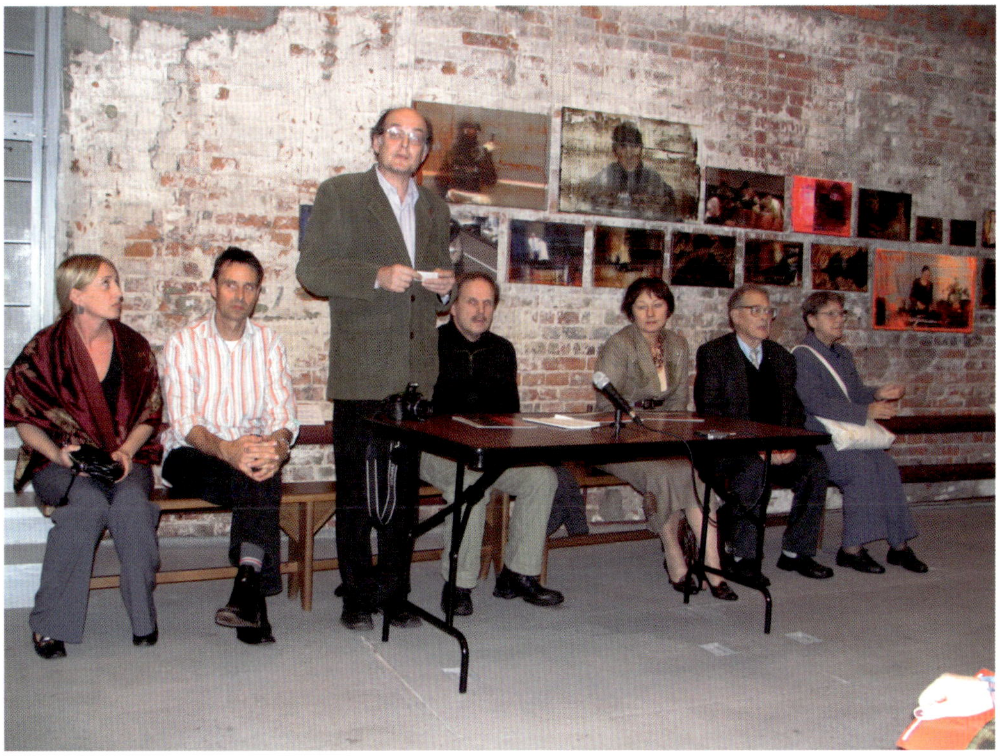

opposite:
57 Hours in the House of Culture, 2010
workshop presentation at
The National Theatre studios in London
with Phyllida Lloyd directing

this page:
57 Hours in the House of Culture, 2006
Opening night of the exhibition at
Andre Sakharov Museum in Moscow
with Yuri Samodurov standing next to
the artist

THE CANTICLES

Photographs by Victor Frankowski

BRIGHTON FESTIVAL 2013
BRITTEN: THE CANTICLES
WORLD PREMIERE.
CO-COMMISSIONED BY BRIGHTON FESTIVAL
AND ALDEBURGH MUSIC

Ian Bostridge, tenor
Iestyn Davies, countertenor
Benedict Nelson, baritone
Richard Watkins, horn
Julius Drake, piano
Sally Pryce, harp
Staged by Neil Bartlett and Paule Constable
with Scott Graham for Frantic Assembly,
Wendy Houstoun & John Keane.

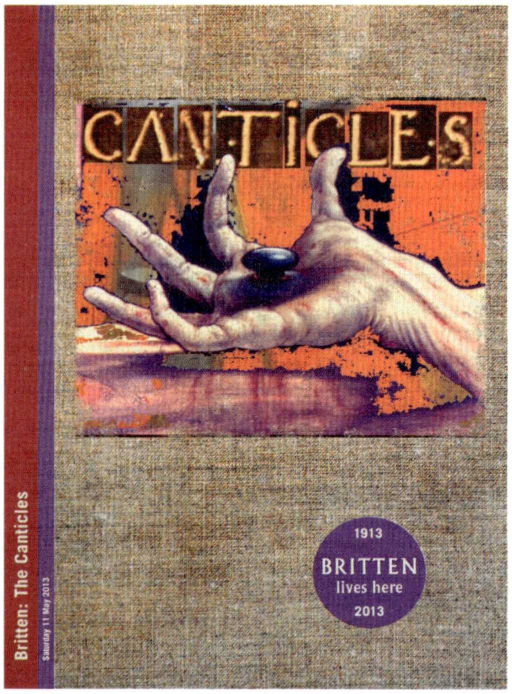

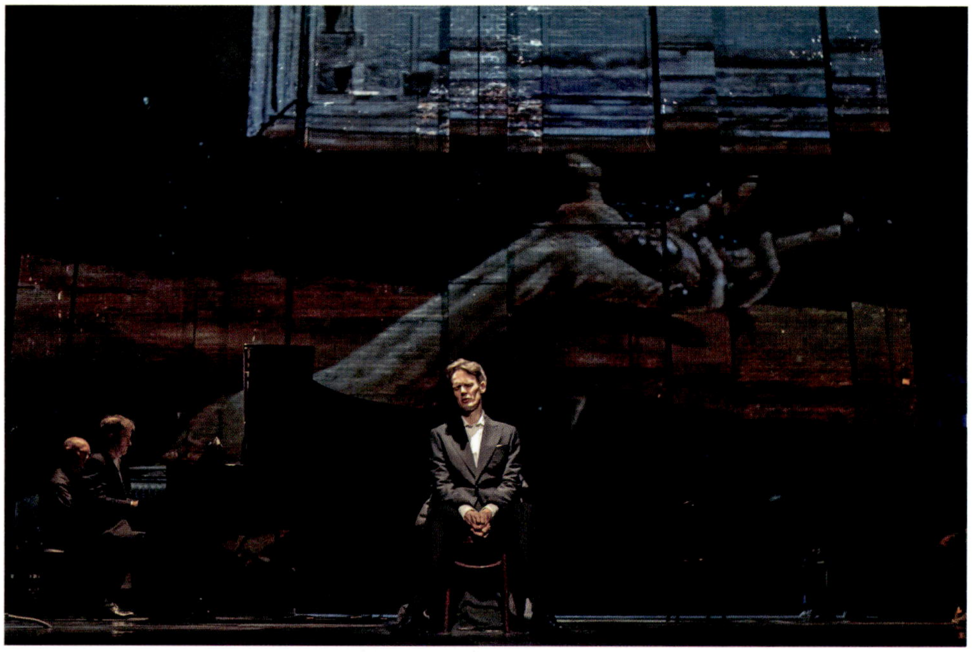

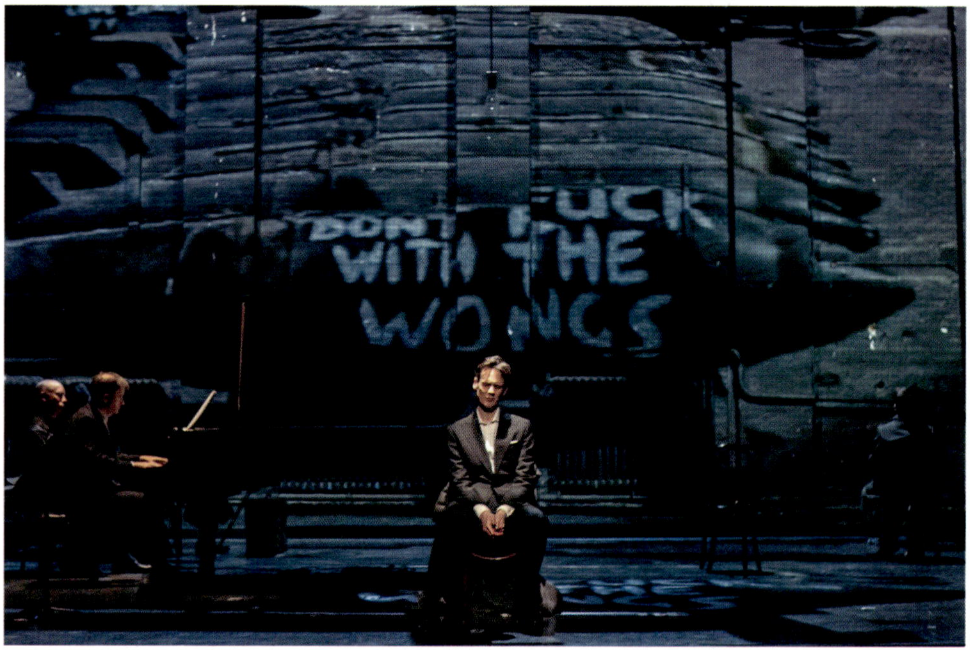

Still images from film projection for Canticle III
'Still falls the Rain' by Benjamin Britten with Ian Bostridge,
Julius Drake, and Richard Watkins

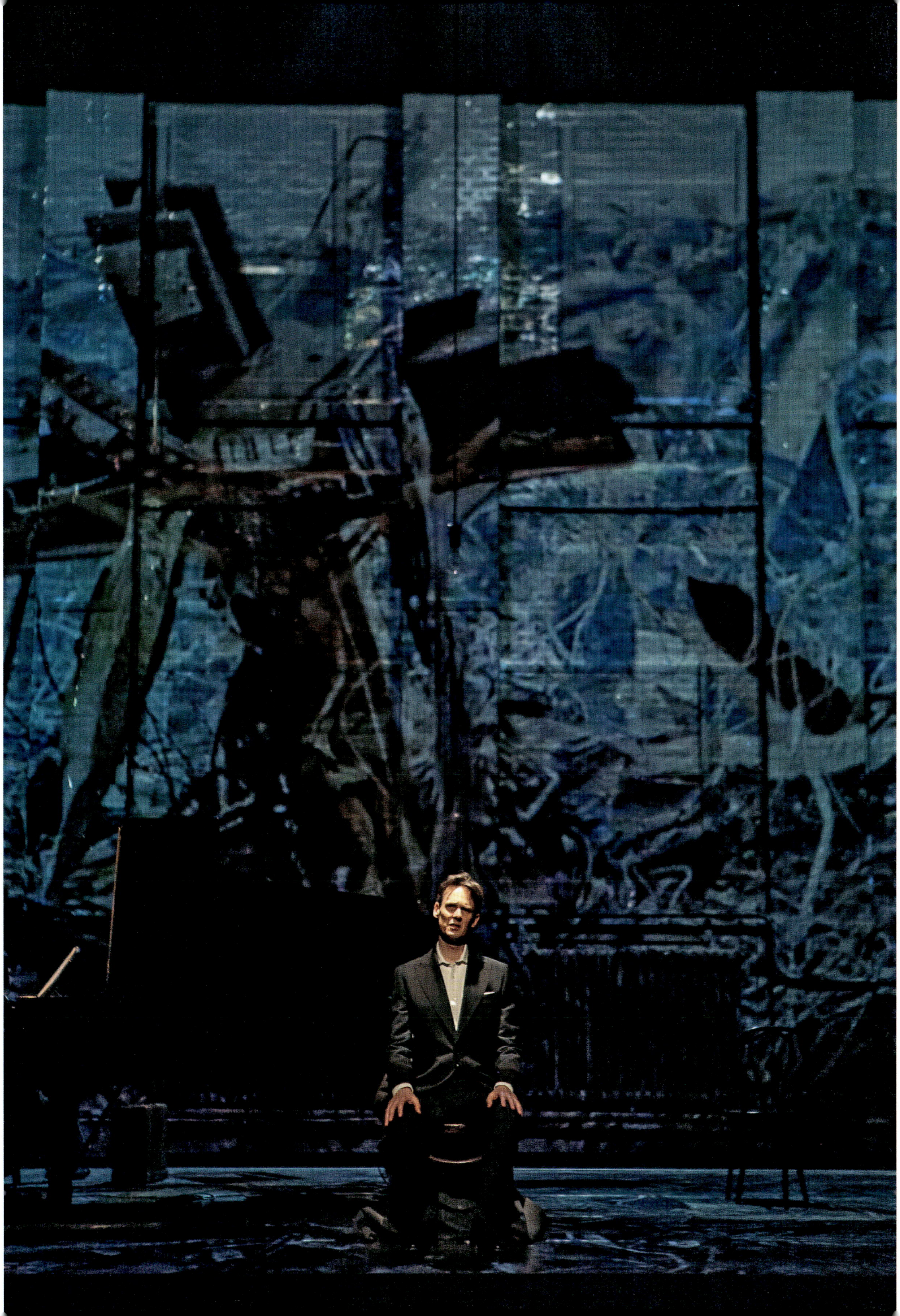

JK: It started with a text from Jonathan Reekie, who was then the director of the Aldeburgh Festival. I'd actually met him when I was looking for a composer for *57 Hours*. And that didn't quite come off, but we established a link. And then a few years later I got a text asking how I'd fancy being part of this Britten project. And I thought: nothing like I've ever done before but let's talk about it. And I chose to do film projection.

ML: Despite your well-known opposition to video art?

JK: Well, I'm not opposed to it as such. And I think video projection in theatre can be extraordinary. And, if you're sitting listening to a 12-minute song and you've got imagery that changes and shifts, there's much more potential. Also, I like what happens when you project photographically on to uneven surfaces, unlikely things happen and I knew it was going to be a brick wall with rough patches and buttresses and what have you. But, when I listened to the piece, I found it quite hard to get into . . .

ML: Partly presumably because it is very religious?

JK: Very. Which is not easy for me. But, as I listened to it, I could build up a bank of images. And, as with *57 Hours*, I was excited by the idea of a collaboration. For someone who works on their own, that's very attractive. I had a meeting with Neil [Bartlett] and then I was given a researcher and a video editor to work with and then later there was a projection guy.

Dame Edith Sitwell, an aristocratic eccentric of statuesque shape, who favoured vivid outfits that often felt like an attempt to anglicise the kaftan and turban, can be seen as an unlikely progenitor of performance poetry. Her work *Facade*, a lengthy rhythmical incantation to the music of William Walton, now seems, in retrospect, like a posh English ancestor of hip-hop.

Triggered by the beginning of the Blitz by German bombers over London, 'Still Falls the Rain' is shaped by a double visual run: a rain-storm above the British capital becomes both the Nazi bombs raining down but also the dark cylindrical nails banging into Christ's cross:

Still falls the Rain---
Dark as the world of man, black as our loss---
Blind as the nineteen hundred and forty nails
Upon the Cross.

Still falls the Rain
With a sound like the pulse of the heart that is changed
to the hammer-beat
In the Potter's Field, and the sound of the impious feet

On the Tomb:
Still falls the Rain

The Keane-eyed critic may note that, just a couple of years on, the artist would make his own connection between war and crucifixion in his other work shaped by poetry: the 'Jump' (previously 'Second Coming') pictures. Sitwell's verse is hauntingly aural: in a Potter's Field (an historical term for a pauper's cemetery), the nails being banged into a coffin and the tramp of feet on ground become pseudo-pulses for the corpses underground. But the work is also strongly visual and, guided by Sitwell's own collision between weather and showers of death, Keane's 'Canticle III' film cuts together newsreel imagery of the Blitz and British women in bomb factories chalking 'Adolf' on the side of one missile with scenes from bombing raids in conflicts and artistic representations of the bleeding Jesus, taken from Matthias Grunewald's altar-piece at Isenheim in Germany.

> JK: I listened to the music and watched YouTube and came up with a wish—list of images: saying this is what I want and what can we get in reality? Certain things suggested themselves—the bomb as rain—and then I started thinking about the munitions factories.
>
> ML: And you didn't create any images of your own?
>
> JK: The only stuff of mine is some of the footage I shot during the Gulf war.
>
> I thought it would be interesting to bring that back to me. I photoshopped the Eisenheim altar-piece. The description of the body of Christ and the wounds was very visceral and so that seemed the appropriate depiction.

The evening of artistically-interpreted canticles was performed at Aldeburgh, Brighton and in London at the Royal Opera House's Linbury Studio. For Keane's contribution, the tenor Ian Bostridge and two musicians—pianist Julius Drake and horn player Richard Watkins—sat on stage in front of a huge screen streaming the film.

> JK: After the first Brighton performance, I was coming home on the train. And, after the performance, we'd done all that post-show back-slap: you were wonderful darling etc. And I told Ian how good he was and he said: 'I was thinking of the film when I was singing it'. And there couldn't be a higher accolade than that. I was just thrilled it worked. And the buzz I felt coming back on the train from Brighton that night is something I will always remember.
>
> ML: This chapter features your two theatrical projects to date. Would you like there to be more?
>
> JK: Yes, if there is the right project, a collaboration I felt I could add something to. There are some theatre productions I go to—we just saw *Golem* at the Young Vic, for instance—and you think that there are certain experiences in theatre that you cannot imagine in any other medium. And I would like to do more.

CHAPTER SEVEN
OVER SIXTY

One consequence of getting older is that so many years come burdened with significance. On September 12, 2014, John Keane reached 60, his birthday now always following the latest anniversary of the attacks on the American east coast that are the historical event on which his most recent work pivots. And 2015 marks the 30 anniversary of his first solo show at Flowers Gallery, called, prophetically of some of the subjects he would tackle in the future, *Conspiracy Theories*. In 2016, the passing of a quarter of a century since the first Gulf War is likely to bring renewed interest and visibility to the paintings that Keane brought back from the front and which cemented his reputation.

The artist continues to look forward: shortly after the last of our conversations for this book, he was travelling to Rwanda, an atrocity zone that has so far escaped his gaze, in his role as Artist in Residence at the department of International Relations at St Andrews University in Scotland.

So the eye moves on but it is also invited, in this phase of weighted dates, to look back.

ML: Being 60—what impact—if any—are you aware of it having?

JK: I think it's mainly psychological. I think being 60—more than any other of the decade birthdays—it's more of a landmark somehow.

ML: Because, in the old days, it would have been close to retirement?

JK: Yes. [Laughs] It would. I think growing older is actually very interesting—there are some things you could obviously do without but the historical perspective on the arc of your life is fascinating. I've got diaries I kept from the age of 14 to about 28, 29. . . .

ML: Which you refused to give me for this book.

JK: Yes. But I've found myself looking at them more and more recently. I think, at this age, when your mind's in neutral, you find yourself looking back more, wondering what happened to people. And I've been re-reading the diaries a lot recently. And it made excruciating, toe-curling reading. But I think that is one of the things about being this age: that you become fascinated by your younger self. What I did learn from reading it was that I seem to have stopped needing to write it when I became happy in my late 20s. What did strike me is that, in adolescence, I seem to have been unable to see myself beyond the age of 30.

ML: In the diaries, is it clear that you're going to be an artist?

JK: Yes, it's obvious that that's what I wanted to do from very early on. It provided a different reality to the one I had from school, family etc.

ML: What relationship do you have with the earlier work now?

JK: Er, er, er . . . it depends: some of it I like. But it's more: if I hadn't done that, I wouldn't be doing this now. The early stuff is not what I'd want to be remembered for. I would hope I've refined, moved on, improved.

ML: But, looking back, it strikes me that there is a remarkable reportage of the times you've lived through.

JK: Good. But I look at it more from the painterly aspect. I think: God, I wouldn't have done that now. It's not—for me—the subject matter but the treatment, how I've executed it. I find some of the early work a bit cartoony and obvious, even if the subject might still appeal to me.

ML: So something like 'Jump' is much more subtle and oblique than some of the earlier war pictures that editorialise more?

JK: Yes, exactly. Although I was just digging out for the photographer for this book some early 20s stuff. In the preoccupations I was showing then there is a direct link, borrowing from photography or television screens and misrepresentation. And in a way I think I've come back to that now, although using computers and blurring. So there is a continuity.

ML: When you're working on pictures, do you think about how they will look in a gallery?

JK: Yes. As I'm working, I am, in the back of my mind, trying to imagine how a collection of work might look in a space.

ML: But do you, as a theatre designer—or a playwright—might, have a sense of an empty room that you're filling?

JK: I think the answer to that is that I fill it as best I can, with work that I have done that might be quite diverse.

ML: Take me through your working day or week?

JK: Well, I pretty much follow office hours, Monday to Friday. I leave the house by half past eight, I'm here by five past or ten past nine. Turn the heating, radio and computers on. Then spend an hour and a half faffing around, reading newspapers online, listening to *In Our Time* or whatever, answering e-mails. Then around 10, 10.30, I start addressing what's in front of me. And that goes on, with distractions, until 6 or so.

ML: And, I've noticed, making times to interview you during this winter, of your awareness of when the light goes. Do you always paint in natural light?

JK: I prefer it. Especially where colour is a factor.

ML: Non-artists never quite understand the significance to artists of natural light. So why?

JK: Because . . . it's a good question, actually. Because it isn't going to be seen in natural light, which maybe defeats the object. It's just a nicer, more even light because studio lights tend to have a yellowish tinge. Natural light is just easier on the eye: there's a greater range and subtlety to the colours.

ML: And it's common these days to read articles by eye doctors arguing that Cezanne had cataracts or TItian was astigmatic or whatever and that's why they painted the way they did. Are you conscious of your eyes changing with age?

JK: Yes, I am. I think I probably have the beginnings of a cataract in my left eye. My eyesight has been pretty good most of my life. But just in the last few years I've started wearing varifocals and my sister has had cataracts and last time I had my eyes done at Specsavers, I was told there might be the start of a cataract.

ML: And, when you're walking here, do you generally know what you'll do that day?

JK: No. Sometimes I get here and don't know what the fuck I'll do and that's difficult. And I think that's the benefit of a routine. I sometimes explain to people that it may look to the uneducated eye as if I spend a lot of time pacing up and down listening to the radio but you don't get the productive time without the time wasted. But then I switch off and go home.

ML: Are you ever unable to finish an image?

JK: Occasionally. Rarely. The way I work now, with the advent of the computer and technology, I've a pretty fair sense of where something is going to go because I can formulate it.

ML: Like storyboarding for a film director?

JK: Yes I suppose so. Everything I do starts on a computer screen and has done for the last 10, 15 years, probably. And to me it's a very satisfying way of working. I realise now that I have eradicated the problem of the blank canvas. Because most of the time I am starting with an image and the creative tension is how I present it, manipulate it, work it into what in the end will be a picture. But there is still the mental blank canvas: what am I going to do now?

ML: Actors and writers and athletes talk about getting 'into the zone', when it's as if the work is doing you. Does that happen?

JK: Yes. Yes. You can't predict or guarantee any of it but, when it does work, it's exhilarating and I put on loud music and dance around. But that's what makes you want to carry on.

ML: We should probably talk about the state of the art world. There's a lot of talk in the papers at the moment about the Turner Prize having gone back into the artistic closet as it were?

JK: I have been quite vocal about the Turner Prize in the past.

ML: Because of their failure to select you?

JK: [Laughs] Well, obviously that's at the root of it.

ML: Seriously, though, do you feel overlooked?

JK: Well, yes, I feel that generally about the art world. The Tate doesn't own anything of mine, for instance. Nor have I ever had any significant support from the Arts Council or the British Council. I heard this new word the other day: the Curatariat, which seemed to me a great coinage — a sort of art-world bureaucracy and establishment which is driven by — well, I'm not sure what it's driven by except a desire to impress other people within that clique. I think the Turner Prize has always been a manipulation. It was set up as a democratic process but I have it on good authority that the public votes were unceremoniously binned. It's chosen by a charabanc of arts insiders who go to certain galleries. It certainly has changed the public perception of modern art: sometimes for good, sometimes for ill. I don't want to appear like someone with a chip on my shoulder. But I do feel that for some reason — whether because I'm a painter or because of the subjects I choose — I am marginalised. I mean, I get by but . . .

ML: I wanted to talk about this. Because the Turner Prize is increasingly seen to represent the triumph — if such it is — of video art. Three of the four 2014 shortlist are video installations. Video artists have won for the last three years . . .

JK: I know. I have a real problem with video art. I enjoy some of it but I really don't want to spend half an hour in a darkened space deciding that I don't really want to see something.

ML: The Duncan Campbell that won the 2014 Turner is an hour long.

JK: I know! Even Adrian Searle [Guardian art critic] said that he struggled with it, for God's sake! And this is what is supposed to engage the public's imagination. I find it rather depressing. There are artists who are state-funded pets, constantly supported, well-represented in all the collections: we could talk about Jeremy Deller or Martin Creed. It's a world that's foreign to me. I don't feel part of it, I don't particularly like most of it.

ML: Although Duncan Campbell said that he would use the Turner cheque to pay his rent because, as a video artist, he couldn't make vast amounts of money by selling his work like a painter.

JK: No, I do see that. If you don't really have a product at the end of it. And, yes, without that, then you can only really survive on grants and subsidy.

ML: How do you feel about Grayson Perry, who seems to me an interesting case. He has become a sort of 'national treasure' but—including his work on TV—does do interesting stuff?

JK: Yes, he does. But would he have been nominated for the Turner Prize if he didn't wear a frock? He is very articulate and he has things to say about the art world. I do quite like his pots, his tapestries are appalling. He is essentially an entertainer. I switched on the Reith Lectures last year and I thought: okay, Grayson, you've got our attention now, let's hear what you have to say about art. And it was introduced by Sue Lawley. And the first thing she said was what he was wearing. And I thought: for fuck's sake! And I switched off.

ML: But the relation of your own work to video art interests me. Because it seems—retrospectively—to be a distillation of paint and video or an attempt to bring the forms together. But was it consciously?

JK: Yes. In that the video—as a still photograph might have been—is the source material. And with video—if it's an event that I'm interested in—I can grab a moment that works visually. For example, in the theatre siege paintings, I went through the footage taken by the terrorists and there were certain frames that seemed to work. But it is a convenient tool. Everything I do is aiming to become a painting.

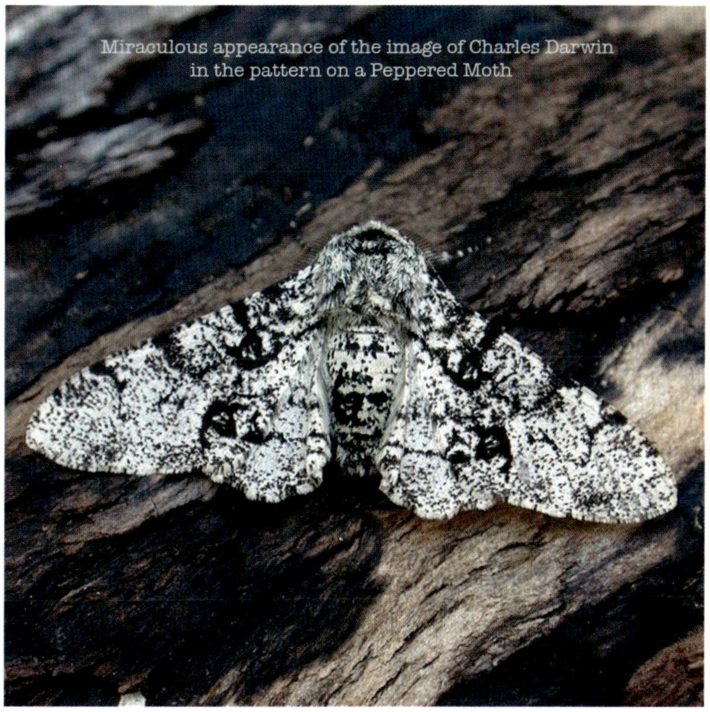

Miraculous appearance of the image of Charles Darwin in the pattern of a Peppered Moth, 2008
Digital print
41 x 41 cm / 16¼ x 16¼ in
Edition of 10

PLATES

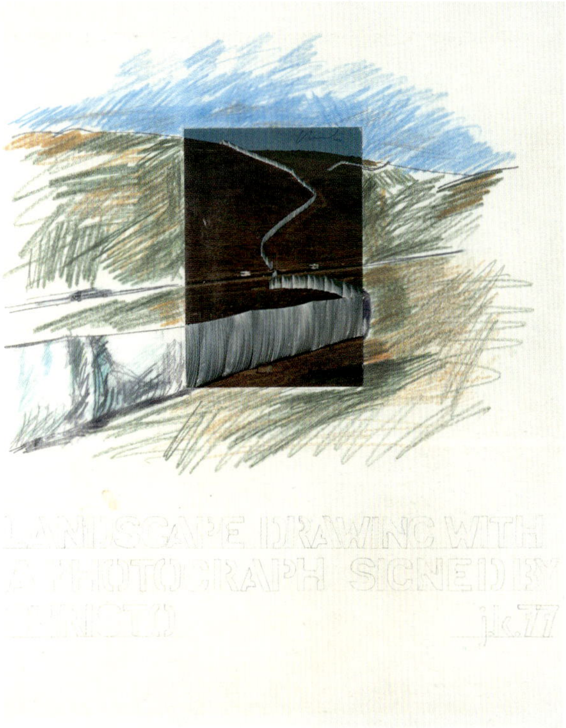

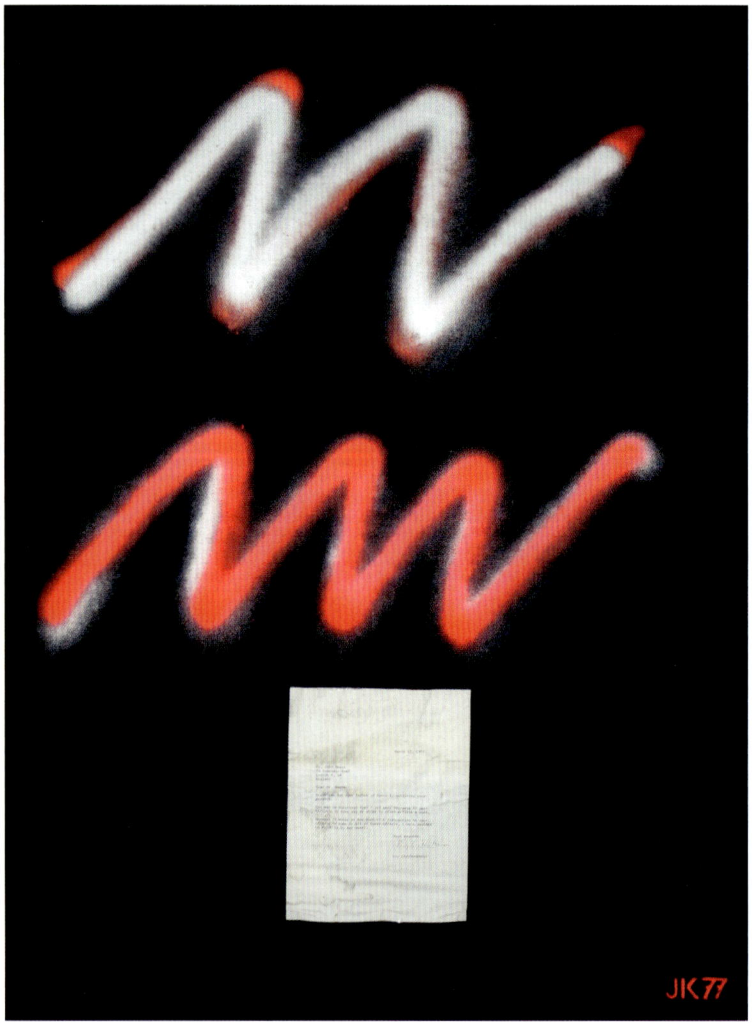

Landscape Drawing with a Photograph Signed by Christo, 1977
Crayon and collage on paper
56 x 42 cm / 22⅛ x 16½ in

Abstract Painting with a letter from Roy Lichtenstein, 1977
Household paint, spray paint and collage on canvas
122 x 92 cm / 48 x 36¼ in

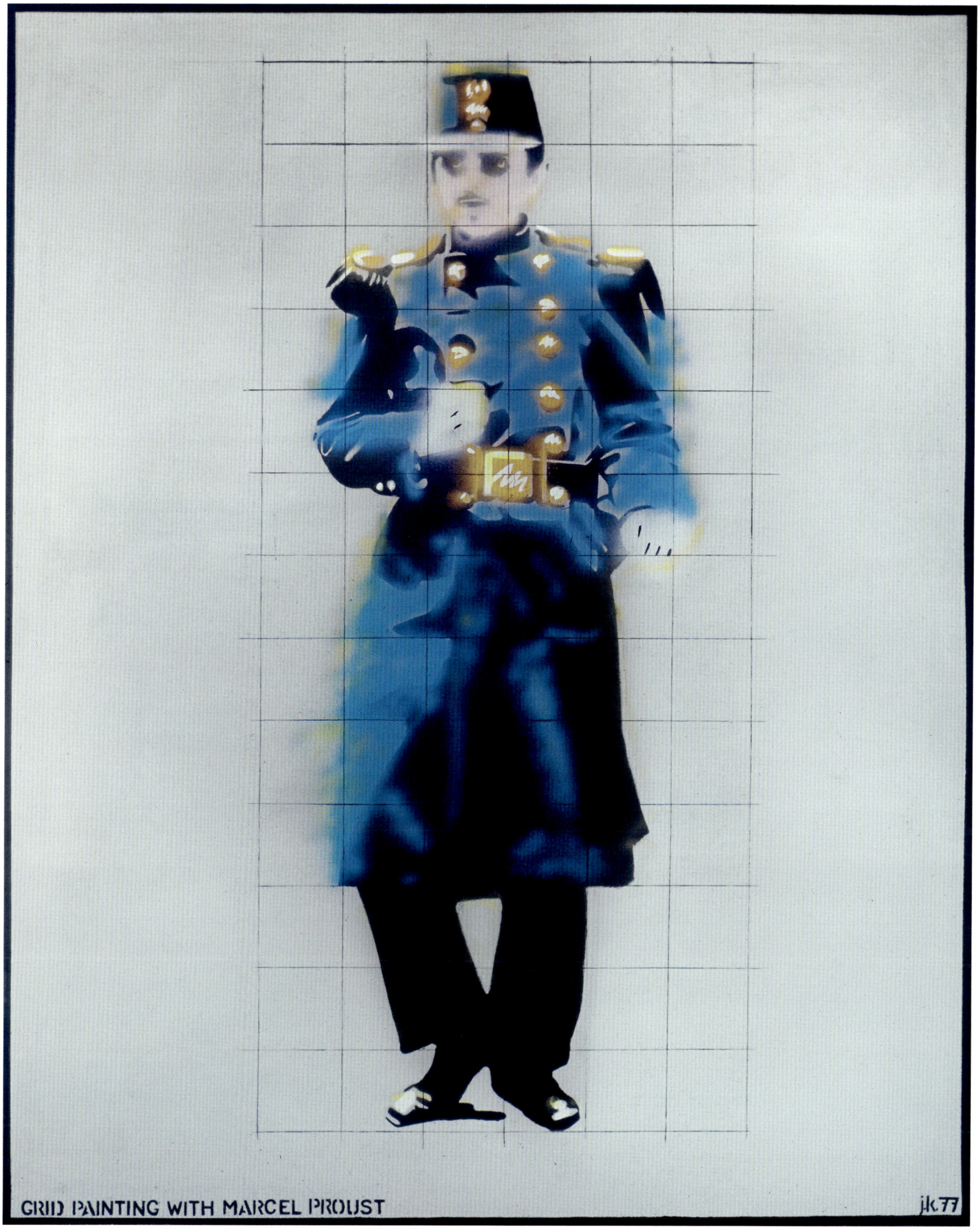

Grid Painting with Marcel Proust, 1977
PVA and household paint on canvas
153 x 122 cm / 60¼ x 48 in

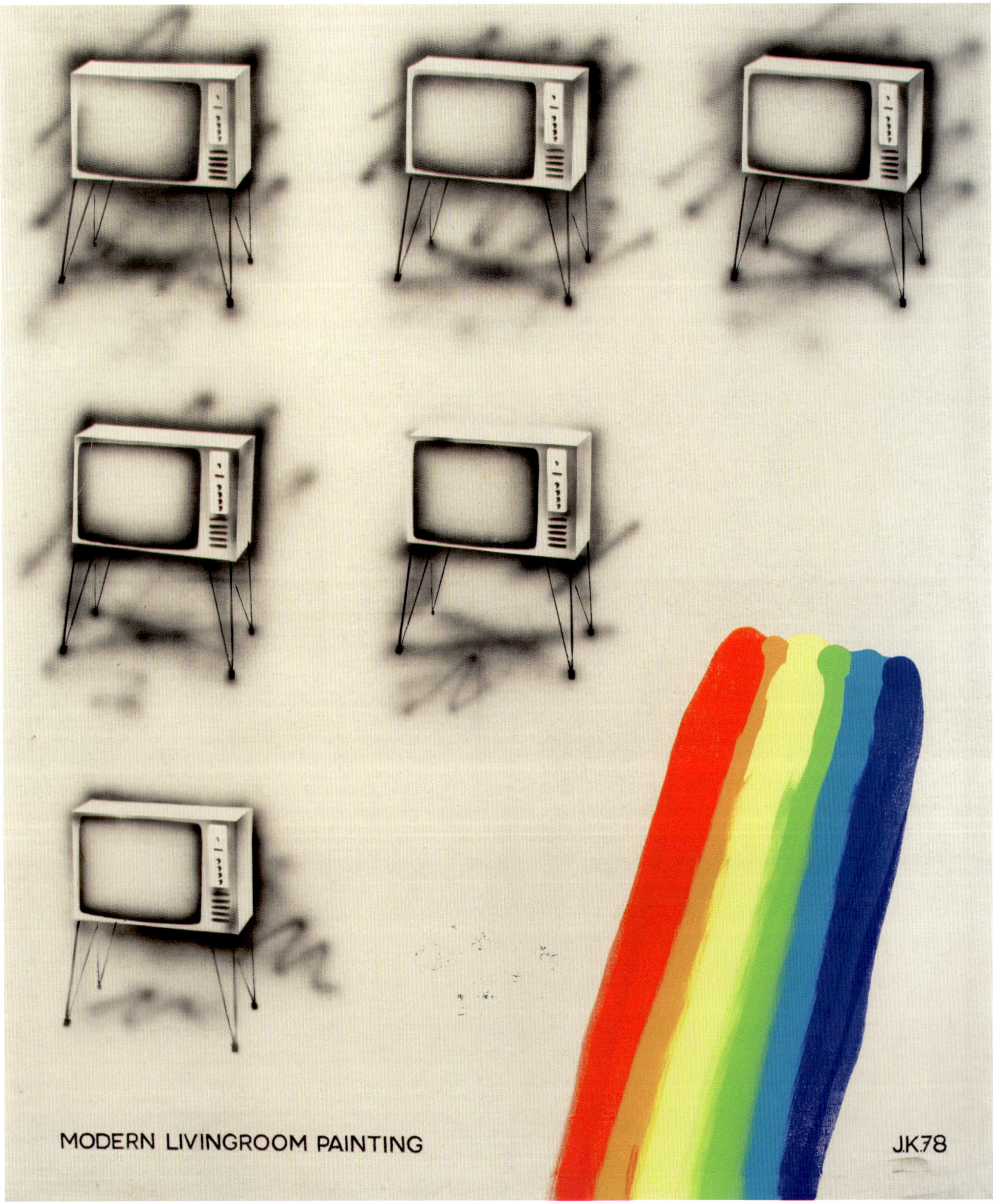

Modern Living Room Painting, 1978
PVA on canvas
183 x 153cm / 22⅛ x 60¼ in

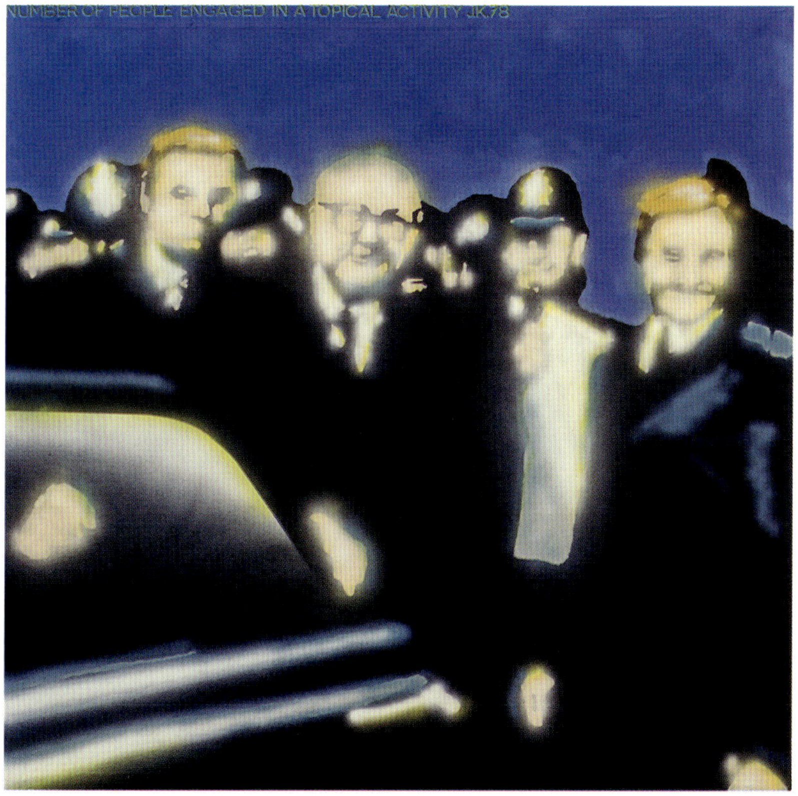

Number of People Engaged in a Topical Activity, 1977
PVA and household paint on canvas
153 x 153 cm / 60¼ x 60¼ in

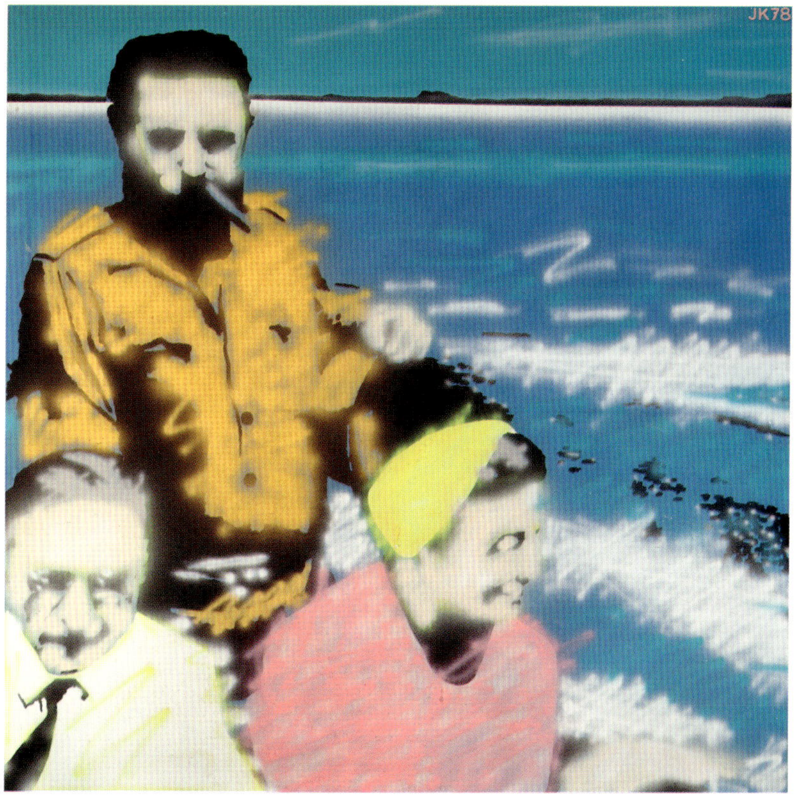

Jean-Paul Sartre & Simone de Beauvoir Speedboating with Fidel Castro, 1978
PVA on canvas
152 x 152 cm / 62¼ x 62¼ in
Private Collection, UK

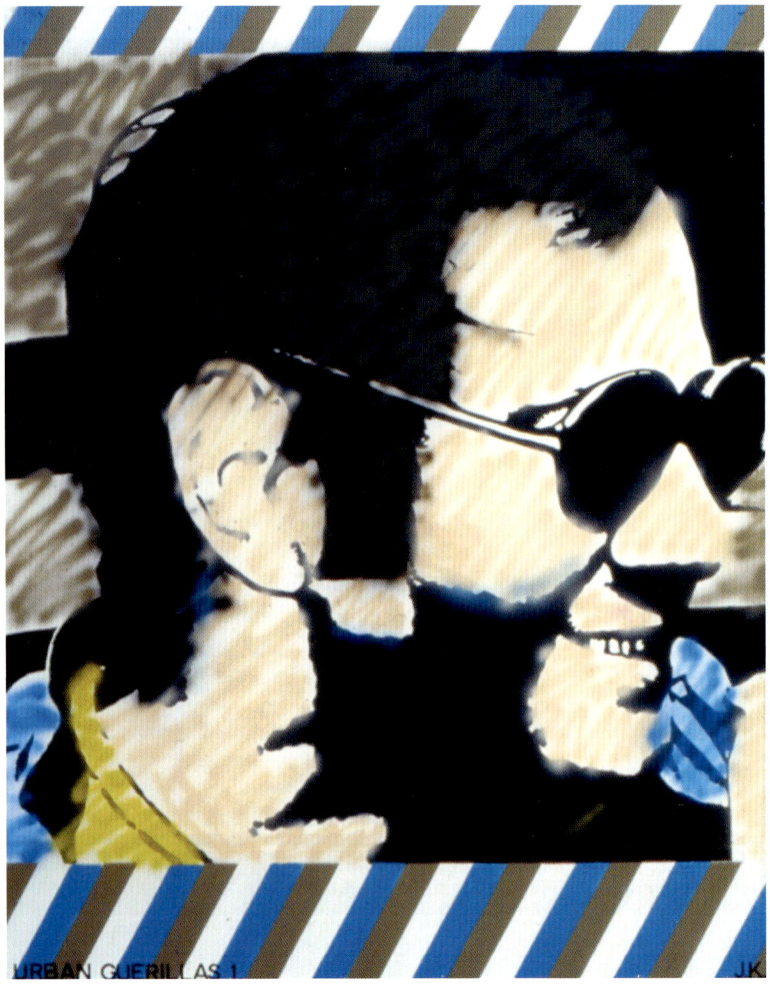

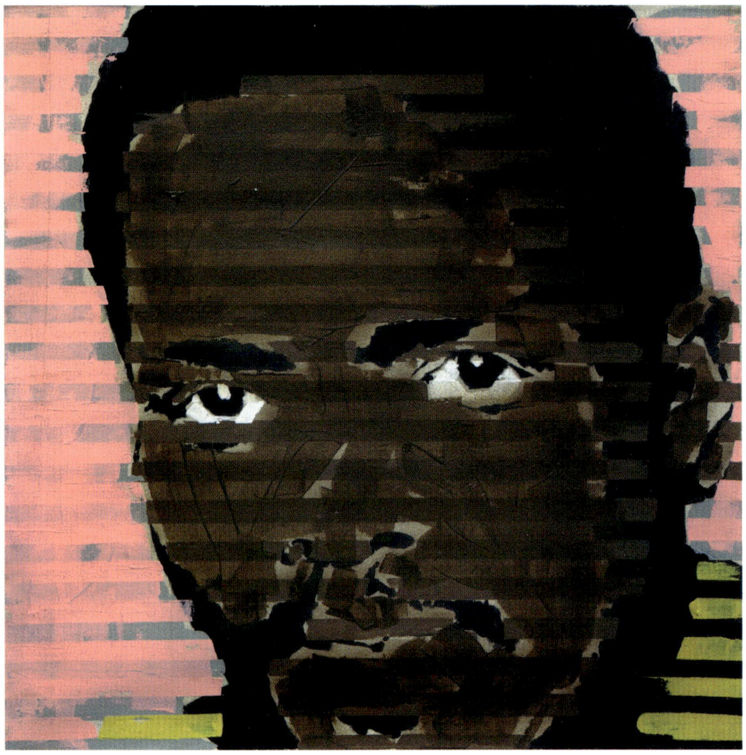

Urban Guerillas 1, 1977
PVA and household paint on canvas
153 x 122 cm / $60\frac{1}{4}$ x 48 in

Steve Biko, 1978
PVA on canvas
60 x 60 cm / $23\frac{5}{8}$ x $23\frac{5}{8}$ in

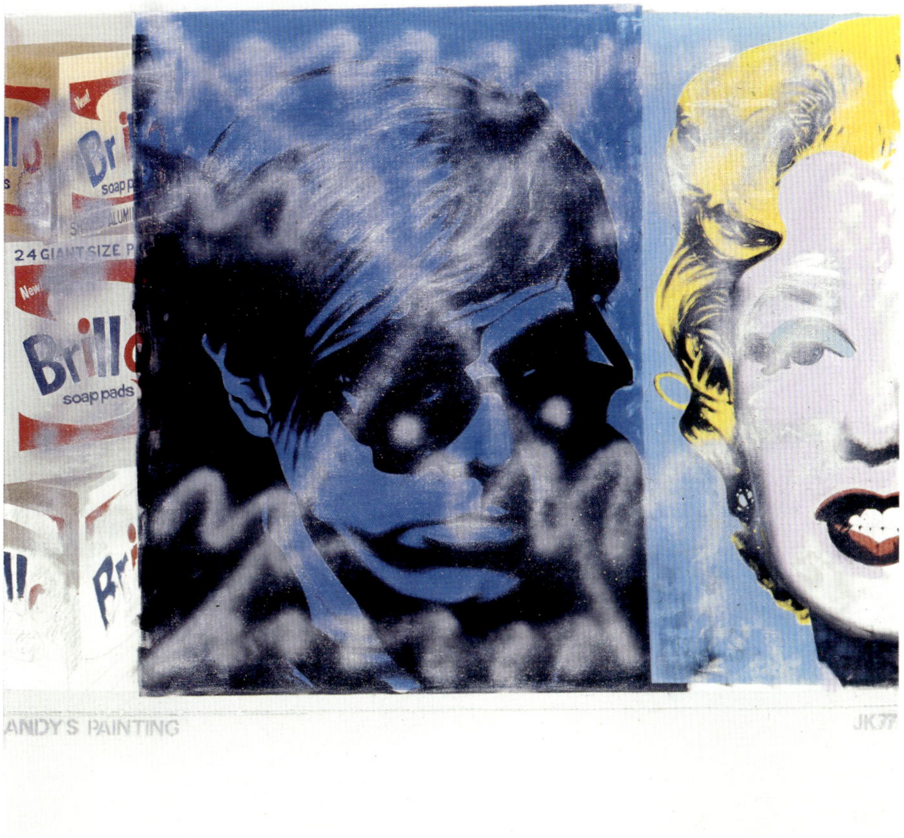

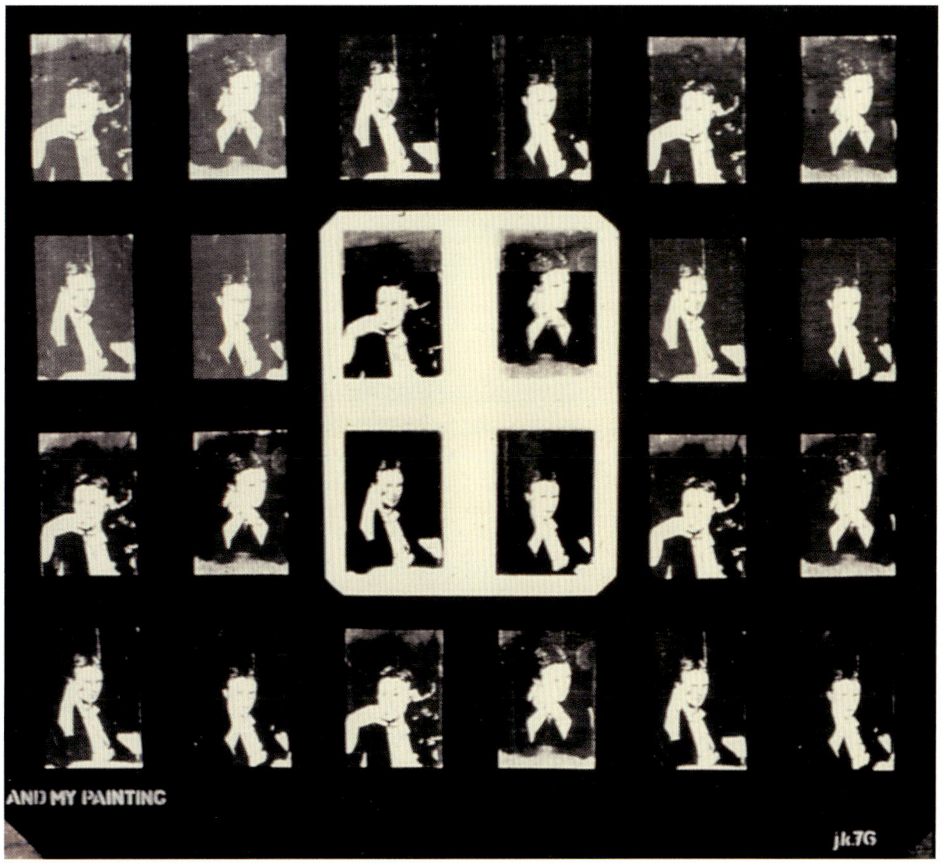

Andy's Painting, 1977
Oil and spray paint on canvas
153 x 153 cm / 60¼ x 60¼

And my Painting . . . , 1976
PVA and silkscreen on canvas
140 x 130 cm / 55⅛ x 51⅛ in

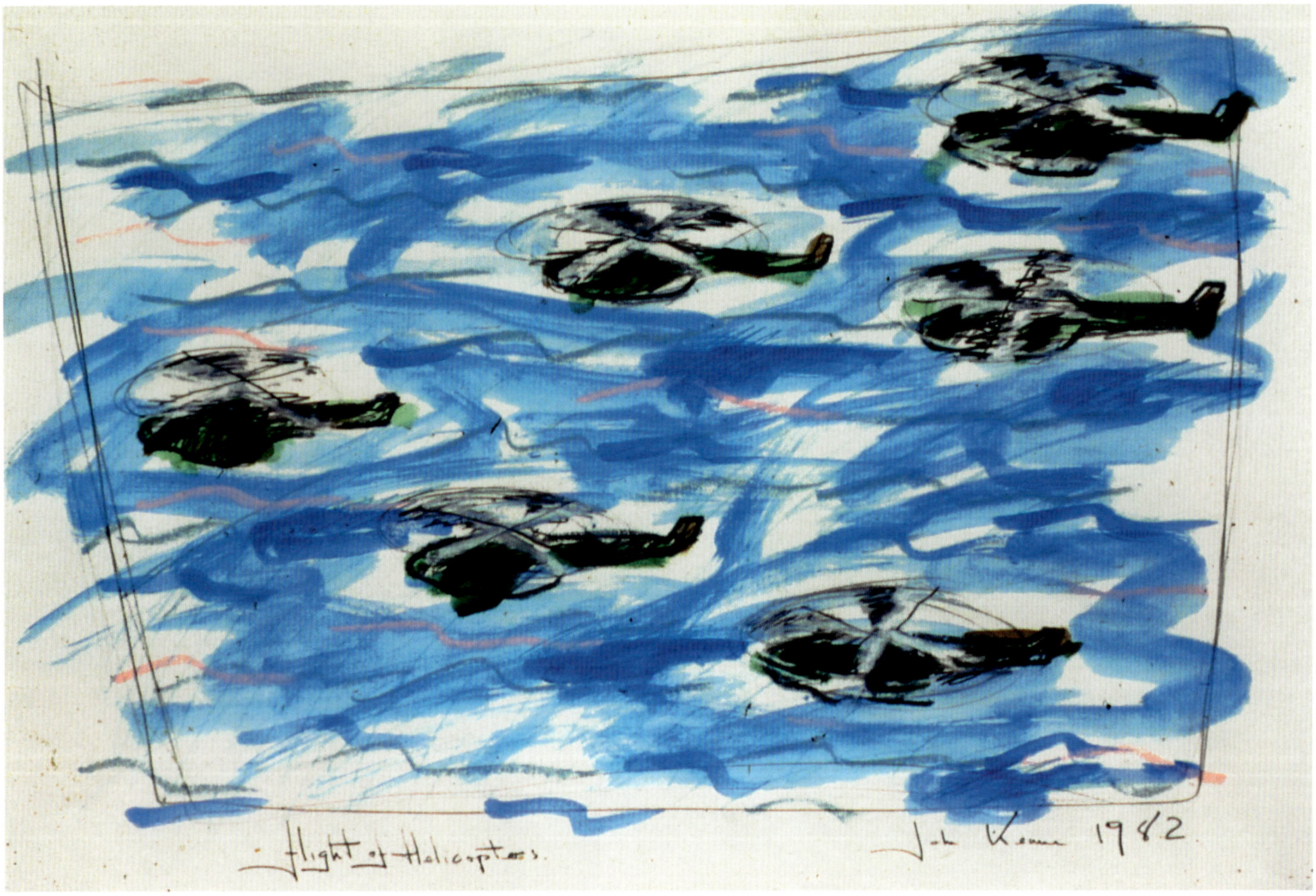

Flight of Helicopters, 1982
Mixed media on paper
56 x 76 cm / 22⅛ x 29 ¾ in
Private Collection, UK

Man with Bomber, 1984
PVA on canvas
183 x 152.5 cm / 72 x 60 in
Collection: David Josephs

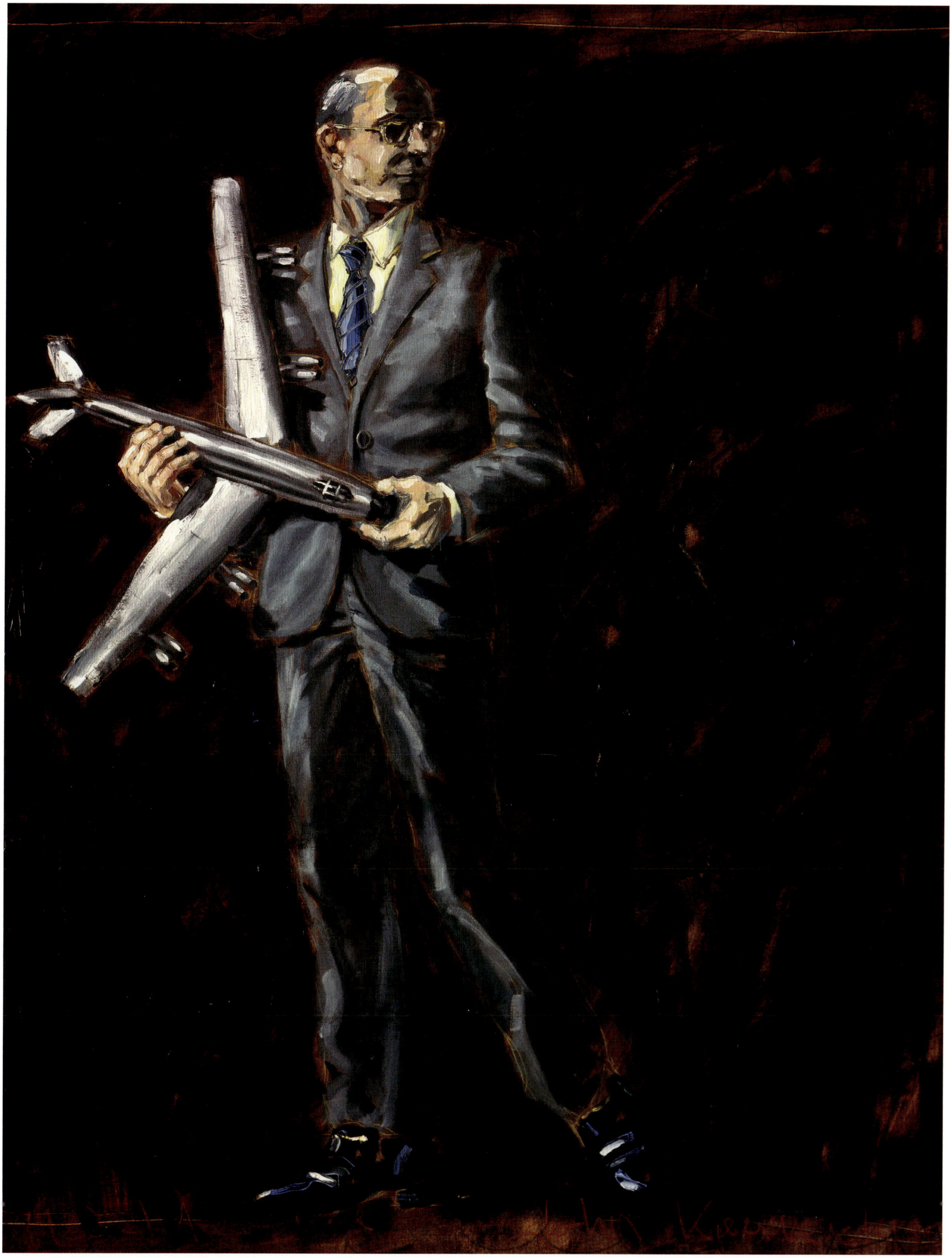

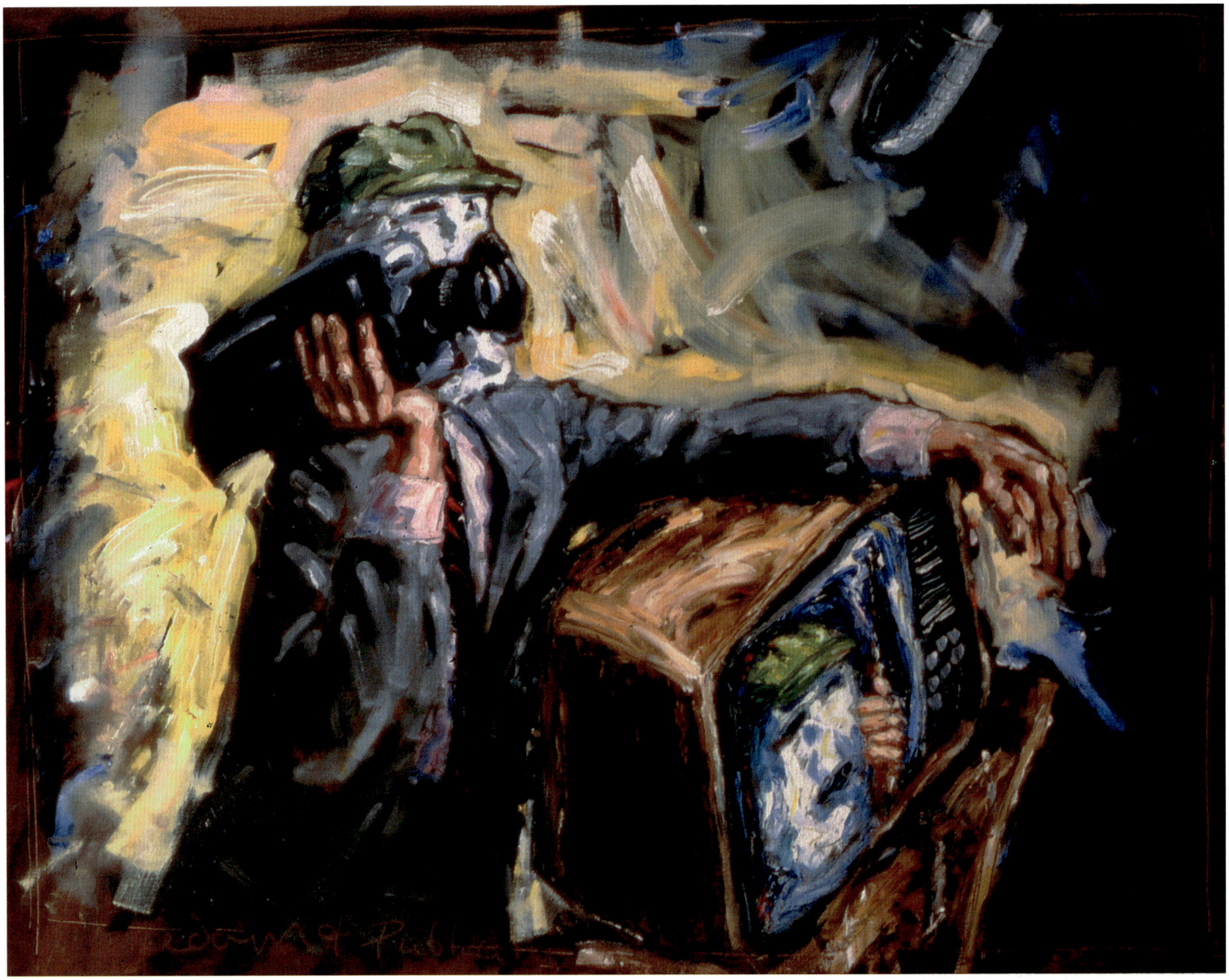

Freedom & Publicity, 1985
Oil on canvas
122 x 152.5 cm / 48⅛ x 60⅛ in
Collection: Nicholas Barker

Romantic Encounter, 1984
PVA on canvas
182 x 152 cm / 71¾ x 59¾ in

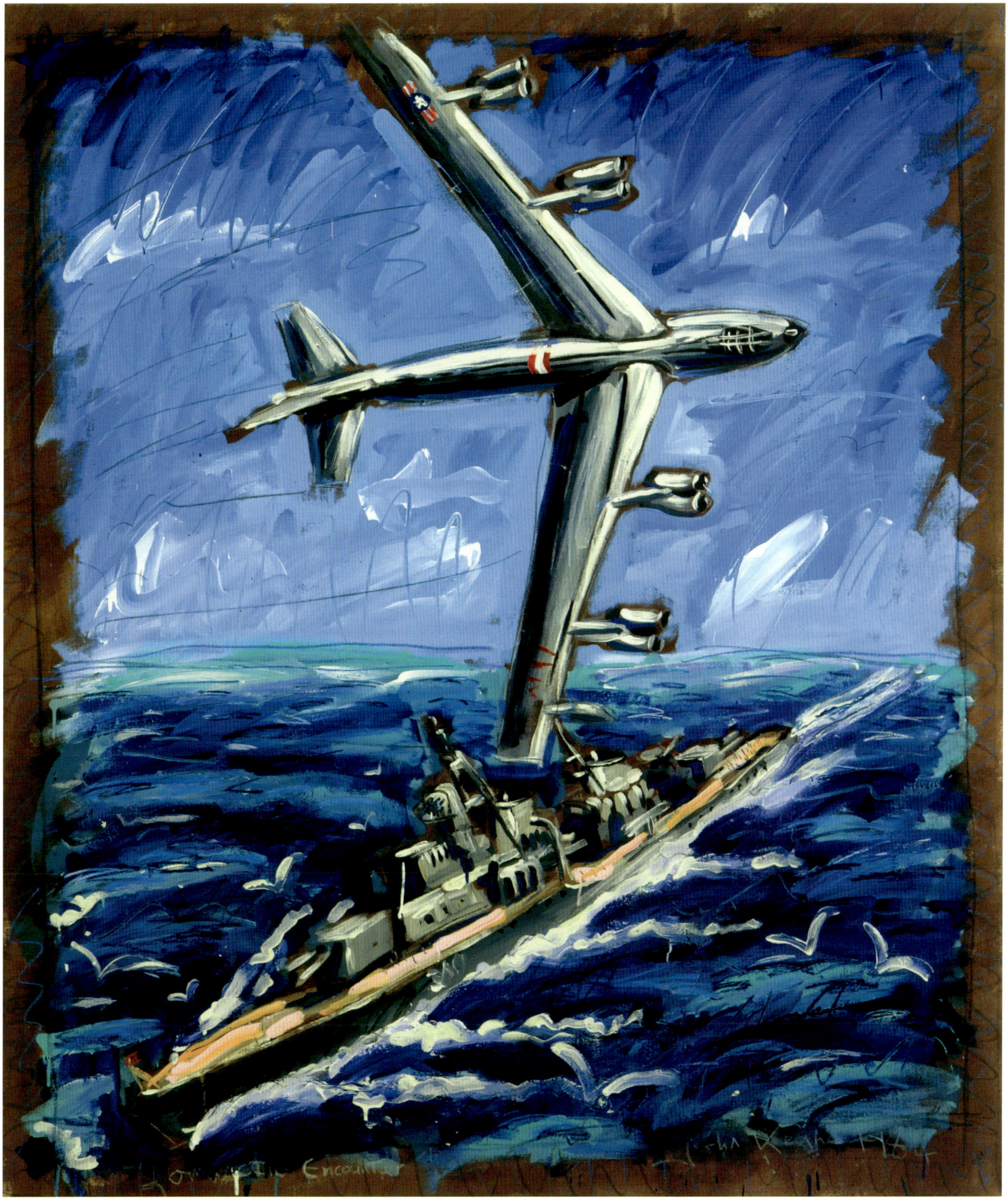

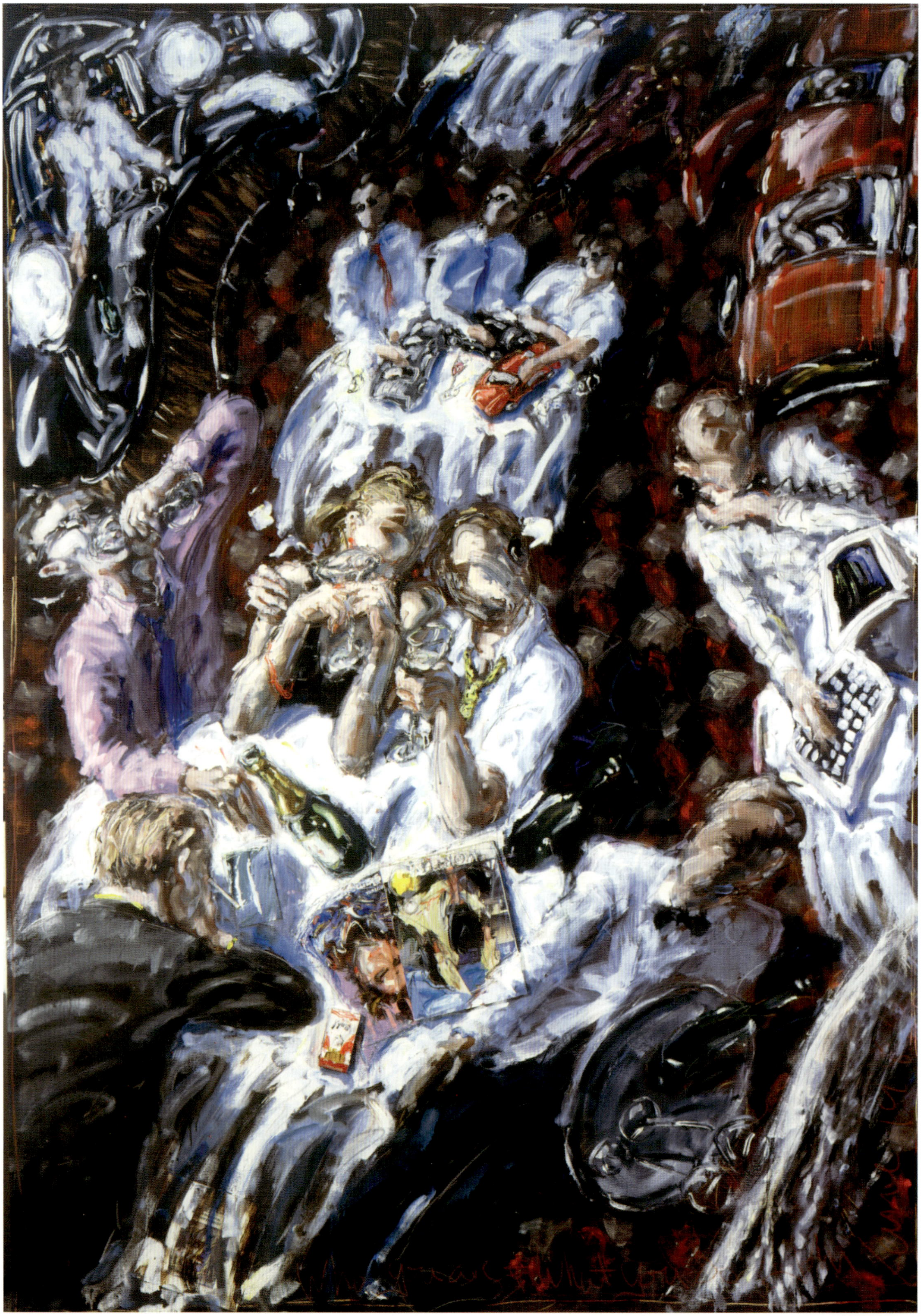

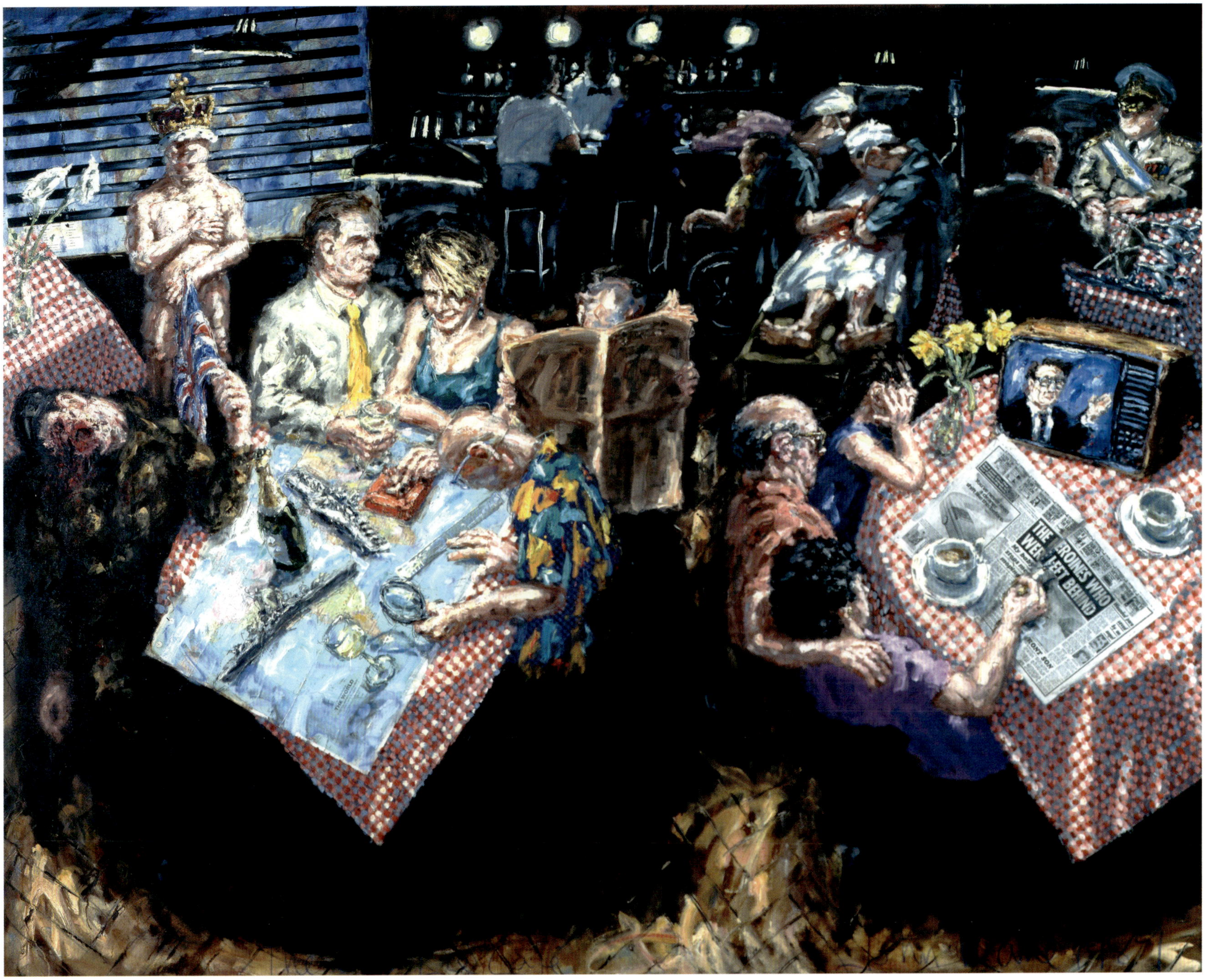

Who you are and what you do, 1986
Oil and collage on canvas
246.5 x 172.5 cm / 97 x 68 in

The Old Lie Cafe, 1989
Oil on canvas
246 x 300 cm / 96¾ x 118 in
Collection: Glasgow Museum

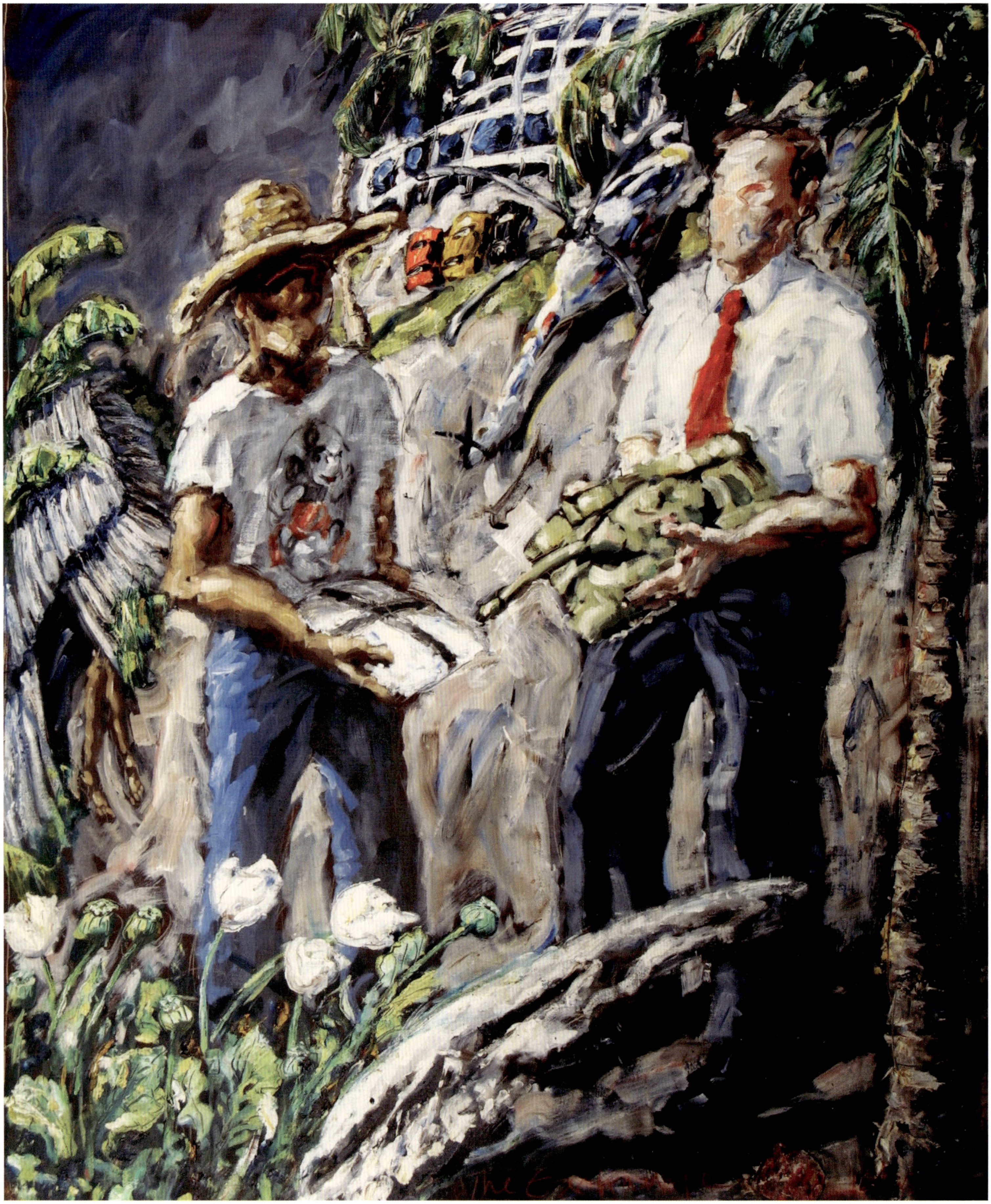

The Exchange, 1986
Oil on canvas
206 x 168 cm / 81 x 66¼ in

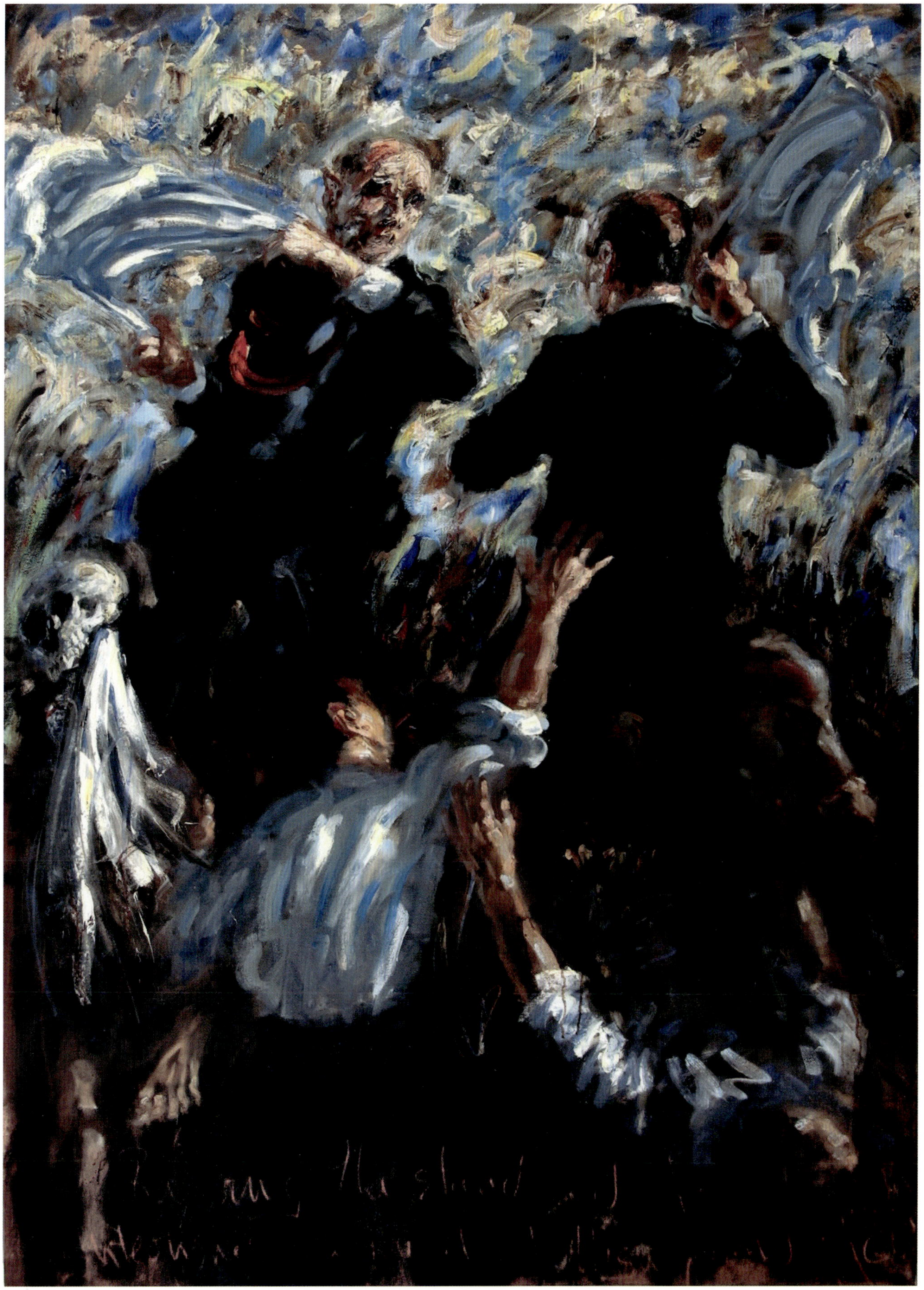

Raising the Standard of Righteousness on the Moral High Ground, 1988
Oil on canvas
214 x 152 cm / 84¼ x 59¾ in
Private Collection, UK

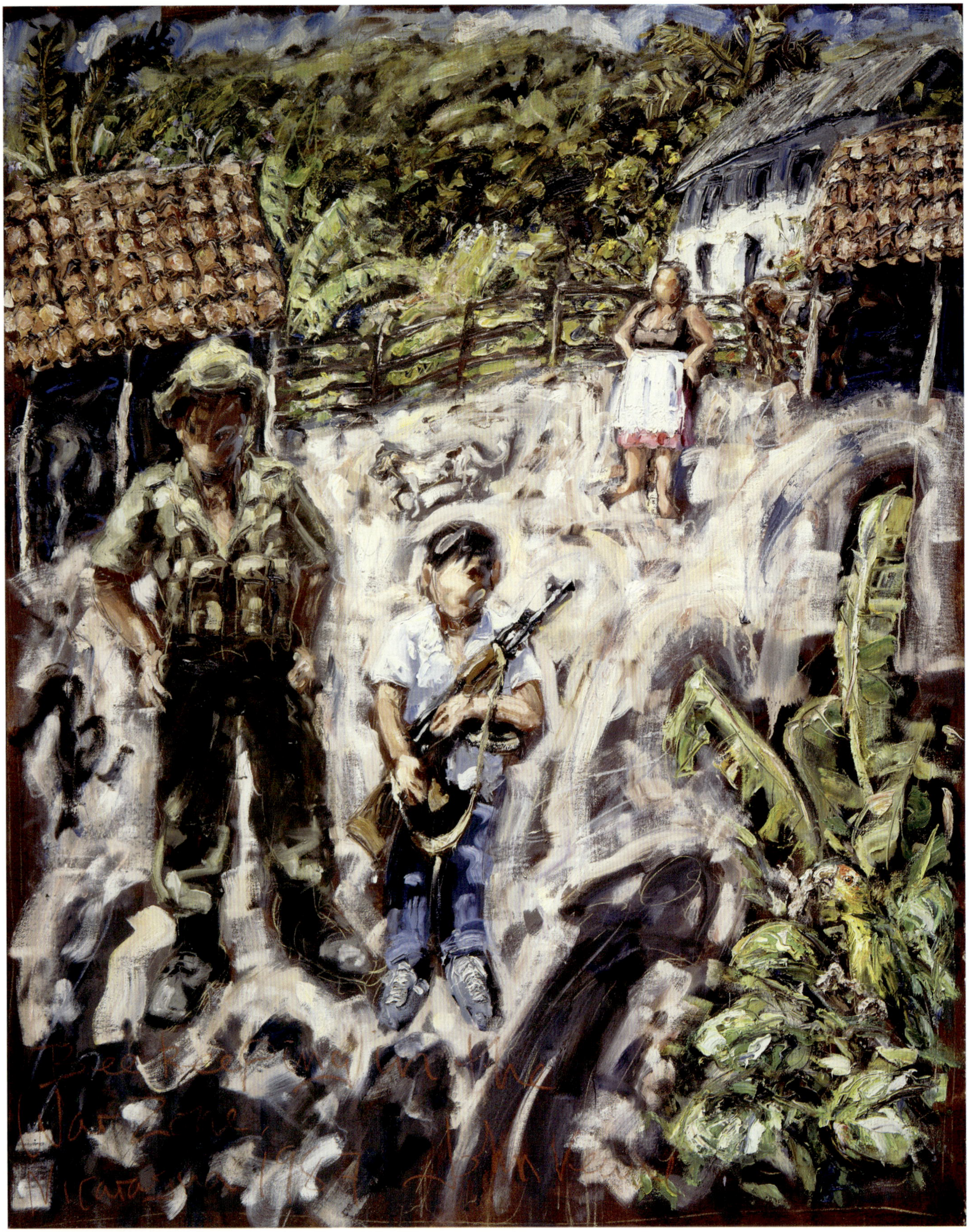

Bee Keeping in the War Zone, 1987
Oil on canvas
195 x 170 cm / 77 x 66⅞ in
Collection: Harris Museum and Art Gallery

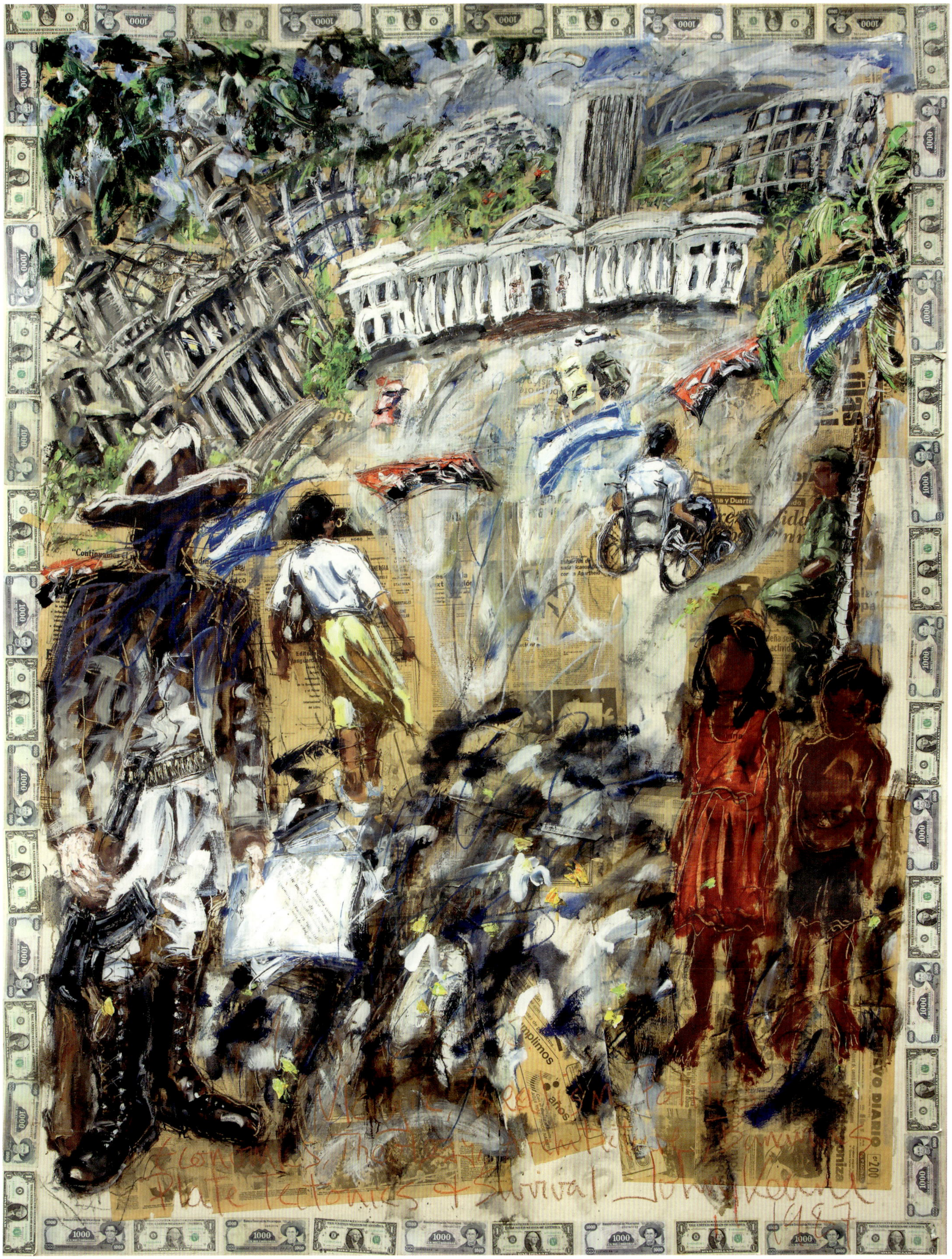

Magic, Realism, Politics, Economics, Theology, Architecture, Bananas, Plate Tectonics and Survival, 1987
Oil and mixed media on canvas
228.6 x 172.7 cm / 90 x 68 in
Collection: Nick Taylor

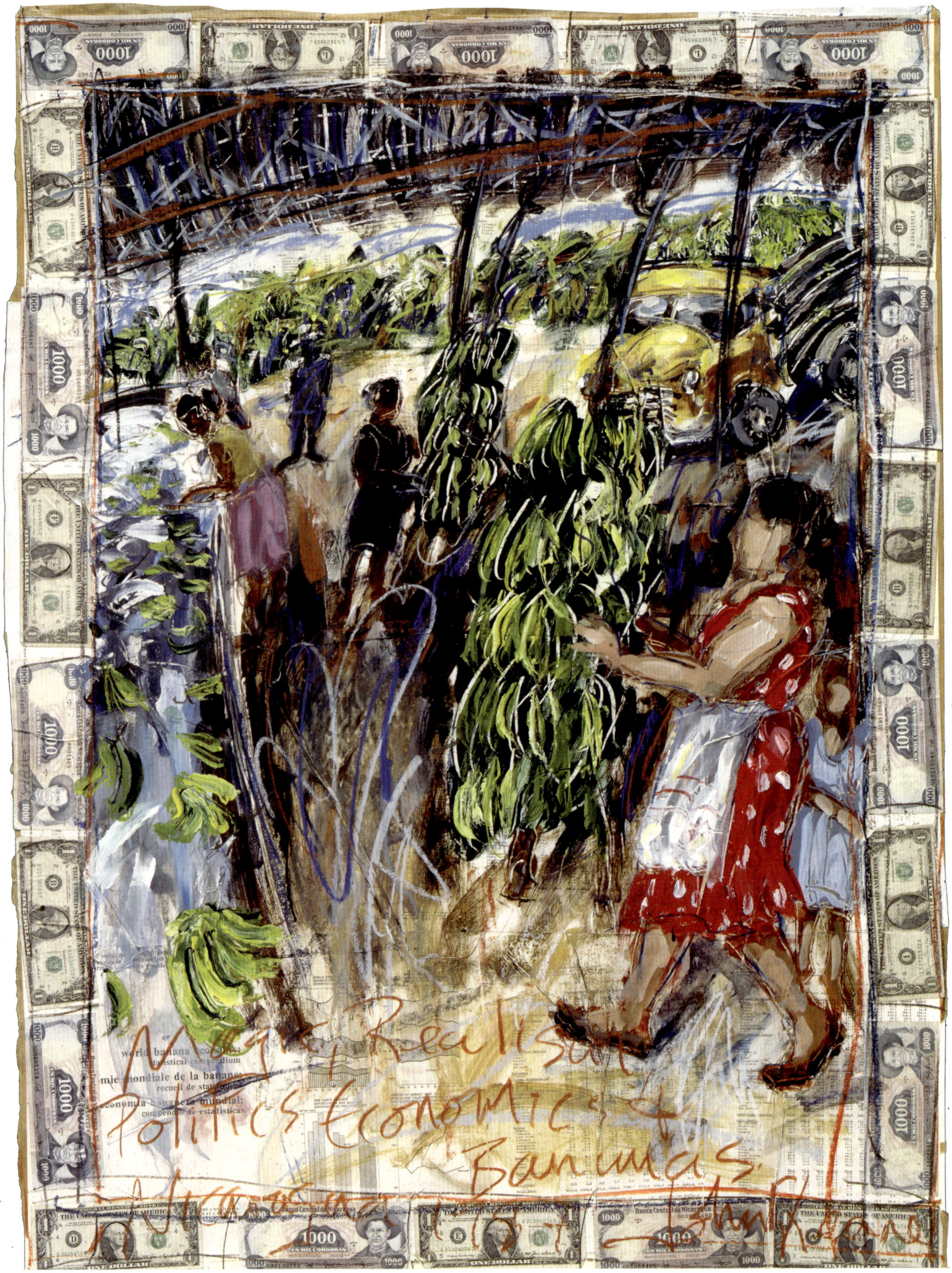

Magic, Realism, Politics, Economics and Bananas, 1987
PVA and mixed media on paper
114 x 83 cm / 45 x 32¾ in
Collection: John Kelly

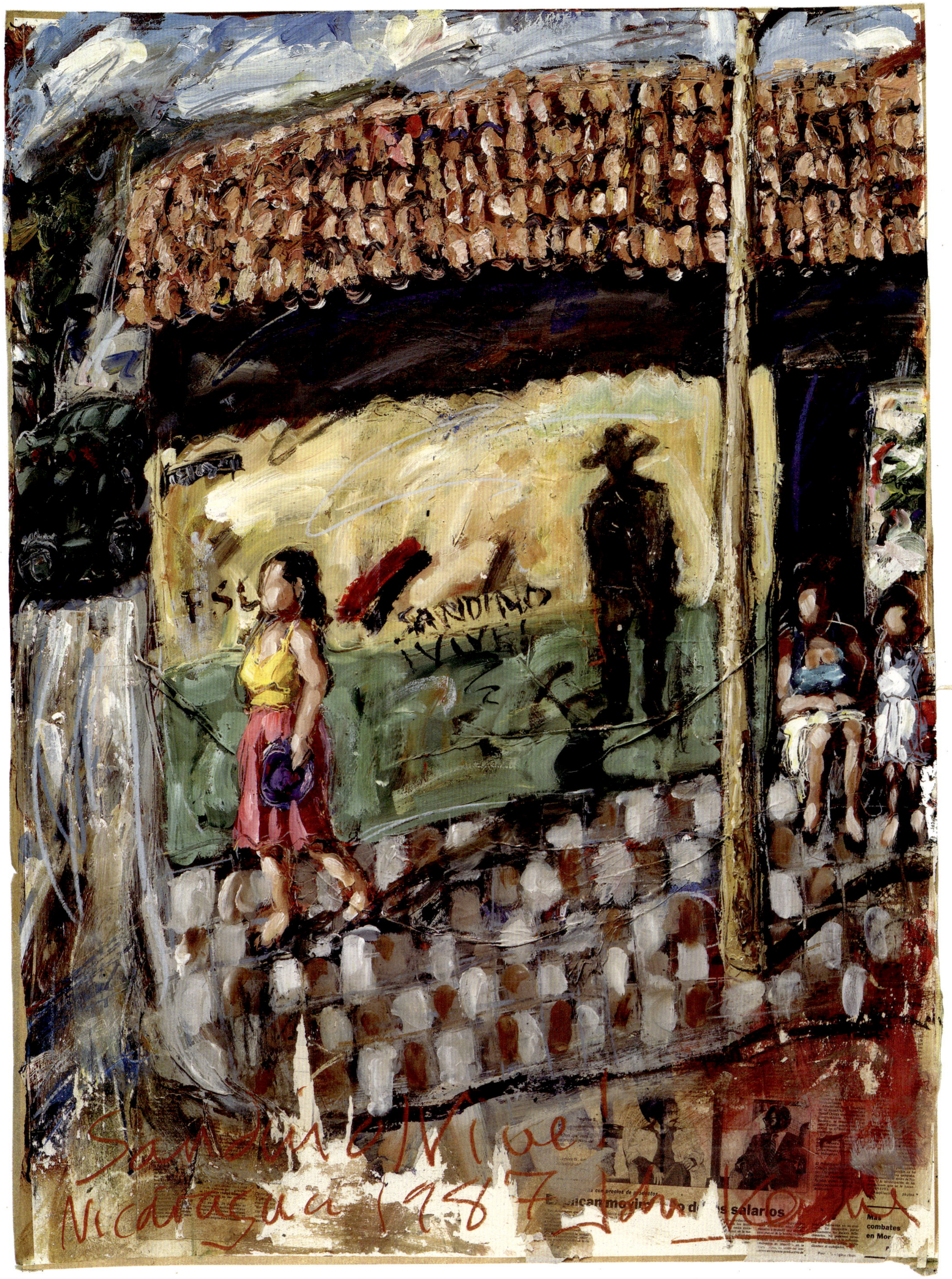

Sandino Vive, 1987
PVA and mixed media on paper
114 x 83 cm / 44⅞ x 32⅝ in
Private Collection, UK

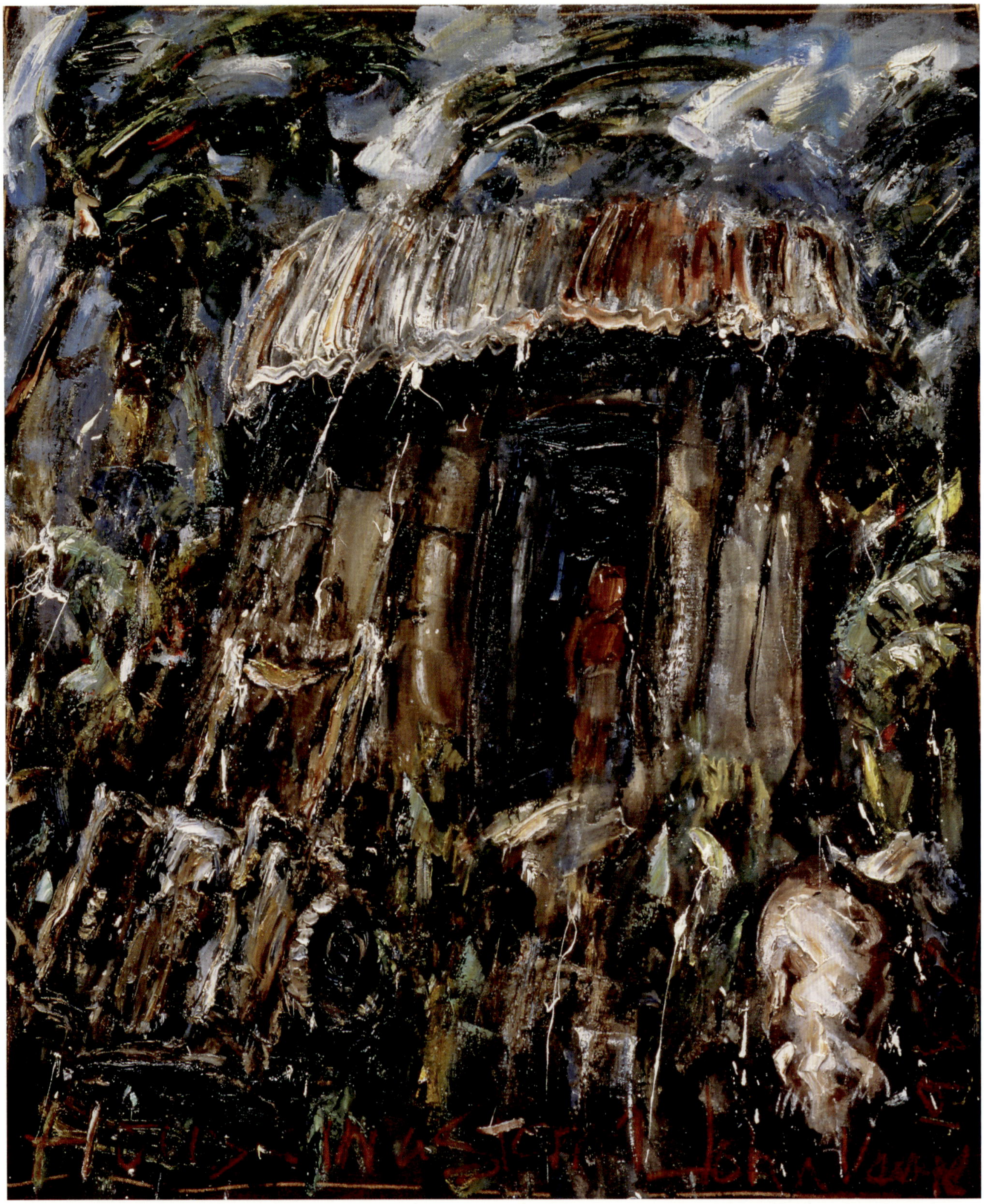

House in a storm, 1987
Oil on canvas
89 x 76 cm / 35 x 30 in
Collection: Angela Flowers

Laser Guided, 1992
Oil on canvas
210 x 173 cm / 82¾ x 68 in

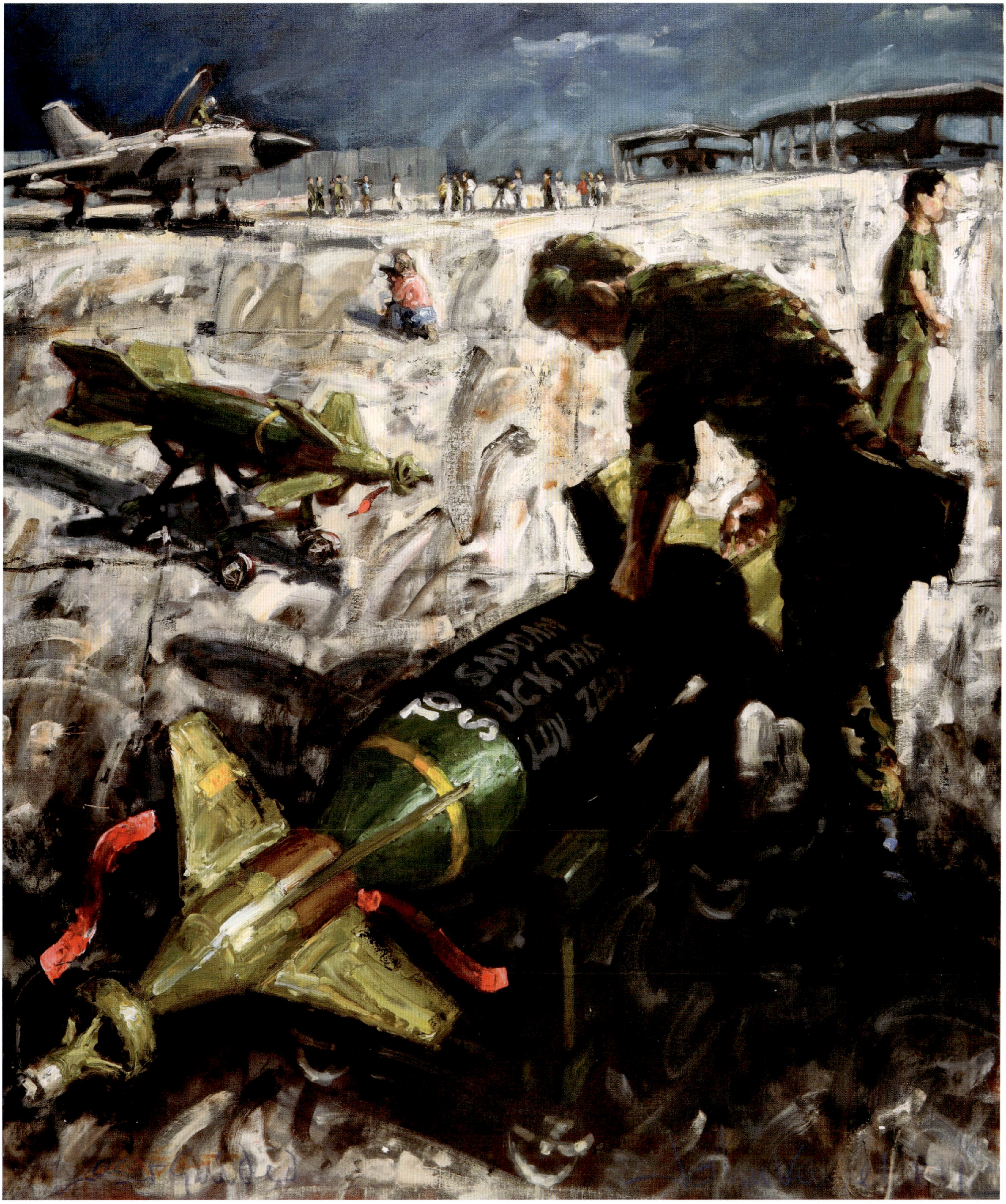
SADDAM
UCK THIS

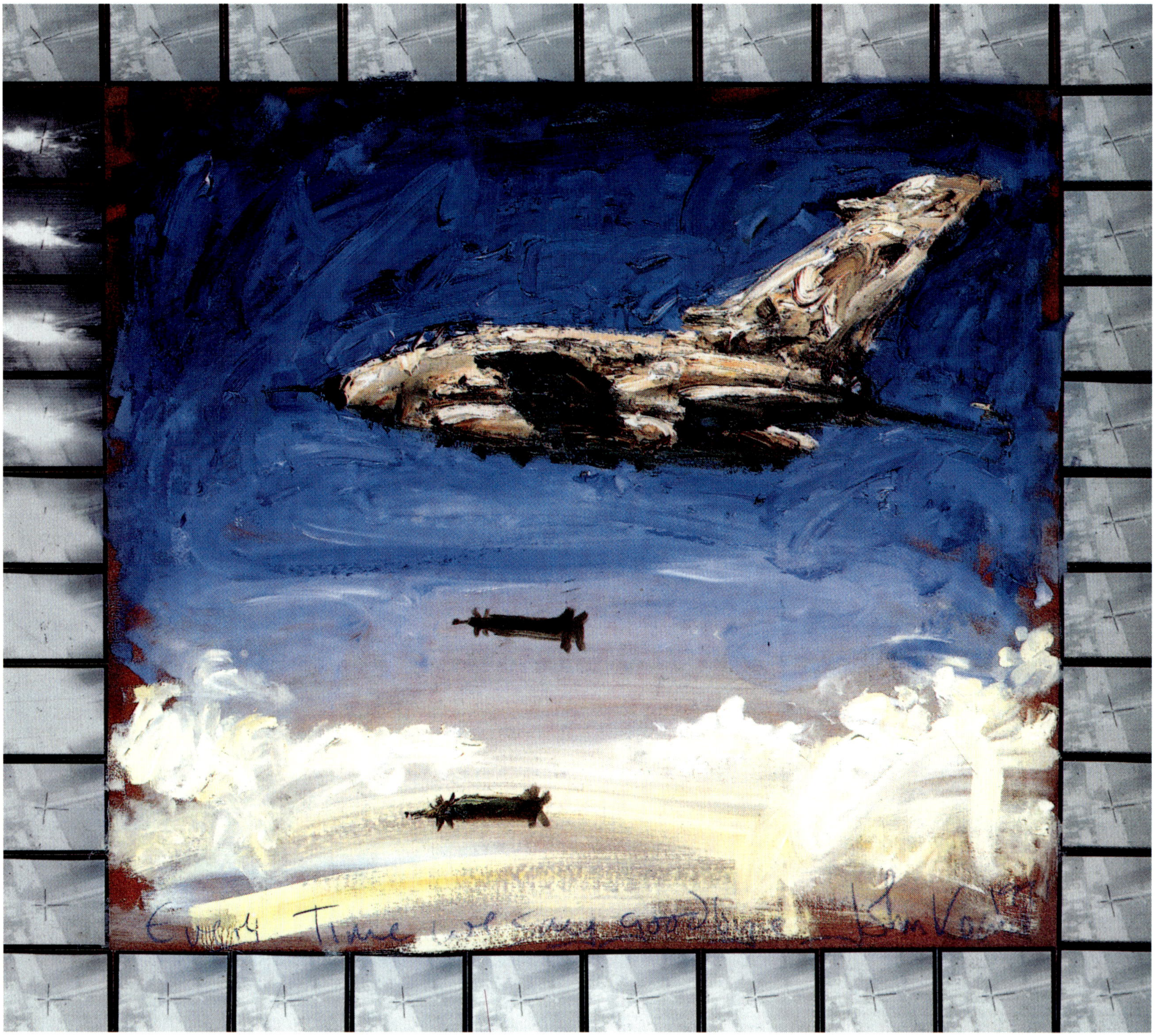

Every Time We Say Goodbye, 1991
Oil and photographs on canvas
128 x 143 cm / 50½ x 56¼ in
Private Collection, UK

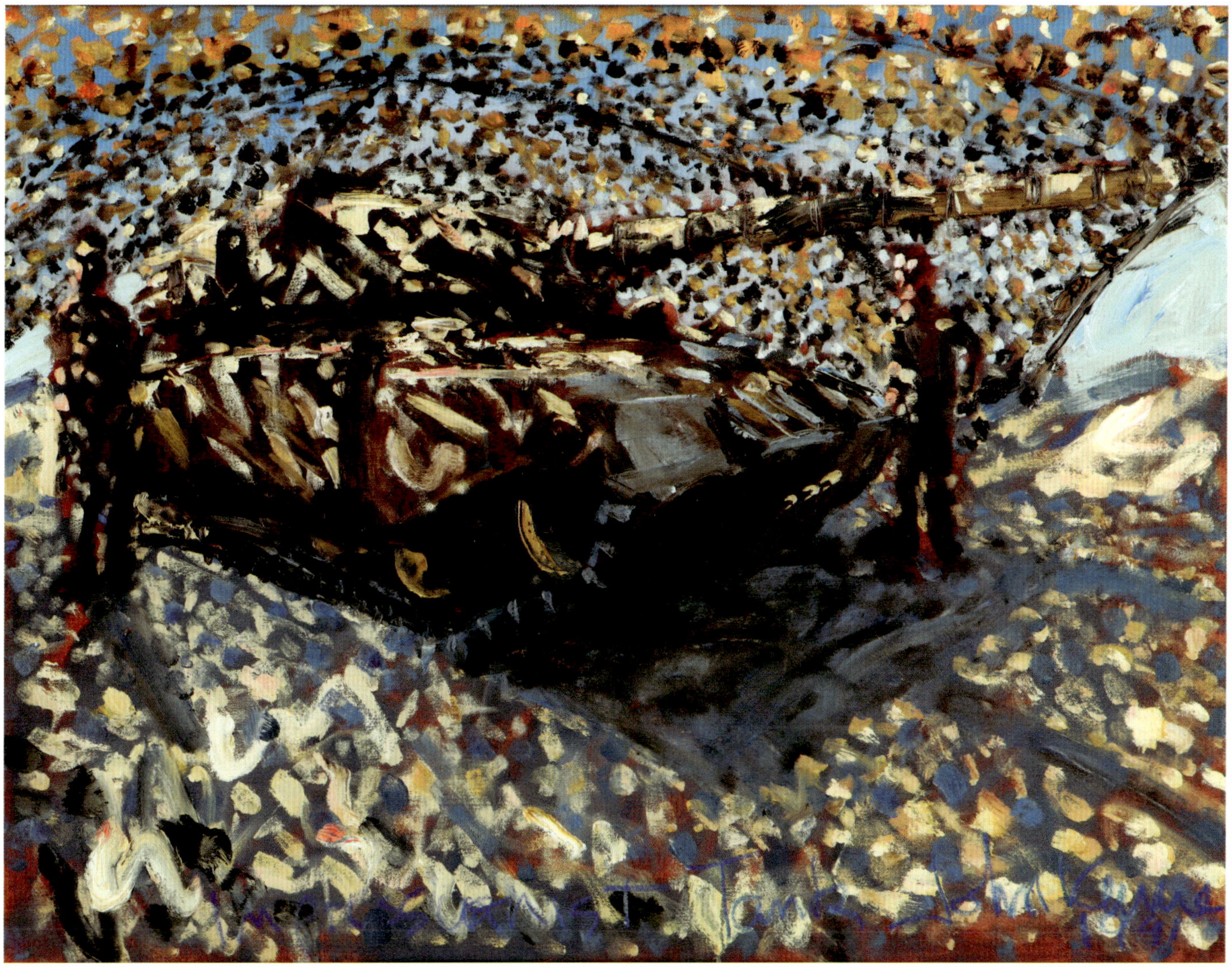

Impressionist Tank, 1991
Oil on canvas
68.5 x 87.5 cm / 27 x 34½ in

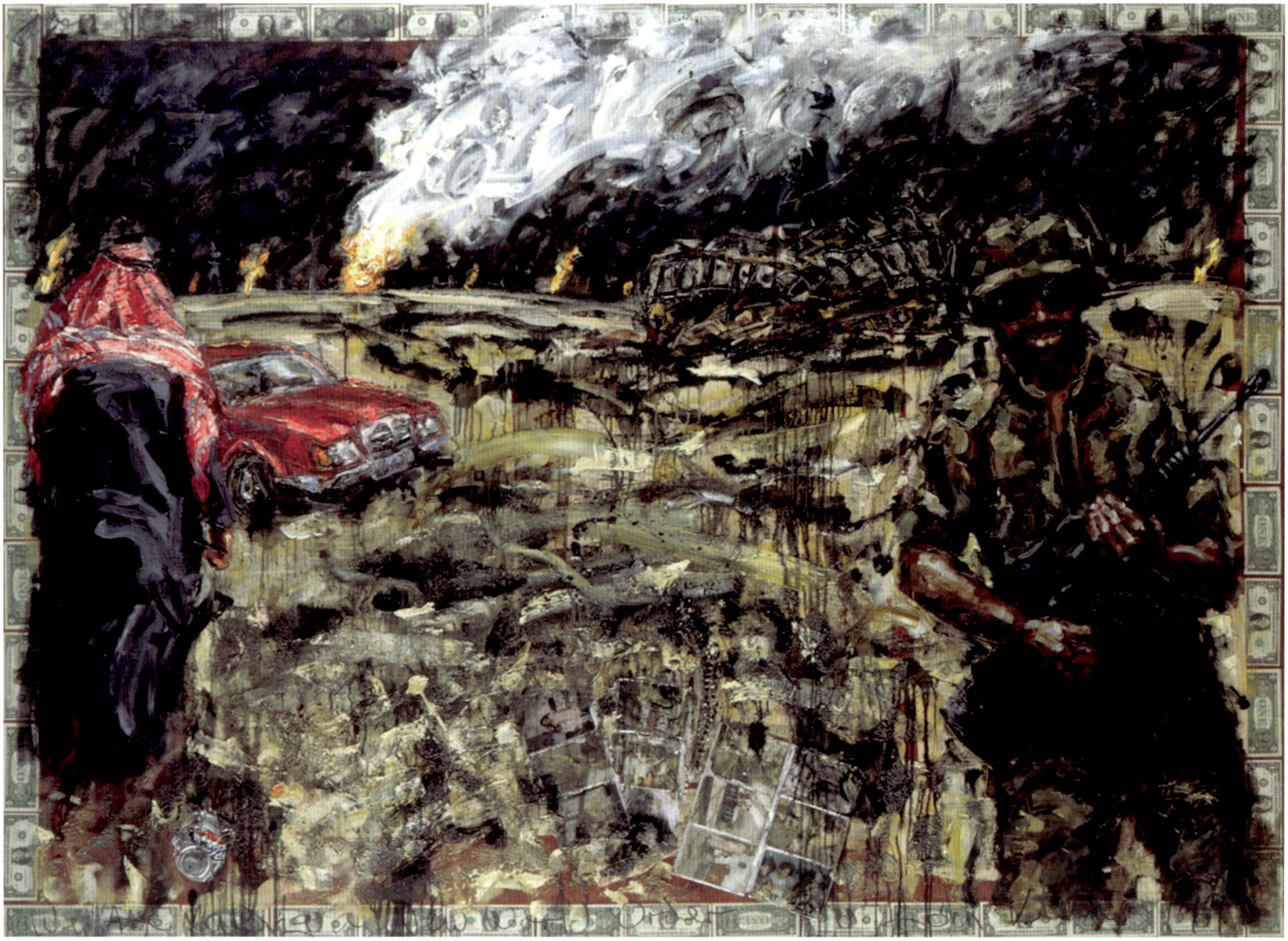

We are Making a New World Order, 1991
Oil, collage and mixed media on canvas
170.5 x 233 cm / 67¼ x 91¾ in
Private Collection, UK

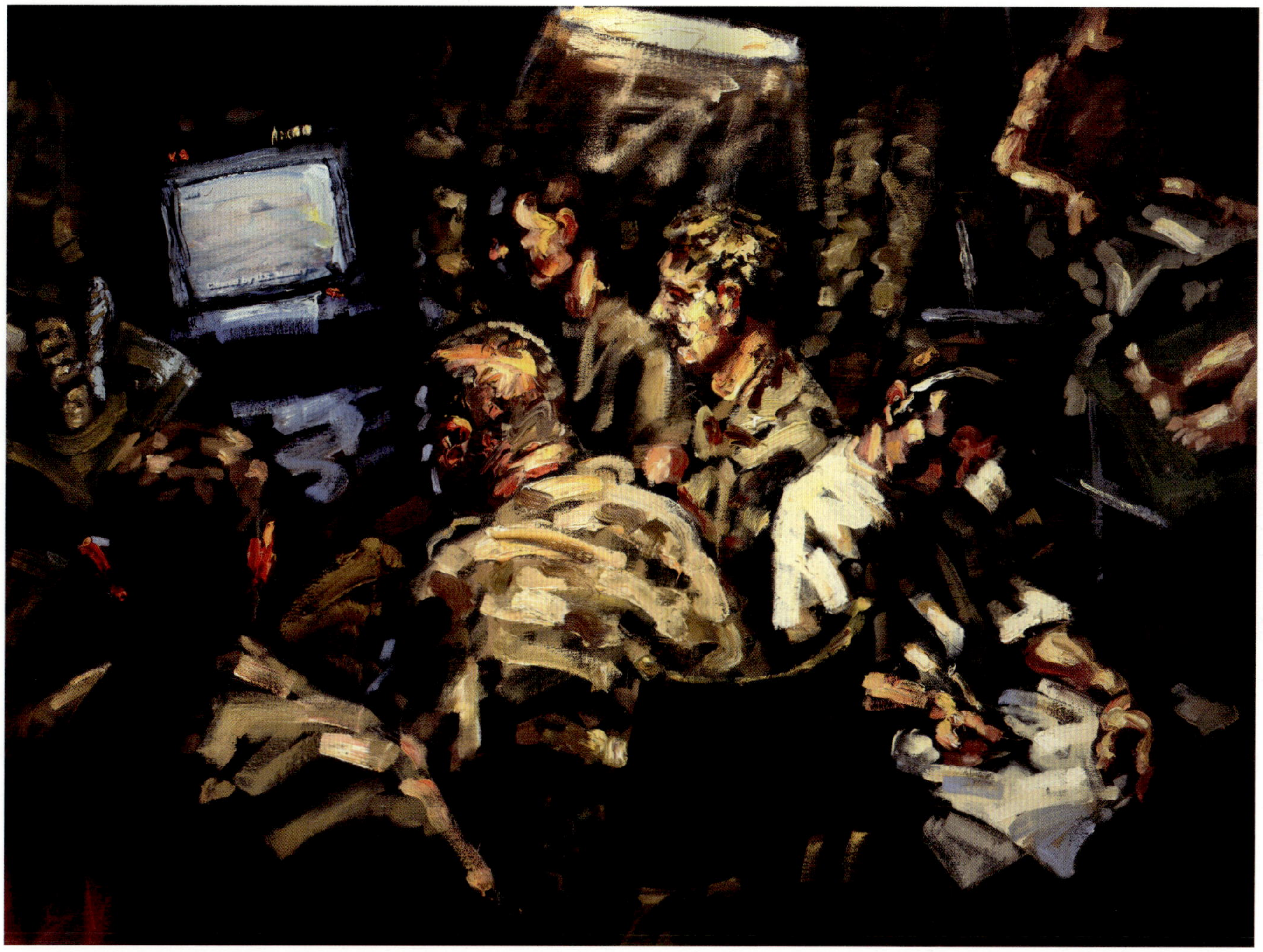

Blackout, 1991
Oil and collage on canvas
71 x 94 cm / 28 x 37 in
Private Collection, UK

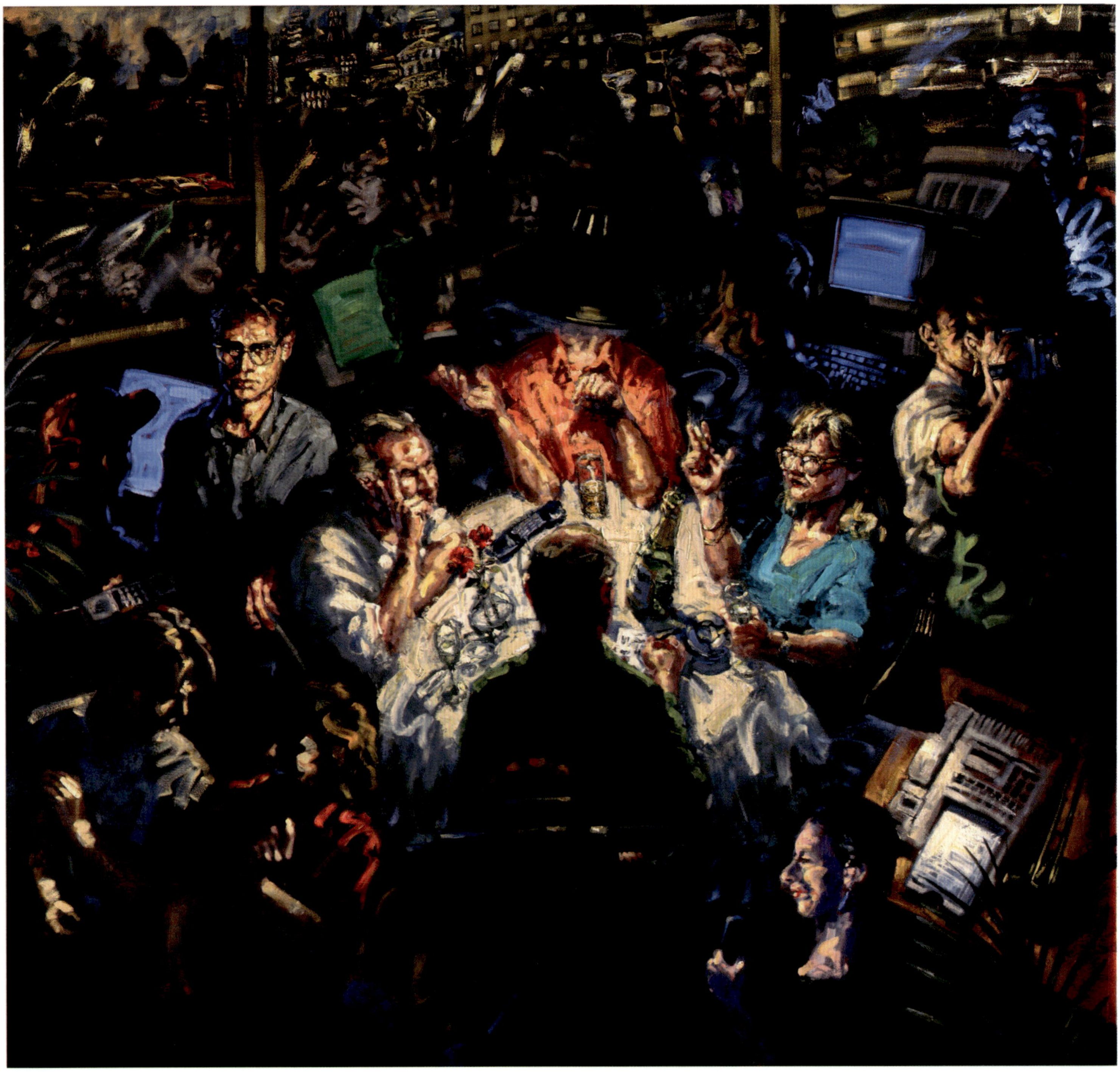

Supping with the Devil, 1993
Oil on canvas
211 x 244 cm / 83 x 96 in

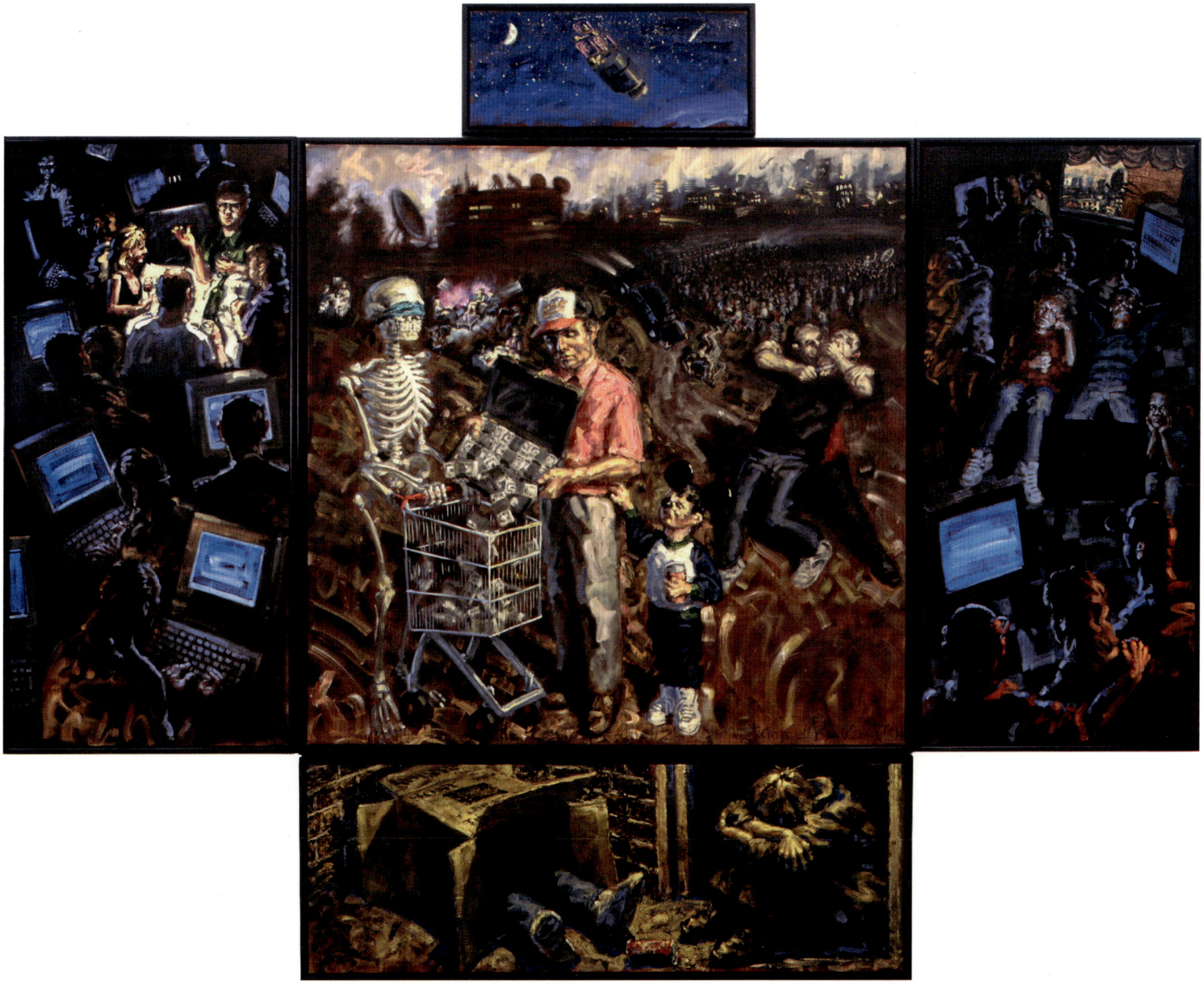

The Struggle for the Control of the Television Station, Five panels, 1992
Oil on canvas
330 x 407 cm / 129¾ x 160 in

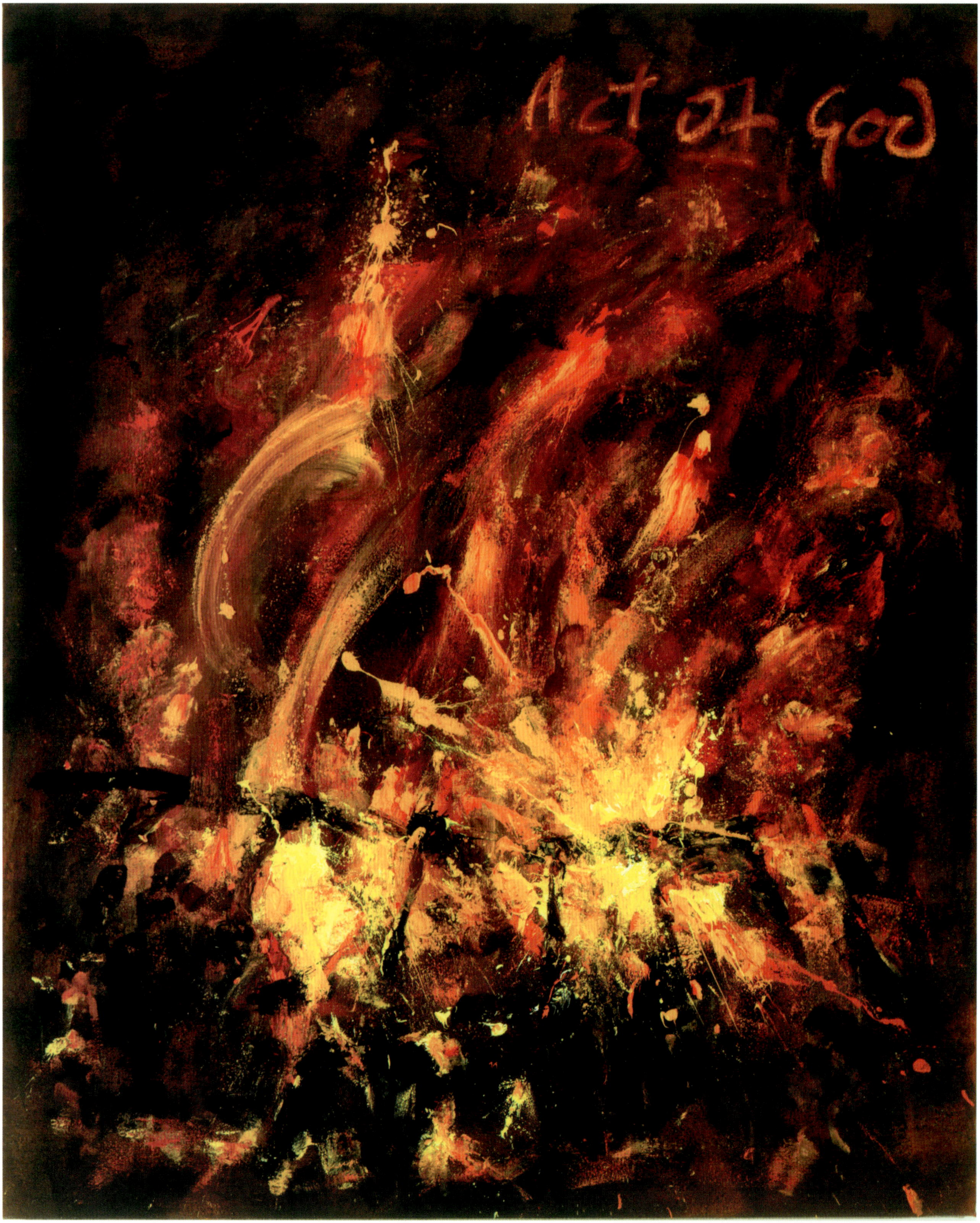
Act of God

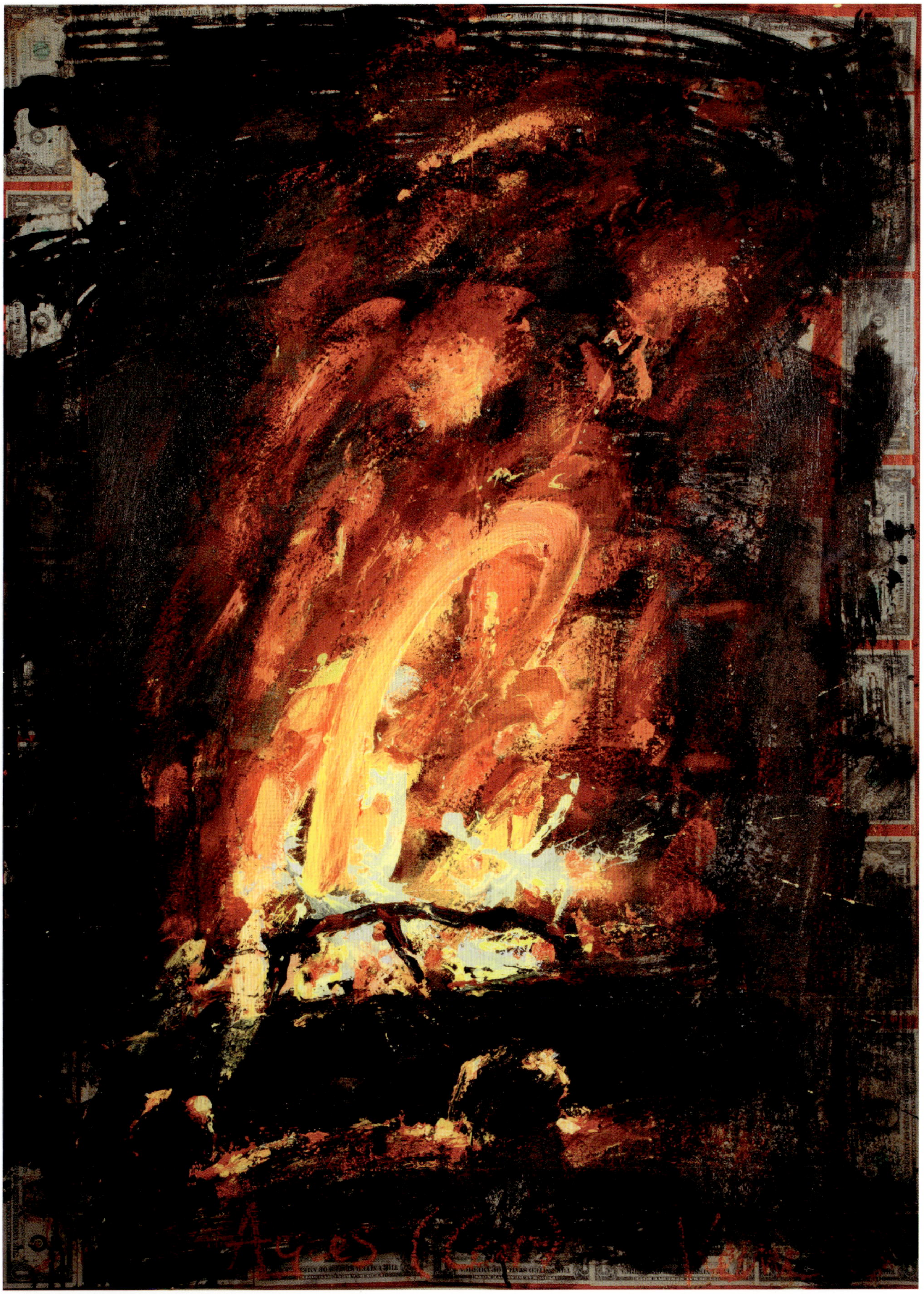

Untitled (Act of God), 1994
Oil and sand on canvas
159 x 127 cm / 62½ x 50 in

Dark Ages (Car), 1993
PVA, sand and collage on paper
114 x 89 cm / 45 x 35 in

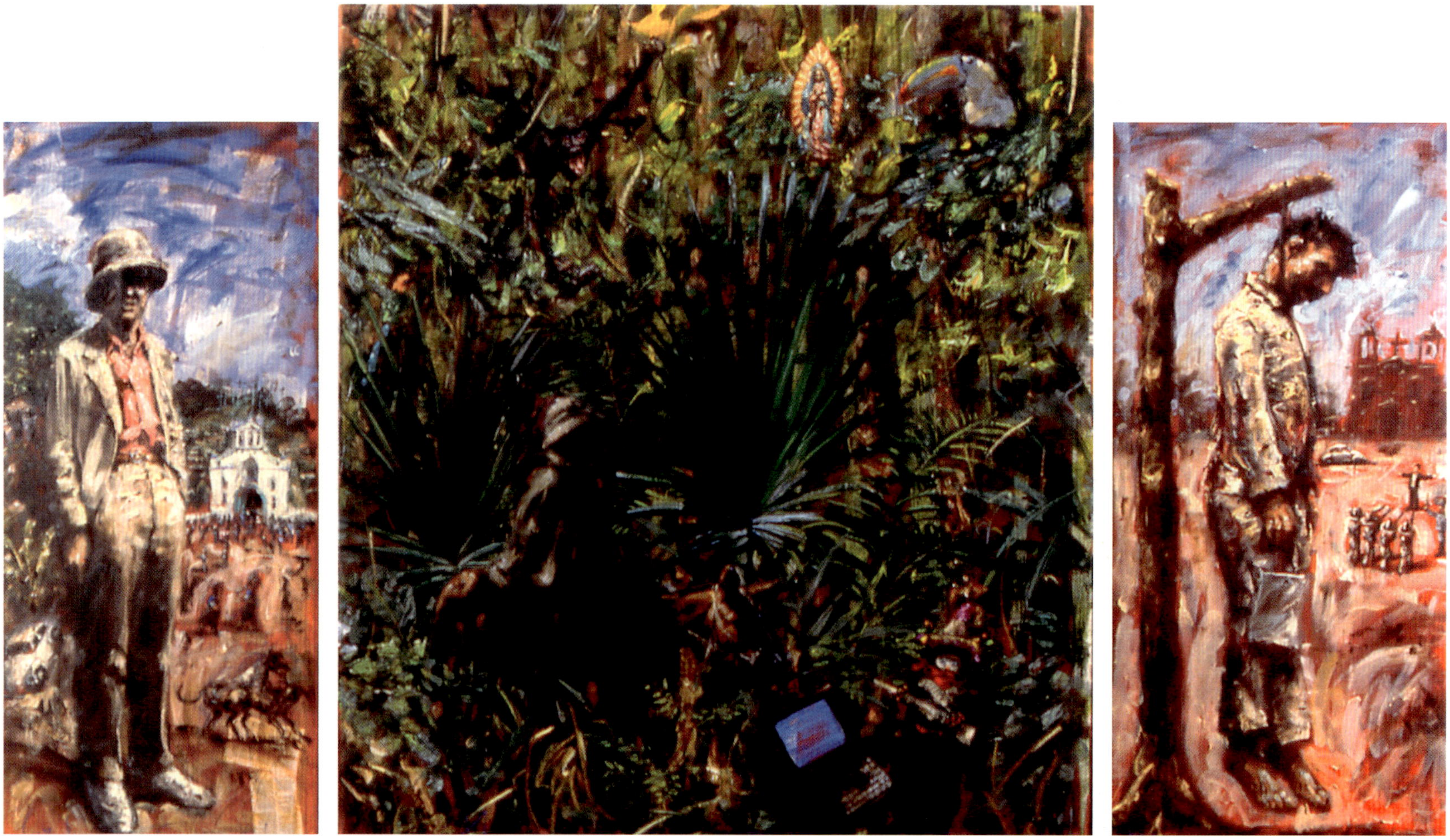

Graham Greene & the Jungle of Human Dilemma (Triptych), 1995
Oil and collage on canvas
239.5 x 414 cm / 94 x 163 in
Private Collection, UK

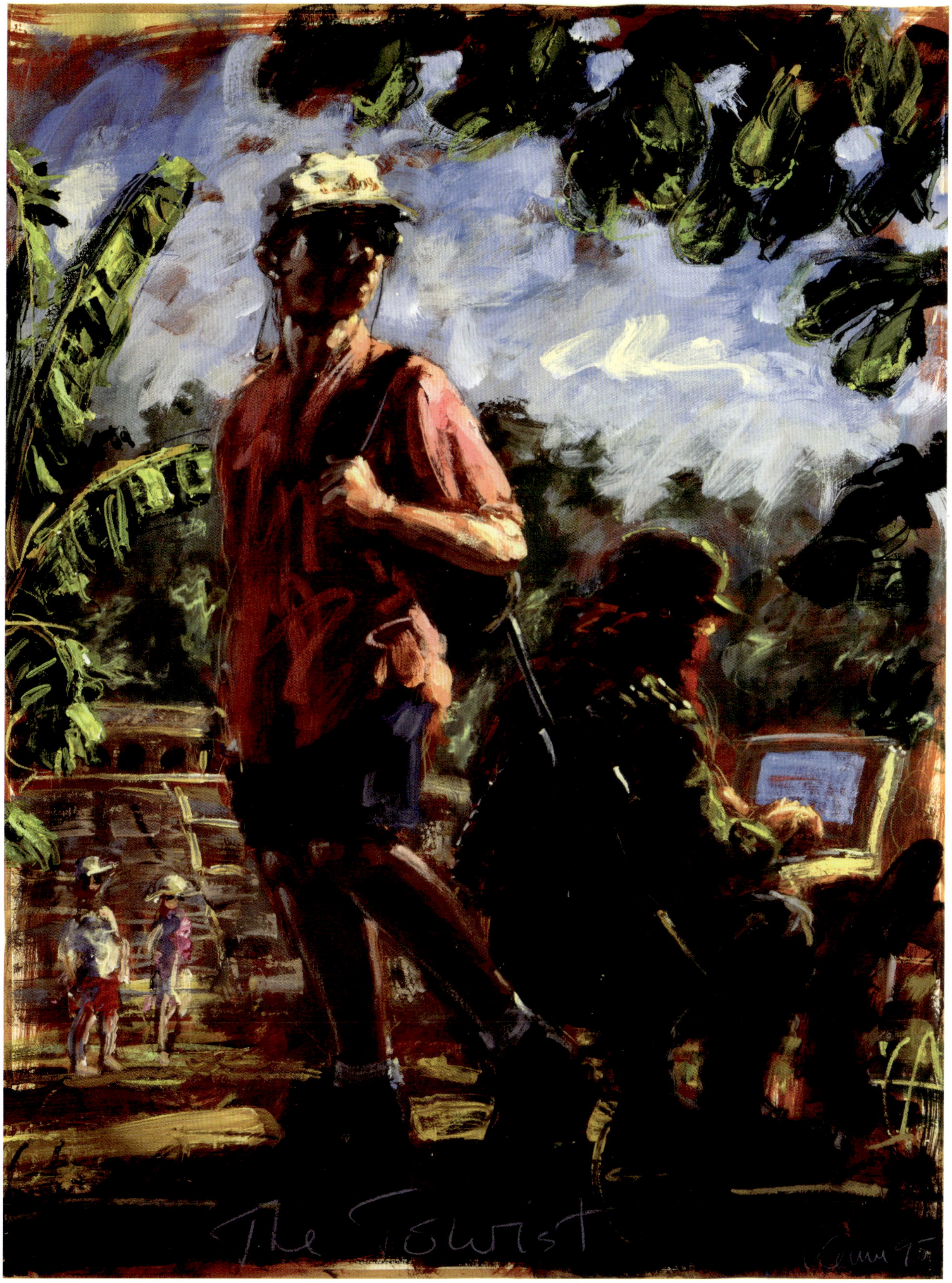

The Tourist, 1995
PVA and mixed media on paper
115 x 85 cm / 45¼ x 33½ in
Collection: Mary Allen

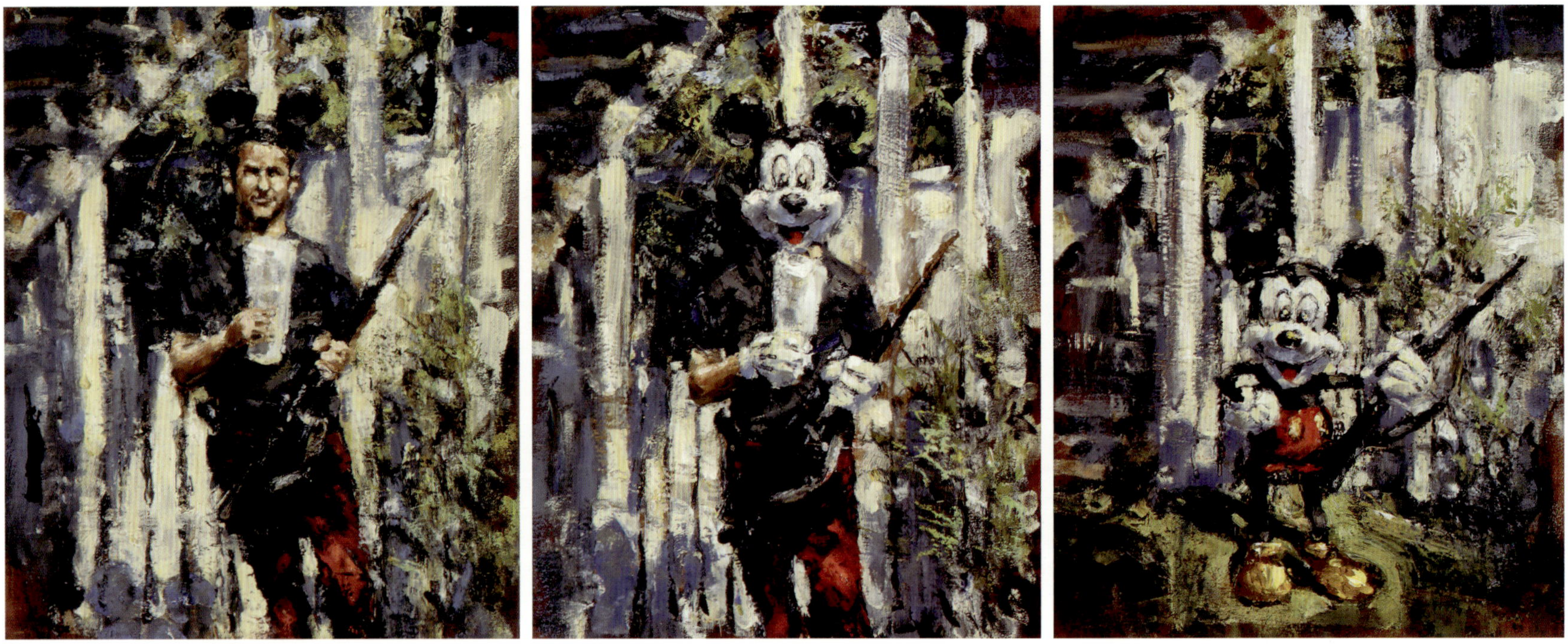

The Painter Never Lies, Three panels, 1997
Oil on canvas,
50 x 40 cm / 19¾ x 15¾ in
Collection: Paul Lyon-Maris

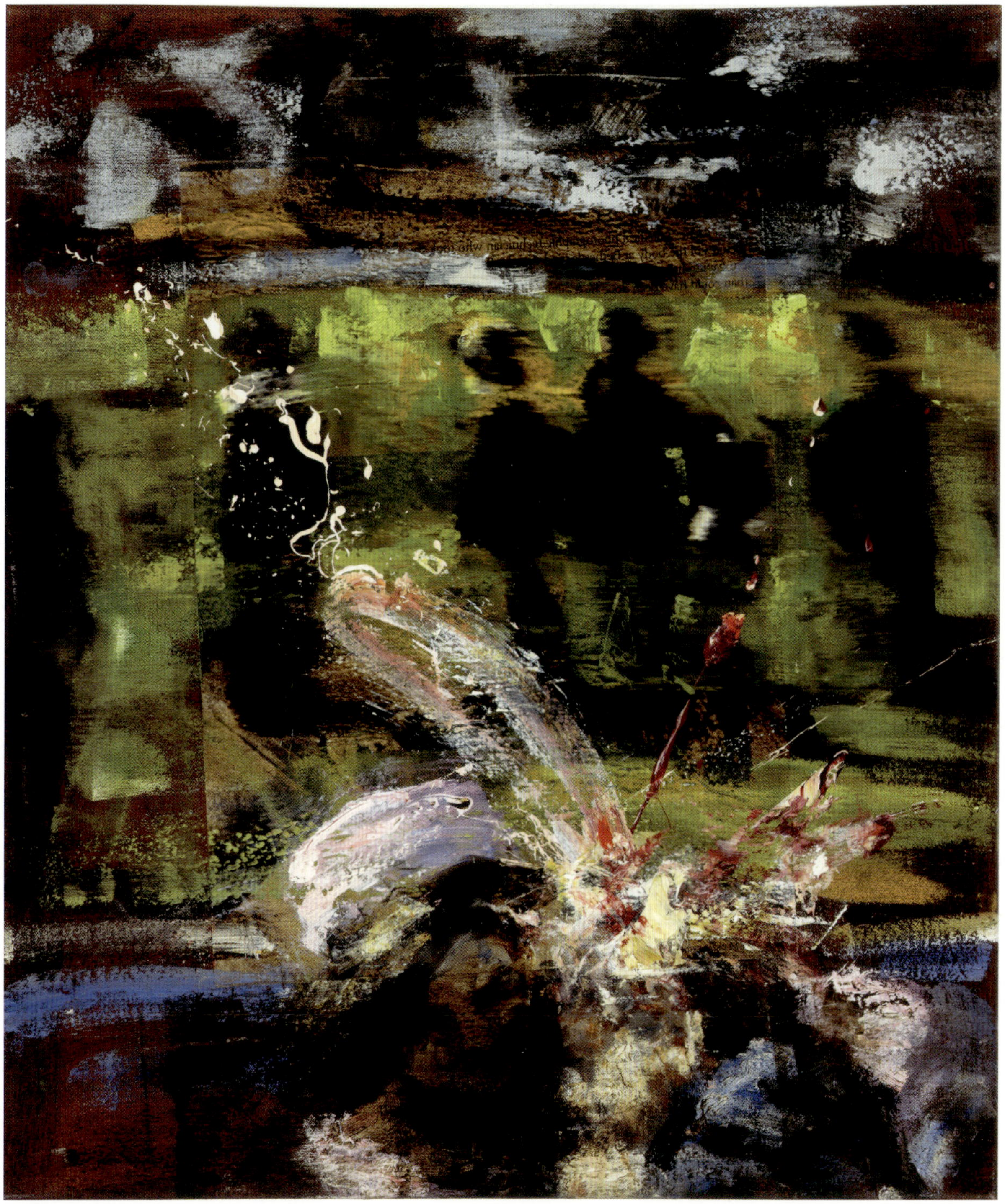

Coup, 1997
Oil and collage on canvas
61 x 51 cm / 24 x 20¼ in
Collection: Philip Knatchbull

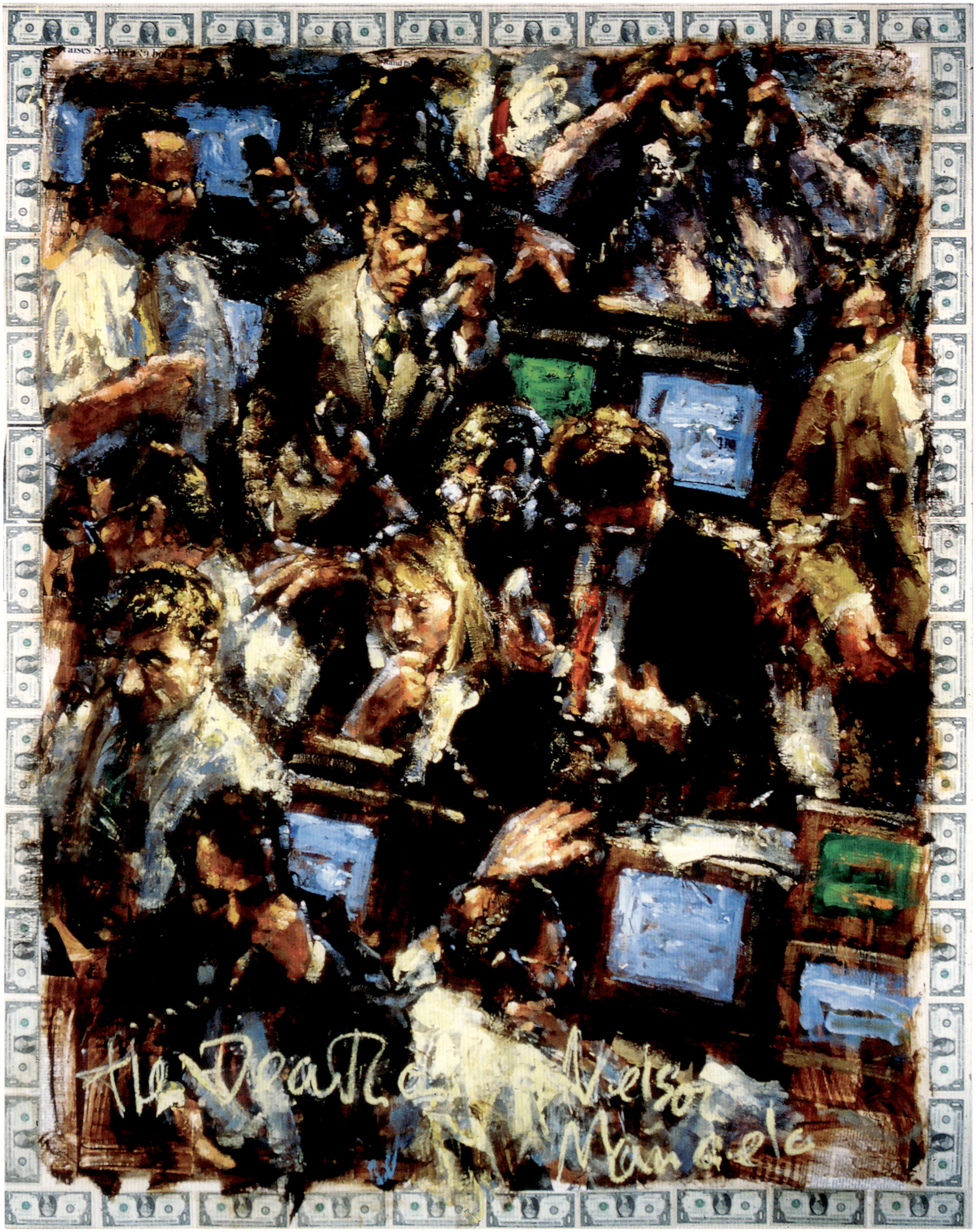

The Death of Nelson Mandela, 1996
Oil and collage on canvas
208.5 x 160 cm / 82 x 63 in
Collection: Berend Rosenboom

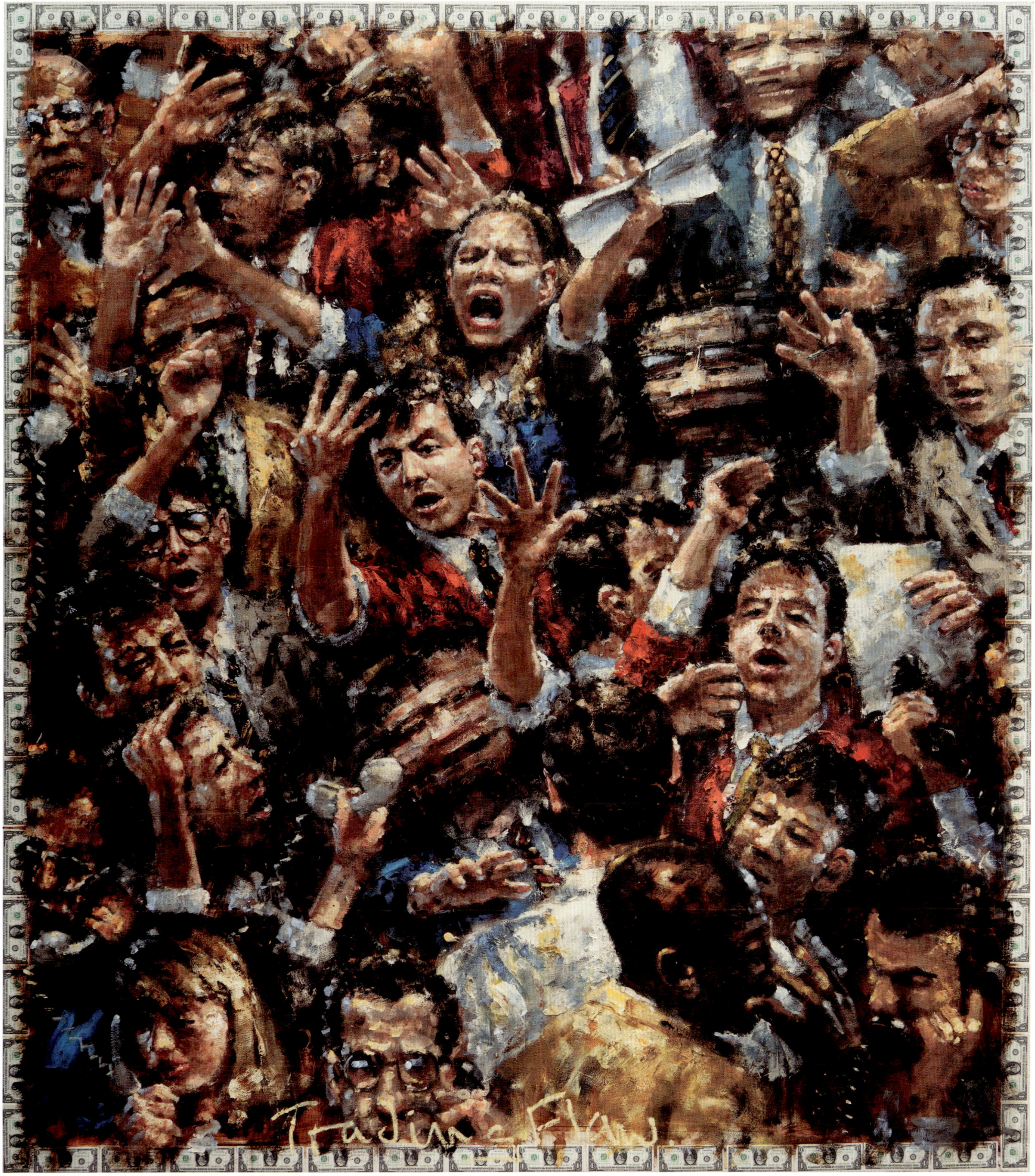

Trading Flaw, 1998
Oil and collage on canvas
274 x 244 cm / 108 x 96 in

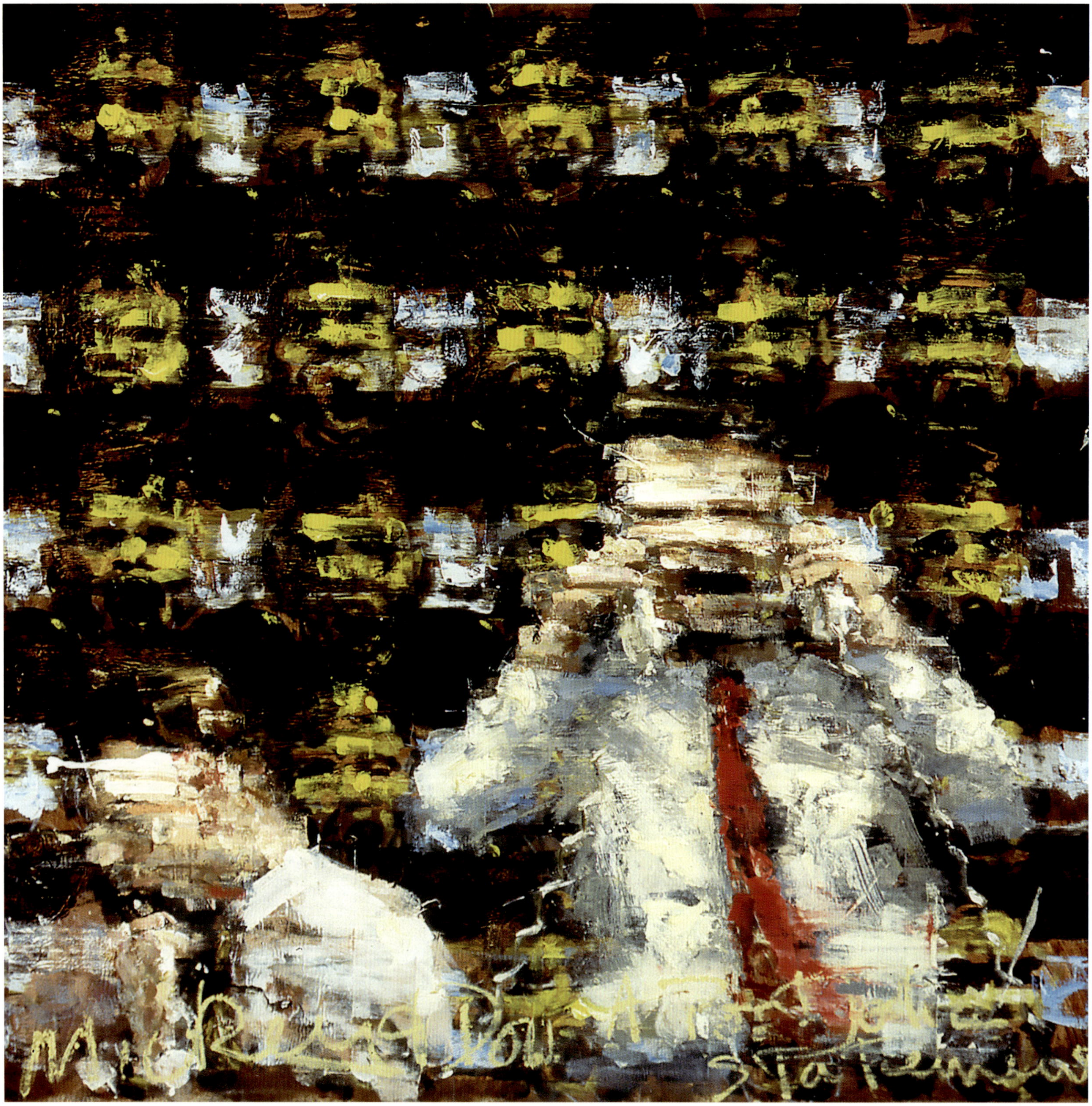

Mickey and Dow (a portfolio statement), 1998
Oil and collage on canvas
147.5 x 152.5 cm / 58 x 60 in
Private Collection, USA

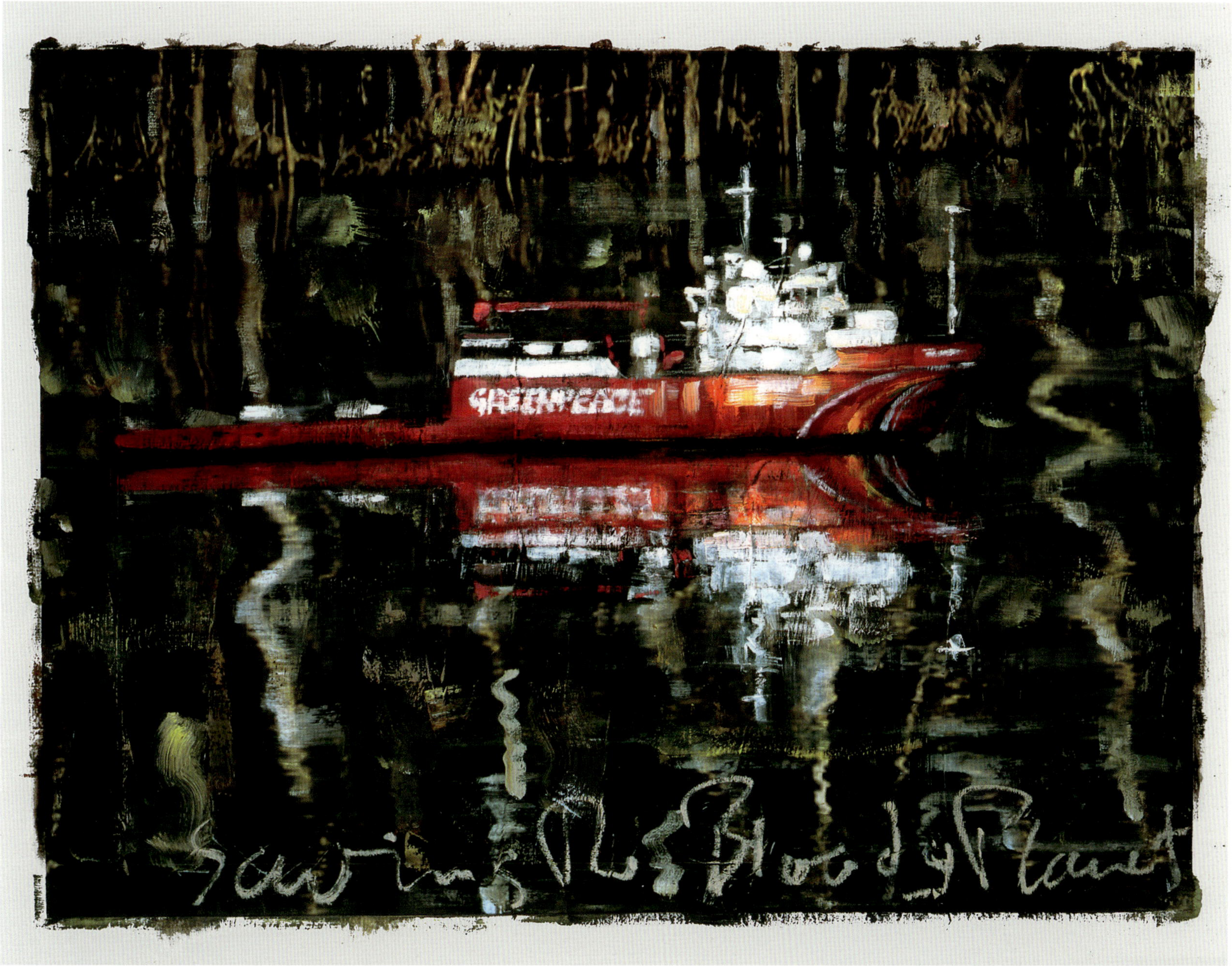

Saving the Bloody Planet, 2001
Oil on inkjet on paper on canvas
83.5 x 114 cm / 33 x 45 in
Private Collection, UK

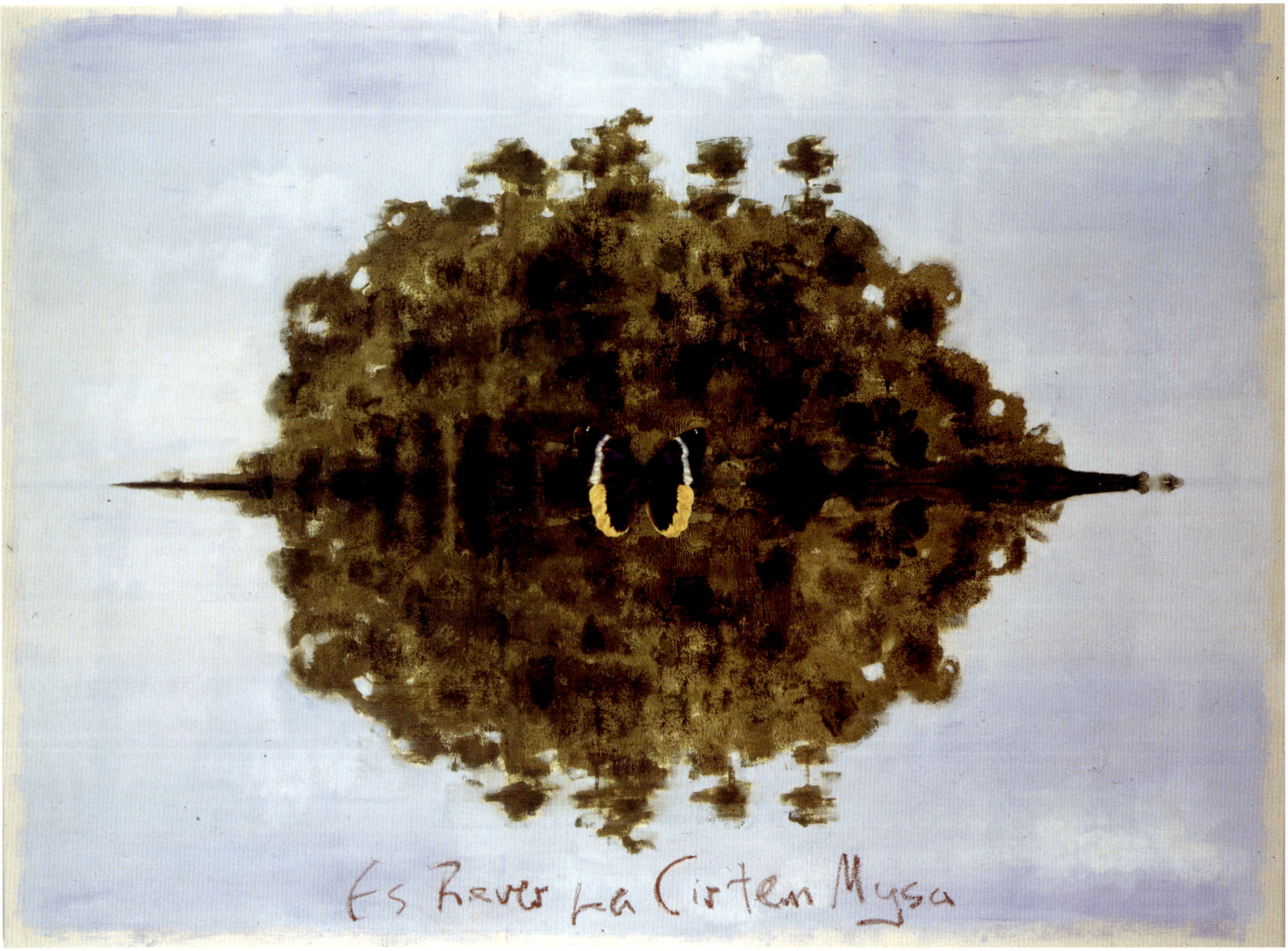

Es Rever La Cirtem Mysa, 1991
Oil on canvas
157 x 208 cm / 61¾ x 81¾ in

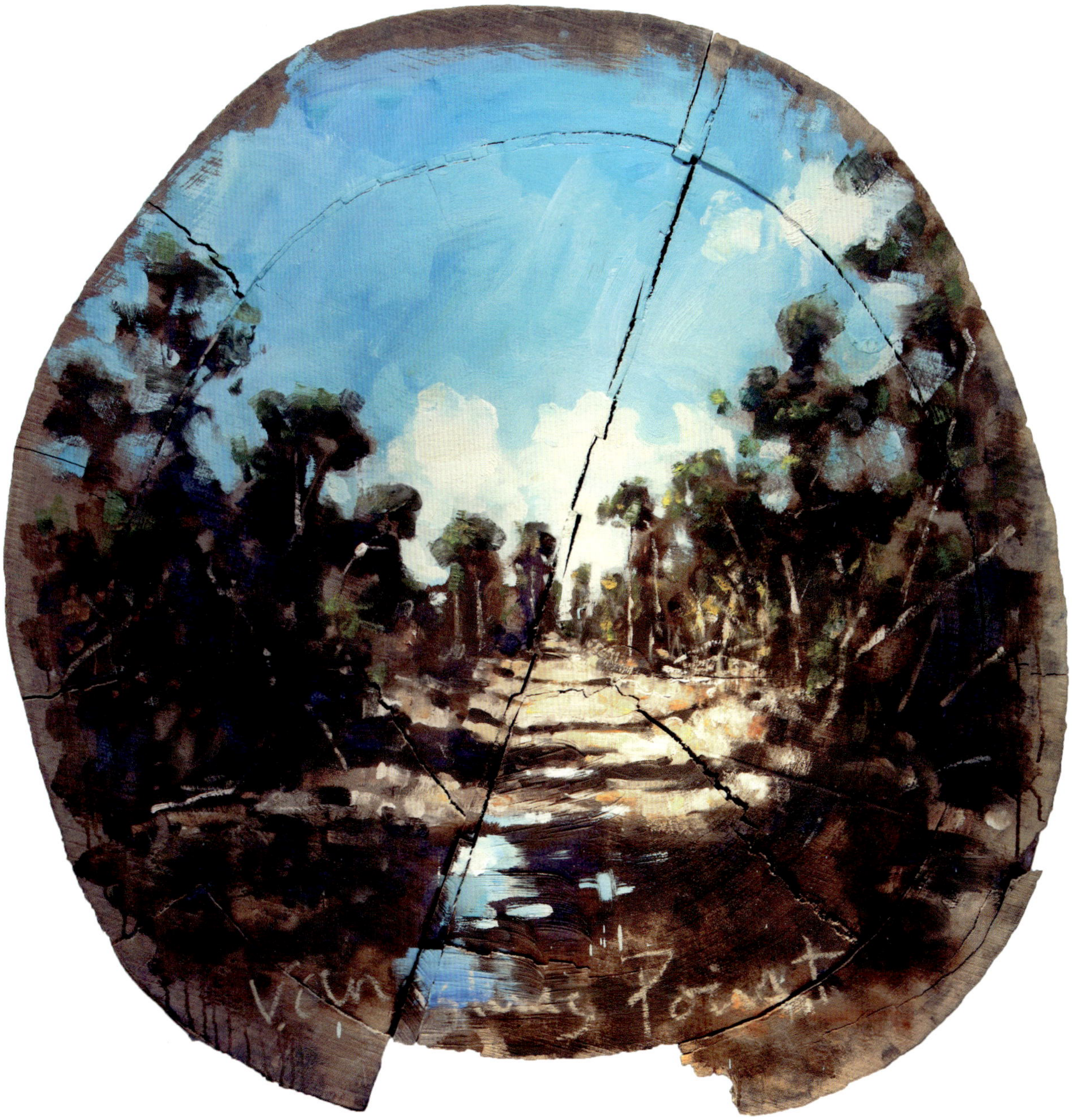

Souvenir 4 (Vanishing Point), 2001
Oil on illegal timber
119.5 x 119.5 cm / 47 x 47 in
Collection: Sara Burns

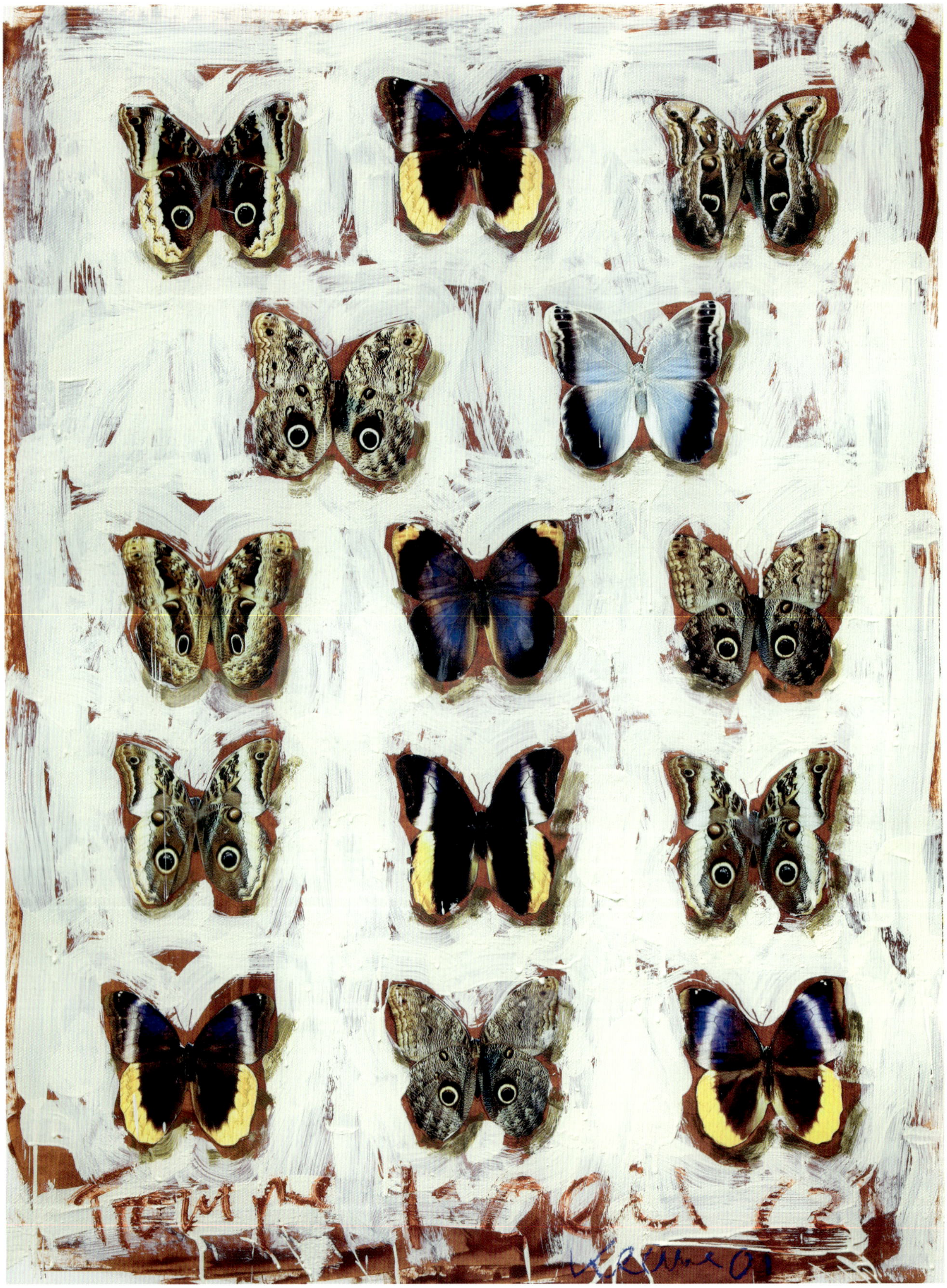

Trompe L'œil II, 2001
Oil, beeswax and inkjet on paper
114 x 84 cm / 45 x 33 in

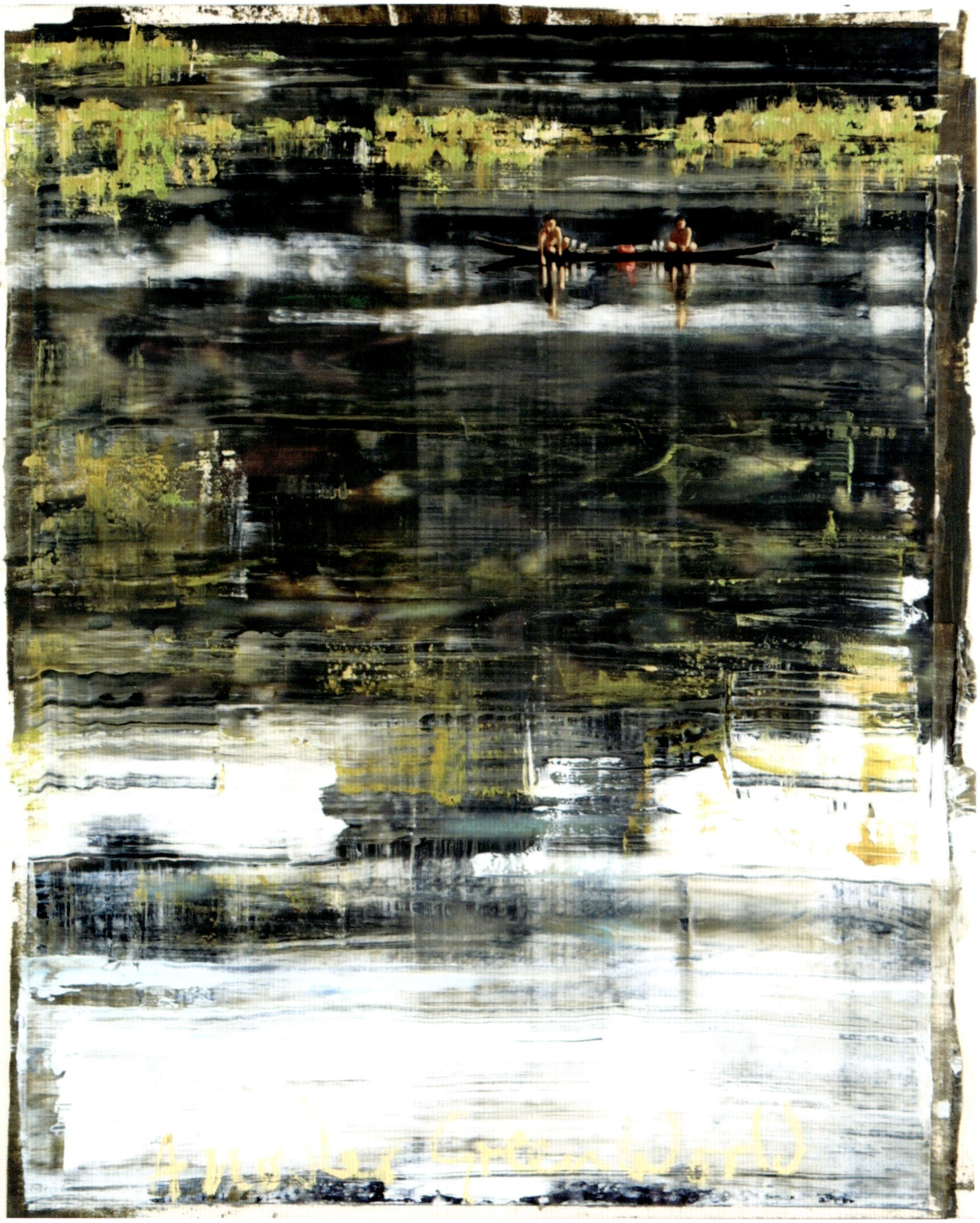

Another Green World, 2001
Oil and inkjet on paper on canvas
82 x 66.5 cm / 32¼ x 26¼ in

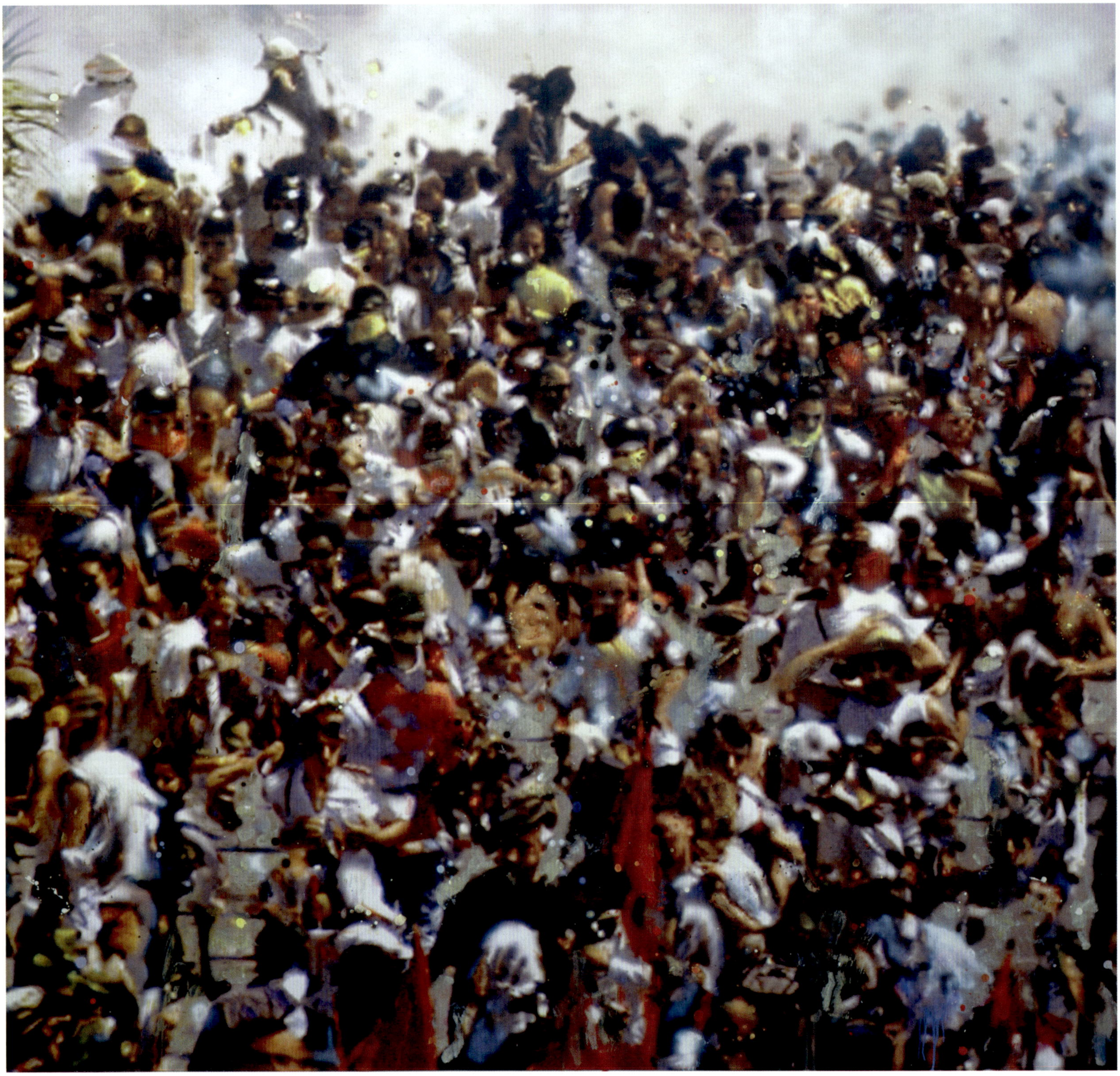

Gas, 2002
Oil and inkjet on paper on canvas
191 x 196 cm / 75 x 77 in

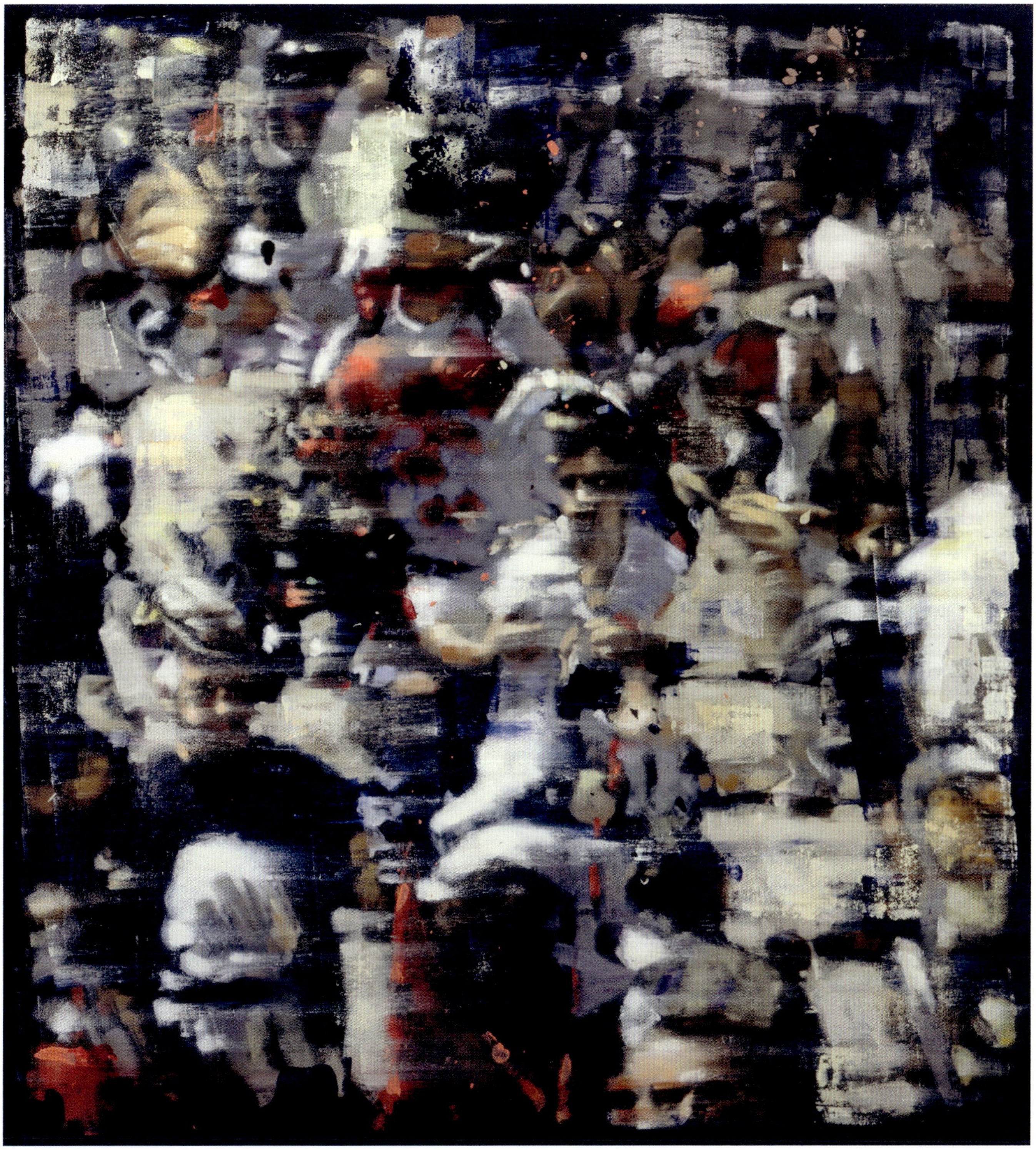

Disturbance (1), 2002
Oil on canvas
123 x 113 cm / 48 x 44 in

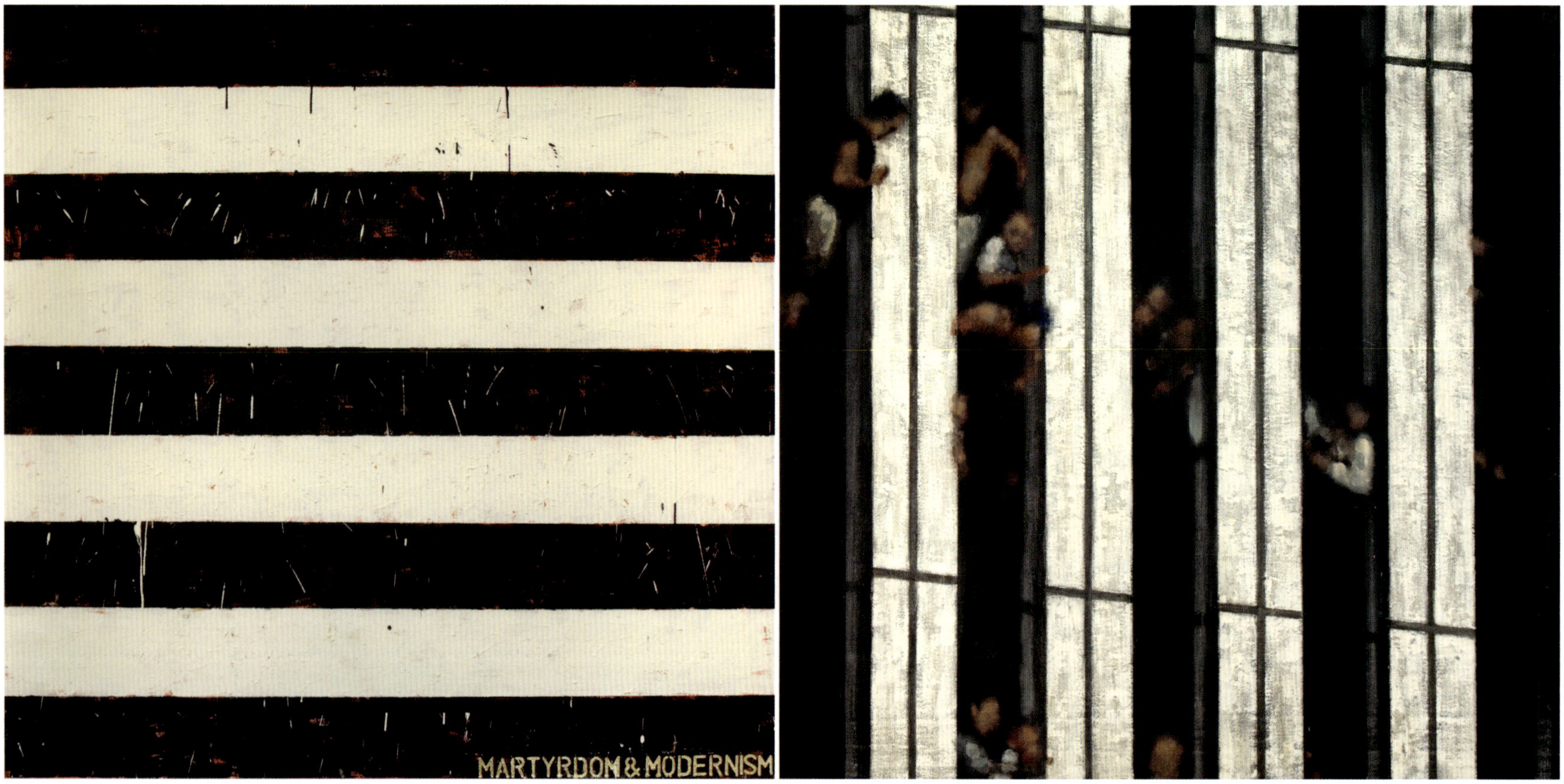

Martyrdom and Modernism, 2002
Oil and beeswax on canvas (diptych)
124 x 246 cm / 49 x 97 in

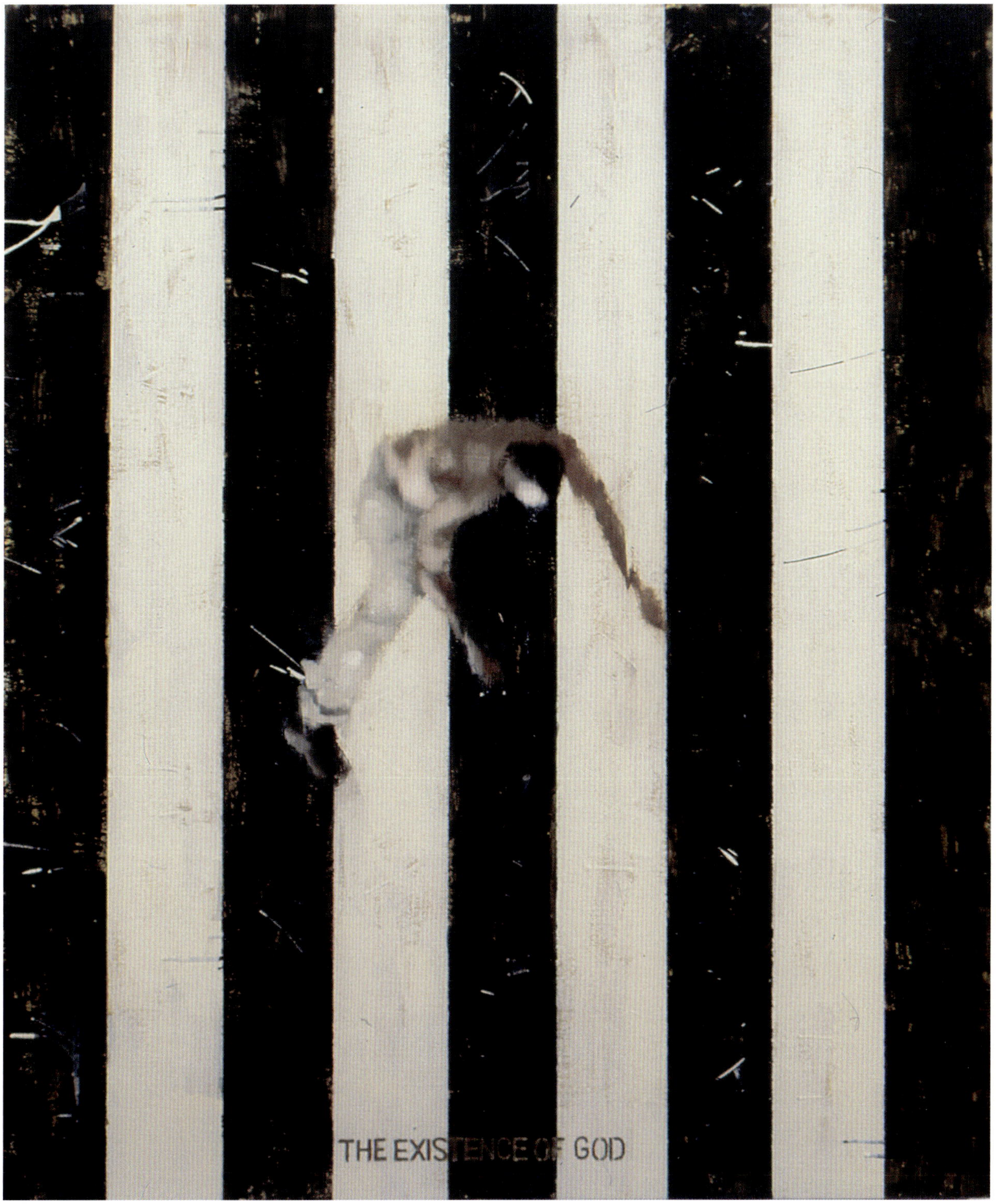

The Existence of God (2), 2002
Oil and beeswax on canvas
112 x 92 cm / 44 x 36 in
Private Collection, UK

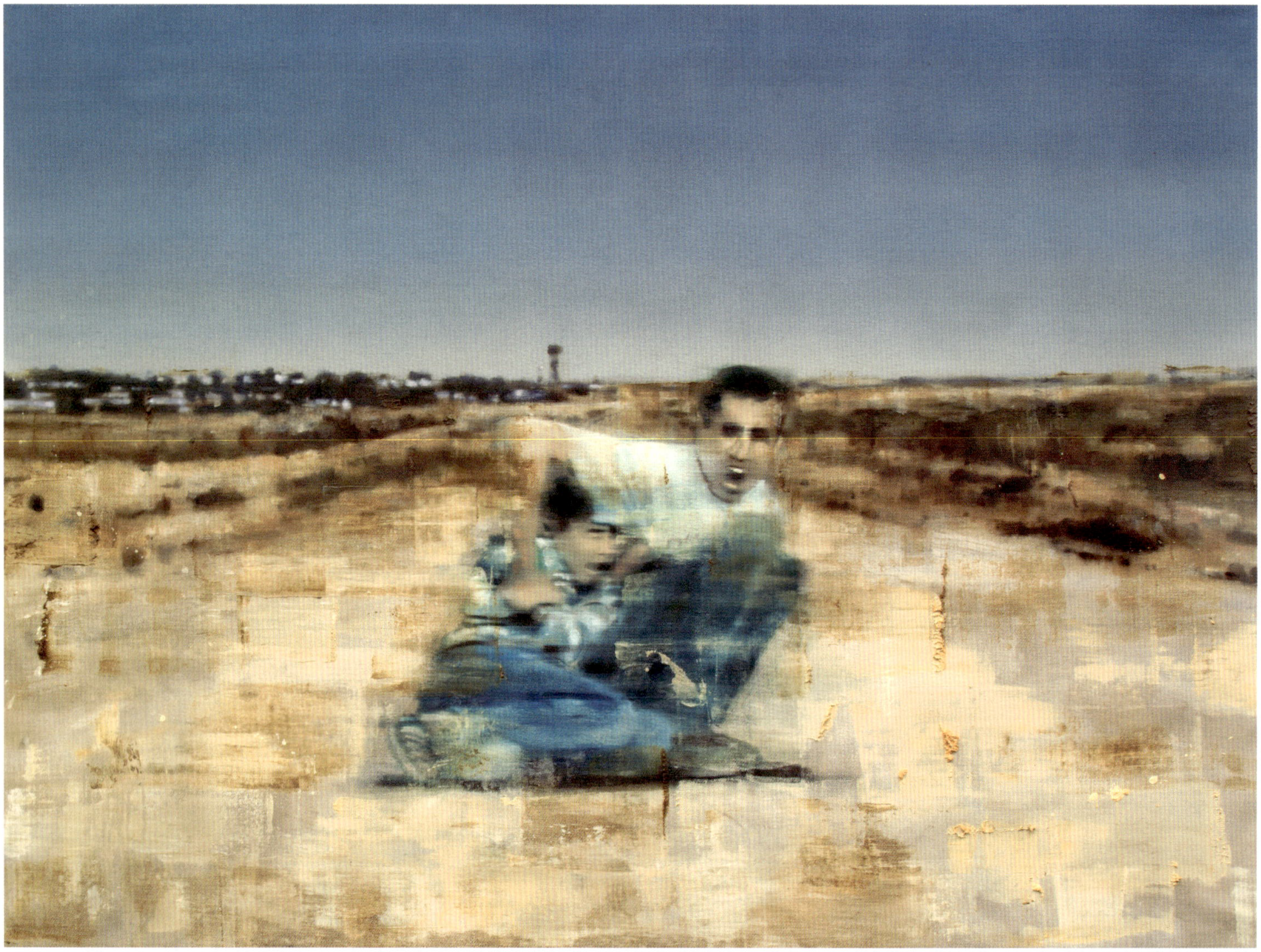

Hopeless in Gaza (Road to a Settlement), 2002
Oil on linen
137 x 183 cm / 54 x 72 in

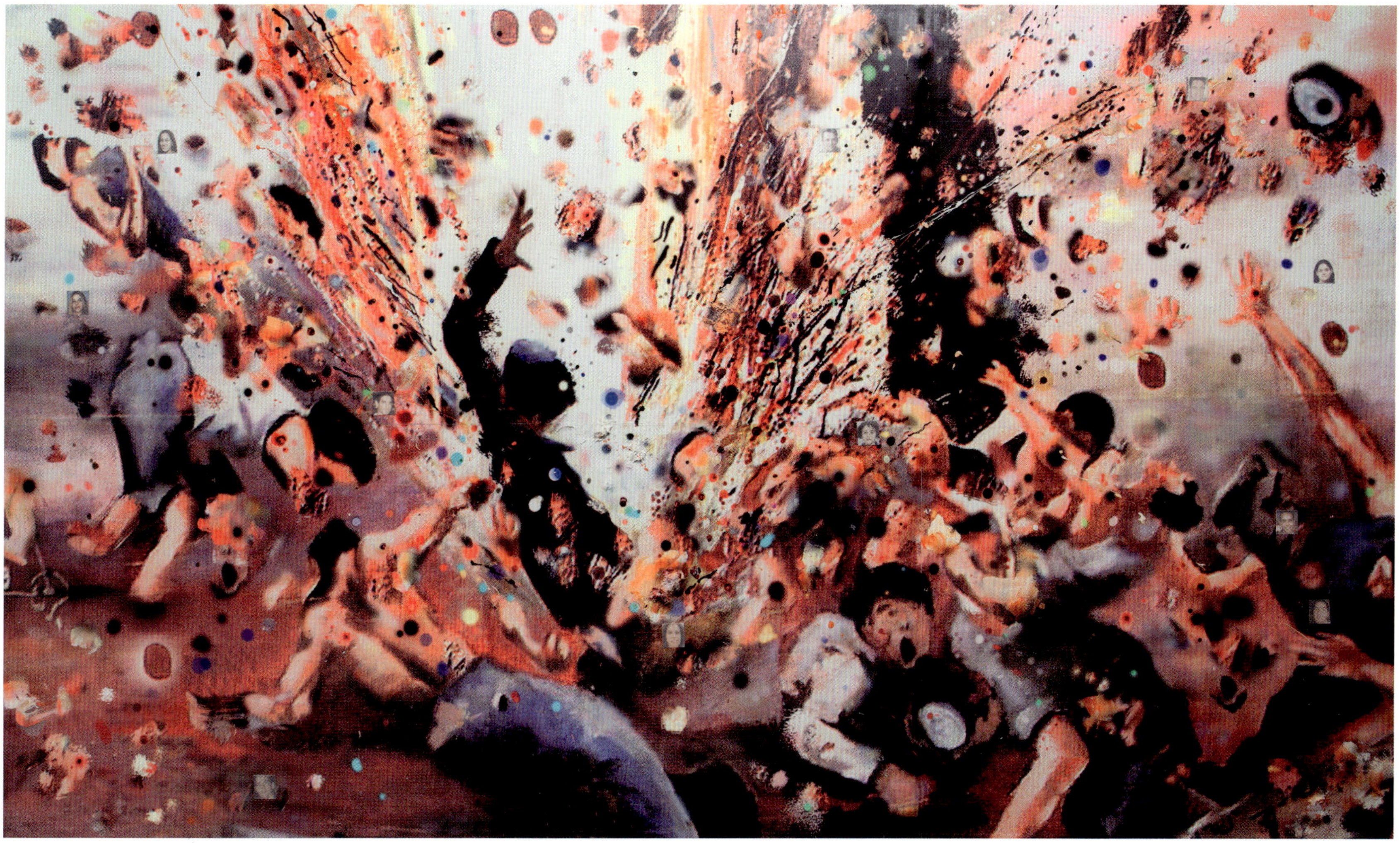

Moment, 2003
Oil and inkjet on paper on canvas
173 x 293 cm / 29½ x 115 in

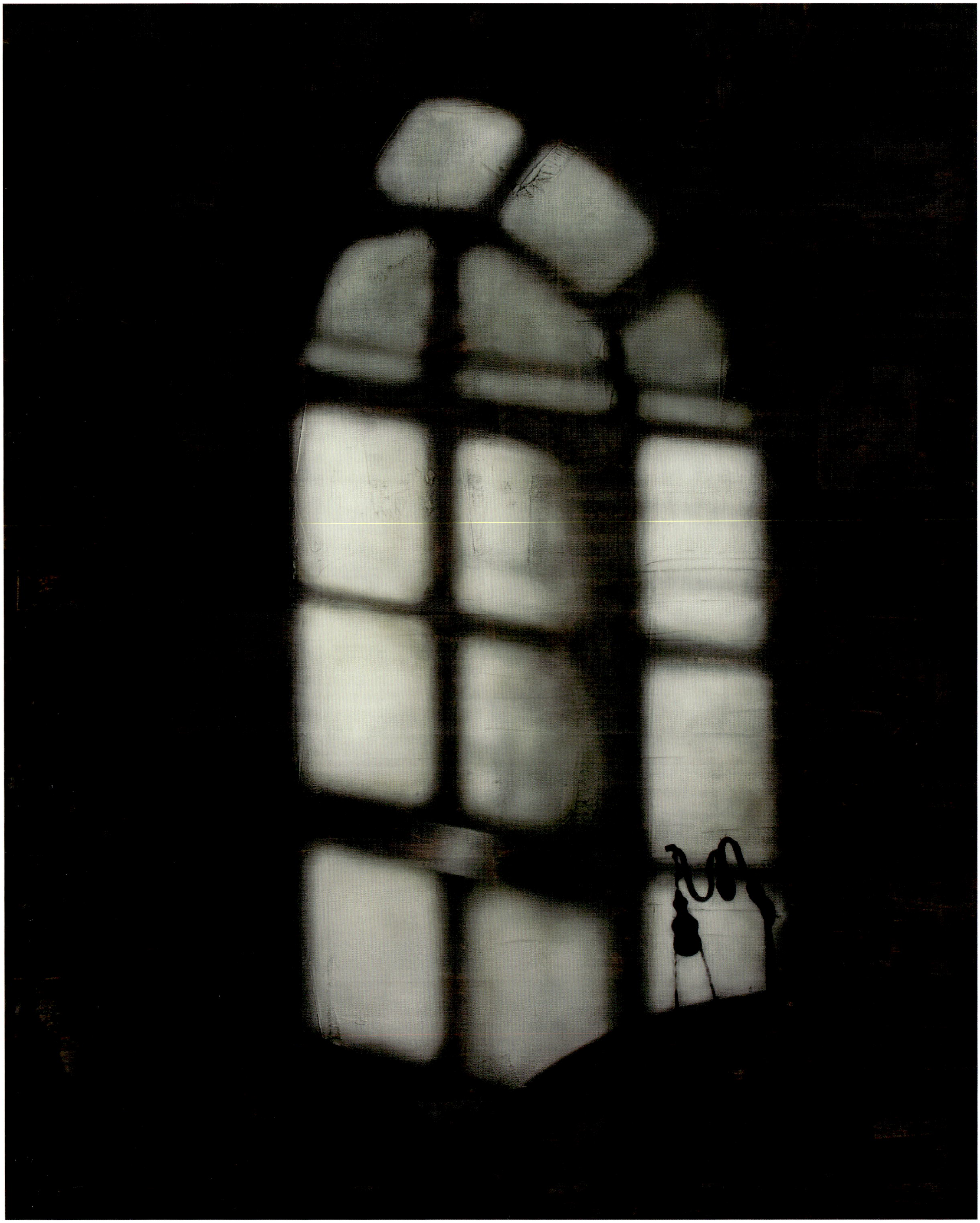

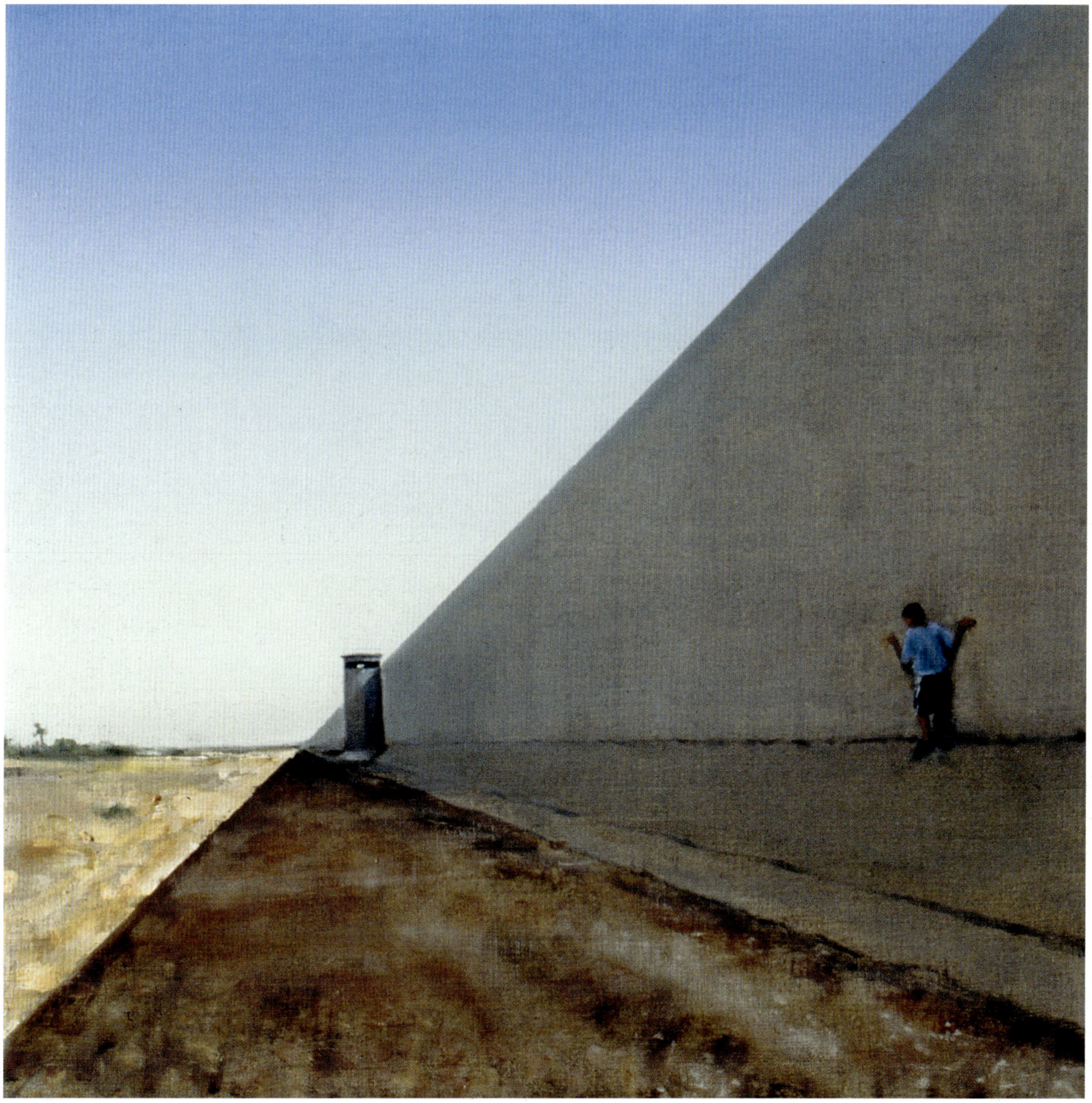

How Still we see Thee Lie! (Darkness and Light in the Church of the Nativity), 2003
Oil and photocopy on linen
198 x 162 cm / 78 x 63¾ in

Security, Impunity, Geometry and Terror, 2003
Oil on linen
61 x 61 cm / 24 x 24 in
Private Collection, UK

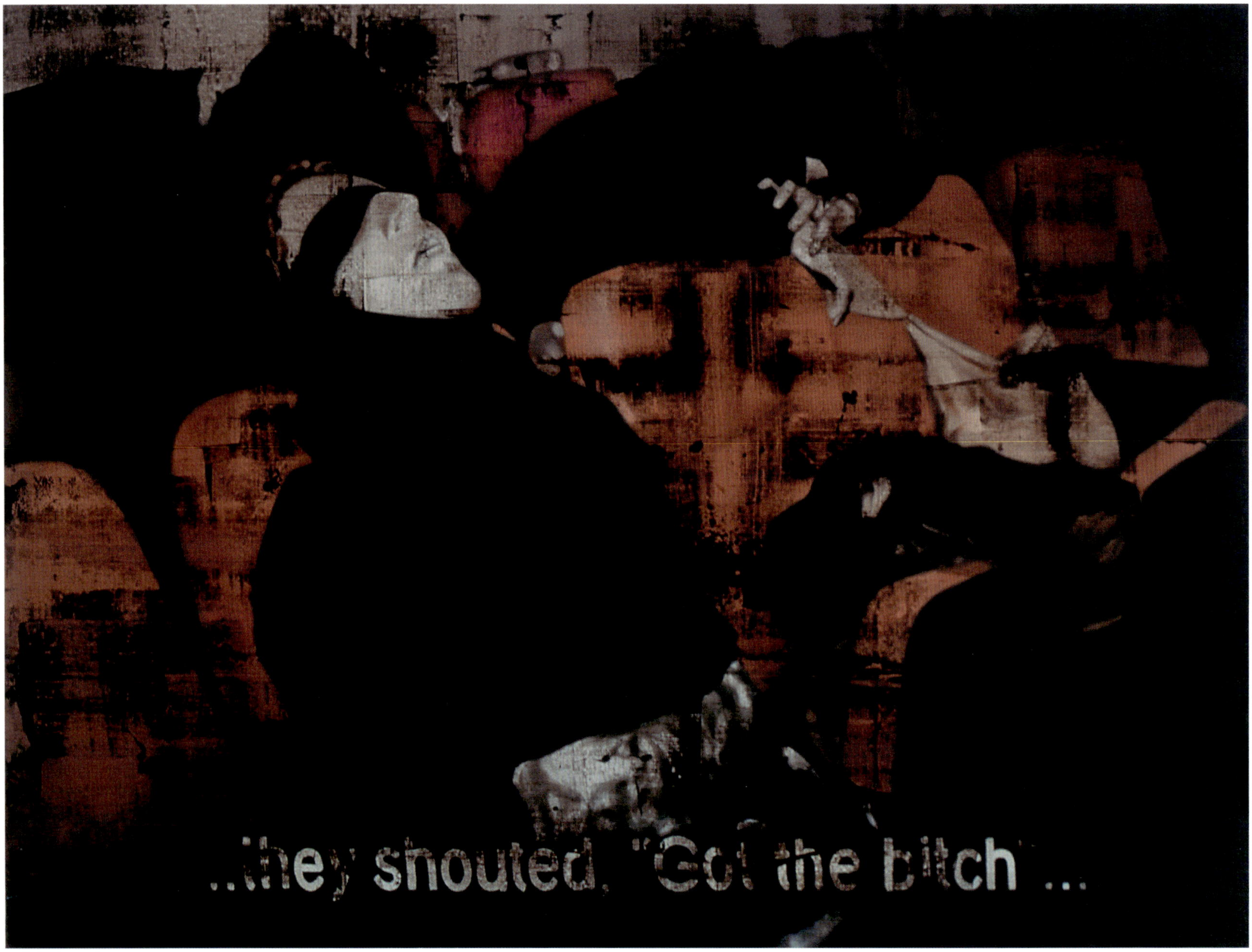

. . . they shouted "Got the bitch". . . , 2004
Oil on linen
212 x 282 cm / 83½ x 111 in
Collection: David Roberts Arts Foundation

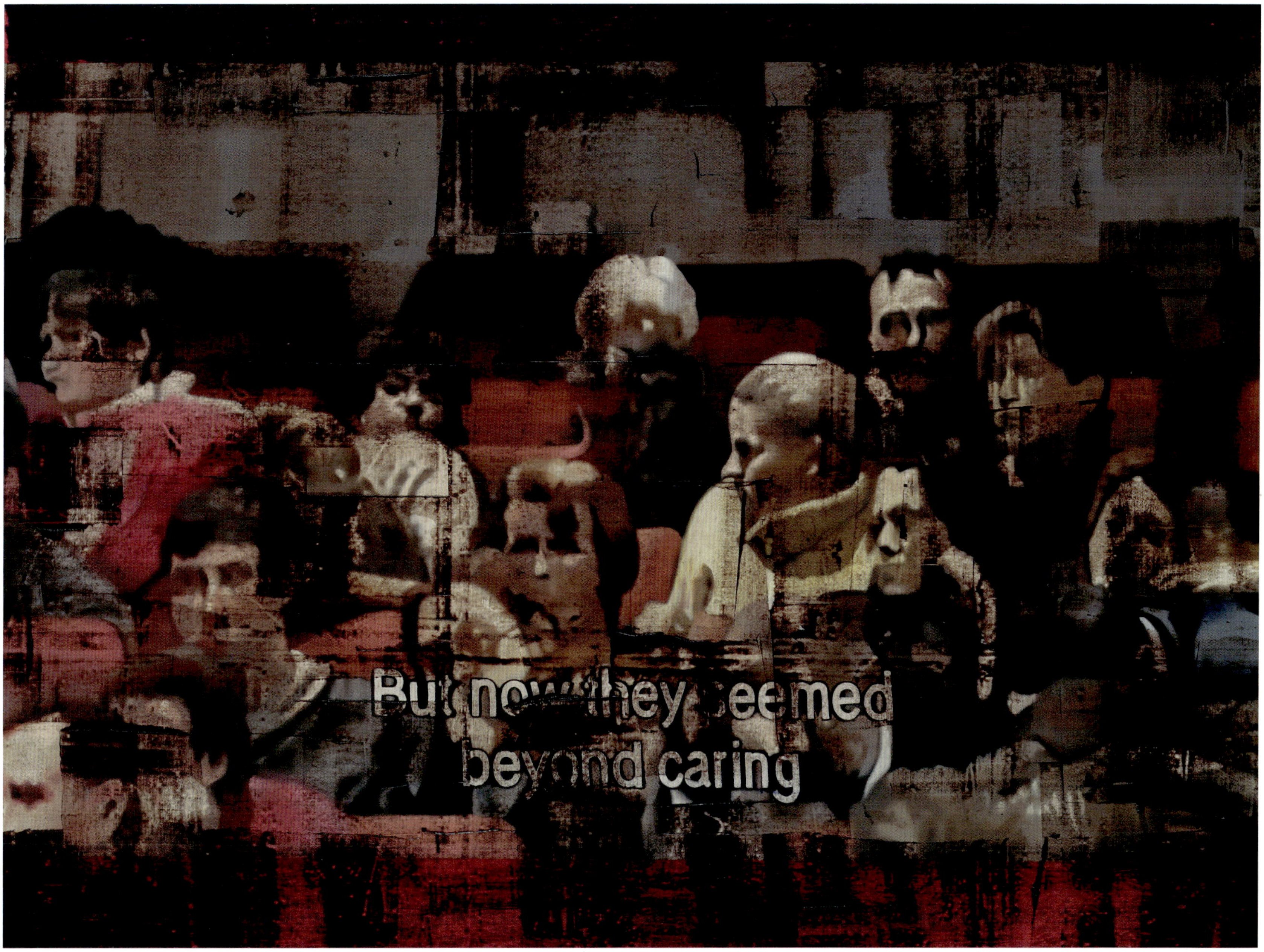

But now they seemed beyond caring, 2004
Oil and acrylic on linen
212 x 282 cm / 83½ x 111 in

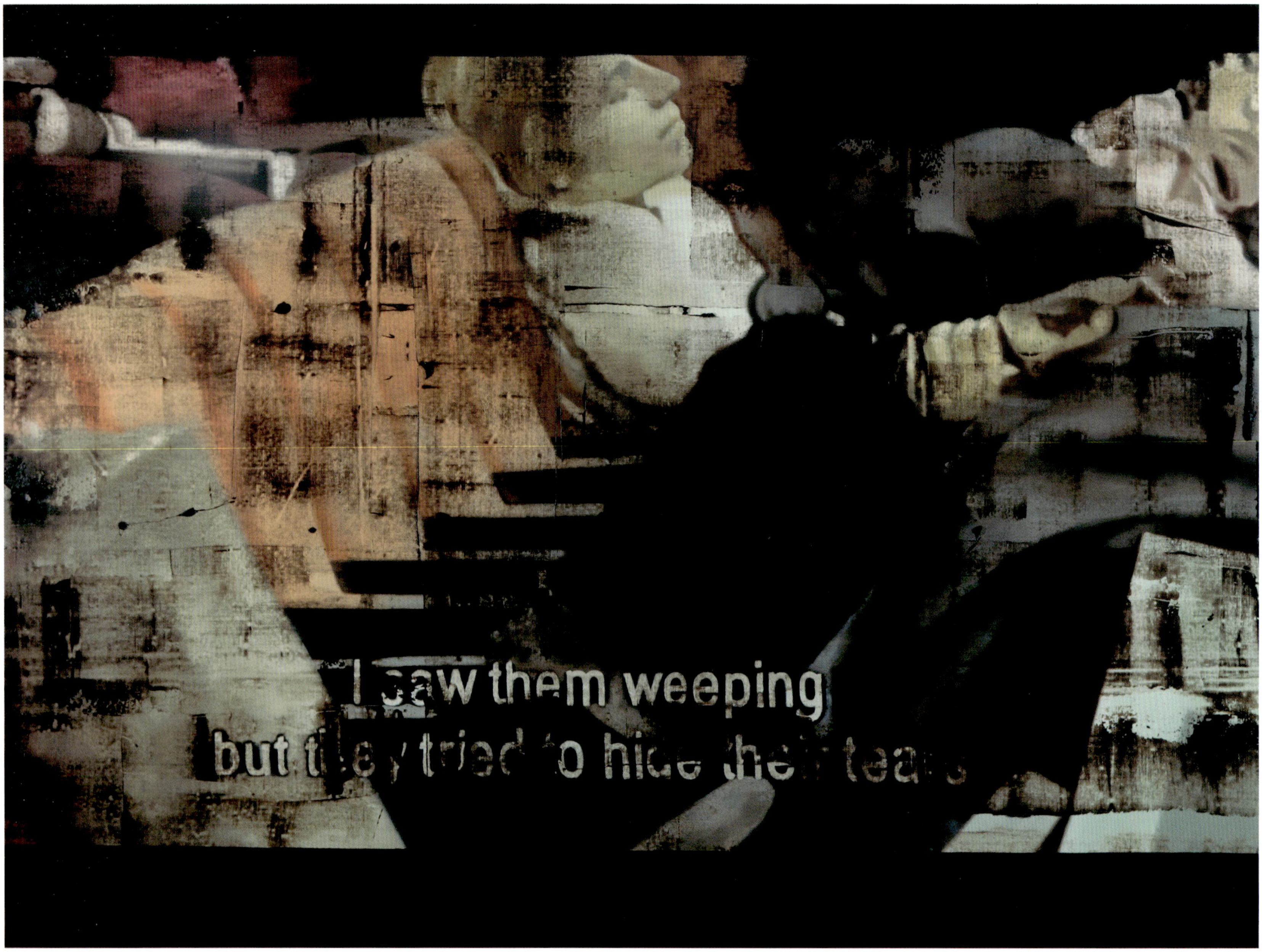

I saw them weeping but they tried to hide their tears, 2004

Oil on linen

212 x 282 cm / 83½ x 111 in

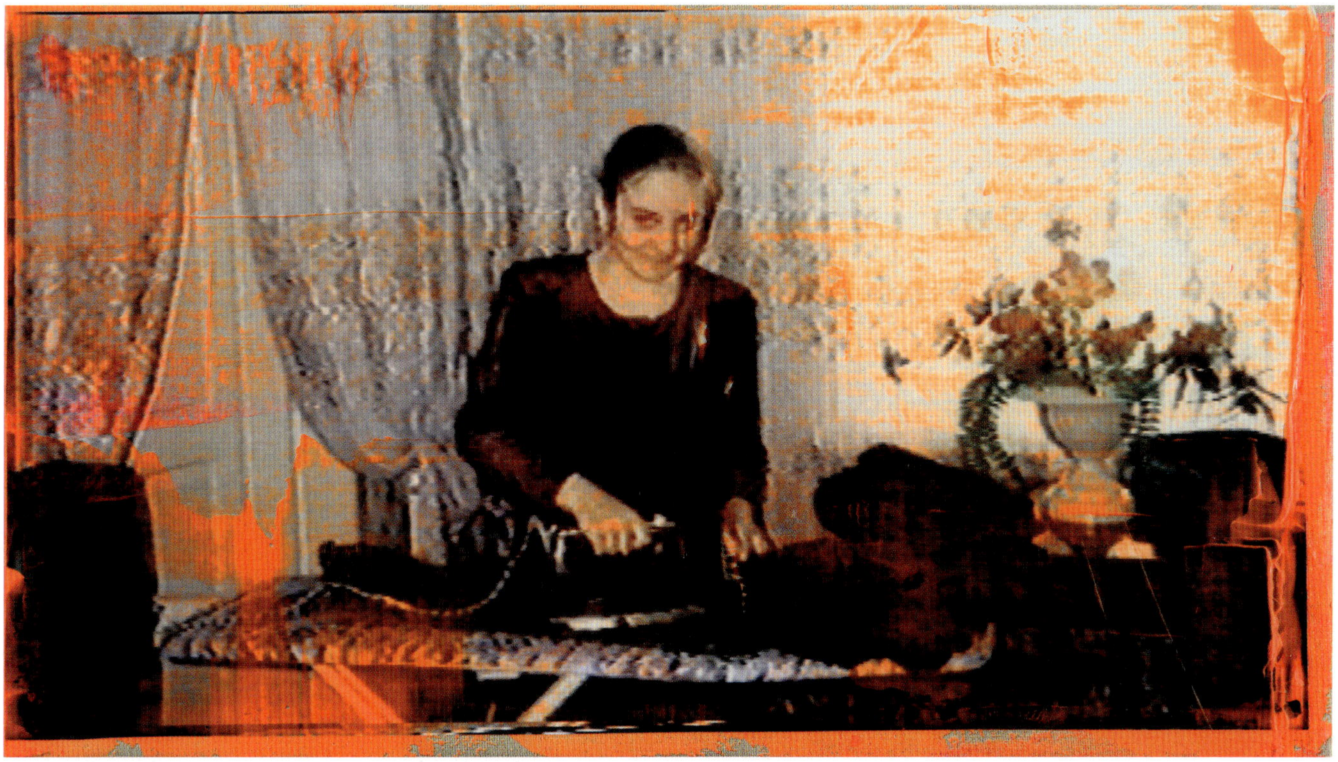

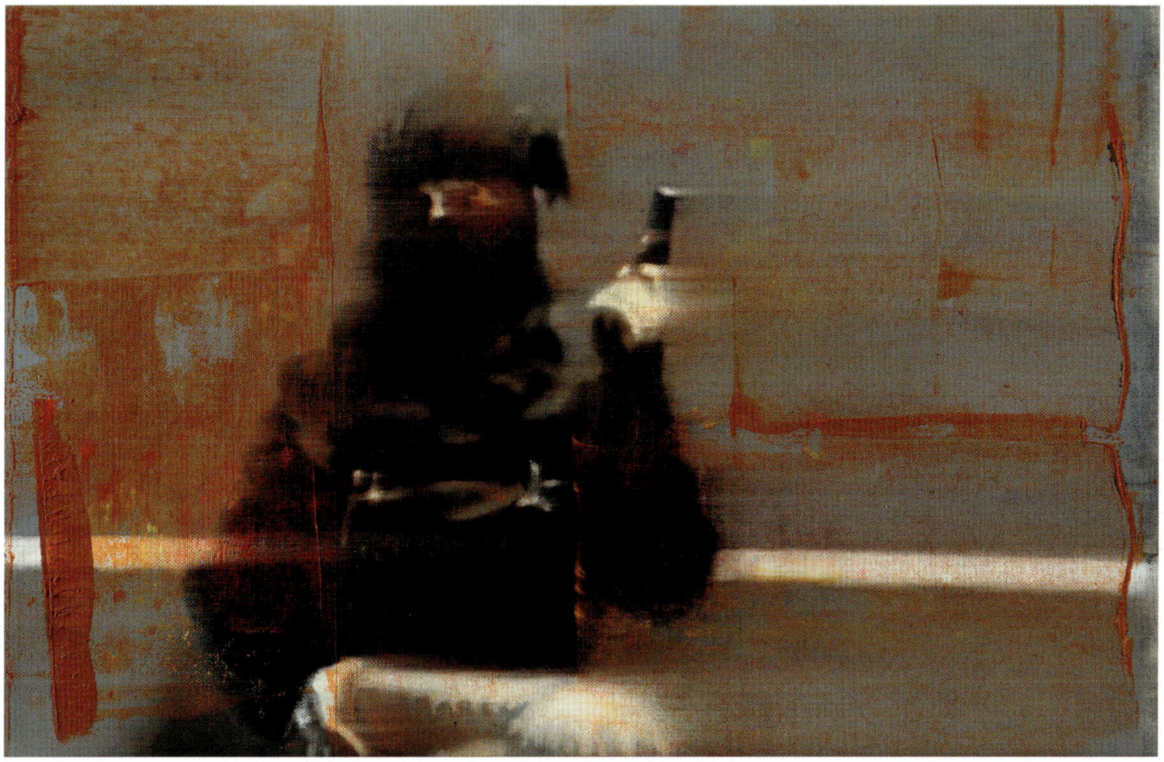

Untitled (Terrorist) 3, 2004
Acrylic on inkjet on paper on jute
47 x 82 cm / 18½ x 32¼ in

Untitled (Terrorist) 4, 2005
Oil on linen
46 x 71 cm / 18¼ x 28 in
Collection: Nick Taylor

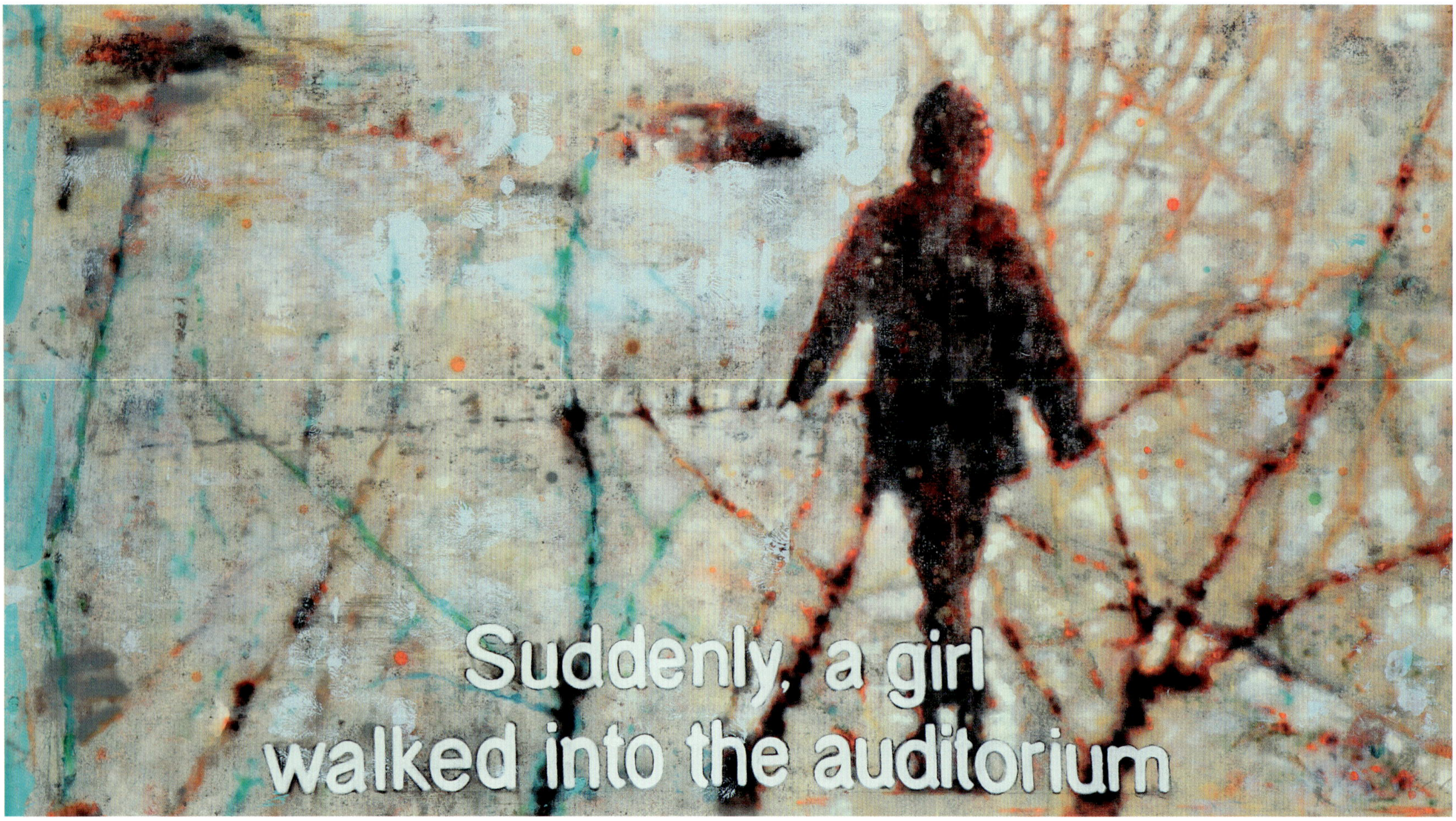

Suddenly, a girl walked into the auditorium, 2004
Oil on linen
114 x 200 cm / 45 x 78¾ in
Private Collection, UK

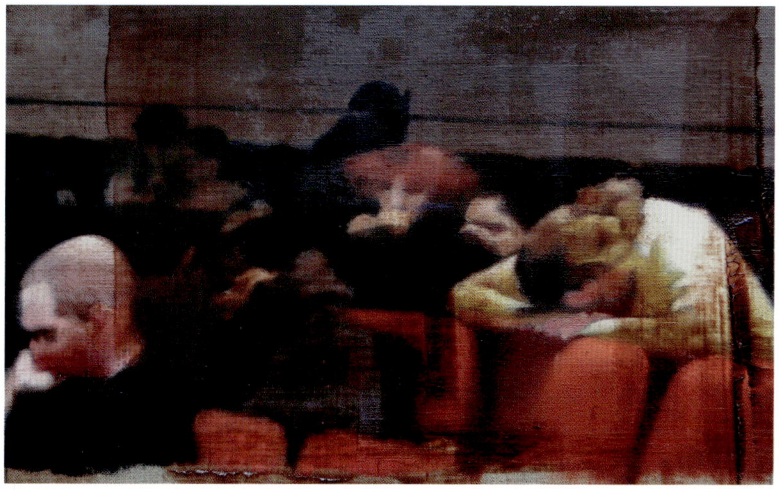

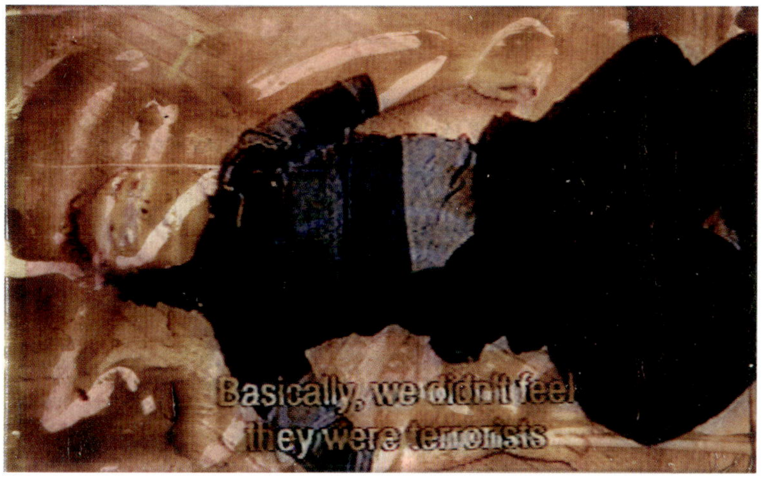

Ten small paintings from the Dubrovka Theatre Siege no.1, 2005
Oil on linen
30.5 x 51 cm / 12 x 20¼ in

Ten small paintings from the Dubrovka Theatre Siege no. 12 , 2005
Oil and inkjet on linen
25.5 x 41 cm / 10¼ x 16¼ in

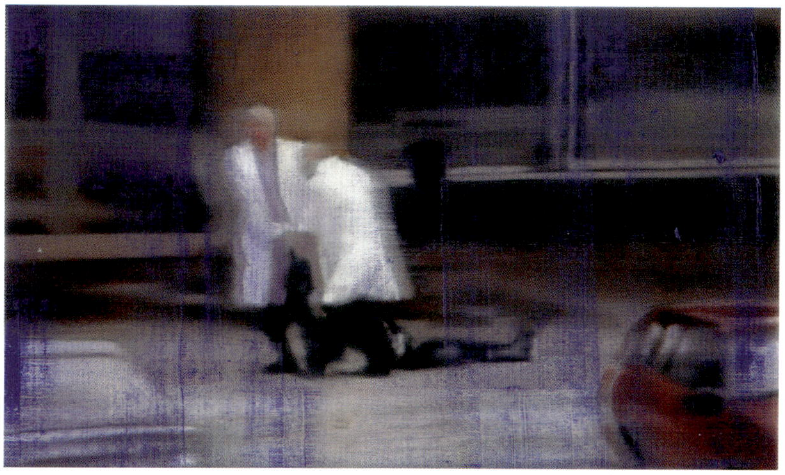

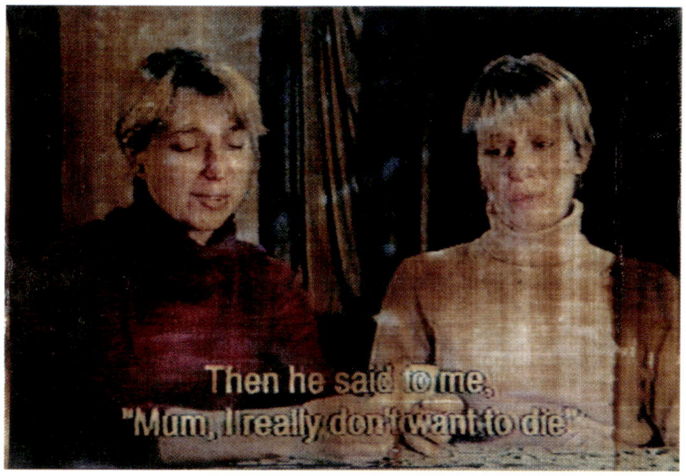

Ten small paintings from the Dubrovka Theatre Siege no. 3
(the Death of Olga Romanova), 2005
Oil on linen
30 x 51 cm / 12 x 20¼ in
Private Collection, UK

Ten small paintings from the Dubrovka Theatre Siege No.10, 2005
Oil and inkjet on linen
28 x 41 cm / 11¼ x 16¼ in

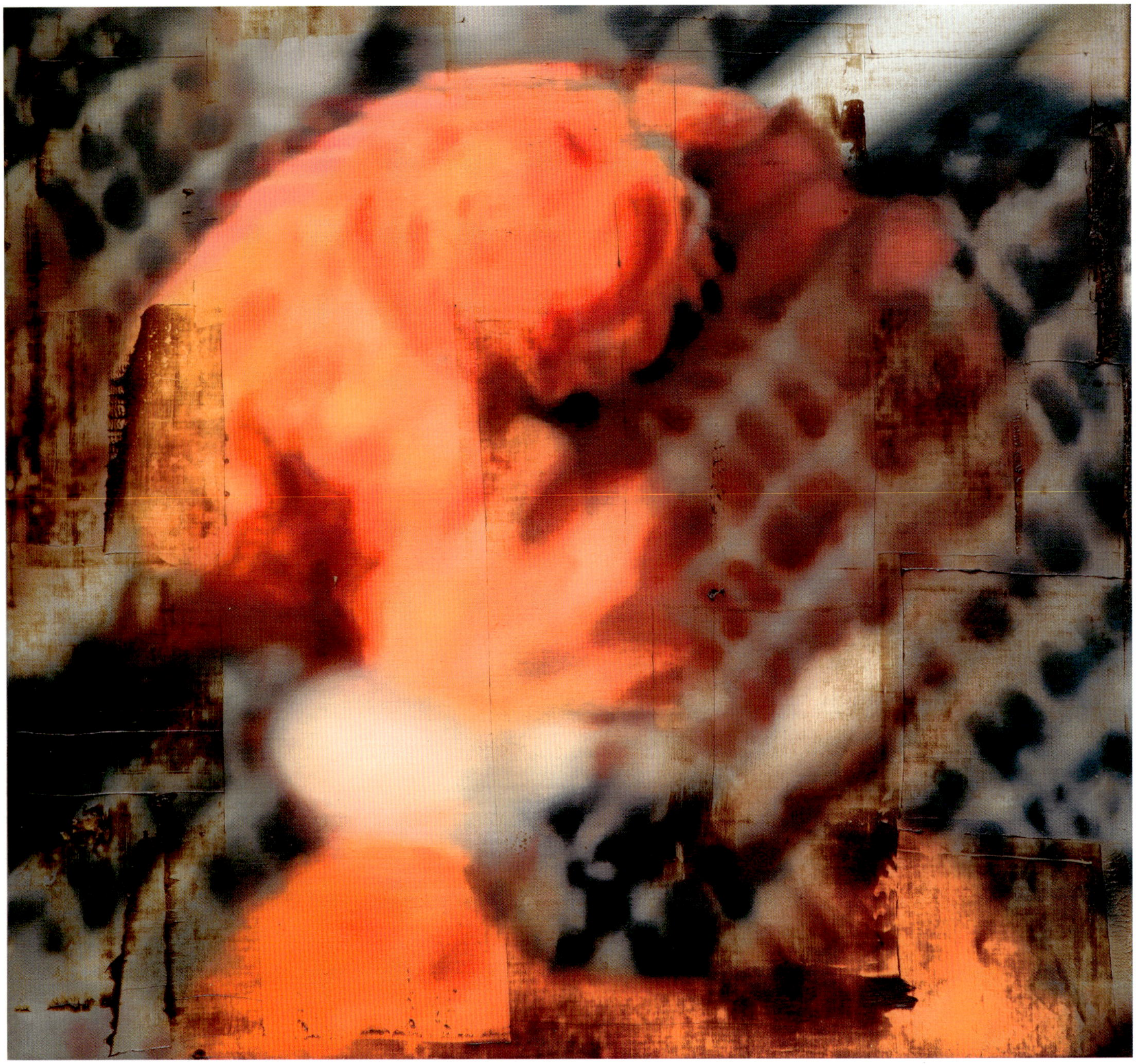

Submission I, 2005
Oil on linen
86.5 x 92 cm / 34 x 36¼ in

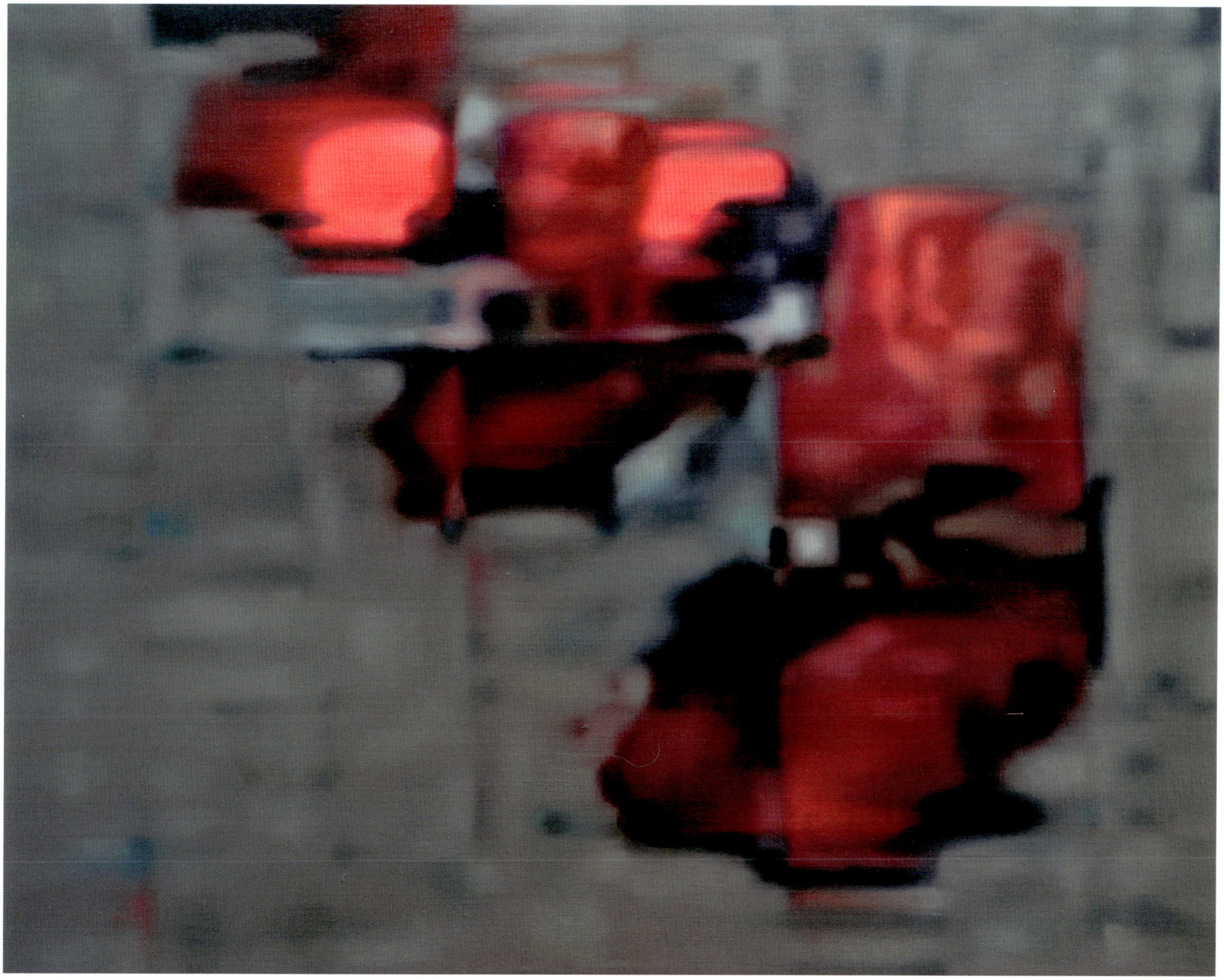

Submission V, 2006
Oil on linen
86.5 x 107 cm / 34 x 42¼ in
Collection: Nick Taylor

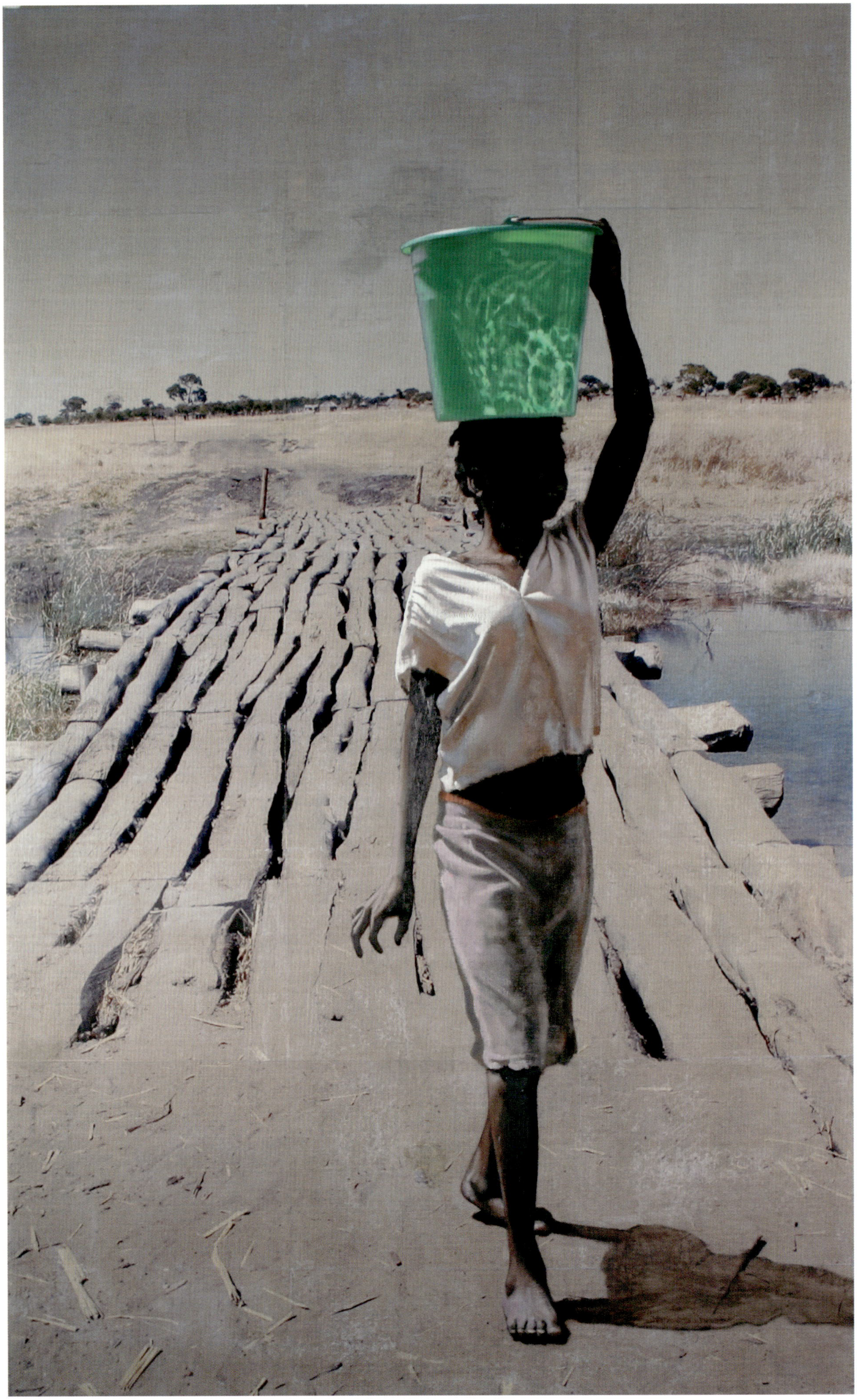

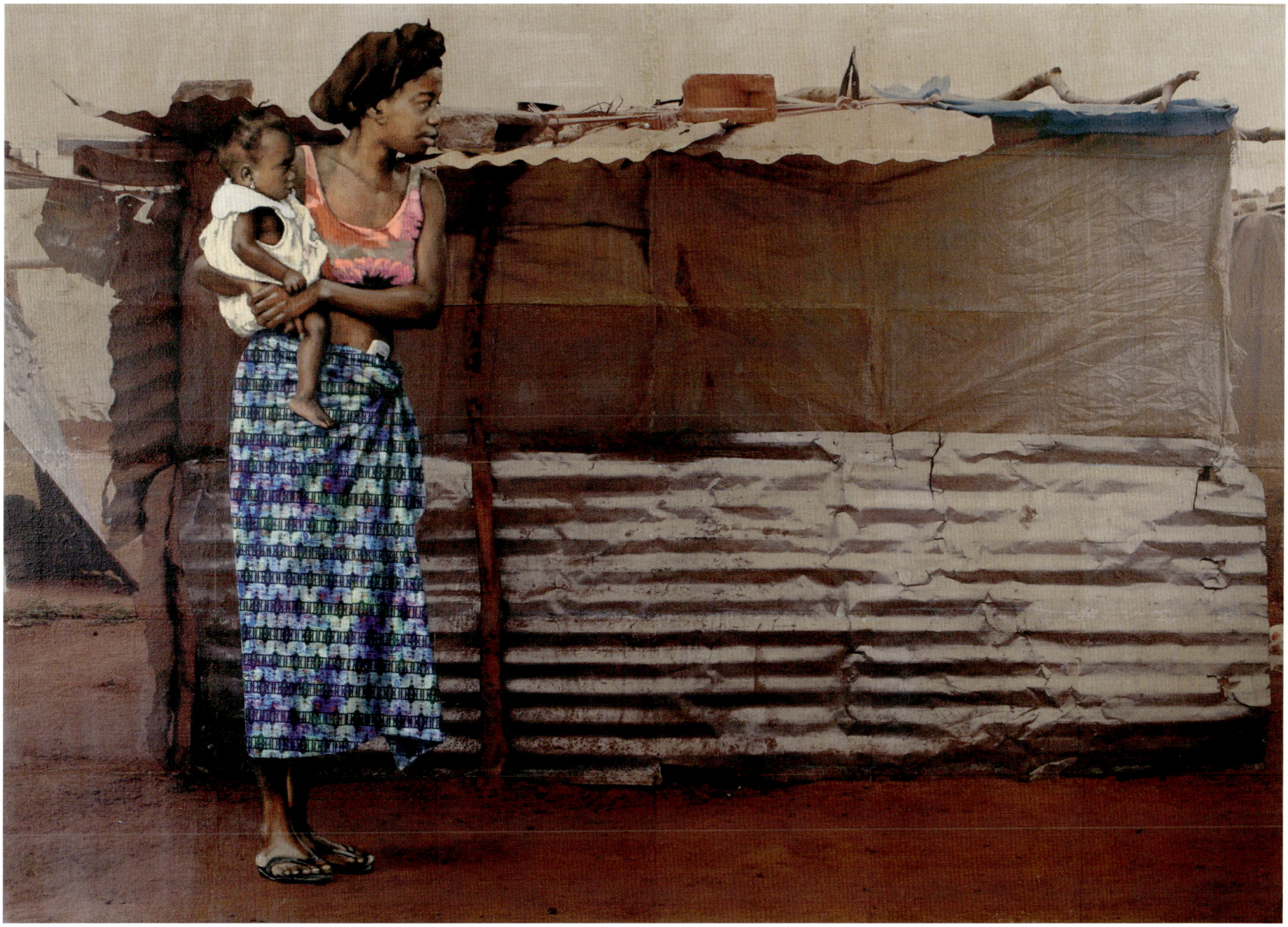

Bridge, 2007
Oil and inkjet on jute
192 x 117 cm / 75¾ x 46¼ in
Private Collection, UK

Shanty, 2007
Oil and inkjet on jute
172 x 238 cm / 67¾ x 93¾ in
Private Collection, UK

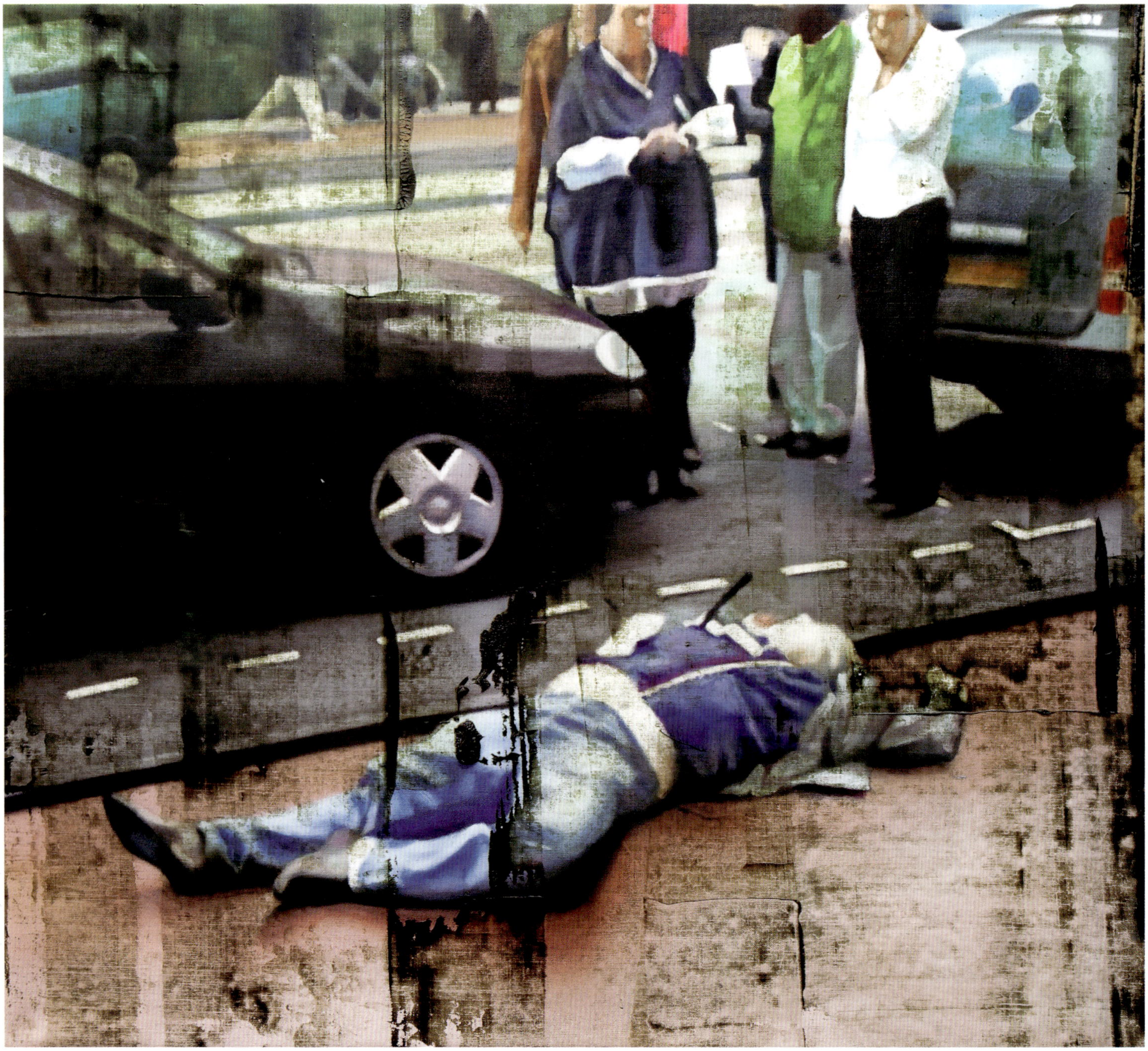

The Death of Theo Van Gogh, 2007
Oil on linen
97 x 107 cm / 38¼ x 42¼ in

Jar Head, 2008
Oil on linen
180.5 x 135 cm / 71¼ x 53¼ in

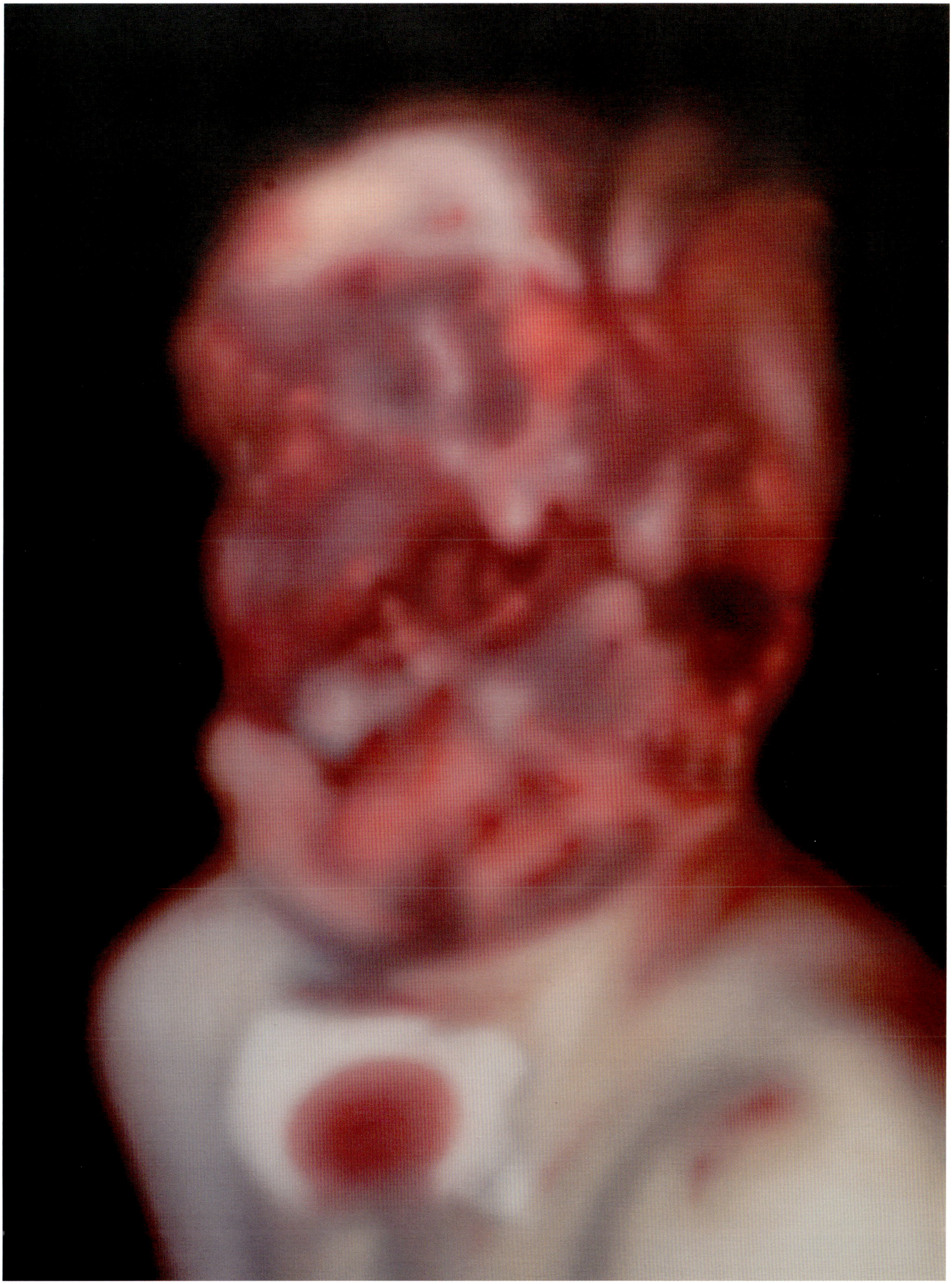

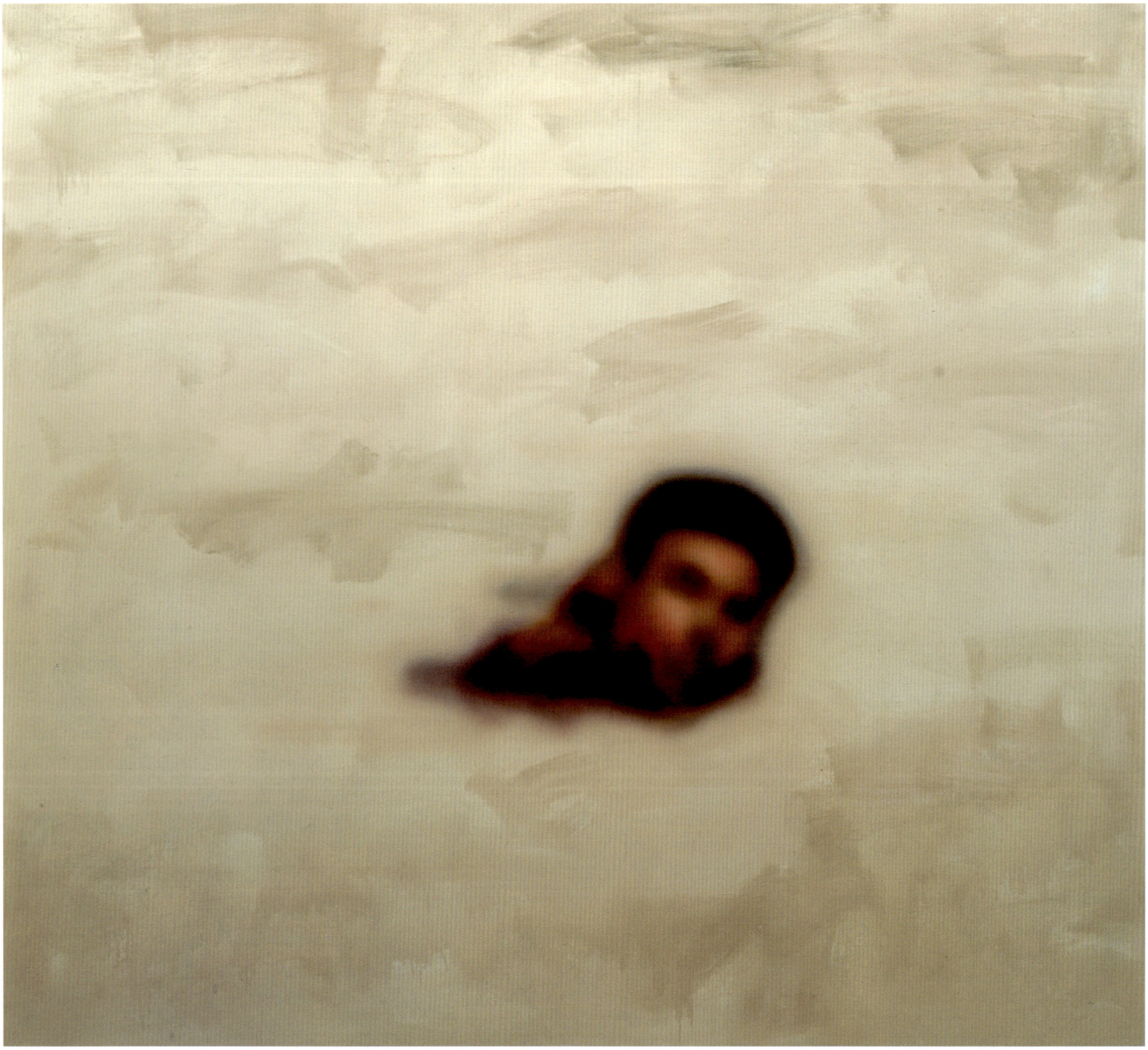

Bomb Head, 2008
Oil on linen
177 x 194 cm / 69¾ x 76½ in

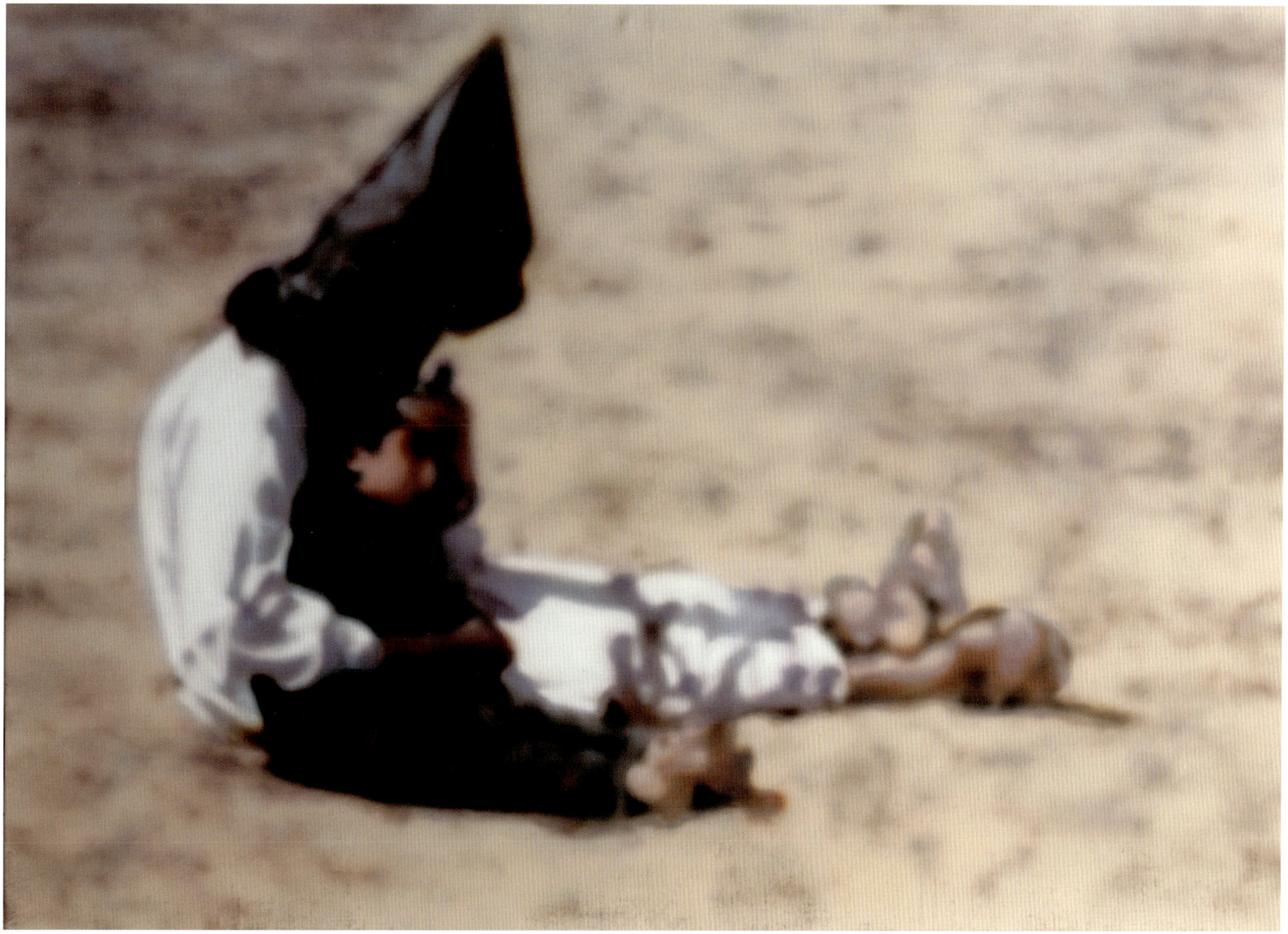

Bag Dad, 2008
Oil on linen
145 x 200 cm / 57¼ x 78¾ in
Collection: Nick Taylor

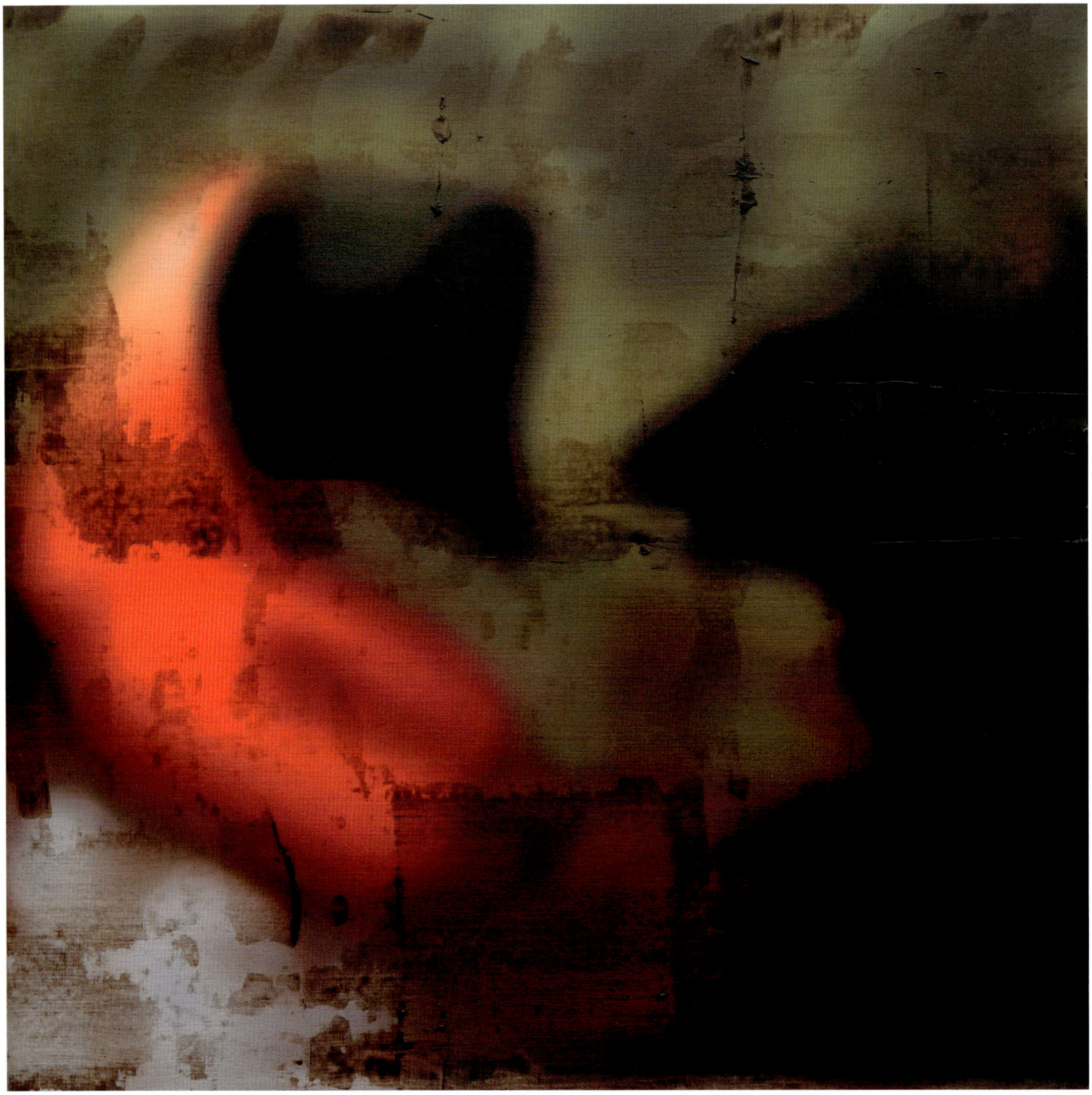

Dog Bag, 2008
Oil on linen
105 x 105 cm / 41½ x 41½ in
Collection: Nick Taylor

Division of Cells, 2008
Oil and acrylic on canvas
195.5 x 155.5 cm / 77 x 61¼ in

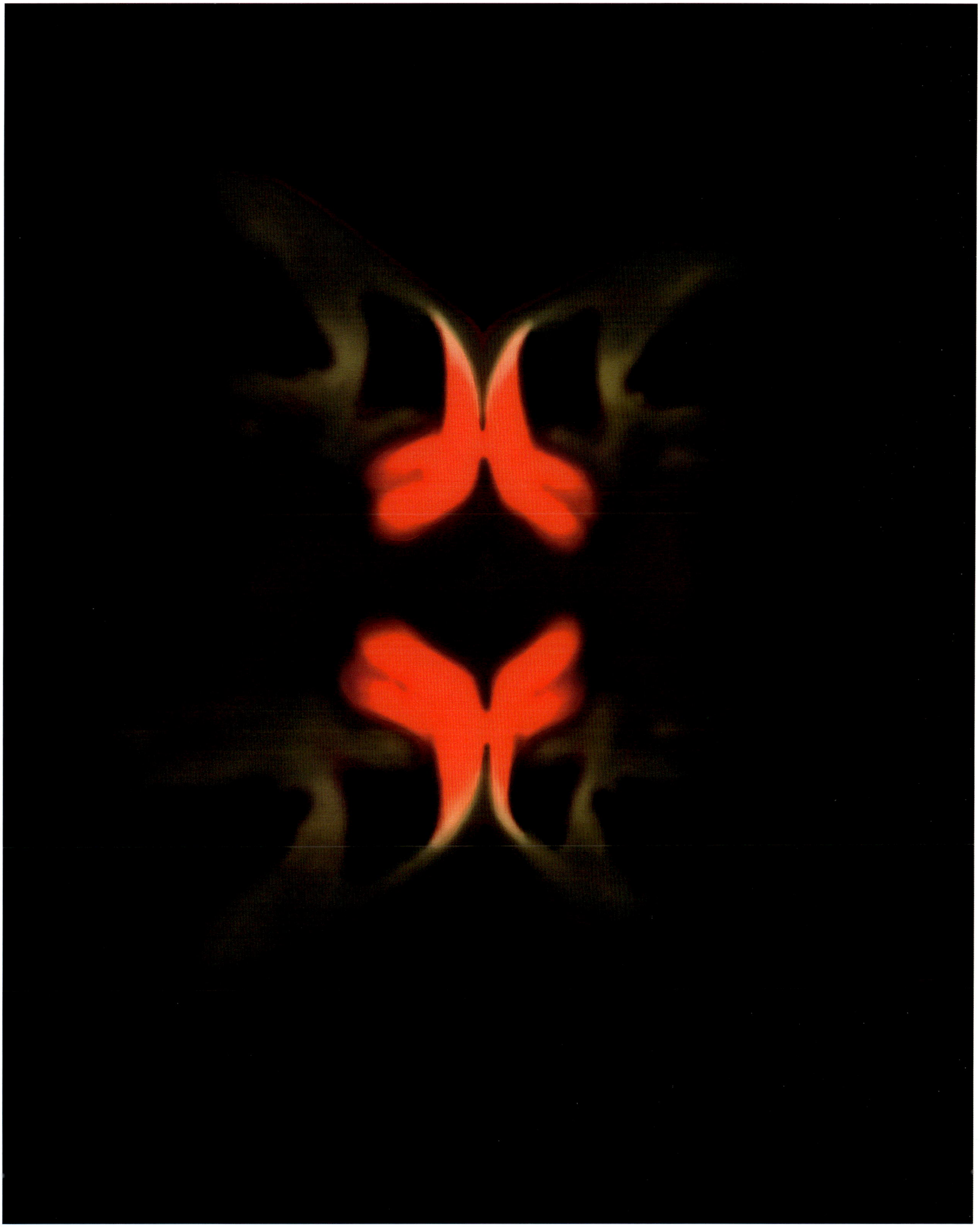

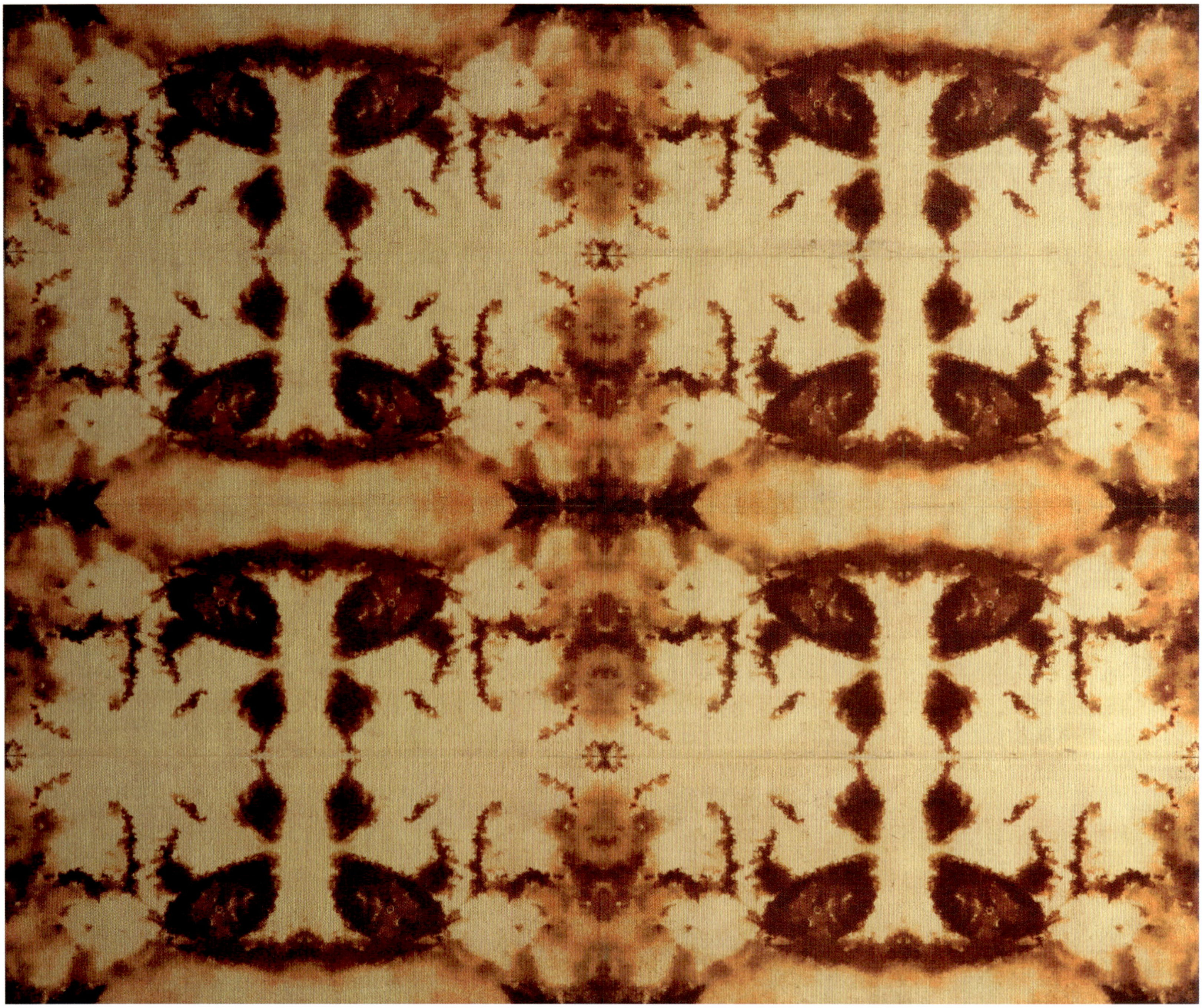

Intelligent Design (The Butterflies in Darwin's Eyes, The Bears in Darwin's Beard), 2008
Inkjet transfer and gold leaf on jute
116.5 x 138 cm / 46 x 54½ in

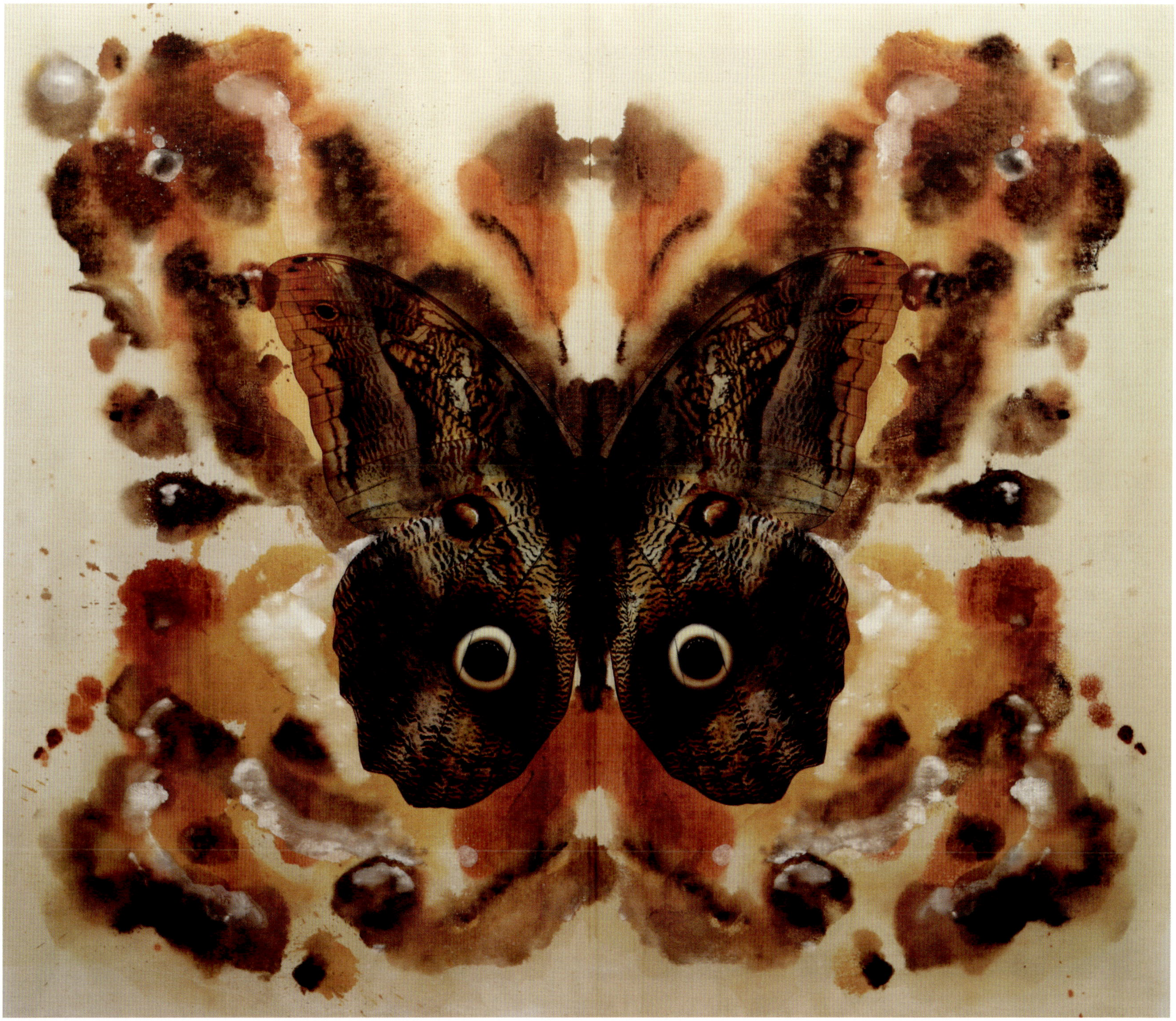

The Predator's Power of Appreciation (3), 2008
Oil and inkjet transfer on canvas
156 x 181 cm / 61½ x 71½ in

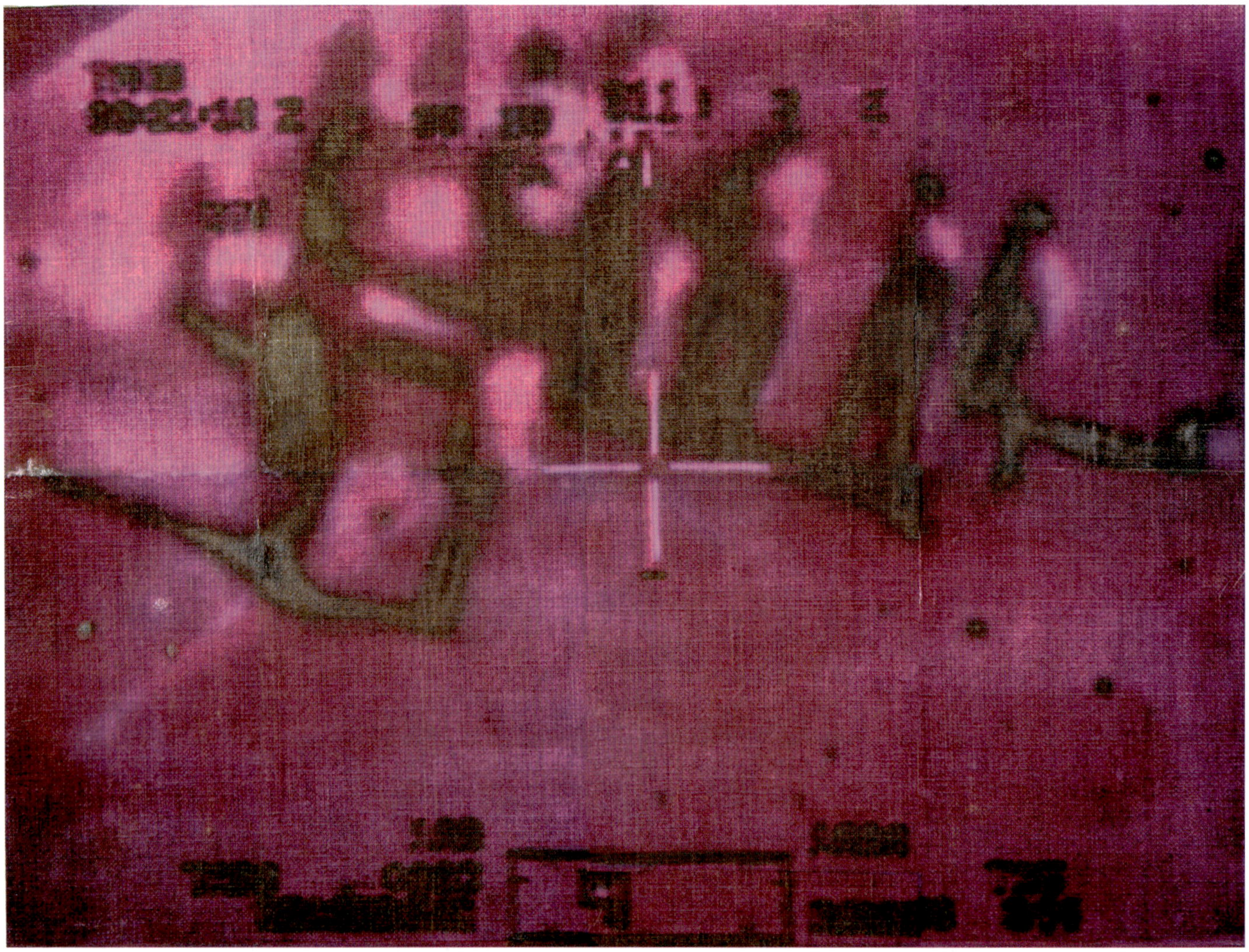

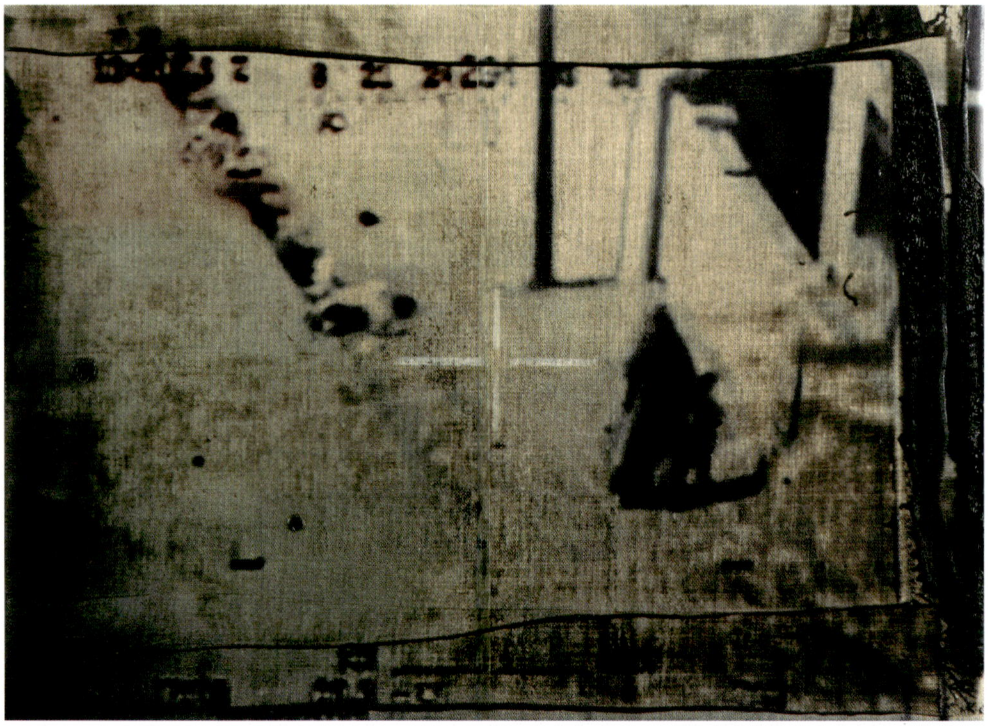

Ghosts, 2011
Oil and inkjet transfer on linen
85 x 113.5 cm / 33½ x 44¾ in

Hindsight 2, 2010/11
Oil and inkjet transfer on linen
41 x 56 cm / 16¼ x 22¼ in

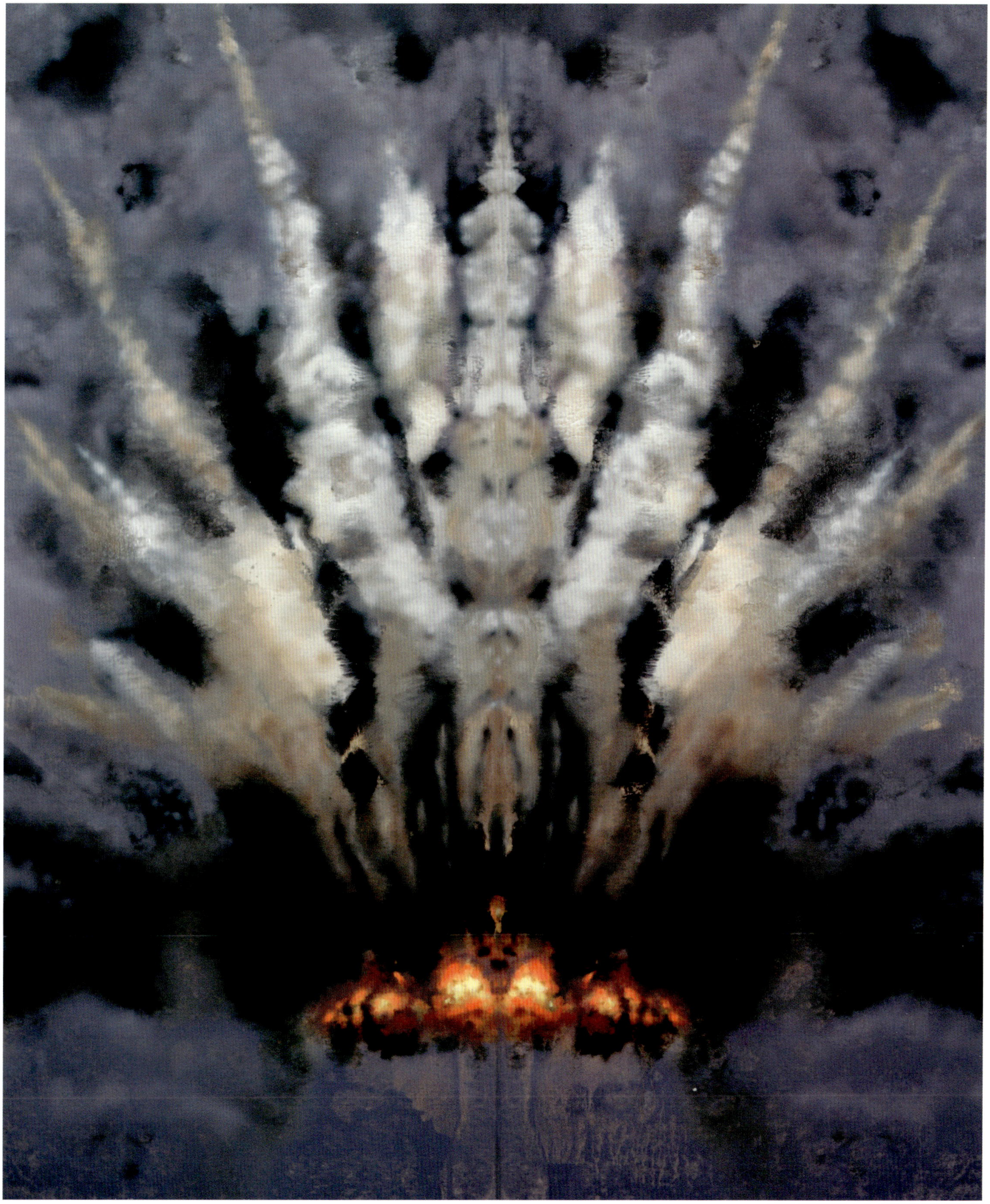

Perfect Explosion (1), 2009
Oil on cotton duct
122 x 102 cm / 48¼ x 40¼ in

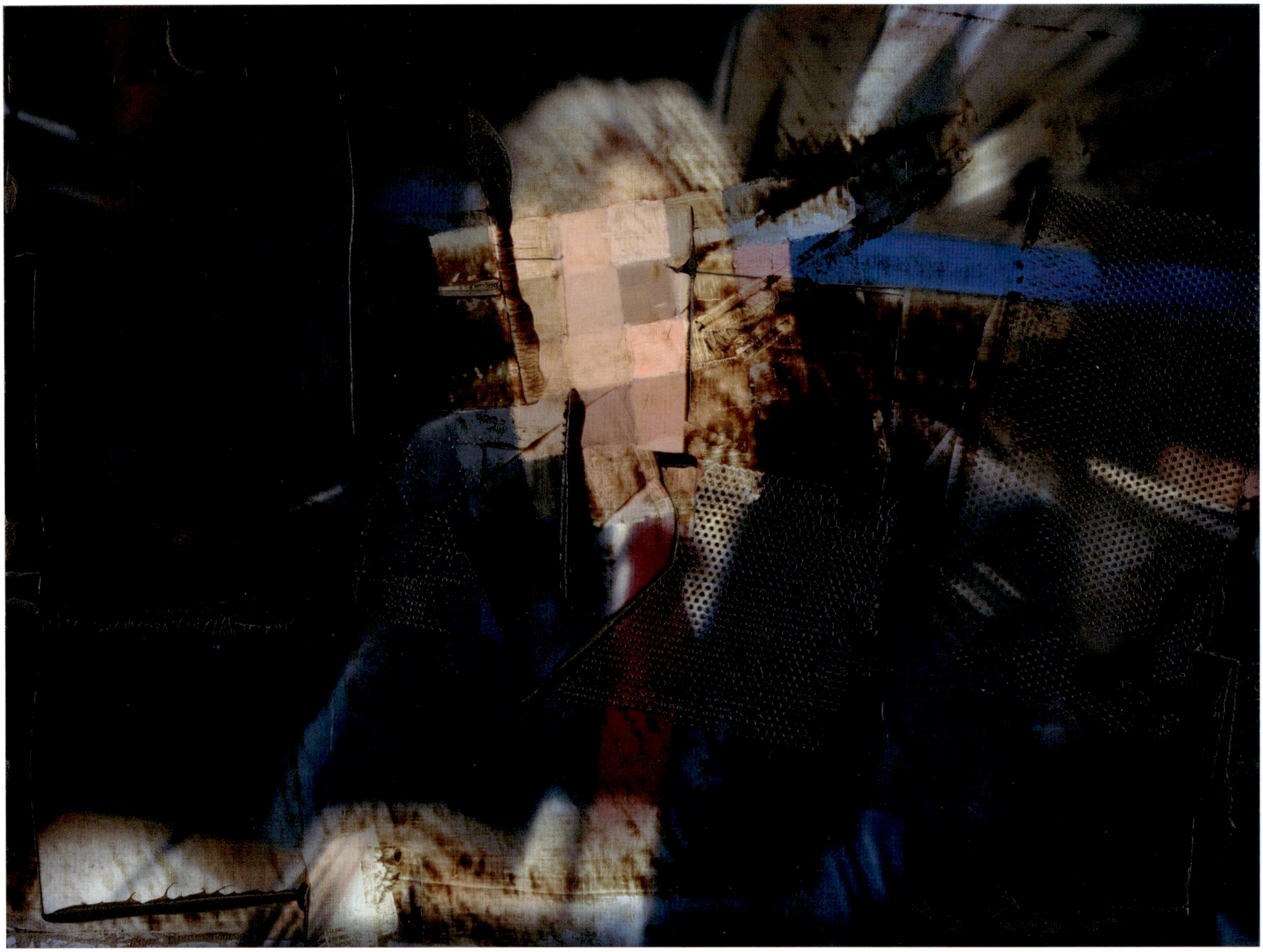

Figure at an Inquiry No.2, 2010
Oil on linen
90 x 120 cm / 35½ x 47¼ in
Collection: Tareq and Anna Islam

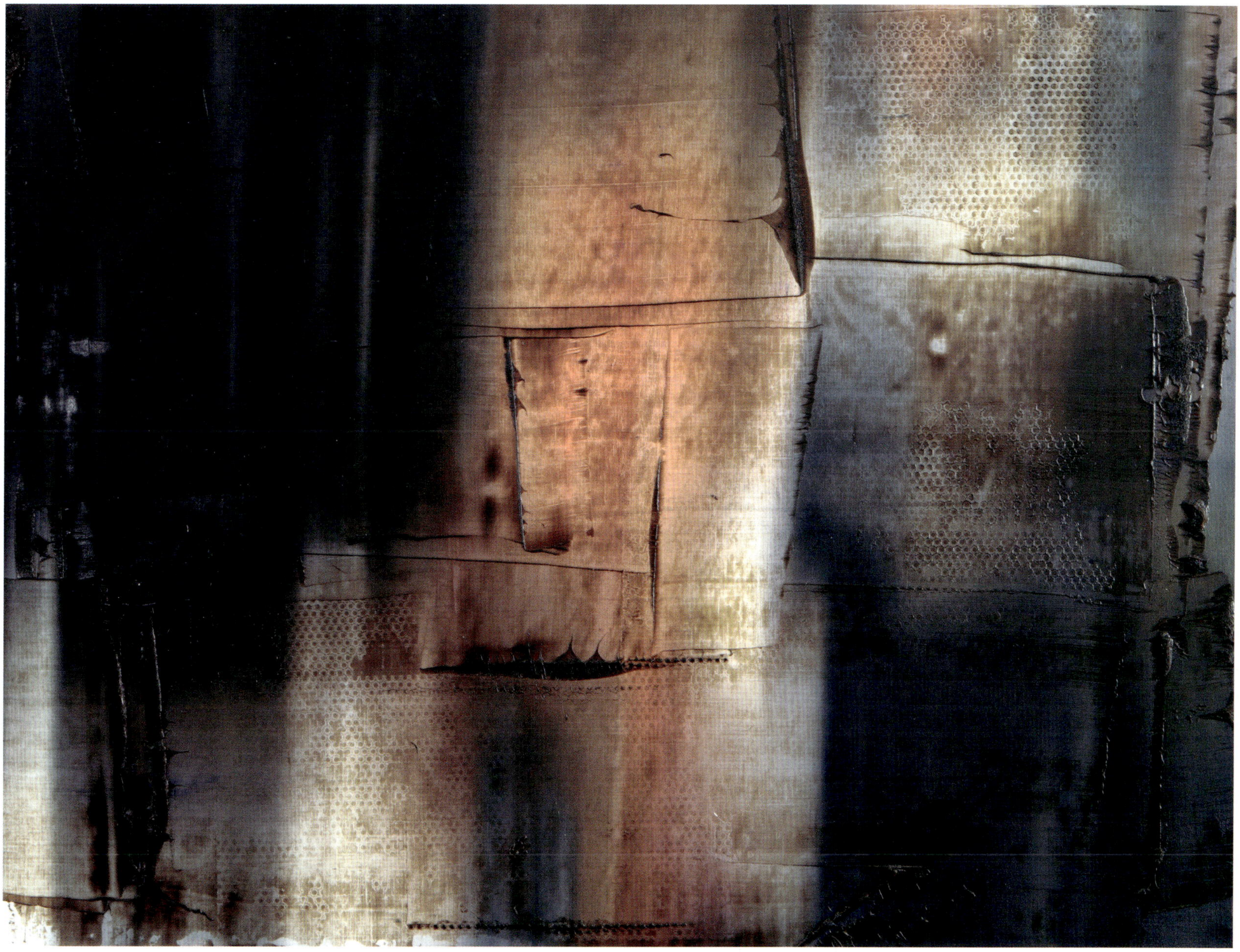

Figure at an Inquiry No.3, 2010
Oil on linen
90 x 120 cm / 35½ x 47¼ in

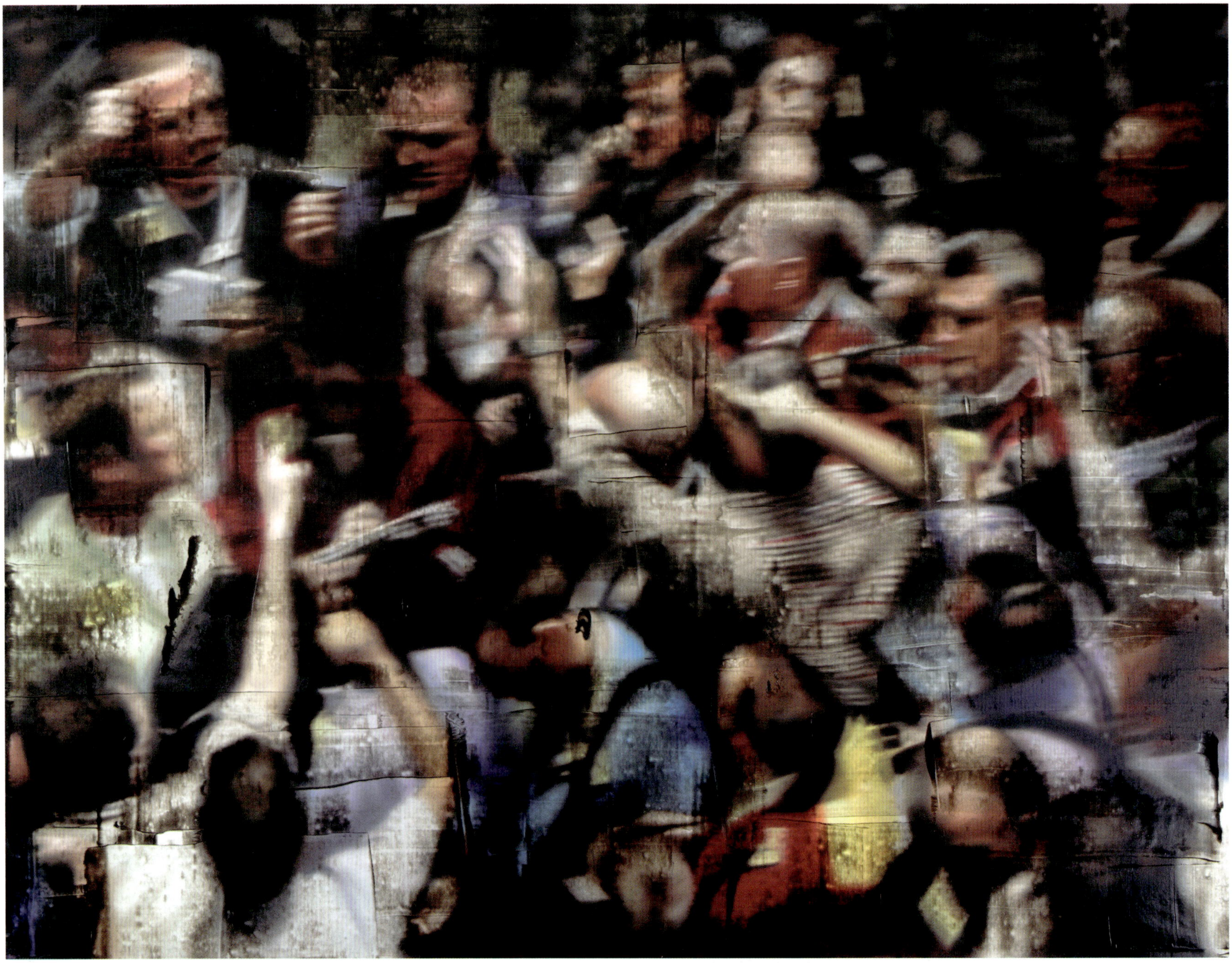

Surface Noise (Economy Stupid), 2010
Oil on jute
205 x 261 cm / 80¾ x 103 in
Private Collection, USA

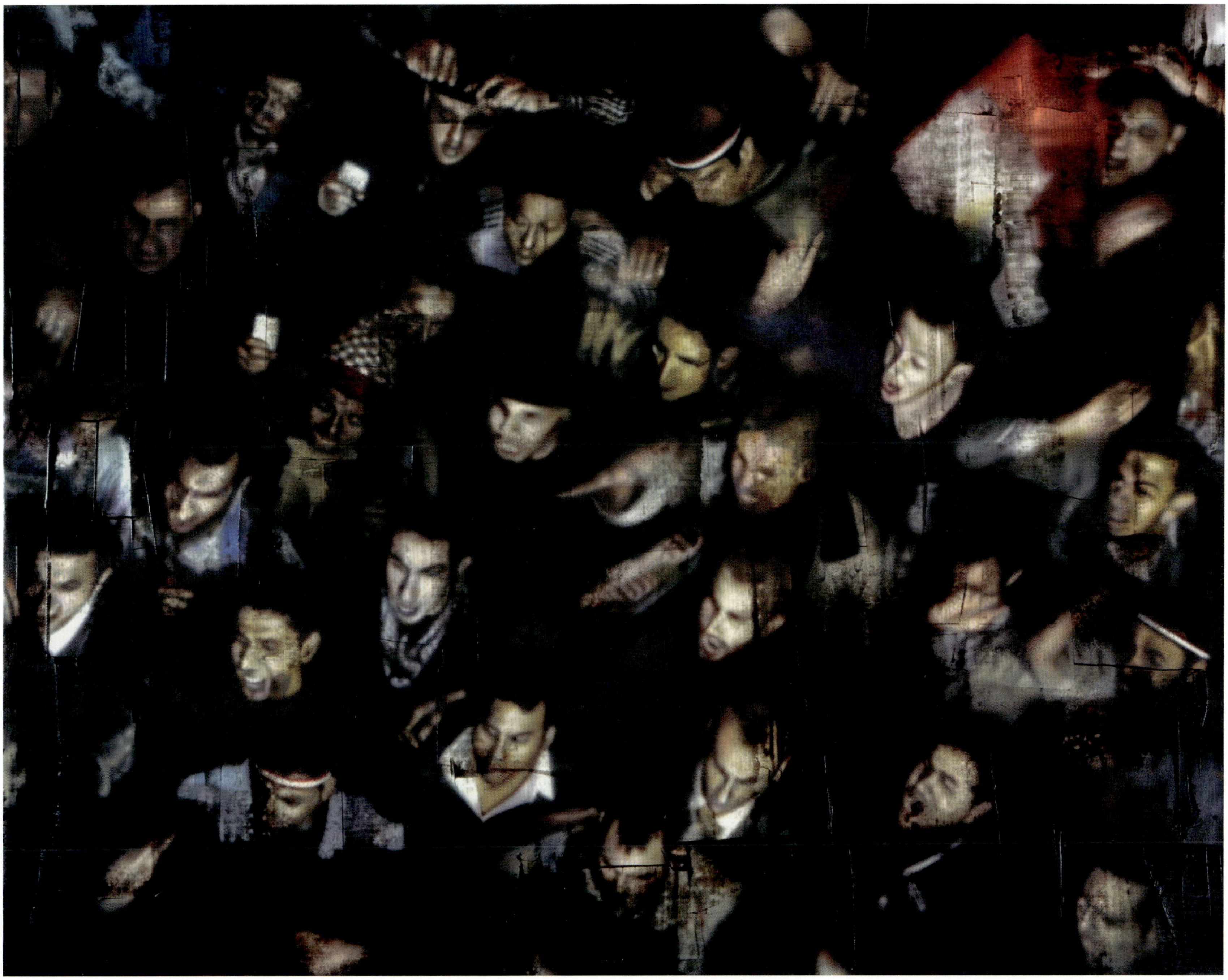

Surface Noise (Freedom + Authority), 2011
Oil on jute
205 x 257 cm / 80¾ x 101¼ in

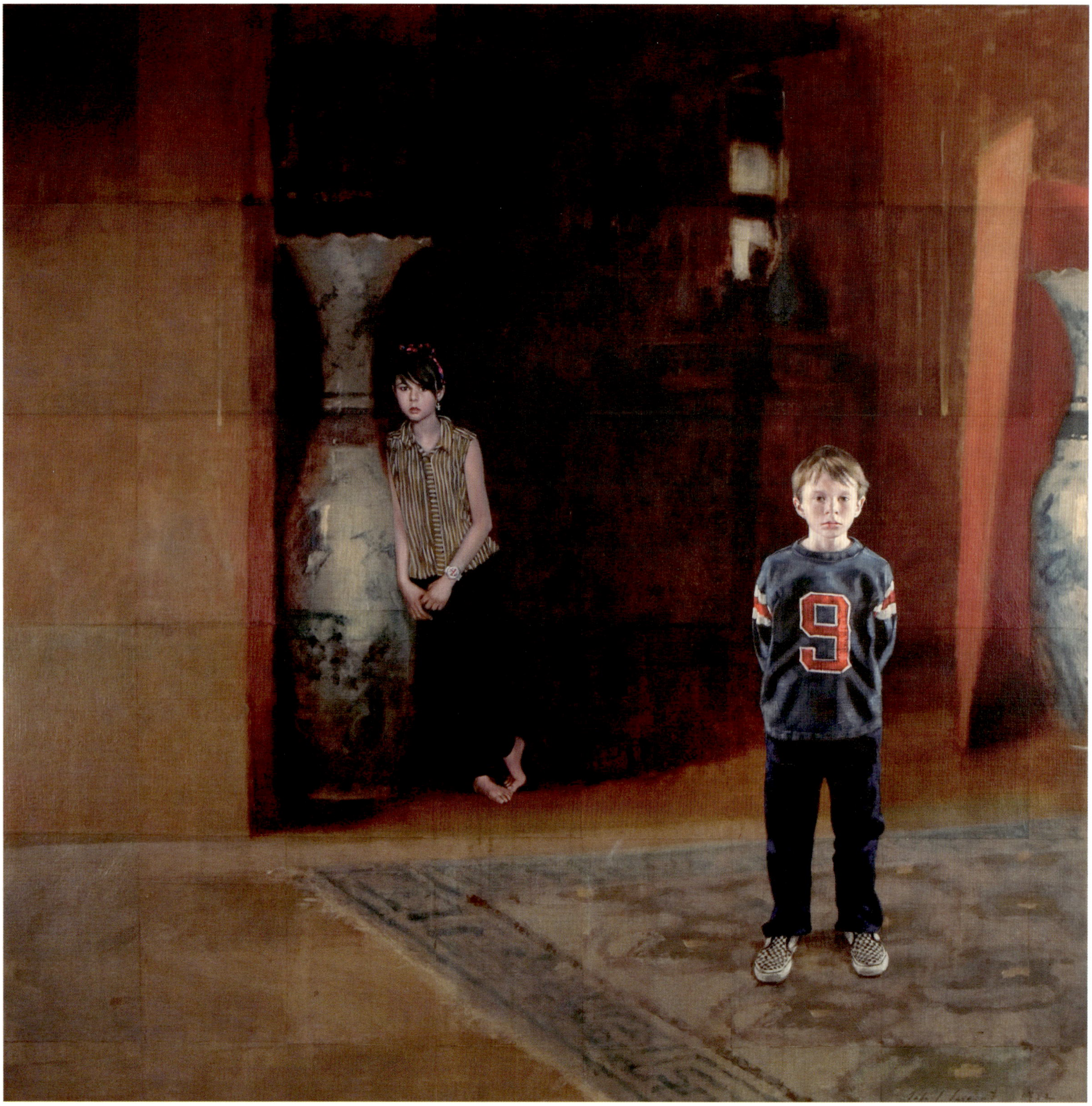

Time Passage No.3 (Fourteen and Nine) after John Singer Sargent, 2011
Oil and inkjet transfer on linen
222 x 220 cm / 87½ x 86¾ in

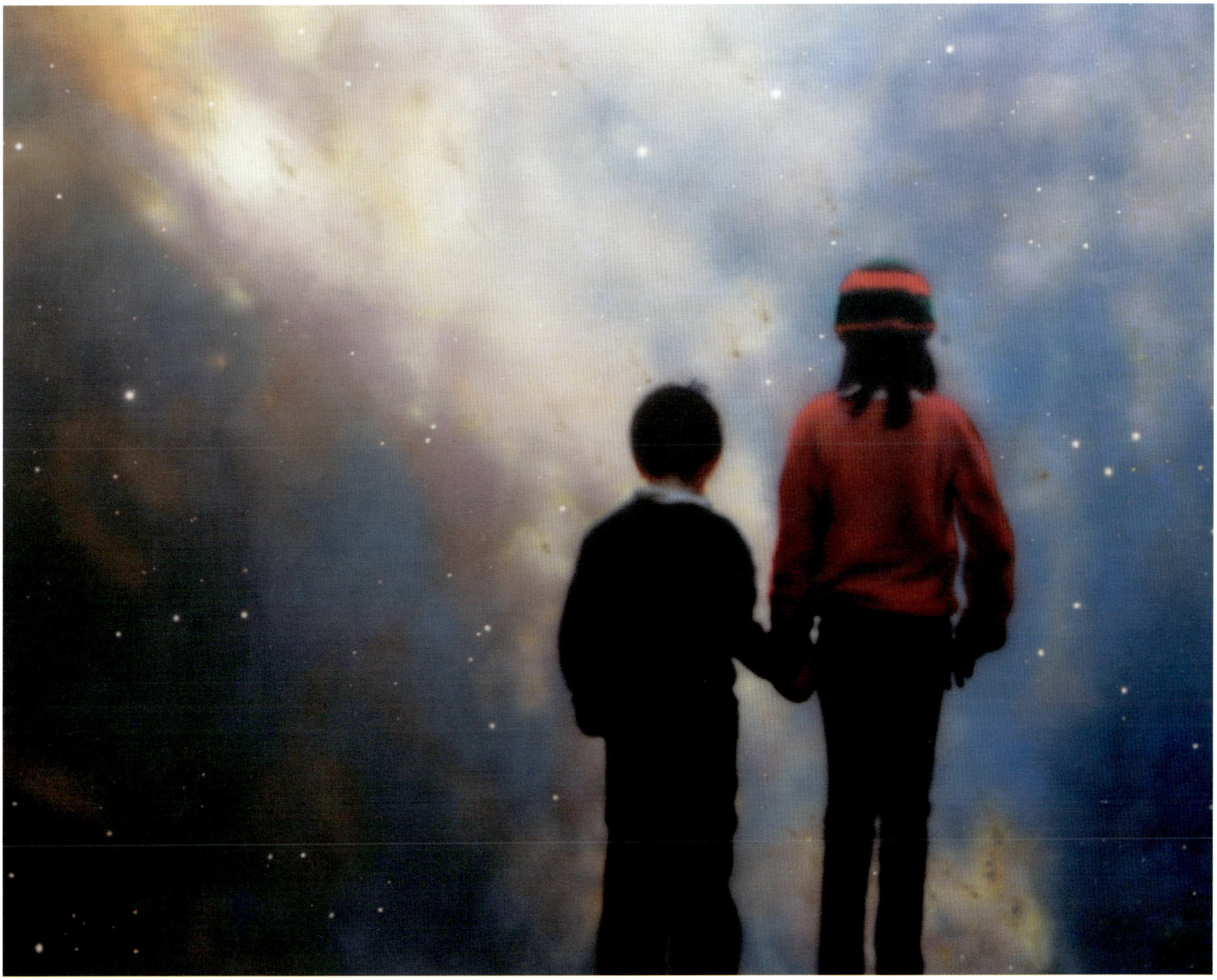

Stardust, 2008
Oil on linen
197 x 245 cm / 77¾ x 96½ in

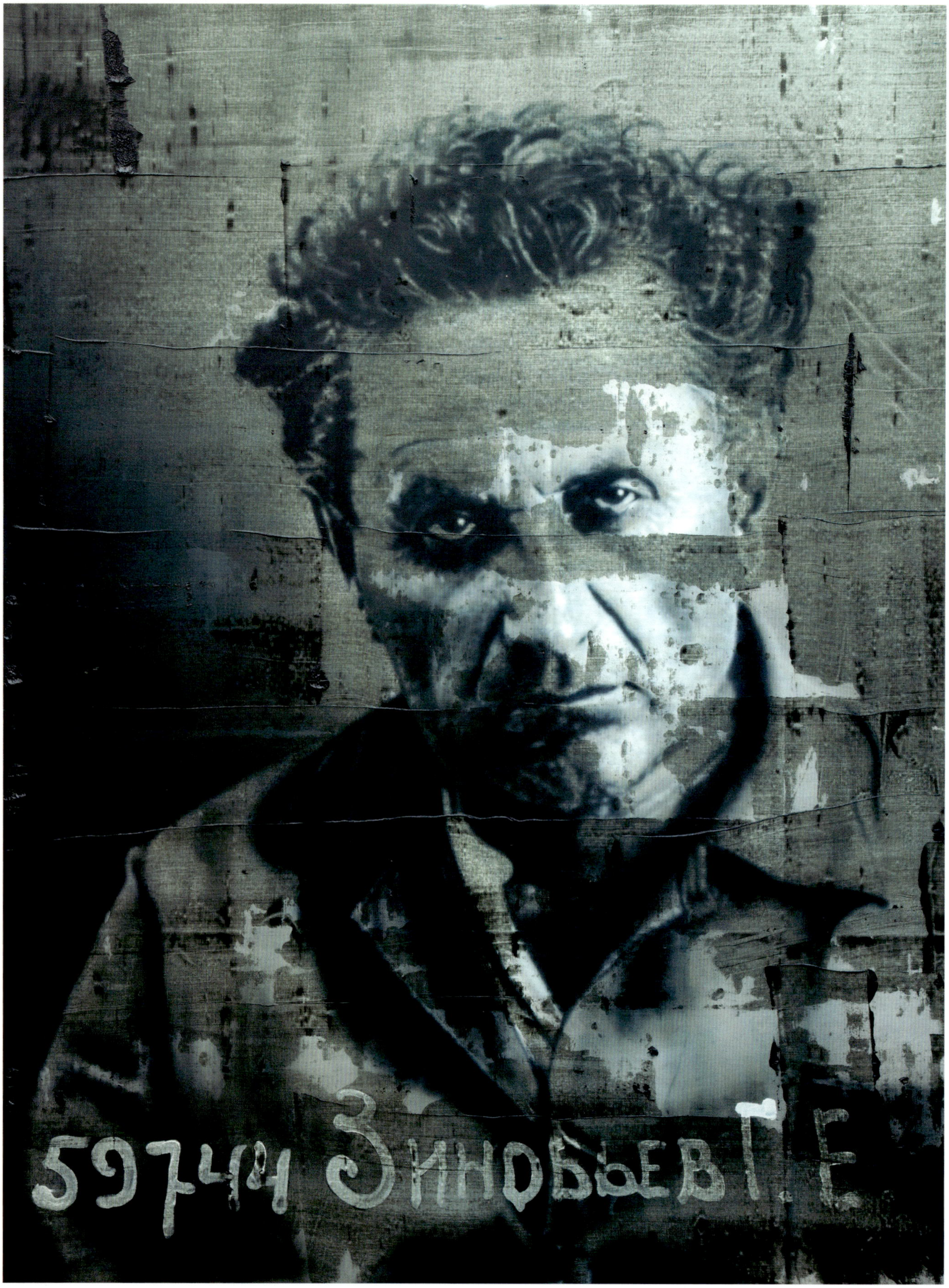

Fear No. 59744, 2012
Oil on linen
200 x 150 cm / 78¾ x 59¼ in
Collection: George Lloyd-Roberts

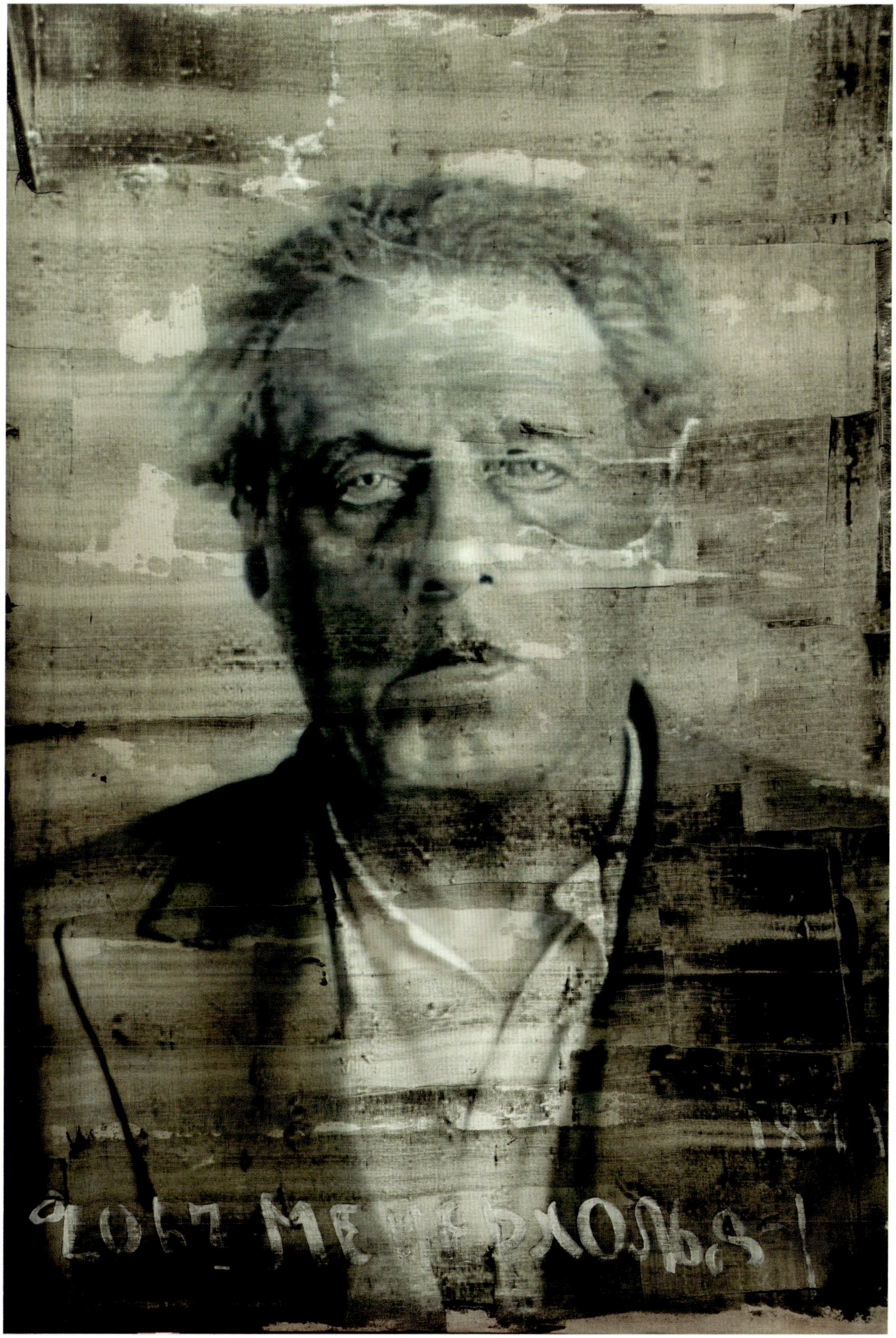

Fear No. 9067, 2013
Oil on linen
200 x 132 cm / 78¾ x 52 in

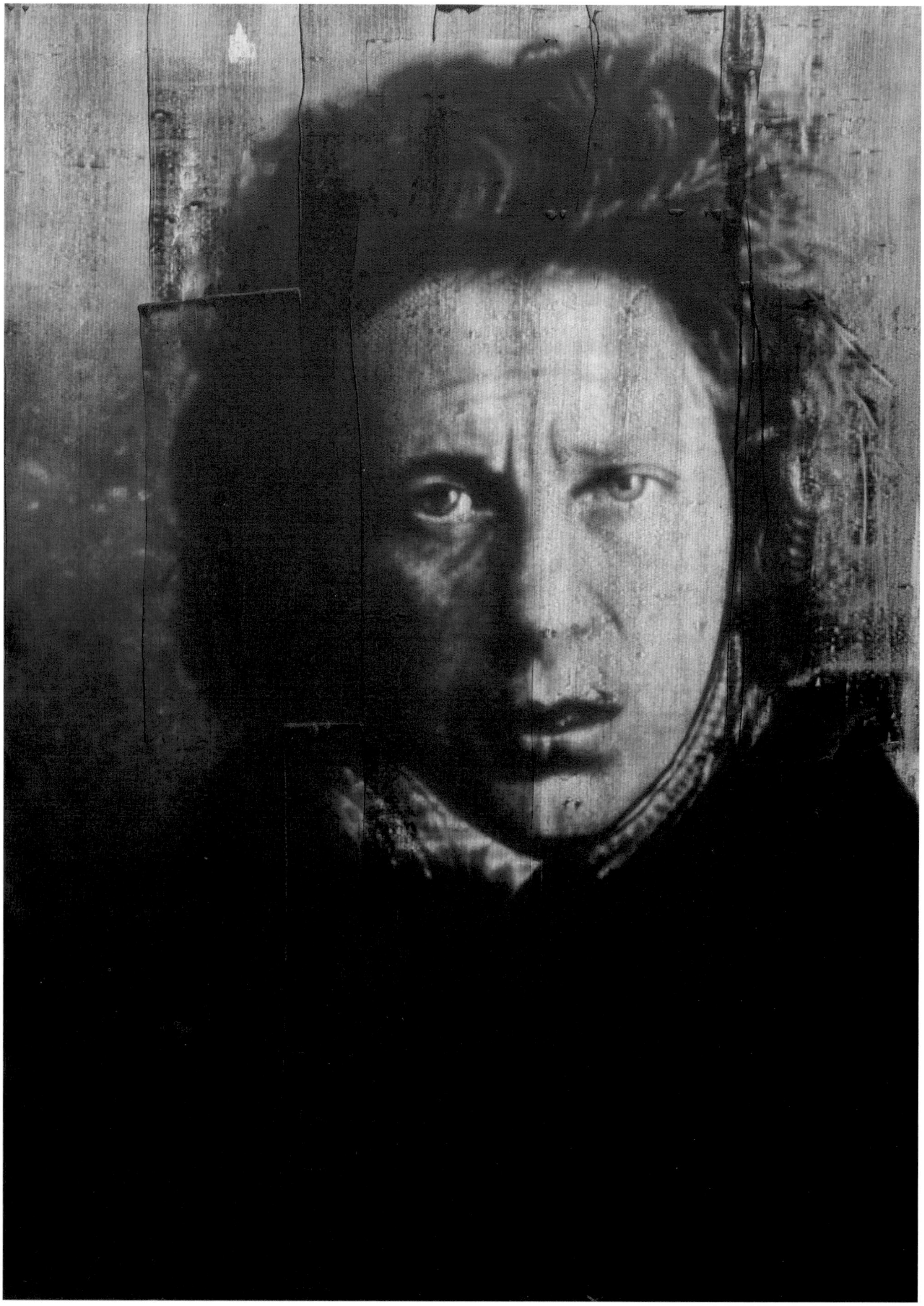

Fear No. 25171541, 2013
Oil on linen
200 x 144 cm / 78¾ x 56¾ in

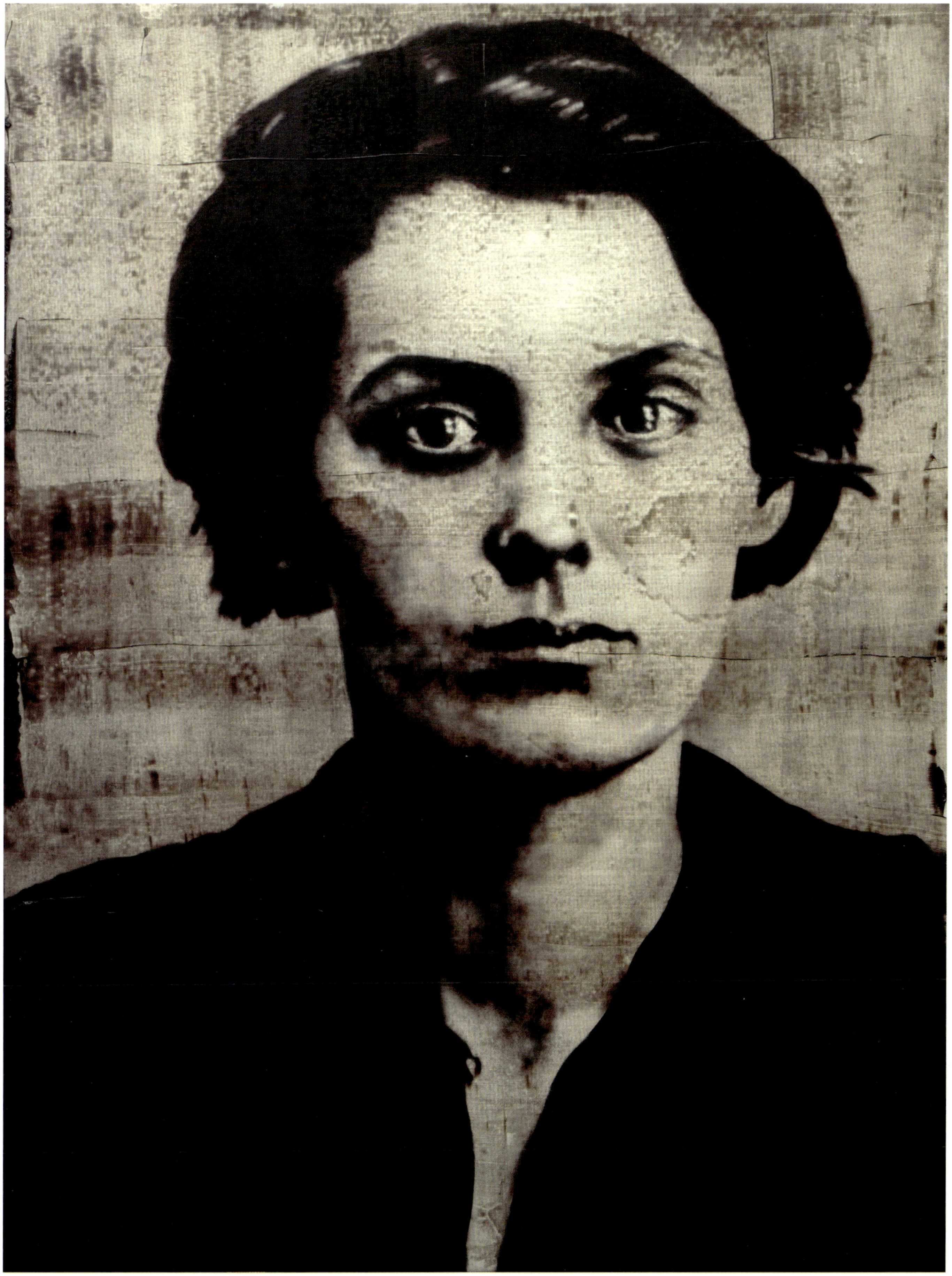

Fear No. 191037, 2013
Oil on linen
200 x 150 cm / 78¾ x 59¼ in

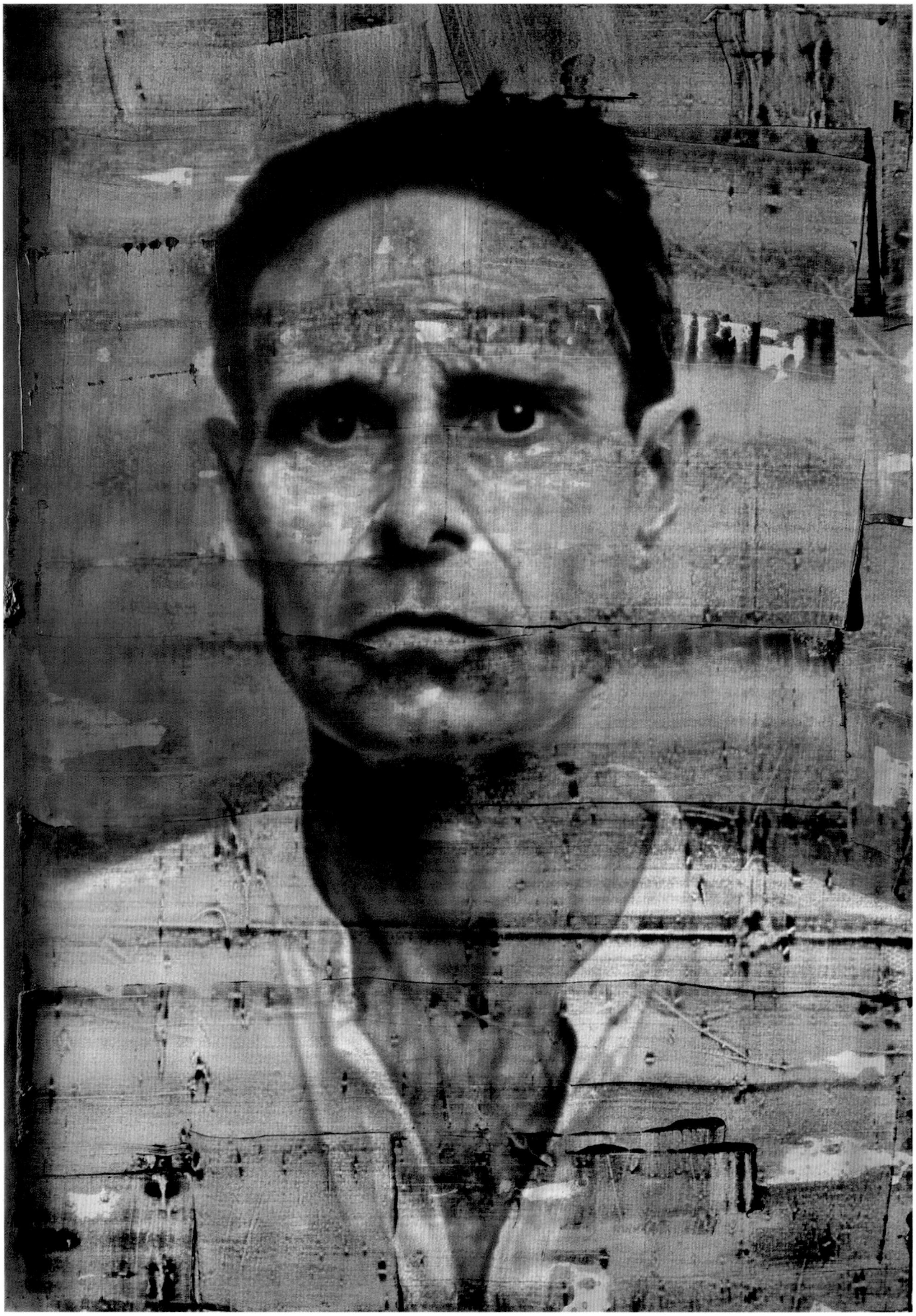

Fear No. 1, 2013
Oil on linen
138 x 200 cm / 54½ x 78¾ in
Collection: Ömer Koç

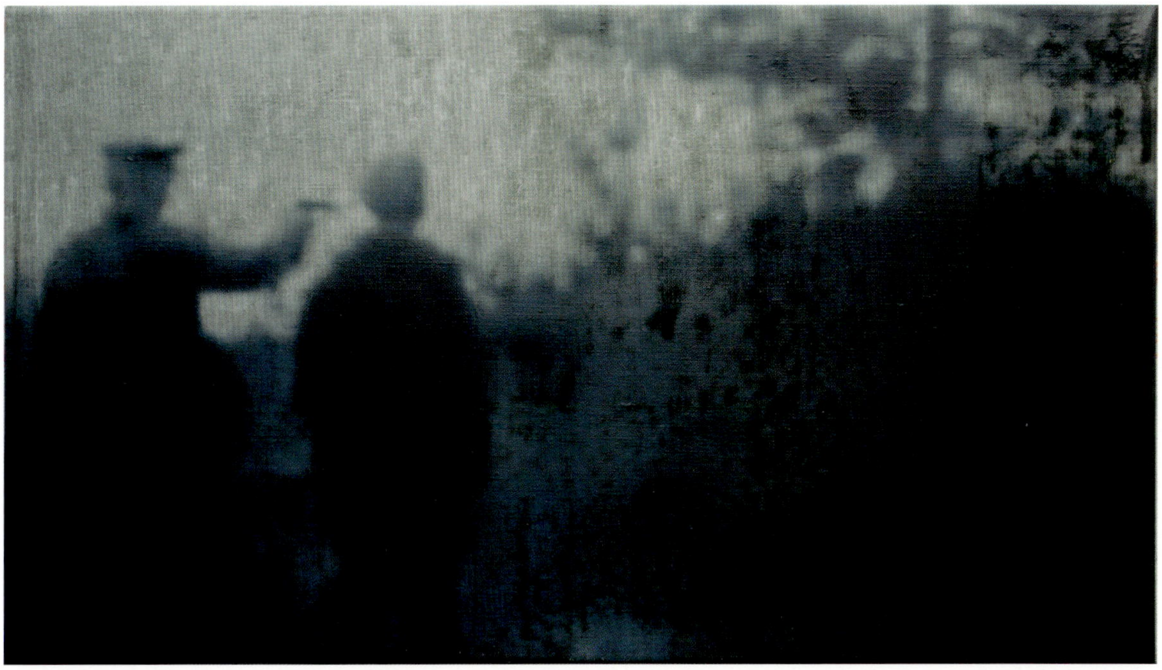

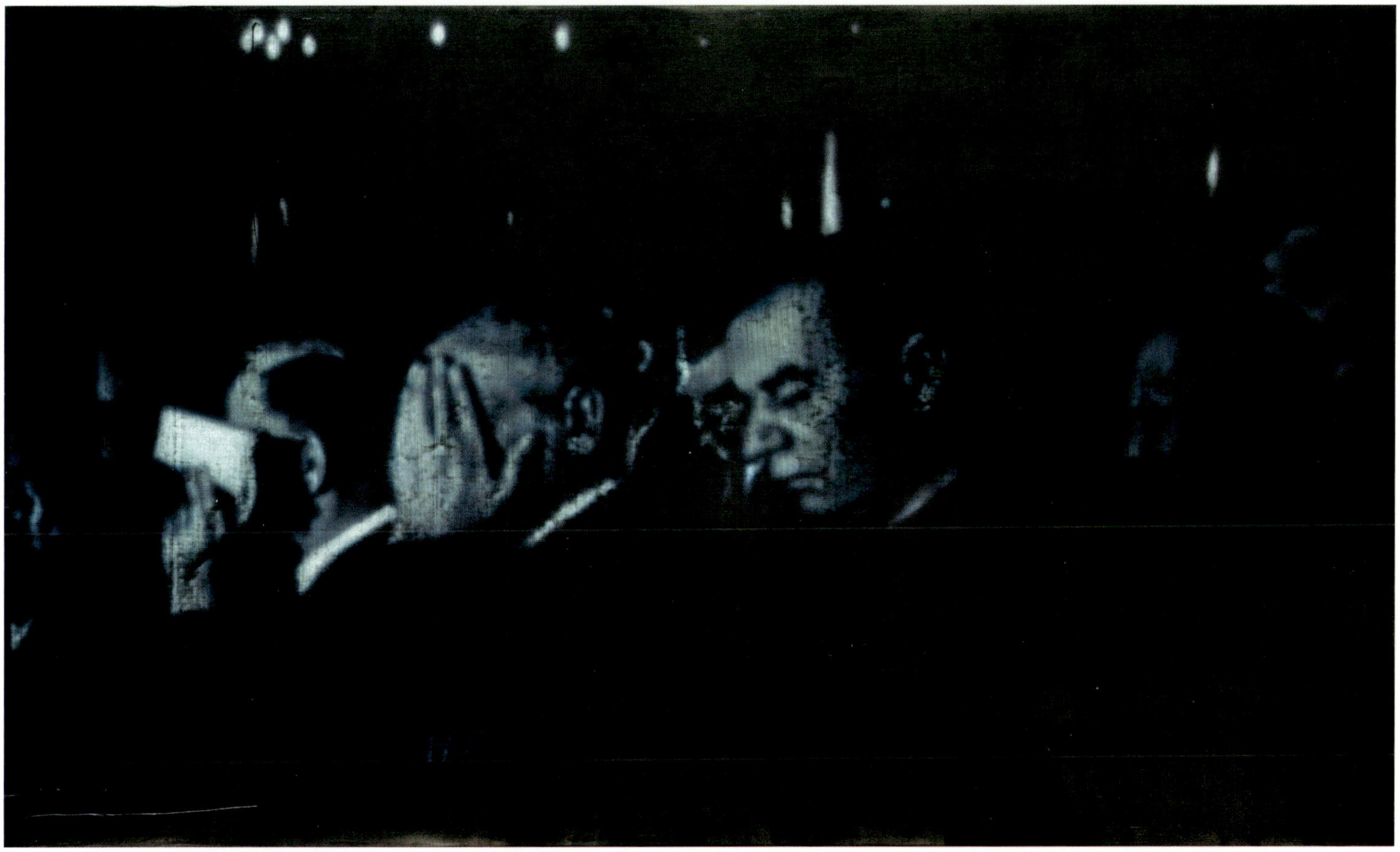

Fear No. 80015302, 2013
Oil on linen
40 x 71 cm / 15¾ x 28 in

Fear No. 15266, 2012
Oil on linen
90 x 150 cm / 35½ x 59¼ in

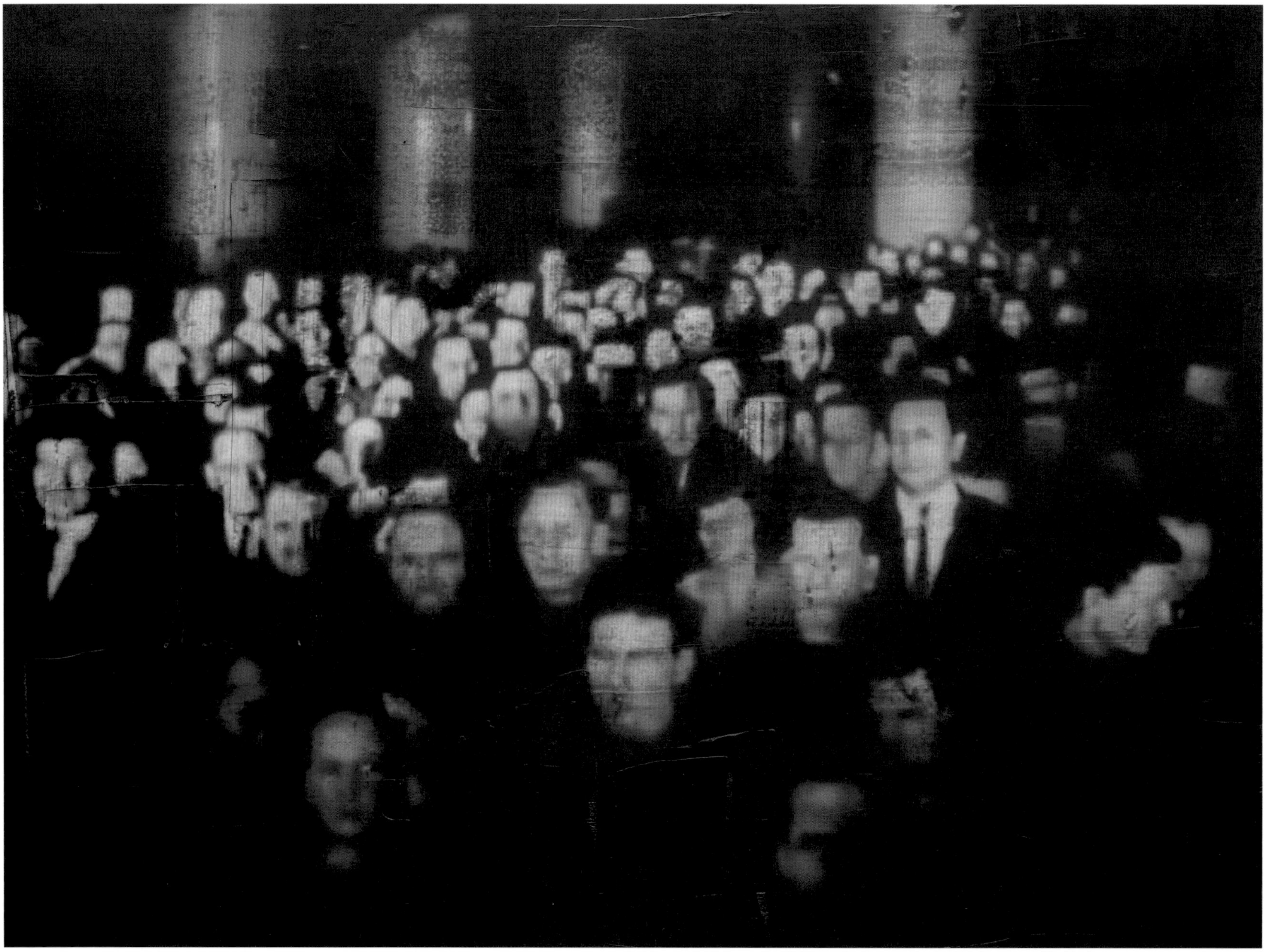

Fear No. 5613, 2012
Oil on linen
210 x 280 cm / 82¾ x 110¼ in

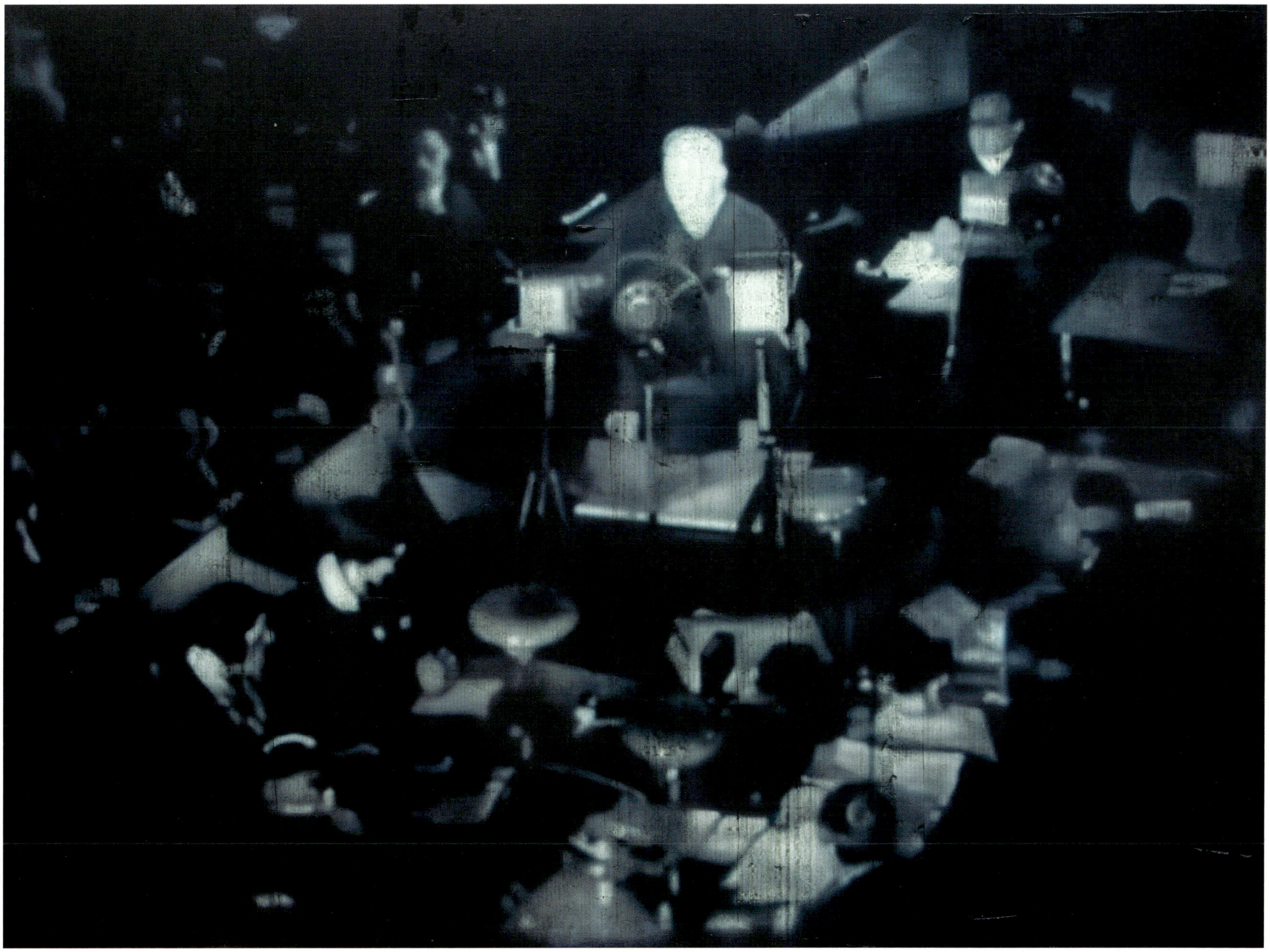

Fear No. 1325, 2013
Oil on linen
210 x 280 cm / 82¾ x 110¼ in

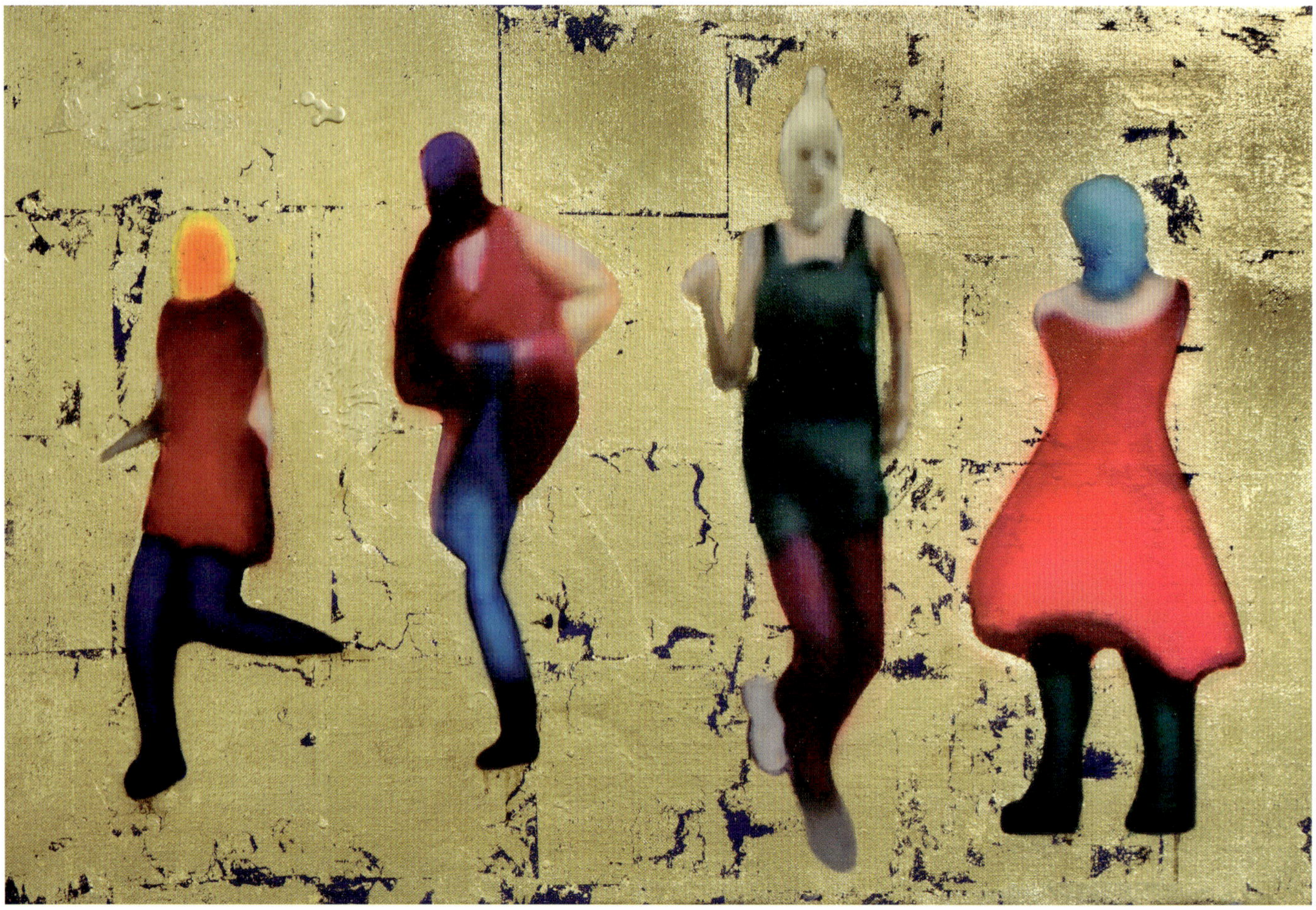

No Fear, 2013
Oil, acrylic & gold leaf on linen
56 x 81 cm / 22⅛ x 31⅞ in
Private Collection, UK

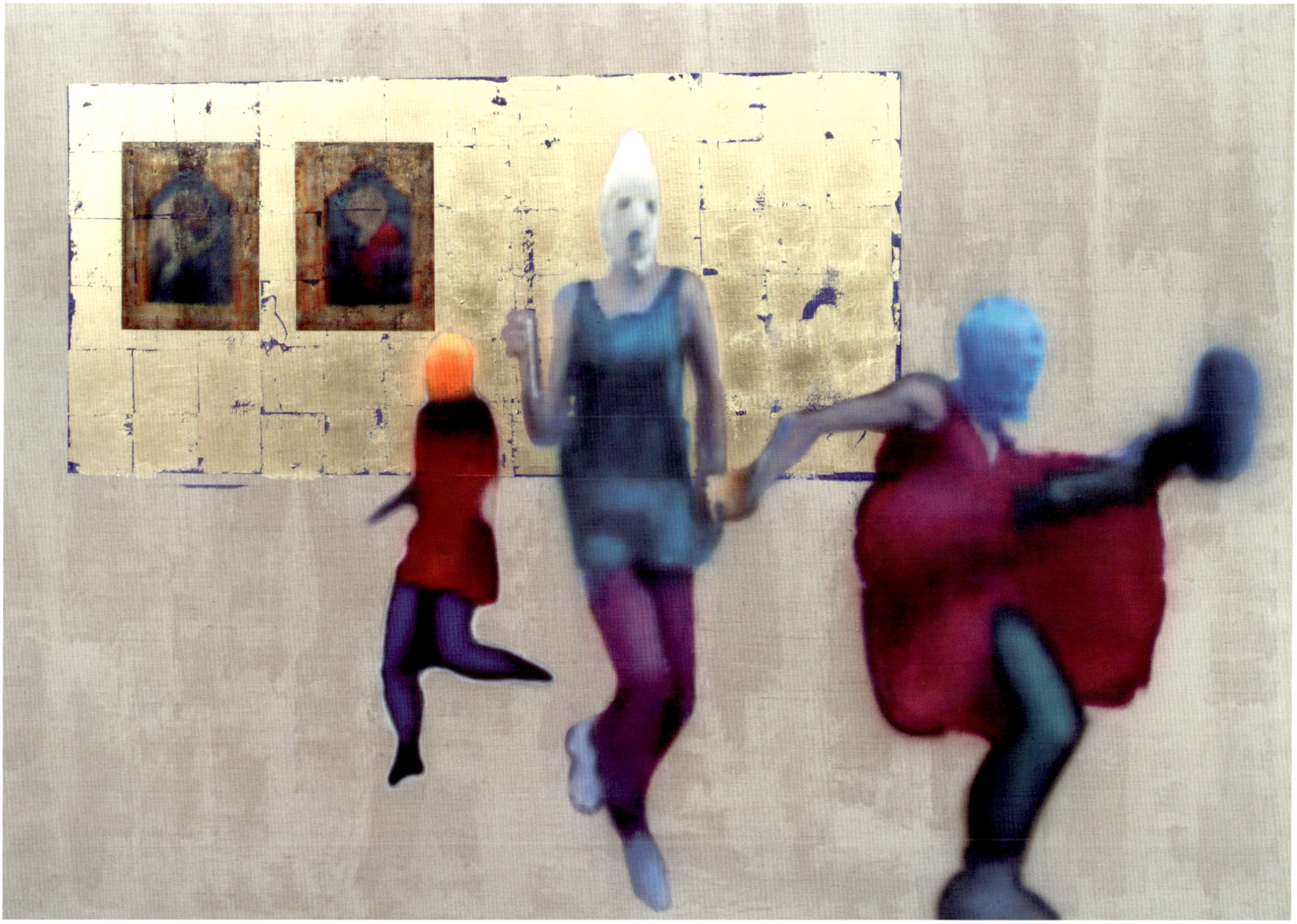

Fear Not, 2013
Oil, gold leaf & inkjet transfer on jute
200 x 280 cm / 78¾ x 110¼ in

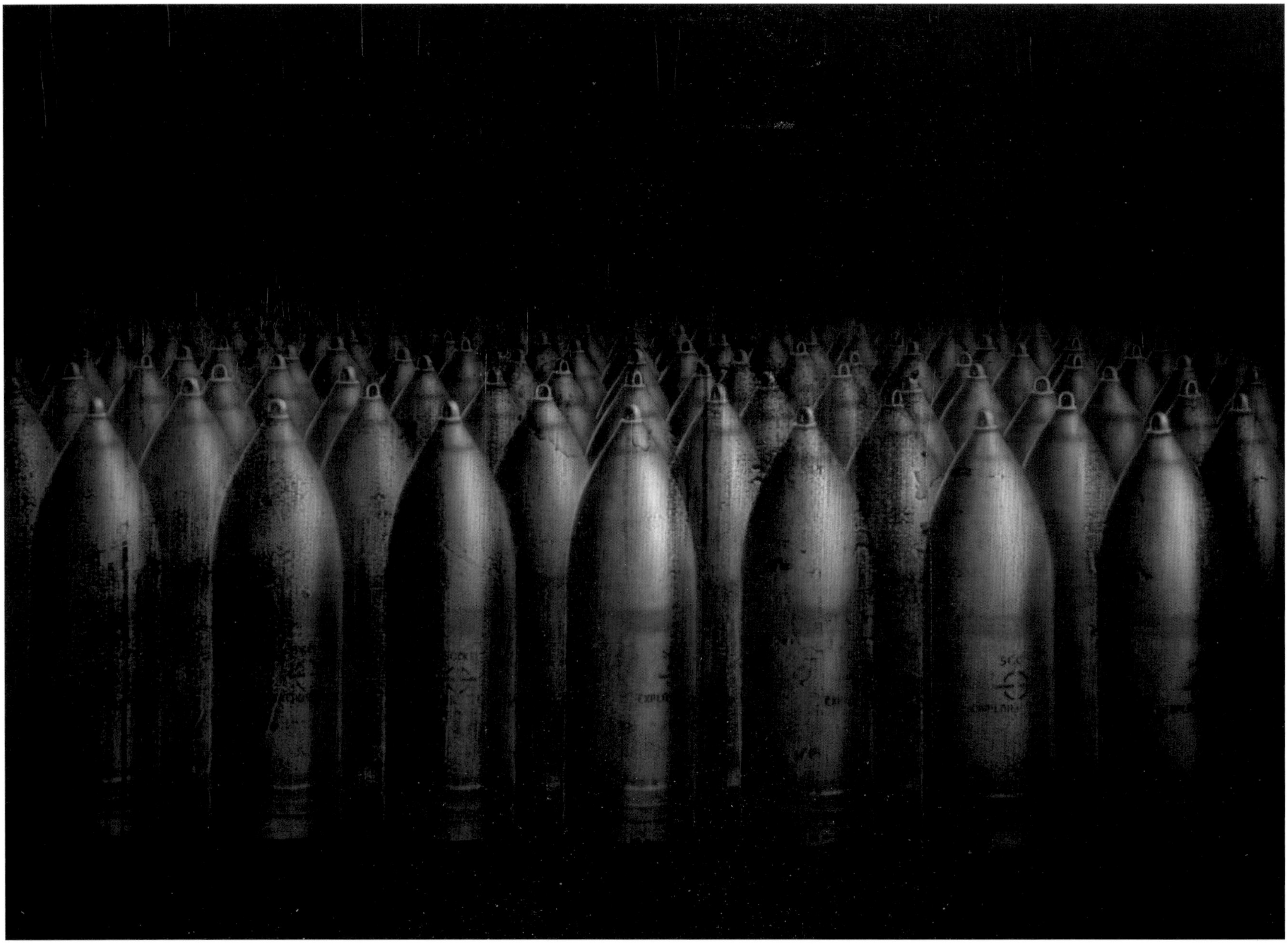

A Hundred Years, 2014
Oil on linen
196 x 267 cm / 77⅛ x 105⅛ in
Collection: Nick Taylor

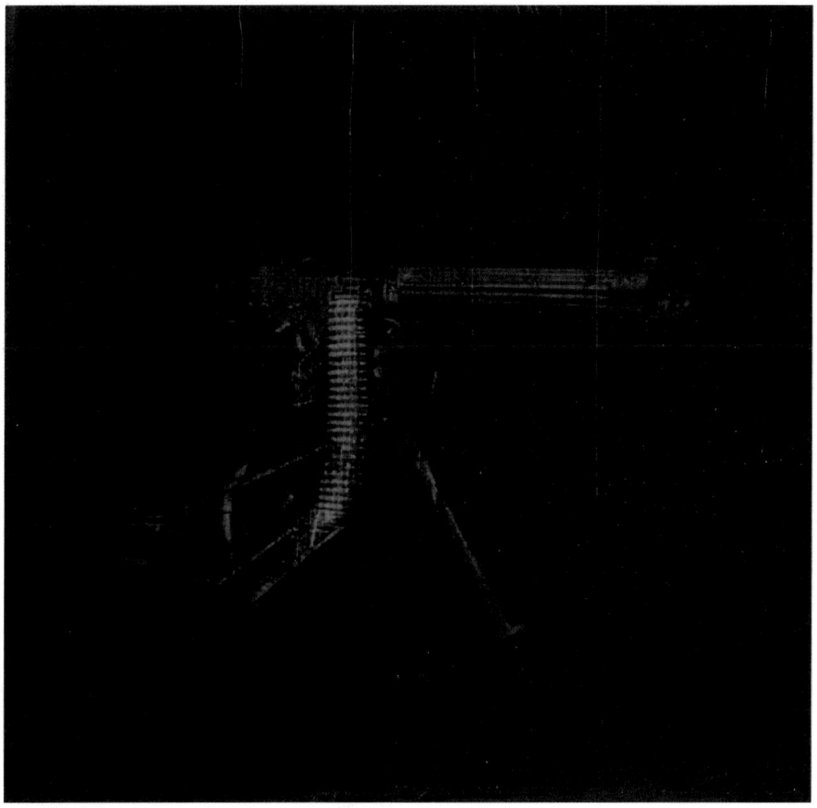

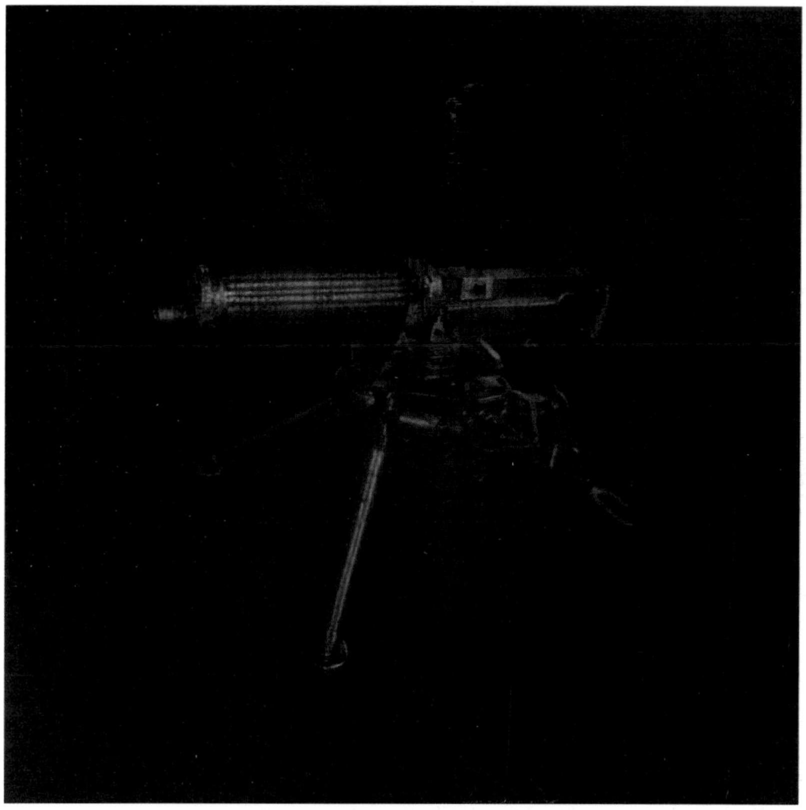

General Purpose (Left), 2014
Oil on linen
150.5 x 150.5 cm / 59¼ x 59¼ in
Private Collection, China

General Purpose (Right), 2014
Oil on linen
150.5 x 150.5 cm / 59¼ x 59¼ in
Collection: Nick Taylor

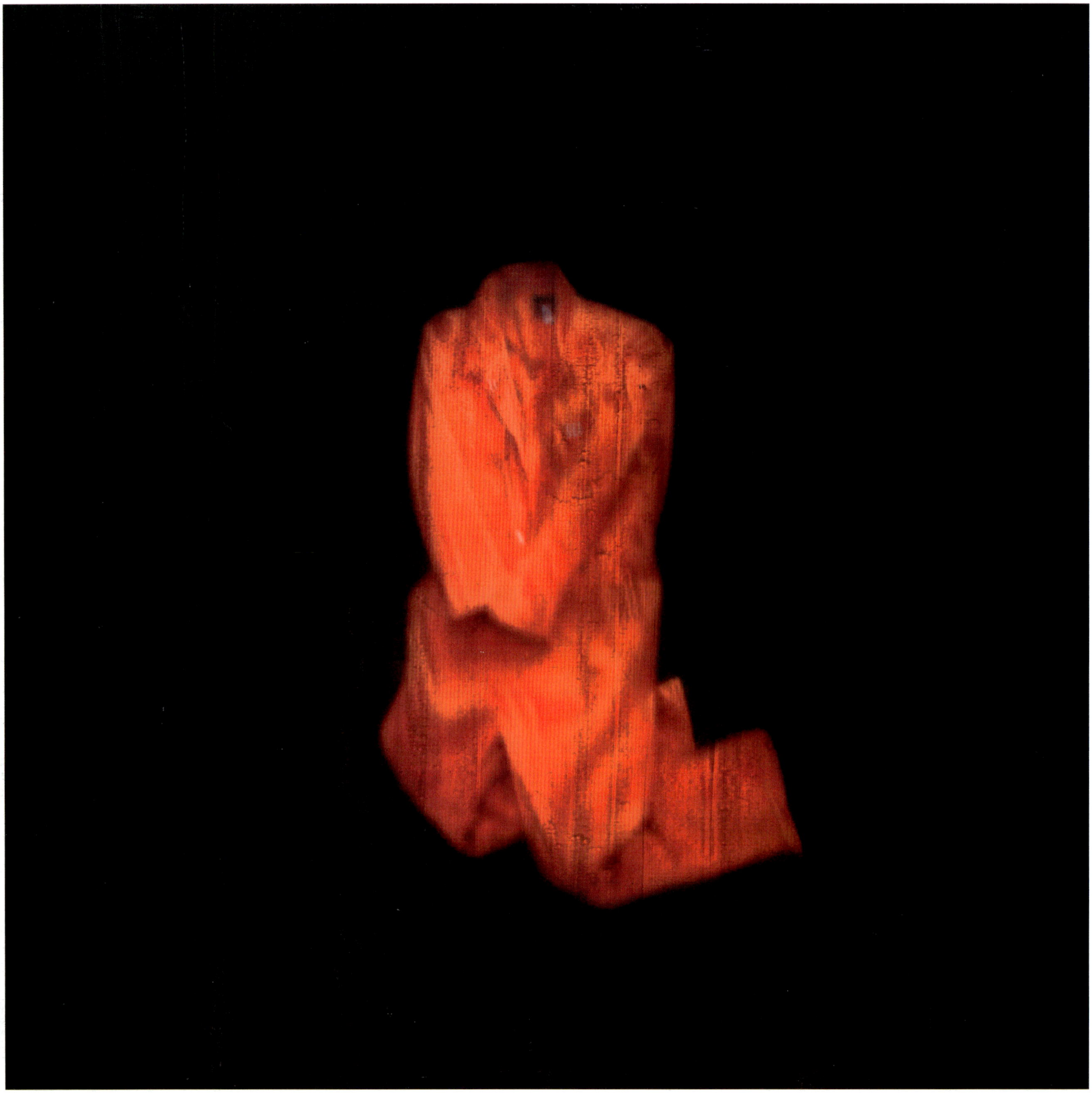

Kneel, 2015
Oil on linen
200 x 200 cm / 78¾ x 78¾ in

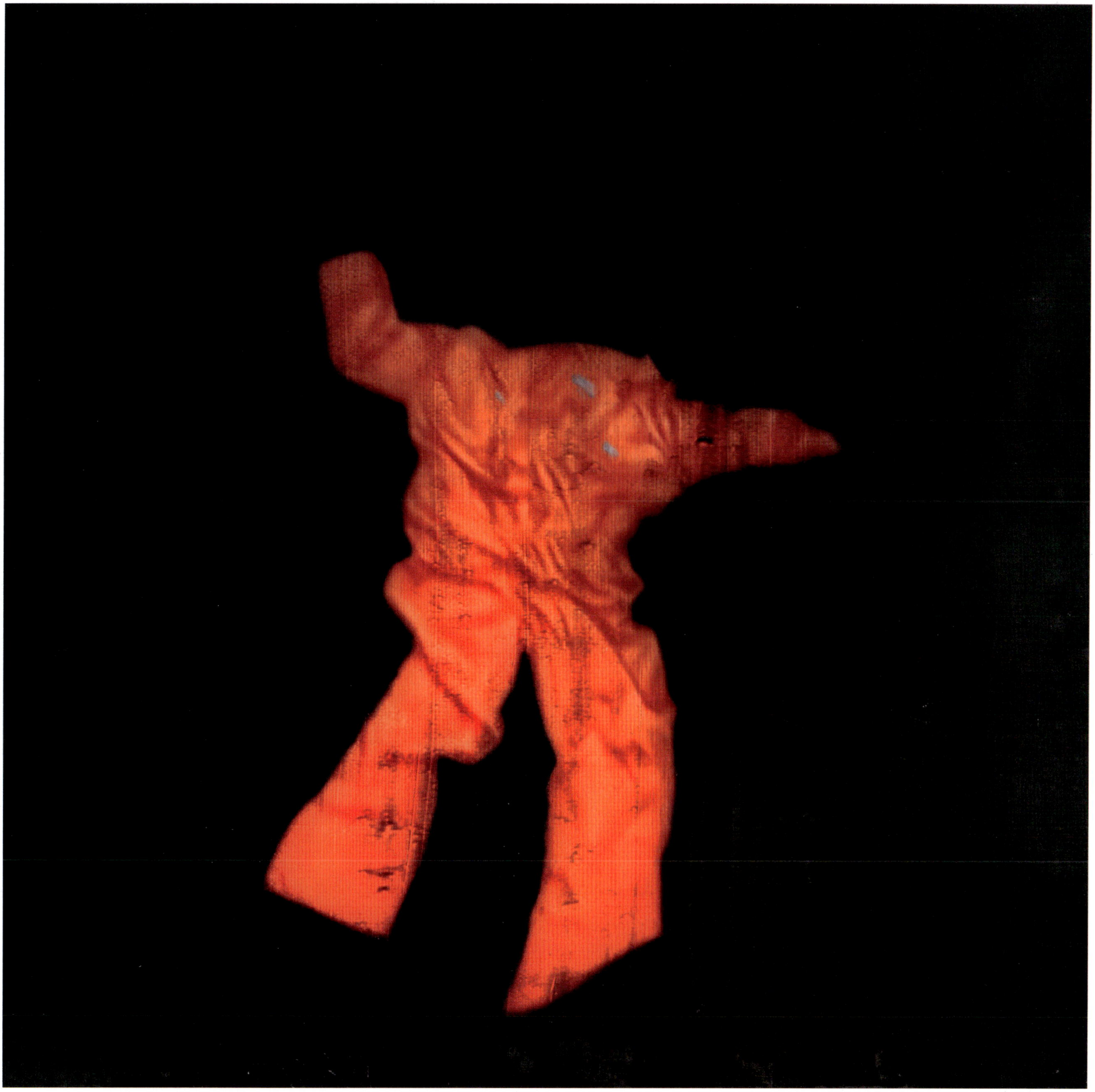

Fall, 2015
Oil on linen
200 x 200 cm / 78¾ x 78¾ in

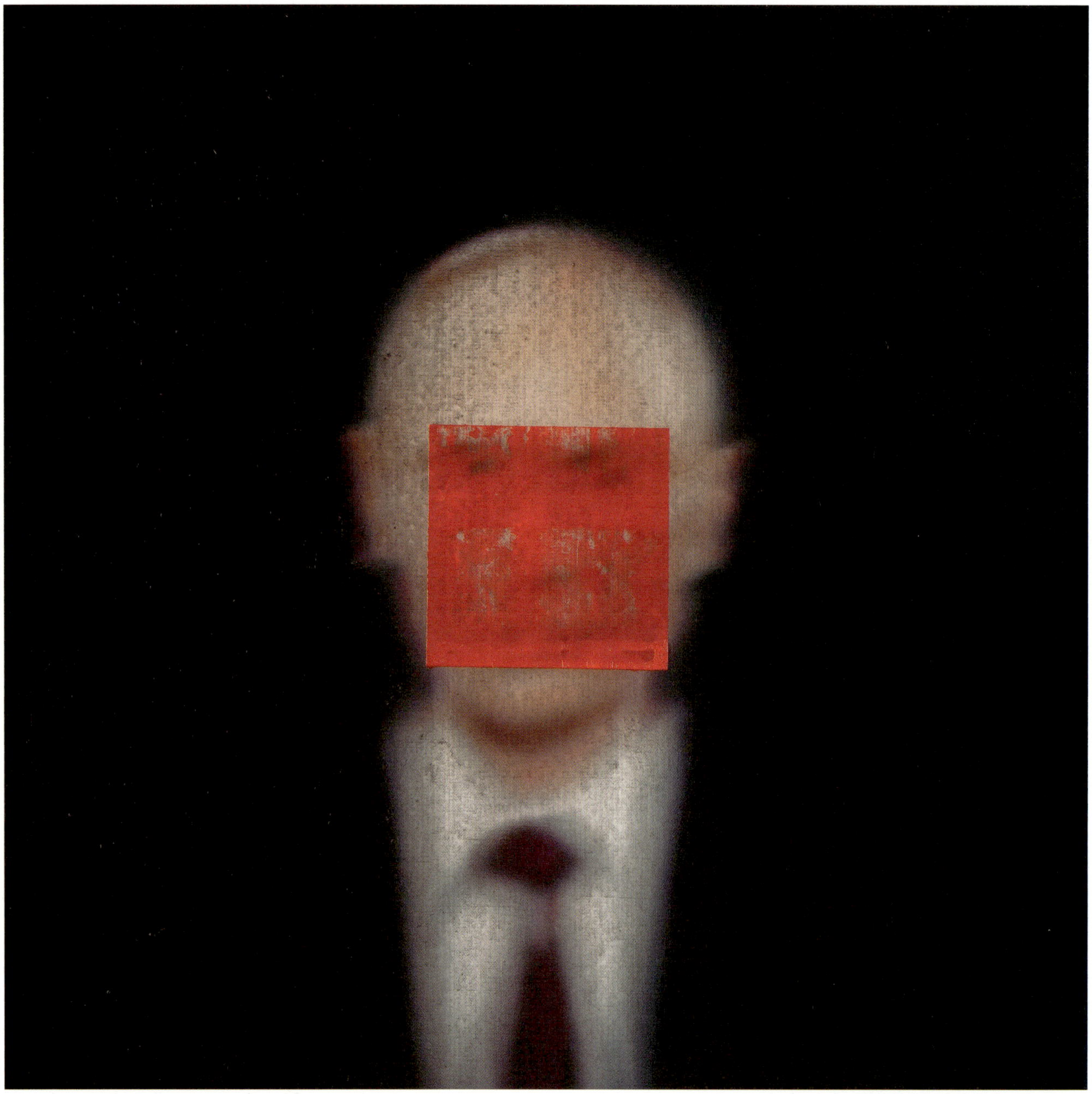

Red Square, 2014
Oil on linen
76 x 76 cm / 29⅞ x 29⅞ in

Putin Variations II, 2014
Oil on linen
76 x 76 cm / 29⅞ x 29⅞ in

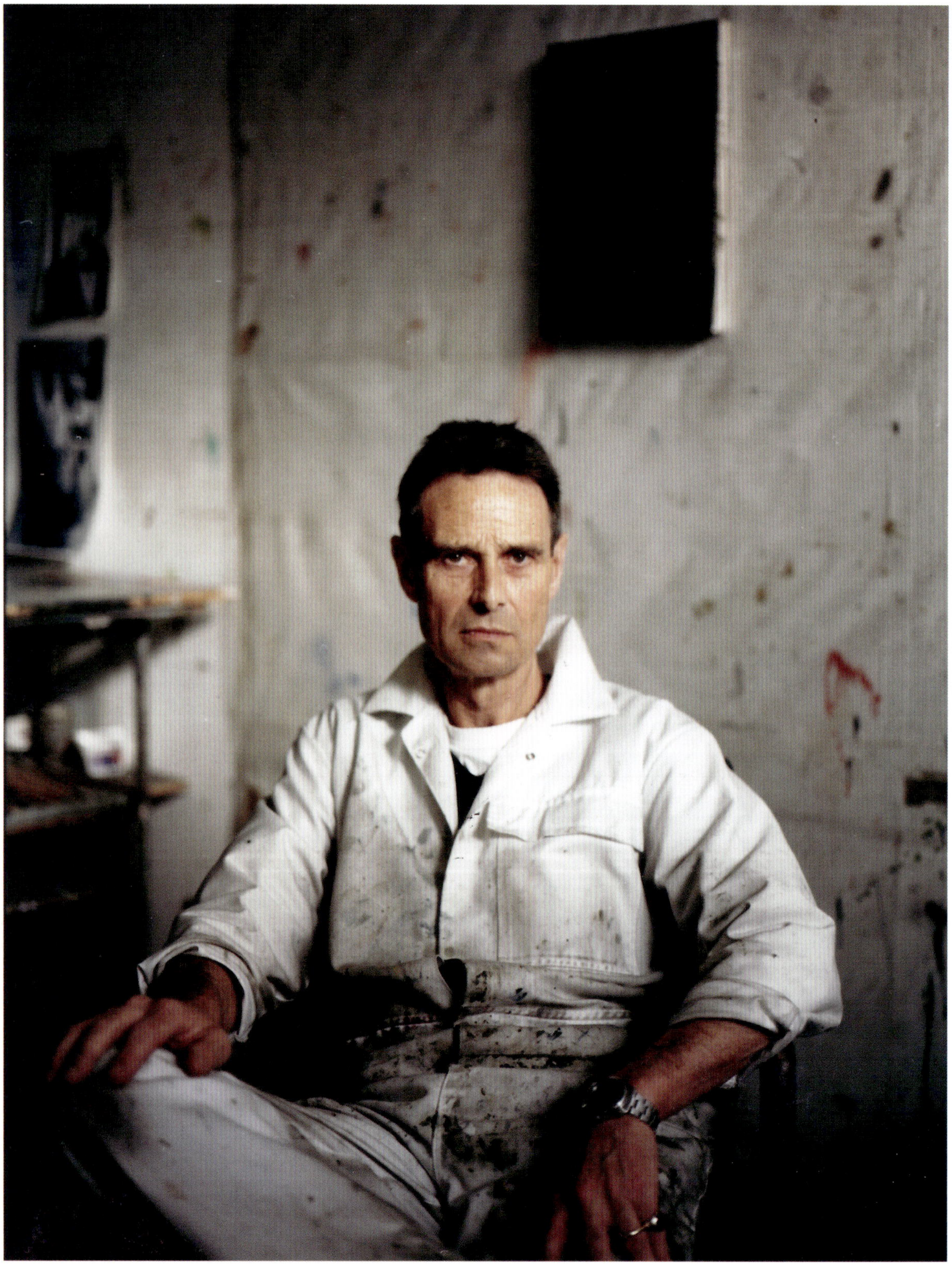

John Keane in his Shoreditch studio, 2014

JOHN KEANE

1954 Born, Hertfordshire
1972–76 Camberwell School of Art
2000– Visiting Professor, The University of Arts in London
2000–11 Visiting Research Fellow, Camberwell College of Arts
2014–17 Artist in Residence, School of International Relations, St Andrews University

SOLO EXHIBITIONS

2015 *Speaking Power to Truth,* Flowers Cork Street, London
The Wisdom of Hindsight, Flowers Kingsland Road, London

2013 *Fear*, Flowers Kingsland Road, London

2012 *Scratching the Surface Joining the Dots,* Flowers Cork Street, London
2010 *The Gulf War 1990–1991*, Photographs, Imperial War Museum North, Manchester
Children in Conflict, Herbert Art Gallery Museum, Coventry

2009 *Intelligent Design*, Flowers Kingsland Road, London

2008 *Angola*, Flowers Cork Street, London

2007 *Guantanamerica,* Flowers, New York

2006 *24 Hours in the House of Culture*, Flowers Kingsland Road, London
24 Hours in the House of Culture, Sakharov Museum, Moscow

2004 *The Inconvenience of History,* London Institute, London; The Naughton Gallery, Queens University of Belfast; Greenbelt Festival; Derby Museum and Art Gallery; Aberystwyth Arts Centre
Back To Fundamentals, Flowers Kingsland Road, London; Hull Museums and Art Gallery, Kingston upon Hull
2003 *Events*, Galerie Behemot, Prague

2002 *Saving the Bloody Planet*, Flowers West, Santa Monica
Recent Events, Flowers Cork Street, London

2001 *Saving the Bloody Planet*, Flowers Kingsland Road, London

2000 *Prints and Monoprints*, Flowers Graphics, London
Making a Killing, Flowers East at London Fields, London
Gwenda Jay Addington Gallery, Chicago

1999 *Trading Flaws and Sporting Mistakes*, Flowers West, Santa Monica

1998 *Truth, Lies & Super 8: The Polyprints*, Riverside Studios, London
John Keane, a Painter in Focus, Ulster Museum, Belfast
Conflicts of Interests, Laing Art Gallery, Newcastle-upon-Tyne

1997 *Truth, Lies & Super 8: The Polyprints,* Flowers East at London Fields, London
John Keane, a Painter in Focus, Wolverhampton Art Gallery

1995 *Works on Paper,* Flowers East at London Fields, London
Graham Greene and the Jungle of Human Dilemma, Flowers East at London Fields, London

1994 *The Struggle for Control of the Television Station*, Galerie Leuenberger, Zurich
Five and a Half Years of Screenprints, Flowers Graphics, London
Fear of God, Riverside Studios, London

1993 *The Struggle for Control of the Television Station*, Flowers East, London; Terry Dintenfass Gallery, New York
Gulf, Norton Gallery, Palm Beach, Florida

1992 *Gulf*, Imperial War Museum, London; Northern Centre for Contemporary Art, Sunderland; Graves Art Gallery, Sheffield; Tullie House, Carlisle; Aberdeen Art Gallery, Aberdeen
Fairy Tales of London, Lannon Cole Gallery, Chicago
Burden of Paradise, Flowers East at London Fields, London
Not the Gulf, Watermans Art Centre, London

1991 *Cloth Caps and Hang Gliding*, Angel Row Gallery, Nottingham London
The Other Cheek?, Arts Council Gallery, Belfast
Before The War, Kelvingrove Art Gallery, Glasgow

1990 *The Other Cheek?*, Flowers East, London

1989 *Divided States*, Terry Dintenfass Gallery, New York
Forum, Hamburg, Germany

1988 *Bee-Keeping in the War Zone*, Angela Flowers Gallery, London
Against the Wall, Turnpike Gallery, Leigh, Greater Manchester
The Accident, commissioned painting and screen-print for Greenpeace, Flowers East, London

1986 *Work Ethics*, Angela Flowers Gallery, London

1985 *Conspiracy Theories*, Angela Flowers Gallery, London
Perspective 1985, Basel Art Fair, Switzerland

1984 *War Efforts*, Pentonville Gallery, London

1982 *Some of it Works on Paper*, Centre 181, London

1980 *Peking, Moscow, Milton Keynes*, Minsky's Gallery, London

1978 *JK:Modern Art French Writers Urban Guerrillas TV Sets Etc.* The Zanzibar, London

SELECTED GROUP EXHIBITIONS

2015 Aesthetica Art Prize Shortlist (Prize Winner), York St. Mary's
Caught in the Crossfire, Guildford House Gallery, Guildford

2014–15 *The Sensory War 1914–2014*, Manchester Art Gallery
Art of the Troubles, Ulster Museum, Belfast
Reality, Modern and Contemporary Painting, Sainsbury Centre for Visual Art, Norwich, Walker art Gallery, Liverpool
Reflections of War, Flowers Kingsland Road, London

2013 *Caught in the Crossfire*, Herbert Art Gallery & Museum, Coventry
Cityscapes, Flowers Gallery, New York
*Catalys*t, Imperial War Museum North

2012–13	*Angela Flowers at 80*, Flowers Kingsland Road, London
2012	*100 Prints*, Flowers Kingsland Road, London
	12 British Artists, Flowers, New York
	Heads, Flowers Kingsland Road, London
2011	*The Art of War*, Chelsea Arts Club, London
2010	*40 Years On,* Flowers Kingsland Road, London
	Standing Room Only, Flowers Kingsland Road, London
2009	Flowers at Palm Beach, Florida
	Meltdown, Flowers Kingsland Road, London
2008–09	*Children in Conflict*, Touring exhibition, Wolverhampton, Aberdeen, Aberystwyth, Coventry
2007	*Conflict*, 20/21 Visual Arts Centre, Scunthorpe
	Beyond the Narrative, PM Gallery, Ealing, London
2006	*Heads*, Flowers Kingsland Road, London
	Occupied Space , Art for Palestine, Gallery 27, London
	Icons and Idols, National Portrait Gallery, London
2005	*35th Anniversary Exhibition*, Flowers Kingsland Road, London
	Flowers West at Keller & Green, Los Angeles
	Paintings from the Nineties, Flowers Cork Street, London
2004	*Six Real Painters*, Flowers Cork Street, London
	Pax Britannica, The Aquarium Gallery, London
2003	*Post-Industrial Landscape*, Museum of Fine Art, Prague
	Events, Galerie Behemot
	John Keane & Peter Howson, Rivington Gallery
2002	*32 Years of Angela Flowers*, London
	Art of the 20th Century, Flowers, New York
	New British Art Part 1, Flowers, New York
2000	*The Times of Our Lives: Endings*, Whitworth Art Gallery, Manchester Milton Keynes Hospital
	Sporting Pictures at the Virgin Lounge
	30th Anniversary Exhibition, Flowers West, Santa Monica
	Flowers Three, Flowers Cork Street, London
1998	*Corps Ville Societe*, La Glaciere, Brussels
1997	*John Keane and Peter Howson*, Galerie Piltzer, Paris
	British Figurative Art, Part One: Painting, Flowers East, London
	After the War was Over, Angela Flowers Gallery (Ireland), Cork
	The Body Politic, Wolverhampton Art Gallery, Wolverhampton
1996	*Monoprints*, Flowers Graphics, London
	The Print Show 1996, Flowers Graphics, London
1995	*Twenty Fifth Anniversary Exhibition*, Flowers East at London Fields, London

1994 *Reflections of Conflict by 16 British and Irish Artists*, Wolverhampton Art Gallery and Museums
An American Passion, McLellan Galleries, Glasgow

1993 *But Big is Better*, Flowers East, London
John Moores 18, Walker Art Gallery, Liverpool
New Figurative Painting, Salander O'Reilly/Fred Hoffman Galleries, Los Angeles

1992 *Artist's Choice*, Flowers East, London

1991 *Angela Flowers Gallery 1991*, Flowers East, London
Inaugural Exhibition, Lannon Cole Gallery, Chicago

1990 *Flowers at Moos*, Gallery Moos, New York
Real Life Stories, Spacex Gallery, Exeter
Where There is Discord, Cleveland Gallery, Middlesbrough
Angela Flowers Gallery 1990, Barbican Concourse Gallery, London

1989 *Big Paintings*, Flowers East, London
Falklands Factor, Manchester City Art Gallery and touring exhibition Leicestershire Schools Exhibition
Confrontation—Three British Artists, Joy Emery Gallery, Michigan, USA
Fourth International Young Artists Competition, Union of Fine Artists, Sofia, Bulgaria
The Thatcher Years: An Artistic Retrospective, Flowers East at London Fields, London
Portfolio Two, Curwen Gallery, London

1988 *New British Painting*, Contemporary Arts Centre, Cincinnatti, Ohio, touring exhibition
Contemporary Portrait, London
Royal Overseas League, London
Wall to Wall Print Show, Pomeroy Purdy Gallery, London
Nutidkunst, Silkesborg Kunstmuseum, Copenhagen

1987 *Southbank Picture Show*, (prizewinner), Royal Festival Hall, London
Athena Art Awards, Barbican Art Gallery, London
Art after Hours, Limelight Club, London
Self-Portrait, Artsite Gallery, Bath
Process and Product, Turnpike Gallery, Leigh, Greater Manchester
Critical Realism, Castle Museum, Nottingham, touring exhibition
State of the Nation, Herbert Art Gallery, Coventry
Heroes, Air Gallery, London
Art for the City, Lloyds Building, London
Which side of the fence?, Imperial War Museum, London
The Big Fight, Vanessa Devereux Gallery, London
The Other Landscape, Southampton City Art Gallery, Southampton

1986 *Artists against Apartheid*, Royal Festival Hall, London
Sixteen, Angela Flowers Gallery, London
Anti-thesis, Angela Flowers Gallery, London
Royal Overseas League, London
Critic's Space, selected by Fenella Crichton, Air Gallery, London

1985 *Contemporary Art Society Market*, 5 Dials Gallery, London

1983–84 *Leicestershire Exhibition for Schools*
TWSA National Touring Exhibition
Whitechapel Open, Whitechapel Art Gallery, London

1983 *Tolly Cobbold*, Fitzwilliam Museum, Cambridge and nationwide tour
Art for Schools, Wells Centre, Norfolk

RESIDENCIES, COMMISSIONS, COLLABORATIONS AND PRIZES

2015 Aesthetica Art Prize Winner

2014–17 Artist in Residence, Department of International Relations, St Andrews University

2013–14 Commemorative First World War coin designs, commissioned by the Royal Mint

2013 Benjamin Britten: The Canticles. A Film for *Canticle 3 (Still Falls the Rain* commissioned by Aldeburgh Music and the Brighton Festival, performed in Brighton, Snape Maltings and the Royal Opera House, Linbury Studio. Directed by Neil Bartlett, with Ian Bostridge

2012 Portraits of Lord Puttnam and Martin Bean for the Open University

2010 Portrait of Sir Victor Blank for Lloyds Banking Group

2009 Portrait of Jon Snow for Channel 4
Portrait of Kofi Annan for the United Nations

2007–10 *57 Hours in the House of Culture* - An opera in development at the National Theatre Studio, London, with Pete Wyer, Phyllida Lloyd and Bryony Lavery

2006 Project with Christian Aid in Angola
Portrait of Greg Dyke for the BBC

2005 Portrait of Sir Bill Morris for the National Portrait Gallery

2002 Project with Christian Aid in Israel and the Occupied Territories

2001 Portrait of Mo Mowlam for the National Portrait Gallery

2000 Project with Greenpeace UK in the Amazon forest

1998 Commissioned painting for The Lowry Centre Trust

1993 Set Design for *Salsa Celestina*, Palace Theatre, Watford
The Lives behind the Lies, commissioned poster for Amnesty International

1991 Official British War Artist, Gulf War, commissioned by Imperial War Museum

1988 Commissioned exhibition about Ollerton Mining Community, by Nottinghamshire County Council

1987 Commissioned poster for London International Mime Festival

1985–86 Artist in Residence, Whitefield School, London

PUBLIC COLLECTIONS

Aberdeen Art Gallery
Arthur Anderson & Co.
Arts and Museum Section of Cleveland County Library and Leisure Department
BBC
Belfast City Council
British Coal

Chase Manhattan Bank, NA
Christie's Corporate Collection
Contemporary Art Society
Dain Rauscher Inc, USA
Detroit Institute of Fine Art, USA
Deutsche Bank
The Economist
Exceed Trust, Aberdeen
The Financial Times
Glasgow Museums: Gallery of Modern Art
Harris Museum and Art Gallery, Preston
Herbert Art Gallery and Museum, Coventry
Hill Samuel Investment Services Group
Hull City Museums, Art Galleries and Archives
Leicestershire County Council
London Borough of Hammersmith and Fulham
The National Army Museum
National Portrait Gallery, London
National Power
Paintings in Hospitals
The Open University
Queen's University, Belfast
Rugby Museum
Trustees of the Imperial War Museum, London
Unilever
Ulster Museum
United Nations
University College of Wales, Aberystwyth
Wolverhampton Museum and Art Gallery
Warwick University

SELECTED TELEVISION

Review Special, BBC2, 9 March 1988
01 for London, ITV, March 1988
BBC Breakfast Time, 23 August 1990
Frank Bough Interview, Sky TV, 30 August 1990
The VIP Show, BSkyB, 5 October 1990
Box Office, Channel 4, 26 November 1990
The Late Show, BBC2, 23 January 1991
Sky News, February 1991
The Late Show, BBC2, 12 March 1991
ZDF, August 1991
The Late Show, BBC2, 20 January 1992
Thames News, ITV, 24 March 1992
Live and Direct, Granada, 25 November 1994
Paul Nash: 'The Man Who Wanted to Fly', Directed by Chris Granlund, BBC2, November 1996

Sky News, November 1996
Antiques Roadshow, with Hugh Scully, BBC1, 1997
Introduction to 'Ice Cold in Alex', Channel 4, 1999
Artsworld Focus, Episode 2, with Richard Coles, Illumina Television, 5 December 2000
Newsnight, BBC1, 26 October 2001
In Your Face, Channel 4, Coluga Pictures, 2002
Artist at War, Directed by Heidi Perry, BBC4/BBC2, 2004
Angola in the Frame, Directed by Dylan Howett, The Community Channel, 2008
The Genius of British Art, with Jon Snow, Channel 4, 2010
The Politics show, BBC1, 2011
BBC London News, 17 October 2013
The Man Who Paints the News, with Dan Damon, BBC World Service, 14 January 2015

SELECTED RADIO

Big City, Radio London, 5 March 1988
Midweek, BBC Radio 4, 19 September 1990
Outlook, BBC World Service, 9 April 1991
Kaleidoscope, Radio 4, 14 April 1991
Tuesday Lives, Radio 4, 12 November 1991
Kaleidoscope, Radio 4, 2 December 1991
The World Today, BBC World Service, February 1992
Diana Luke Show, GLR, March 1992
Outlook, BBC World Service, 27 May 1992
Omnibus, BBC World Service, November 1992
Night Waves, BBC Radio 4, 7 July 1993
Kaleidoscope, BBC Radio 4, 30 September 1994
Peter Curran Show, GLR, November 1994
From our own Correspondent, Radio 4, 25 February 1995
From our own Correspondent (Georgia), BBC World Service, 2 November, 1997
Front Row (Saving the Bloody Planet), BBC Radio 4, June 2001
Front Row, BBC Radio 4, 9 October 2001
Work in Progress, BBC Radio 3, July 2001
Excess Baggage, with Arthur Smith, BBC Radio 4, 28 September 2002
Personal Touch, BBC Radio Scotland, 10 November 2002
Sitting Pretty (with Mo Mowlam) BBC Radio 4, 11 April 2002
Front Row (Frida Kahlo), BBC Radio 4, June 2005
Front Row, BBC Radio 4, 29 March 2006
Front Row, BBC Radio 4, 27 June 2006
Front Row (Mark Rothko), BBC Radio 4, 23 September 2008
The Essay (The Father Instinct), BBC Radio 3, 26 April 2011
Nightwaves, BBC Radio 3, 11 January 2012
Saturday Review, BBC Radio 4, 14 January 2012
The Strand, BBC World Service, 11 January 2012
Front Row, BBC Radio 4, 12 January 2012
Front Row (Art Under Attack), 30 September 2013
Private Passions, BBC Radio 3, 29 June 2014
Free Thinking. BBC Radio 3, 14 January 2015

ACKNOWLEDGEMENTS

My thanks and appreciation to:

Mark Lawson
Alex Danchev
Brian Eno
Katy Homans
Alexandra Peake
Juliette O'Leary
Antonio Parente
Matthew Flowers
James Ulph
Angela Flowers
And all the staff at Flowers Gallery

My thanks also to Rosemary McGowan, Calypso Keane and Theo Keane, who had nothing at all to do with the production of this book.

Mark Lawson's work as a broadcaster includes *Mark Lawson Talks To* (BBC4), *Front Row* and *Foreign Bodies* (Radio 4) and *Late Review* (BBC2). He is a columnist, critic and feature writer for *The Guardian* and theatre critic of *The Tablet*. His books include the travelogue *The Battle for Room Service* and the fictions *The Deaths, Enough is Enough, Going Out Live, Idlewild* and *Bloody Margaret*.

Alex Danchev is the author of a number of acclaimed biographies, most recently CÉZANNE (2012), and an influential collection of essays, ON ART AND WAR AND TERROR (2011). He is Professor of International Relations at the University of St Andrews.

Brian Eno is a composer and light artist who lives in London.

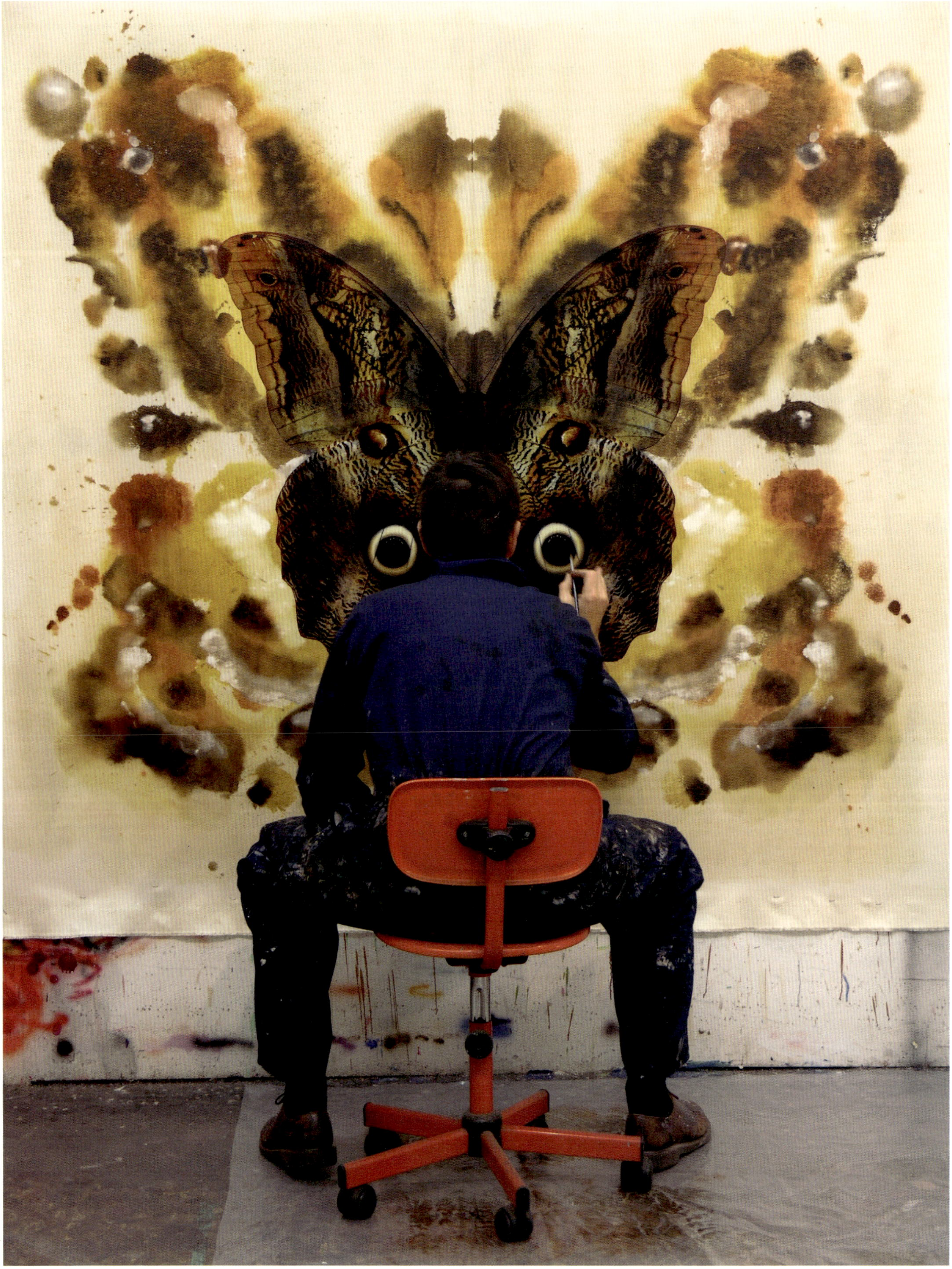

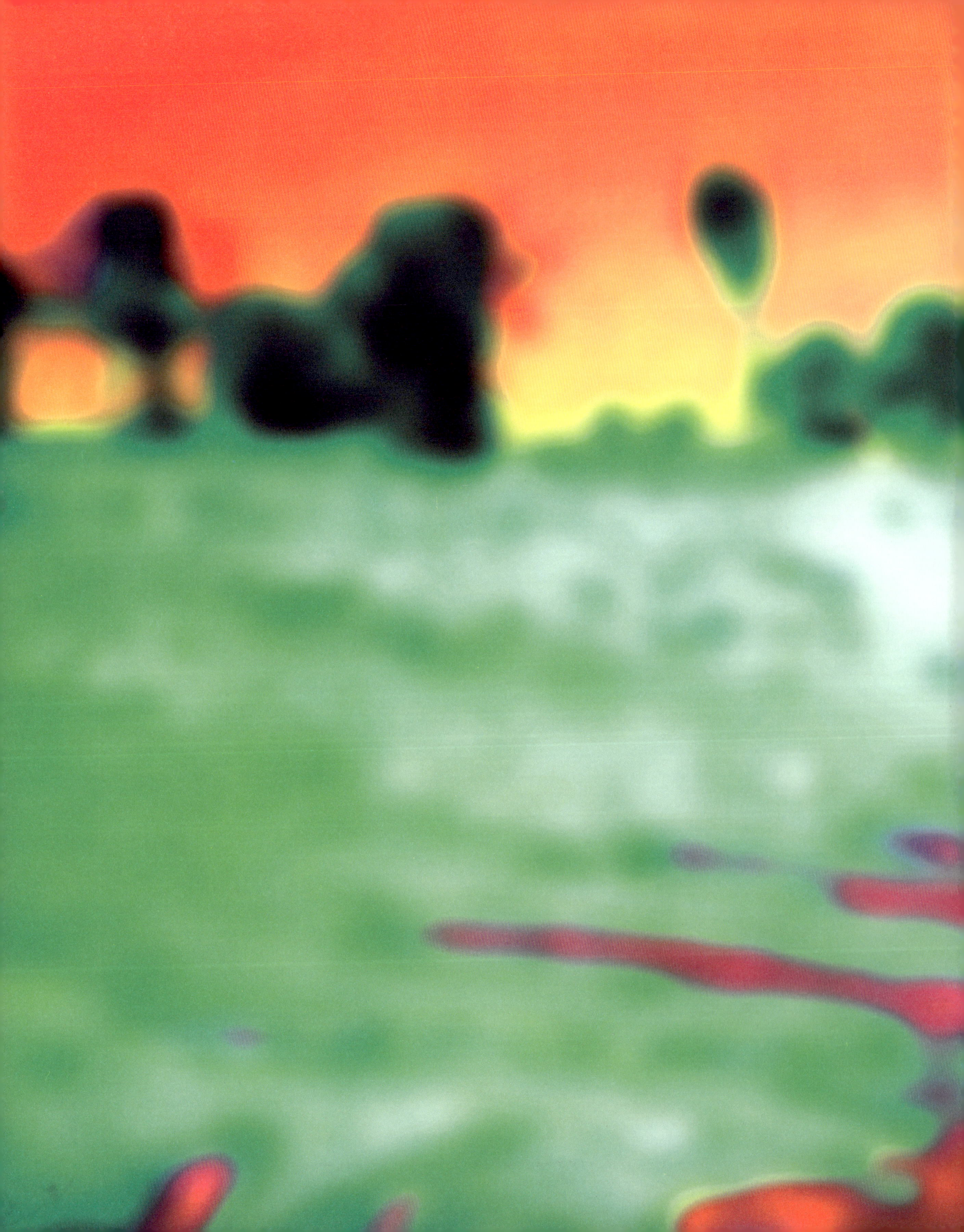